BECOMING A WARRIOR
in GOD'S LAST DAYS ARMY

GOD'S ANOINTED WARRIORS

UNVEILING MYSTERIES
in the BOOK *of* REVELATION

DR. DONALD BELL

MAJOR USMC, RET.

God's Anointed Warriors

Becoming a Warrior of Christ in God's Last Days Army

December 2015
Copyright © Dr. Don Bell

Cover created by:

Rick Schroeppel
Elm Street Design Studio
ElmStreetDesignStudio.net
Rick@ElmStreetDesignStudio.net
615.283.8317

ISBN 978-1-943412-08-2

Published by -

Wilderness Voice Publishing, LLC
Canon City, Colorado USA
www.wvpbooks.com

"A voice crying in the wilderness - proclaiming the good news of the coming Kingdom!"

This book is dedicated to the memory of Russell John Berg, who possessed a passionate heart for justice, righteousness, honor, and integrity and spent much of his time walking moment-by-moment alone with God. He was my very first mentor in the ways of the Lord. Russ was a man gifted with strong, spiritual discernment who saw the lateness of the hour and who initially encouraged me in the study of eschatology. His warrior spirit is reflected in the following poem that he wrote in 1982.

- Dare to be the man –
    Who will look inside!
    Who will bow to his pride!
    Who will seek the truth!
    Who will bow before God!

- Dare to be the man –
    Who will suffer reproach!
    Who is called a fool!
    Who has lost his friends for Christ!
    Who will bow before God!

- Dare to be the man –
    Who resists temptation!
    Who makes time for prayer!
    Who will sacrifice!
    Who will bow before God!

- Dare to be the man –
    Who will speak the truth!
    Who will not retreat!
    Who is lowly and meek!
    Who will bow before God!

- Dare to be the man –
    Who will suffer trials!
    Who in weakness is strong!
    Who gains strength in tribulation!
    Who will bow before God!

- Dare to be the man –
    Who will yield to God's call!
    Who gives all for all!
    Who will give his life!
    Who will be a living sacrifice!

    --Russell John Berg

Acknowledgments

I am very grateful to my wife, Gery, my sons, Jeff and Bucky, and their wives, Colleen and Bree, and my daughter, Christian, and her husband, Robert, for their steadfast support in the writing of this book. I am also indebted to those close friends who provided valuable insights concerning the editing, designing and marketing of the book: Charles Pretlow, Rick Schroeppel, David Gorospe, Bob Maratas, and Bill Gremmert. Last, but certainly not least, I want to thank a host of encouragers throughout this writing endeavor: Cleveland Futch, Mike Stoltenberg, Jim Ray, Rod Graciano, Tim Taylor, Bill Sparks, Vern Johnson, Chuck Shank, Phil Fernandez, William Bartley, Steve Hjelmstad, Jesse Hjelmstad, Neil deLeon, Philip DeLeon, Darren Lawrence, Kevin Hearon, Tyrone Harris, Tom Hanna, Ron Robbins, Tracy Krueger, Rick Tomlinson, Mark and Jacqueline deMers, Ed and Maria Roberts, Mike and Brenda Keith, all the staff at the Bell & Futch CPA firm, and the entire Bell, Gorospe, Ereth, Evans, and Robinson families. This is my family.

It is also fitting to express my gratitude to my close friend Chris Berg for directing me toward the Lord at a very critical time in my life and then introducing me to his father, my early mentor. Additionally, I wish to acknowledge the impact that Western Reformed, Westminster West, and Faith Evangelical Seminaries have had on my life. Finally, my thanks to Dr. Michael Adams, president of Faith Evangelical Seminary; who encouraged me to complete my Doctor of Ministry degree and write a dissertation that later formed the foundation for this book.

**Becoming a Warrior of Christ
in God's Last Days Army**

"GOD'S ANOINTED WARRIORS"

TABLE OF CONTENTS

Chapter 9 – Confrontation Between the Woman 133
and the Dragon (Revelation 12)

Chapter 10 – Three Beasts – An Unholy Trinity (Revelation 13) 143

Chapter 11 – Mystery Babylon the Great (Revelation 17 - 18) 157

Chapter 15 – Equipping Warrior Leadership 229
in the Kingdom of God

Chapter 16 – Understanding "The Problem of Evil" 253

INTRODUCTION

MISSIONAL ASSIGNMENT:
REACHING OUT TO CHRISTIAN WARRIORS

The primary mission of this book is to provide warrior-spirited Christians with insights into extremely important events recorded in the book of Revelation. These are end-time events that are quite mystifying but extremely critical for the twenty-first-century Christian to understand. Hopefully, this book will encourage many Christians who are discerning that troubling times are about to descend upon the United States, as well as the entire world, to begin preparing now. Those who are spiritually prepared will be among the Christian leadership who will stand strong in the midst of these catastrophic events by continually seeking the Lord's guidance.

I realize that the contents of this book will not be appreciated by many in the churches of today. Yet, there are also those within these churches who are searching for an understanding of their role in the Army of God during the time of coming tribulations.

These are men and women:

- Who deeply desire to be uncompromising, anointed witnesses for the Lord Jesus Christ in order to be a shining light in the lives of both believers and unbelievers in the midst of great darkness and,
- Who deeply desire to play a visible role in the strengthening and growth of God's kingdom during a time when the attack upon His people will greatly intensify and,
- Who deeply desire to make a glorious impact within the kingdom of God during their short life span upon this earth and,
- Who deeply desire to hear our Lord Jesus Christ say, "Well done, good and faithful servant" when they enter into His presence.
- When that occurs, these Christian warriors will know that their calling in this life has been completely fulfilled. Well done!

PACIFISTS ARE TEACHING ESCHATOLOGY

Throughout most of the twentieth century, the subject of eschatology (end-times teachings) certainly has been a key factor in contributing to the disunity among many churches. Theologians have been debating controversial issues of eschatology for centuries; yet advocates of each of the different viewpoints state that their respective views are all clearly supported by Scripture, and they all attempt to provide the interpretations that support their personal viewpoints. Most recent books on biblical prophecy are, as a rule, simply restatements of what has been previously published. Yet, there is common ground on one issue among most of the differing views of eschatology, and that is that Christians need not be concerned about preparing themselves for times of tribulation. Instead, they teach that the church will be raptured prior to tribulation, or that the tribulation is simply an ongoing experience throughout the Christian age, or that it already occurred in AD 70 with the destruction of Jerusalem. These are all warm and fuzzy teachings that put the church to sleep and fail to challenge Christians to prepare for the reality of those tremendous tribulations which will precede the second coming of our Lord. There has been much written about the end times and the book of Revelation over the centuries, with view after view contending against one another, and yet little is happening within the church as a result of all this writing. The Lord's people are not being prepared by the church for the Day of the Lord as commanded by our Commander in Chief, Jesus Christ.[1]

TARGET AUDIENCE – WARRIOR-SPIRITED CHRISTIANS

The target audience for this book is for men and women, who possess a strong love for the Lord and who, like the sons of Issachar, are a remnant of the people of God who understand that a tremendous crisis is rapidly approaching and are not yet certain of their calling.[2] We are right on the verge of devastating events that will create great fear and chaos throughout the world and especially in our comfort-seeking nation. Many Christians are aware that over the last few years world events have been rapidly accelerating downhill toward what many recognize as a time of tribulation like the world has never before experienced.[3]

This book is intended to provide direction, preparation, and encouragement that you are not alone, for our Lord is raising up many others who, like you, are to be a light within your community.[4] We are under attack, and the battle is rapidly intensifying, and Christians need to understand what enlistment as soldiers in the Army of God truly entails. The focus of this presentation is to reach out to those who sigh and groan over the abominations that are committed in this world, with the hope of raising up strong, strategic leadership among these Christians who will lead many to prepare for those terrifying events that precede the second coming of our Lord.[5]

This is truly an exciting time for this generation; a time of opportunity to stand and fight for the kingdom of God against a spiritual enemy that will soon launch the most powerful offensive attack against the church since the beginning of time. But first, we must learn to walk through the valley of the shadow of death without fear, knowing that our Lord walks right alongside of us.[6]

Introduction

Although there are different levels of commitment among soldiers comprising an army, as there are within the Christian church, the author uses the term "mighty warriors" as representative of those Christian soldiers who will run to the frontlines of the battlefield without regard for personal consequences. Also, the terms "soldiers, warriors, and warrior-spirited Christians in the Army of God" are all used synonymously within this book to convey a similar heart that is totally sold out to the Lord —hearts that will never compromise their faith in Jesus Christ even if it leads to martyrdom. They are the ones who possess the attributes of true leadership within the world of Christianity.

THE PURPOSE FOR THE "BOOK OF REVELATION"

Christians who truly believe that our Lord is in control of these coming events need not be kept in the dark concerning the times that lie before us. For The Lord Jesus Christ, our Commander-in-Chief in the Army of God has already provided detailed intelligence concerning those events which will precede His return to set up the Kingdom of God throughout the entire earth. This intelligence has been primarily recorded in the Book of Revelation which is a writing that has confused many in the church over the centuries. Yet, our Lord promises great blessings to those who <u>read</u>, <u>hear</u> and <u>keep</u> the prophetic messages communicated in the Book of Revelation.

<u>Listen to His words at the beginning of this Book:</u>

- *__Blessed__ is the one who <u>reads aloud</u> the words of this prophecy, and __blessed__ are those who hear, and who <u>keep what is written</u> in it, for the time is near. __(Revelation 1:3)__*

Obviously, this revelation from Jesus which was recorded by the apostle John is of extreme importance. Jesus provided this information to His people in order that they would not be kept in the dark about future events, but prepared to stand for His glorious name in the midst of increasing evil throughout the world. We need to understand the blessings promised by Jesus to those who read aloud (teach), hear (learn), and keep (obey) the words prophesized in this great book which reveals the development of both the kingdom of God and the kingdom of the world until the coming of our Lord Jesus.

<u>Also, in the very last chapter of the bible, Jesus again reminds us:</u>

- *"And behold, I am coming soon. __Blessed__ is the one who keeps the words of the prophecy of this book." __(Revelation 22:7)__*

However, to "keep" the words recorded in the Book of Revelation, you have to become familiar with it, not ignore it. Over my years as a Christian, these promised blessings of Jesus have inspired me in the continuing study of the Book of Revelation together with the Old Testament prophetic books as well as numerous fine books, many of which are recorded in my bibliography. These studies have evolved into my authoring of this book which is intended for those of our 21st century generation who are seeking for a more clear understanding of the mystifying events recorded in the Book of Revelation.

Thus, one of my mission objectives for writing this book is to encourage other warrior-spirited Christians to study the Book of Revelation with fresh eyes - and to not be misled by modern-day beliefs that tends to keep our heads buried in the sand. I certainly understand that none of us has all the answers and I know that the various scenarios presented in this book will certainly not be 100% correct. However, I am convinced that the challenges which the church will soon face will be just as difficult, if not worse than the chaotic events described in this book.

Now, what is the purpose for the Book of Revelation? Well, the Book of Revelation together with other prophetic books is intended to provide the Lord's people with:

- Understanding—of the times & purposes for these events.
- Direction—for our ministerial calling in the midst of these events.
- Preparation—to "be ready" both spiritually & physically.
- Encouragement—to be a glorious light within our respective environments during these times.

Understanding, Direction, Preparation, & Encouragement – that's what we need to take away from this prophetic book and also to share these insights with others whom the Lord brings before us.

Certainly, the Book of Revelation has been a blessing to those truly committed churches throughout the centuries. It provided encouragement for many Christians concerning God's purposes in the midst of challenging times leading to persecution and martyrdom. This resulted in an uncompromising faith as they continued to look forward to the time of the New Heavens & Earth where they would abide forever with their Lord. But also, since the Book of Revelation was written over 1900 years ago, millions of Christians over the centuries could not relate these prophetic events to their respective generations. Thus, the importance of the Book of Revelation has been pretty much ignored or downplayed by developing non-offensive theologies that would not scare or offend their respective churches.

However, we cannot continue to ignore or downplay these prophetic events any longer. I truly believe that we are currently at a point in biblical history where many of these mysteriously challenging events recorded in the Book of Revelation will actually take place within our current generation. These are events which will precede the coming of our Lord Jesus to setup His millennial kingdom on earth. Exciting, but also challenging for this generation of Christendom.

Introduction

GENERAL OUTLINE AND PURPOSE OF THIS BOOK

Numerous fine books have been written on the subjects of Christian leadership, the kingdom of God, and the state of the church, along with the more popular books concerning eschatological events. This book presents an overview of all of these subjects but combines them in such a way that allows the readers to more clearly relate these subjects to our present circumstances.

The first chapter of this book provides a brief testimony of the author's Vietnam experience and how it removed his heart from the world and subsequently, into the kingdom of God.

- A summary overview of a nation gone terribly astray.
- A vision received from the Lord revealing a worldly attack on the 21st century church.
- And a calling for Christian soldiers to rise up and join our true Commander-in-Chief, Jesus Christ, on the battlefield.

After establishing these foundational teachings, the next thirteen chapters move through the book of Revelation, as well as portions of several Old Testament prophetic books, attempting to provide understanding of what Christian warriors of this generation will soon face and how to answer His calling to the spiritual battlefield. Following this:

- The fifteenth chapter will provide important insights on how to lead and prepare other American Christians to stand strong in the midst of the Great Tribulation.
- The sixteenth chapter addresses the age-old "problem of evil" as well as providing some insights into God's purposes for allowing evil to continue up to the coming Day of Judgment.

Additionally, there are seven pertinent appendixes which will assist us:

A. In our understanding of the spiritual warfare between the "worldly (beast) kingdom" and the "kingdom of God" which has been taking place from the beginning of history up to the present day.
B. Understanding the Mystery concerning the Kingdom of God in the midst of the World.
C. Insights into "Discerning the Time" for our 21st century generation.
D. Understanding of the importance of "fasting" for spiritual growth plus suggestions on how to proceed.
E. A sample letter that may assist in reaching out to non-believing family and friends.
F. In our ministerial calling to searching hearts in our respective neighborhoods and workplaces.
G. In the planning of physical preparation for our families who will face challenging times.

Although I have borrowed from many Christian writers, whose works are listed in the bibliography, they are in no way responsible for what I have made of their works. All Scripture references are from the English Standard Version (ESV) of the Bible unless otherwise noted. Also note that it is important to read the associated Bible passages in the book of Revelation together with the related chapters in this book. Although, I don't pretend to know the exact nature of the coming tribulation events, I am absolutely certain of the following two truths:

- Judgment will first come to the household of God before coming to those in the world.[7]
- We may not know the exact times of these approaching events, but our Lord assures us that those of His people who walk in His light will know when the time is dawning. And today, there are many worldwide who are hearing His call to "prepare."[8]

This book is not intended to be an apologetic for theological discussion; it is meant to feed the hungering, warrior spirit within that Christian remnant who are aware of the tremendous challenges that lie before us and are seeking guidance as to what we are about to confront and how to prepare for it. It is intended for those who discern the times and hear the call to prepare for a leadership role in the Army of God during the time of coming tribulations. Thus, this book will not effectively speak to the entire body of Christ, nor will it be welcomed by many.

My approach to addressing these end-time events is from a military perspective since much of who I am today is the result of my twenty years in the Marine Corps. The Lord has put a deep burden in my heart, and that is to arouse a remnant of Christian warriors to visualize their heritage and purpose in life. The common purpose for all volunteers in the Army of God is to prepare in the boot camp of life in order to allow the light and glory of our Commander in Chief, Jesus Christ, to be clearly manifested on the battlefield that lies in the midst of this world.

"Christian warriors, we are called to stand strong for the Kingdom of God!"

CHAPTER 1

AMERICA - "A FORMER CHRISTIAN NATION"

The western world, which was unknown in biblical times, has evolved to be the strongest representative of the world of Christianity under the new covenant and certainly America, where missionaries have been trained and sent worldwide, has been the most influential nation in the promotion of Christianity throughout the world.

Godly leaders founded this country under the biblical principles of justice, truth, and religious freedom. These founding fathers were Europeans seeking freedom from religious persecution within the countries of Western Europe. They were the early pilgrims who pursued and honored the Lord. Our present-day heritage of freedom, peace, and prosperity is the fruit of our forefathers' obedience to and love for, the Lord Jesus Christ and His heavenly Father.

The Lord obviously has raised up America to be a powerful and glorious witness for the Kingdom of God and over the last four centuries, she has greatly influenced most of the nations of the world with the gospel truths of Jesus Christ.

MARINE CORPS COMBAT EXPERIENCE – "VIETNAM"

America was the country that I grew up in – the country where I went to school and developed into a young patriotic American. I loved my country. Subsequently, when I graduated from high school at age 17, I decided to enlist in the Marine Corps with some of my classmates. Although I was a young teenager who was suddenly confronted with some very intense and challenging training – I gave it my all and eventually matured into a young "teenage man" who was proud to be a Marine. I was totally committed to our government and those in authority over me as well as my Marine buddies. I loved the Marine Corps, although my initial plan was to leave when my enlistment was up and enter college. However, this plan was suddenly changed for shortly before my enlistment was up, I was among a few enlisted men selected to attend officer training at Quantico where I was subsequently commissioned. As it turned out, I ended up serving 20 years in the Marine Corps including two tours in Vietnam.

During officer training at Quantico, we were called to swear an oath of allegiance that we would dedicate ourselves to the following combat priorities for Marine Corps officers. These priorities were:

- 1st: - The mission(s) assigned by our commanders
- 2nd – The lives of those men under our authority
- 3rd – We were to place our own life last

1st Vietnam Tour: In 1965, I was among one of the first Marine units sent to Vietnam where we made a beach landing at a place called Chu Lai. At that time, I was a young lieutenant and a committed American patriot who totally believed in the calling of our country to stop the aggression of communism in South Vietnam. During that tour in 1965, I was absolutely committed to prioritizing my country, and the men under my command, before myself. I do believe that I was totally committed to sacrificing my life if called to achieve victory and/or protect my men.

2nd Vietnam Tour: In 1969, I was the commander of a company-size unit on the DMZ, which was on the border of North Vietnam; as well as a place known as the Rockpile - both were highly volatile combat areas. However, by this time our government and many in our country had shown that they no longer were supportive of our efforts in the war.

A war that could have easily been won in a couple of years was dragged out in Washington D.C. by wimpy politicians and a liberal media. As a result, many of us in the military know that thousands of lives were lost needlessly over those Vietnam years. And as a small unit commander I had to write personal letters to wives and parents of those men under my command who were killed. Obviously, this was very hard.

This weakness within our government inspired a movement of war protestors which voiced an unrighteous hatred for those in the military. They even gathered in groups at airports to mock, spit at, and ridicule the military returning home from Vietnam. They hated those of us who went to war out of love and patriotism for our country. Never before in American history has our government, together with the news media shown such a lack of support for the military troops that answered the call of their country. Such cowardice! Our government had quietly succumbed to the cries of this massive drug-infested hippie culture crying out: *"Make love, not war!"*

As I witnessed some of my men and a close friend killed during this 2nd tour, inwardly my combat priorities changed:

- 1st – Lives of men under my command
- 2nd – Myself
- 3rd – Assigned mission

We were no longer prioritizing our country, we were protecting ourselves. This was not the result of fear; it was the result of a loss of support from and respect toward those in the highest leadership offices of our country who allowed the hippie protestors to determine the direction of the war. Obviously, when I returned home, I was a different person. And I pursued a wild lifestyle during my remaining years in the Marine Corps. Looking back, I now realize that I was searching for future direction that would be meaningful.

Now with this background, I feel a need to share a brief testimony concerning my relationship with our Lord in order that you will have a better understanding of the man who is sharing some very hard and challenging truths in this prophetic book.

A LIFE-CHANGING TESTIMONY: "BORN-AGAIN IN A HOT-TUB"

Following retirement from the Marine Corps, I was working in California and a very close friend, together with his dad, encouraged me to attend church. At this time of my life, I had recently been married and fathered a son who was now a year old. Yet, I was still a very stubborn and arrogant man who believed that church was for wimps, not warriors. However, my marriage together with the birth of my son had somewhat softened my heart and out of respect for my friend and his dad, I reluctantly agreed to go - but only for one service. Obviously, I wasn't a God-fearing man back in those Marine Corps days. In fact, as previously mentioned, I lived a pretty wild life following my 2nd tour in Vietnam. But there came a day when I was changed forever.

It was November 6, 1979, and because I'd given my word to my friend, I attended a church service without any expectation that it would be meaningful – although deep in my heart I was quietly searching. Now, I remember that the focus of the pastor's sermon had to do with the sacrifice of Christ on the cross and His desire to have an ongoing relationship with each of us. Surprisingly, it touched me quite deeply as I never considered that God wanted a personal relationship with me. Later, as I was talking with some men after the service and sharing my interest, one of them gave me a bible and suggested that I go home and read the gospel of John.

Well, I left church that morning somewhat fired up, but without any real expectation that the bible would do much for me, <u>but I was wrong</u>. Early that same afternoon, I sat down in a hot tub out in our backyard, expecting to read a couple of bible verses and then switch to a more interesting detective novel. <u>Again, I was wrong</u>! I opened to the first chapter of John's gospel, which begins:

- *In the beginning was the Word, and the Word was with God, and the Word was God. He was in the beginning with God. All things were made through him, and without him was not any thing made that was made. In him was life, and the life was the light of men.*

All of a sudden the truth of those words impacted me and I knew the Lord was speaking to me through His Word. I never had been so impacted in the spirit like this, but it was just the beginning. For when I got down to verse 14 and read:

- *And the Word became flesh and dwelt among us, and we have seen his glory, glory as of the only Son from the Father, full of grace and truth.*

At that point I cried out. "Oh my gosh - Jesus, Jesus, that was You wasn't it!"

The reality of those words struck me like lightning and the Spirit of God dropped upon me like electric current flowing through my body over and over. Up to this point in life I believe very few men had a harder heart than I did, but as I read these words, my heart was broken and I wept for the first time since I was a young boy.

My years on the front lines of the Vietnam conflict never broke me down like this; I thought I was too tough for "wimpy" things like the bible. I kept reading and weeping and reading and weeping, constantly crying out, "My God, my God, I didn't know these things; please, please forgive me." I could not stop - the Spirit of God continued to pass through me like a strong electric current over and over, and I was completely overwhelmed. This continued on for twelve hours, until 1:00 AM the following morning. By then I had read through the books of John, Acts, Romans, and part of 1 Corinthians. And I probably shed more tears than there was water in the hot tub! I was completely broken, but I had fallen deeply in love with the Father and His Son, our Lord Jesus Christ.

Before this occurred, the bible was just another book in Grandma's bookcase, but it was at this point that I came to understand deep in my spirit that it was truly God's Word speaking to us.

Now, I've traveled the tough, sinful road of the unbeliever, and I do understand that until one truly seeks the Lord, the bible will have little credibility. Yet, that all changes for those who will seek Him with a searching heart. For then, the Word Himself, the Lord Jesus Christ, reveals that the words in scripture come to us from a loving Father who calls us to Himself.

AMERICA – "A NATION GONE TERRIBLY ASTRAY"

Today's America, our once beloved country, has rejected our Lord and has evolved into a idolatrous nation who worships other gods - gods of money, entertainment, and immoral pleasures. These are the primary American idols of the 21st century. A country that was founded on biblical principles established by almighty God has now chosen to throw off our Christian heritage and embrace the principles of Sodom and Gomorrah.

Today, we are a country:

- Where prayer and Bible study are no longer permitted in our schools. Although our college campuses are floating in New Age & Islamic teachings.
- Where the presence of our Lord is not welcome in governmental facilities. Even military chaplains are being warned not to pray in the name of Jesus. However, again Islamic and New Age-style religions are quietly being embraced.
- Where the American news media has lost all credibility over being honest with the public. It has brainwashed many of our citizens into embracing corrupt government agendas leading to a major disregarding of our constitutional freedoms.
- Where abortion clinics have butchered tens of millions of babies over the last 38 years and now our tax dollars fund abortion clinics across the world. This child sacrifice has been made lawful in order to support "lustful addiction" to sexual immorality resulting in the continuing slaughter of young, innocent victims.
- Where violent and demonic television, movies, video games, coupled with widespread drugs has spawned a dangerous belief system within our youth culture. So many of our youth of today are "technology smart" but "life stupid."
- Where the voice of demons sounds quite pleasant. They are heard on television, in the newspapers, on the internet, in our courtrooms, in our schools, and even in many of our churches. These are voices which embrace a "godless" lifestyle that has given rise to a dangerous drug-influenced American culture that welcomes adultery, abortion, pornography, homosexuality, and same-sex marriages as a normal way of life.

Sin and lawlessness have replaced righteousness and justice in our once great and mighty land. America has fallen into the same trap as ancient Israel which led to their ultimate downfall. Power and riches has led a former nation of God into a great apostasy. Sadly, our nation no longer worships the Lord who established our religious freedoms.

This is not a time to place our hopes in upcoming elections or promised changes by our existing government. Those in the most powerful positions of governmental and economic authority have little regard for the constitution of our country and they will not relinquish their authority through an election process. The United States as a democratic nation is rapidly disappearing – constitutional law will soon be ignored. As Christians, we cannot continue to put our trust in financial institutions or government promises. All this is of the world and Jesus Christ, our true Commander-in-Chief is calling us to let go of this world. It's getting worse and worse and yet, many in today's churches will undoubtedly continue in their comfortable blindness until the time comes when the 21ˢᵗ century American culture turns their hatred toward the Lord into a violent persecution of His church.

LACK OF PREPAREDNESS IN THE AMERICAN CHURCH

Now why isn't the Christian church in America standing stronger against this ungodly, worldly invasion of our beloved country? In answer to this question I wish to **share an impacting vision that I received from the Lord in 1982:**

- *"I was up walking during a period of early morning intercessory prayer when suddenly a trance-like vision appeared before me revealing a tremendously huge, marble-like boulder emanating brilliant and beautiful light. It was overwhelmingly glorious and the Lord immediately revealed to me in my spirit that this was His church which He dearly loved. It was so gloriously captivating that I immediately fell in love with it.*
- *But as I began to walk toward it, I saw that there was a small, black piece of evil attached to the bottom of it. I suddenly became angry and wanted to tear it off, but as I approached this tiny evil "thing" attached to the church, it suddenly began to grow larger and larger and octopus-like tentacles came out of it which penetrated the boulder-like church over and over. As it continued to grow, the tentacles of this "black octopus-like demon" continued to swallow the "light of the church" until sometime later there remained only a small remnant of light (approximately 10 percent) that was not consumed by this darkness. In the final scene, this demonic beast was continuing to go after this remaining remnant and I knew that it would not be satisfied until it had consumed the entire church. When I came out of the trance, I was weeping deeply, knowing that I was feeling the grieving emotions emanating from the heart of Jesus Christ for His church."*

This vision probably lasted about ten minutes but a few years later, when it was revealed to me that this demonic monster was <u>symbolic of the kingdom of the world,</u> it has definitely contributed to my understanding of what is continually happening within the traditional church of the 21ˢᵗ century.

I realize that the world has always had a grasp on portions of the true church – however, I've come to understand that the purpose for this vision was to communicate how it was going to rapidly consume the majority of the church in our generation. Now 30 years later, many of today's Christians do recognize that there has been a rapid increase of apostasy within numerous American churches which have become more and more liberal-minded as they continue to fall in love with the pleasures of this world. The great prosperity experienced in this nation has lulled many of God's people into following a cross-less, painless gospel that accommodates selfishness and laziness within Christians which allows the thoughts and intents of the heart to remain unchallenged.

To summarize this vision:

- The church of this present generation (the glorious, marble-like boulder) is under attack from the worldly kingdom (the black, octopus-like demon), whose influence is rapidly creeping in and consuming much of the traditional church community.
- The "dark remnant" of the church will soon unite and turn against the "glorious light' represented by those Christians who will never compromise their faith as they proclaim Jesus Christ as the eternal Son of God and only those who believe and follow Him will enter into the eternal Kingdom of God.
- Many within the deceived worldly church will soon join with the worldly government(s) in their war against the remnant of Christianity who will not compromise their faith.
- It appears that only a small, holy remnant will remain pure and respond to our Lord's call to the spiritual battlefield during the catastrophic times that lie shortly before us.
- However, I do believe that in the midst of the disastrous times that will soon descend upon our nation, this "pure light" will be powerfully released into darkness and many within both the deceived church community as well as many in the world will come to the truth of the gospel and embrace Jesus Christ as their Lord and King.

All of this is becoming more and more visible in America as the citizens of the kingdom of this world will actively confront the citizens of the kingdom of God. For those of this generation who hear our Lord's calling, this can truly be a challenging but also an exciting time – a time of opportunity to stand strong for the kingdom of God against an enemy that will soon launch the most powerful offensive attack against the church since the beginning of time.

A PACIFIST CHURCH IS UNPREPARED FOR WARFARE

The great majority of the twenty-first-century American church is not preparing for the challenging events that the Lord Jesus Christ warned us about—events that precede His second coming to physically establish the kingdom of God on this earth. Most leaders within today's churches acknowledge the truth of the future return of the Son of God, yet they continually ignore the multiple warnings concerning the tremendous warfare the church will face in both the natural and spiritual realms which precede His coming. Although the church may admit to the reality of warfare between the kingdom of God and the world, it continues to function as if it is only passively involved. Most allusions to spiritual warfare simply emphasize the assurance of complete victory at the second coming of Christ and avoid speaking of our lifelong participation in this spiritual war. Thus, the church busies itself with the more tangible and legalistic aspects of religion, preferring to believe that Christ has already achieved total victory over these evil forces and that there is nothing more to do except attend church regularly and await that time when we will be united with Him in heaven.

Compounding the problem, these same church bodies are impervious to their lack of spiritual strength, thinking themselves strong because of the vastness of their resources or the correctness of their doctrine. No matter what is said from the pulpit, more often than not, the normal vision and programs of these churches are primarily focused upon internal growth rather than the transformation of people and cities outside of their walls. Thus, many in the body of Christ are living as if there is no ongoing warfare or that we are already in possession of the ultimate victory. This mind-set is certainly similar to that found in the parable of the five foolish virgins who failed to maintain oil in their lamps and when the night came, they found themselves locked out from the presence of the Lord.[9] In truth, a tremendously violent war is accelerating, and individual Christians must either stand strong and be uncompromising in their faith as soldiers of the kingdom or they will become spiritual casualties in the days that lie shortly before us. Additionally, I would highly recommend Charles Pretlow's tremendously impacting book, *Discernment,* for those who desire additional insights into the realm of spiritual warfare within both the world as well as the church. Now contrary to what numerous religious pacifists believe:

JESUS CHRIST IS THE "LORD OF HOSTS"

Few Christians realize that the true meaning of hosts in both Hebrew and Greek is "a gathering army organized for war." God is called the Lord of hosts 242 times in the bible. This is far more than any other name that identifies the character of our Lord. Jesus Christ was the greatest and mightiest warrior that ever walked this earth. He fought against the dark forces in this world because of His deep love for us and He is calling for warrior-spirited Christians of this generation to join Him in His fight for the souls of others.

I'm continually reminded that the leadership priorities of Jesus Christ are very similar to those taught to Marine Corps leadership. <u>For Example</u>:

- <u>Marine Corps Leadership Priorities</u>:
    1. The mission(s) assigned by our commanders
    2. The lives of those under our authority
    3. We were to place our own life last
- <u>Priorities of Jesus during His life on earth were</u>:
    1. The mission(s) assigned by His Father
    2. The lives of all those who choose to follow Him
    3. He placed His own life last

<u>Look at this parallelism with the two greatest commandments of our Lord:</u>

1. God is our primary focus on the battlefield of life - love Him before all else.
2. Prioritize others before ourselves with a heart of true love.

Throughout the New Testament, Jesus calls us time and again to the frontlines of the spiritual battlefield. He doesn't tell us that we won't be wounded or even killed because of the world's hatred, but He does tell us that He walks alongside us through the Valley of the Shadow of Death and we will not be killed until our calling is complete. Until then a thousand may fall at your side and ten thousand at your right hand, but harm will not touch you until your assigned mission is complete. This was certainly true of His disciples whom He dearly loved. They were among the first Christians who were martyred, but only after their mission in this life was complete.

A MILITARY PERSPECTIVE OF A GREAT LEADER

A leader does not abide in his tent while his men bleed and die upon the battlefield. A leader does not dine while his men go hungry or sleep when they stand at watch upon the wall. A leader does not command his men's loyalty through fear or purchase it with gold; he earns their love by the sweat of his own back and the pains he endures for their sake. That which comprises the harshest burden, a leader lifts first and sets down last. A leader does not require service of those he leads; he provides it to them. He serves them, not they him.[10] These certainly are the leadership traits inherent within the greatest Leader that ever walked on this earth and who currently serves as the true Commander in Chief over the Army of God.

- *By this we know love, that he laid down his life for us, and we ought to lay down our lives for the brothers.* **1 John 3:16**

JESUS' TEACHINGS – "MAKE WAR, BECAUSE WE LOVE!"

Surely this is not the time for God's people to withdraw into passivity—to refuse to look at the reality of a rapidly decaying society that affects all of us and our loved ones. We are in Christ and He is in us, which means that His aggression against Satan must be expressed through us. We are not free to play the role of civilians, living as if there were no war. Our military role is pictured to us throughout the Bible—for the history of Christianity in every age is one of conflict. The pathway the disciple treads as he follows the Lord is one of intense and challenging warfare. Warrior-spirited Christians is the author's description of those disciples who will be called by Jesus Christ to minister in the midst of the end-times tribulation with an anointing of unprecedented power. Thus, in contrast to these liberal world-view voices who cry "make love, not war," Jesus Christ, our true Commander-in-Chief calls us to: **"Make war, because we love!"**

Satan knows that his time is running short, and he is accelerating his efforts in a desperate last-ditch attempt to defeat the redemptive purposes of God. Although our spiritual weapons are as powerful today as they were in the early church, our strategies have to be reevaluated in the light of contemporary times, for the technologies of today are mighty weapons being used in the strategies of Satan against the kingdom of God. Therefore, we must have a deeper understanding of today's spiritual warfare if we are to properly prepare for His coming—for we have been commanded to stay ready and alert by our true Commander-in-Chief, Jesus Christ Himself.

WHAT OUR MISSION "IS NOT"

Soldiers in the army of God need to understand that we are not forces of a revolution attempting to establish a righteous government in this present world. This world is not our home; until it is finally liberated, it belongs to the enemy. In fact, soldiers in God's army are despised by the world.

- *Do not love the world or the things in the world. If anyone loves the world, the love of the Father is not in him. For all that is in the world— the desires of the flesh and the desires of the eyes and pride in possessions—is not from the Father but is from the world. And the world is passing away along with its desires, but whoever does the will of God abides forever. **1 John 2:15-17***

Our army is probably better characterized as guerillas behind enemy lines with a mission to proclaim the true gospel message of Jesus Christ, as the Son of God, to those currently in the world. As soldiers in this army, we will be continually ridiculed, scorned, and persecuted; yet the greater the persecution, the more powerful the gospel message becomes as the evilness of the world becomes more and more visible to the masses when they witness the tremendous hatred toward those who possess a heart of love.

<u>Our assigned mission is to lead those held in captivity by the world:</u>

- Out of darkness into the light
- From deception to truth
- From evil to righteousness
- From eternal damnation and misery into eternal life and joy.

We thought this was our mission in Vietnam – to free the South Vietnamese from the bondage of communism – but America, who is a worldly kingdom, turned their back on those who were fighting to free others. Many of the South Vietnamese, who had supported and trusted America, were subsequently tortured, raped, and murdered when the communists took over. Our government betrayed the South Vietnamese who had placed their trust in us. But the kingdom of God, led by our Lord will never betray His soldiers fighting to free others. Jesus Christ will continually encourage and strengthen us to "make war, because we love."

<u>There is a significant difference between soldiers of the world & soldiers in God's army:</u>

- Soldiers of the world may die carrying out a mission to kill the enemy and take prisoners captive.
- Soldiers in the kingdom of God may die carrying out a mission to love the enemy and release prisoners from spiritual captivity.

All Christian soldiers in the Army of God do lose some battles now and then, but they continue to be strengthened by their experiences and do not succumb to self-pity.

21ST CENTURY CHRISTIANS NEED TO EXPECT "CHALLENGING ORDEALS"

Christian soldiers who follow Jesus Christ in the army of God must understand, and internalize the following truths if they intend to prevail in their spiritual assignments:

- The great warriors of the bible always went through periods of darkness before they were brought into the purposes of God.
- Between those places where we receive the promise and the fulfillment of the promise, there will be a challenging wilderness experience that few Christians understand when it rises up before them.
- The purpose of the wilderness journey is to conform us more and more into the image of Jesus Christ and to bring us to a place of maturity where He can trust us with more authority.

- Many Christians will never walk in the promises of God to which they were called because, like the ancient Israelites, they will fall into whining, grumbling, and complaining about their wilderness experiences.
- Remember warriors, there is no victory without a battle. We must see every test as a great opportunity and no matter how dark it seems to get, the light will surely dawn, just as the sun comes up in the morning.

Some historical examples of Warriors standing for the Kingdom of God:

God's Warrior(s)	versus	Satan's Warrior(s)
David	versus	Goliath – a 9'6"giant in full armor
Moses	versus	Pharaoh - a powerful monarch
Joseph	verses	10 brothers & Pontiphar's wife
Moses, Joshua & Caleb	verses	Two-million whining Israelites
Gideon & 300 Men	verses	Army of 15,000 Medianites
Elijah on Mount Carmel	versus	Ahab, Jezebel, & 450 Prophets of Baal
Esther & Mordecai	verses	Haman, an Assyrian-plot to kill all the Jews
Christian Martyrs	verses	Holy Roman Empire & Bloody Monarchs
In the 21st Century		
Christian Warriors	verses	World Governments & False Religions
For 6,000 years:		
Kingdom of God	verses	Kingdom of World

Now these biblical warriors did not start out in church leadership positions – they received leadership anointing as they continually sought the Lord's direction for their lives. The above events certainly stand out, but we need to remember that the whole history of the church is a battlefield where God's people are confronted again and again by Satan's chosen vessels.

As the previous examples demonstrate, Satan's champions will always visibly appear to be more numerous and powerful than God's champions. Yet, warrior-spirited Christians standing uncompromisingly for our Lord will always prevail in the strength of the Lord. The praying believer will never faint during hard times. On the contrary, he will grow stronger and stronger – because he trusts in God before he trusts in men.

- *He gives power to the faint, and to him who has no might he increases strength. Even youths shall faint and be weary, and young men shall fall exhausted; but they who __wait__ for the Lord shall renew their strength; they shall mount up with wings like eagles; they shall run and not be weary; they shall walk and not faint.* **Isaiah 40:29-31**
- The Hebrew word: "**wait** = "kaw-vah." This means to patiently look for. In other words: continually seek His face and develop that personal one on one relationship with Jesus and your heavenly Father.

Christian warriors need to remember that this is a Holy War and that the required power for victory is not found among its human participants, but in the power of God. Thus, believers need to understand the power of prayer which may be likened to that wrestling which took place between God and his chosen warriors throughout history. This is the "ongoing battle" that should be taking place within each member of the Body of Christ.

That warrior spirit may be knocked down on occasion, but will always seek the strength of the Lord in order to get back up and again run to the battle. **These are the Christian warriors who will "never quit."**

A CALLING FOR CHRISTIAN WARRIORS

The Lord is calling many among His people to champion His kingdom purposes, both on the spiritual and earthly battlefields. This book is intended for those Christians who possess a warrior spirit deep inside and are searching for their individual mission within the Army of God. Men and women who really want to stand strong for the Lord in the face of a world that is becoming increasingly darker year by year. These are Christians who will not shy away from being counted among those in His army who can identify with the following passage.

- *"If the world hates you, know that it has hated me before it hated you. If you were of the world, the world would love you as its own; but because you are not of the world, but I chose you out of the world, therefore the world hates you. Remember the word that I said to you: 'A servant is not greater than his master.' If they persecuted me, they will also persecute you. If they kept my word, they will also keep yours."* **(John 15:18-20)**

Now, warrior-spirited Christians must recognize that they are up against an enemy who is incredibly powerful—one whom the great majority of the world's population ignorantly embraces. Since the days of mankind's fall in the Garden of Eden, there has been ongoing warfare between Satan and his vast and powerful army of darkness and the eternal purposes of our Lord. Over and over, the Scriptures reveal that there is a violent, ongoing war occurring in the spiritual realm in which the people of God on earth must actively participate. The New Testament Christian, like the Old Testament Israelite, continues to be engaged in a battle, and it is a battle:

- *...not directed against flesh and blood, but against the rulers, against the authorities, against the powers of this dark world, and against the spiritual forces of evil in the heavenly realms.* **(Ephesians 6:12)**

Christians have been brought into the story of life at this time in the history of the world in order to enlist in the Army of God. Believers need to put on the armor of God and allow His light to shine through them in the workplace, their neighborhoods, and their families. These places are the true front lines of the battlefield.

- *You are the light of the world. A city set on a hill cannot be hidden. Nor do people light a lamp and put it under a basket, but on a stand, and it gives light to all in the house. In the same way, <u>let your light shine before others, so that they may see your good works and give glory to your Father who is in heaven</u>. (**Matthew 5:14-16**)*

In the wilderness, Israel lived a wandering lifestyle that God had led them into for a season of time. They were on their way to being restored, but they continually responded in a negative way. They developed a victim mentality and constantly grumbled about their state of discomfort. They had sunk into a maintenance mentality, trying to stay alive, rather than a victory mentality of ruling and reigning with God. They seemed to believe that when they entered the Promised Land that all fighting would cease and their worries would disappear. They had no idea that they were the weapon in God's hands that would establish the rule of God on earth. This sounds like much of the contemporary church.

Believers have not been put on this earth simply to be saved and then to sit around living life as usual. We are being presented with the opportunity that Jesus offered His disciples: making an eternal impact for the kingdom of God and becoming a warrior-spirited soldier in His army. If believers decide for greatness, it will cost everything they have and are, for they may even have to give up their very lives. The choice is momentous, but amazingly, it is for every believer to make.[12]

<u>God's Valiant Warriors are called to:</u>

REMAIN STEADFAST IN THE FOLLOWING TRUTHS

1. **God speaks to His people in this life through both the Old and New Testaments. The bible is God's revelation concerning <u>Who He Is</u> and <u>Who We Are</u> together with the relationship that exists between God and man. The Scriptures are NOT man's witness that God exists, but God's witness to man. It contains God-breathed words that are true in every respect; there are no contradictions or superfluous information.**

- *All Scripture is breathed out by God and profitable for teaching, for reproof, for correction, and for training in righteousness, that the man of God may be competent, equipped for every good work. (**2 Timothy 3:16-17**)*

2. **Jesus Christ is truly divine and existed from all eternity as the Son of God. He is the Word of God that was present when creation was spoken into being.**

- *In the beginning was the Word, and the Word was with God, and the Word was God. He was in the beginning with God. All things were made through him, and without him was not any thing made that was made. In him was life, and the life was the light of men. (John 1:1-4)*
- *And the Word became flesh and dwelt among us, and we have seen his glory, glory as of the only Son from the Father, full of grace and truth. (John 1:14)*
- *He was foreknown before the foundation of the world but was made manifest in the last times for your sake, who through him are believers in God, who raised him from the dead and gave him glory, so that your faith and hope are in God. (1 Peter 1:20-21)*

3. Jesus Christ is God's Son who came to earth to pay the penalty of death for all those who believe on His Name.

- *"For God so loved the world, that he gave his only Son, that whoever believes in him should not perish but have eternal life. (John 3:16)*

4. Jesus Christ is the one and only way to eternal salvation. There is no other way.

- *Jesus said --- "I am the way, and the truth, and the life. No one comes to the Father except through me. (John 14:6)*
- *And there is salvation in no one else, for there is no other name under heaven given among men by which we must be saved." (Acts 4:12)*

5. Mankind is a natural born sinner who cannot enter the kingdom of God unless this sin has been washed away by the shed blood of Jesus Christ.

- *Therefore, just as sin came into the world through one man, and death through sin, and so death spread to all men because all sinned— (Romans 5:12)*
- *---for all have sinned and fall short of the glory of God, (Romans 3:23)*
- *---but God shows his love for us in that while we were still sinners, Christ died for us. Since, therefore, we have now been justified by his blood, much more shall we be saved by him from the wrath of God. (Romans 5:8-9)*

6. One must be truly "born again" in order to enter into the Kingdom of God. These are those who truly repent (turn from their sins) and render obedience (walk in the truths of God).

- *Jesus answered him, "Truly, truly, I say to you, unless one is born again he cannot see the kingdom of God." (John 3:3)*
- *That which is born of the flesh is flesh, and that which is born of the Spirit is spirit. Do not marvel that I said to you, 'You must be born again.' (John 3:6-7)*

7. <u>Who are the true sons of God?</u>

- *Whoever confesses that Jesus is the Son of God, God abides in him, and he in God. (1 John 4:15)*

- *No one who denies the Son has the Father. Whoever confesses the Son has the Father also.* **(1 John 2:23)**

- *No one born of God makes a practice of sinning, for God's seed abides in him, and he cannot keep on sinning because he has been born of God. By this it is evident who are the children of God, and who are the children of the devil: whoever does not practice righteousness is not of God, nor is the one who does not love his brother.* **(1 John 3:9-10)**

- *By this we know that we abide in him and he in us, because he has given us of his Spirit. And we have seen and testify that the Father has sent his Son to be the Savior of the world. Whoever confesses that Jesus is the Son of God, God abides in him, and he in God.* **(1 John 4:13-15)**

- *The Spirit himself bears witness with our spirit that we are children of God, and if children, then heirs—heirs of God and fellow heirs with Christ, provided we suffer with him in order that we may also be glorified with him.* **(Romans 8:16-17)**

8. Come Out of the World

- *Do not love the world or the things in the world. If anyone loves the world, the love of the Father is not in him. <u>For all that is in the world— the desires of the flesh and the desires of the eyes and pride in possessions—is not from the Father but is from the world.</u> And the world is passing away along with its desires, but whoever does the will of God abides forever.* **(1 John 2:15-17)**

- *"If the world hates you, know that it has hated me before it hated you. 19 If you were of the world, the world would love you as its own; but because you are not of the world, but I chose you out of the world, therefore the world hates you.* **(John 15:18-19)**

- *Who is it that overcomes the world except the one who believes that Jesus is the Son of God?* **(1 John 5:5)**

The time is coming when God's warrior-spirited watchmen will hear the following call from our Lord:

- *Arise, shine, for your <u>light</u> has come, and the glory of the Lord has risen upon you. For behold, <u>darkness</u> shall cover the earth, and <u>thick darkness</u> the peoples; but the Lord will arise upon you, and his <u>glory</u> will be seen upon you.* **Isaiah 60:1-2**

The First Step in Becoming a Warrior-Spirited Disciple in the Kingdom of God: **"LET GO OF THE WORLDLY KINGDOM"**

CHAPTER 2

WARNINGS FOR THE CHURCH IN AMERICA

(First Read: Revelation 1—3)

BETRAYAL ARISES FROM WITHIN

One of the most eye-opening teachings in the Bible is found in the Lord Jesus' informing His disciples that when the nations commence persecuting the church prior to His second coming, many will fall away and eventually hate and betray those who remain. This is primarily the consequence of many false teachers who are solidly established within the organized church system but whose teachings continually lead their devoted followers astray.[13] Here our Commander in Chief is alerting His people that many of the enemy are within their midst, yet His words are largely ignored within the American church. This is somewhat understandable since few pastors could possibly believe that members of their congregation, or fellow pastors, would ever align with the kingdom of the world in their hatred toward the church. However, this is such a huge event that God's kingdom people will face in the near future that it simply cannot be ignored any longer. Preparation to deal with this issue will be discussed in a subsequent chapter, but for now let's address how such a catastrophic event could possibly happen.

THE LETTERS OF JESUS TO THE CHURCH

An overview of the letters Jesus dictated and gave to the seven churches in Asia Minor should provide a clearer understanding of the circumstances that will cause people to either remain steadfast in their love for Christ or fall away when confronted with life-threatening pressures. The characteristics of five of these churches will be briefly discussed within this chapter; however, I would highly recommend David Ravenhill's excellent book, *The Jesus Letters*, for those who desire additional insights.

Now, contrary to the theories of some theologians, it is extremely important to understand that these letters from Jesus to the church in Asia Minor are also meant for the entire Christian church from the first century until the present day. Jesus speaks of spiritual ailments and misunderstandings concerning sin that have historically plagued and continue to weaken the Christian churches. Christian soldiers need to stand back and take an unbiased and truthful look at the American church today, and hopefully they will see that Jesus is not only speaking to the churches in His day but is also speaking to us. Our generation needs to awaken to the tremendous weaknesses in our churches today, for the love of so many of our people has, unknowingly, grown cold.

THE CHURCH OF EPHESUS IN AMERICA
(First Read: Revelation 2:1-7)

If one were to only read the first three verses, it would appear as if the Ephesian church was a prime example of the type of church that is very pleasing to the Lord. The Ephesian church was obviously a very influential body that gave a tremendous effort to Christian ministry. However, these initial accolades from Jesus are followed by a "but," which tells us that we are about to hear what really is on Jesus' mind. There was a time many years before when the Ephesian church was passionate in their relationship with Jesus; however, their passion had now faded and been replaced by other priorities. Doctrinal purity and the letter of the Word had become more important than the Spirit of the Word, which is necessary to develop that moment-to-moment intimacy with the Lord. We the church need to understand the importance of devoting ourselves to Him. Note the following insights by Charles Stanley.

- *I believe with all my heart that it is impossible to be both goal-oriented and God-oriented at the same time. One orientation will always take precedence over the other. When our desire to achieve takes the lead, several things happen in our relationship with God. He becomes a means to an end rather than the end. We tend to use God rather than worship Him. We find ourselves seeking information about Him rather than transformation by Him.*[14]

Very subtly, the church can become like the Pharisees and their followers, who prided themselves in their hard work and doctrinal purity. Now the Ephesian church certainly baptized, fasted, paid tithes, and kept the Sabbath, which in their minds was evidence of their spirituality; yet they were blind to the presence of the Lord in their midst. This was a church that needed to pay attention to the following warning given by Jesus: *"Unless your righteousness exceeds that of the scribes and Pharisees, you will never enter the kingdom of heaven."*[15]

It was a church strong in doctrine, faithful in discipline, obviously intellectual, and abounding in the work of the Lord; yet there was a certain defect in its inner life that was so serious that it would lead the church to utter ruin before God unless it repented. Ministry was increasing, but the spiritual life of the church was ebbing away. Outwardly, the church had grown; inwardly it had become weak. Certainly, there was a remnant of those within the church who knew the love of Christ, but they no longer were the leading element within the church. The subject of spiritual growth in the knowledge of the Lord Jesus was silently becoming of secondary importance. Such routine priorities as whether the services were faithfully attended, the sacraments were properly applied, the church bulletins were read, the budget was paid—all questions that pertained to the external life and activities of the church—was its primary focus.[16]

Such churches and seminaries, with their prideful spirit of independence and the worshipping of their respective denominations, are very prevalent in the Western world today—yet, they have no idea of their lack of readiness for the coming Day of the Lord. When this type of church is confronted with persecution from a worldly government, the majority will not have the spiritual strength to stand against it and will in fact compromise the gospel message in order to maintain their status within the new governmental system. This is so serious to the Lord that He tells the Ephesian church that unless they repent and return to their first love, He will remove them from their place.

THE CHURCH OF SMYRNA IN AMERICA
(First Read: Revelation 2:8-11)

Now here was a congregation of warriors for Christ. As we contemplate the tribulation, the poverty, and the slandering that this church was experiencing day after day and year after year while maintaining their faithfulness to Christ, it should be an awakening to us in the Western world. It is probable that the Smyrna church had earlier experienced a falling away of many in their congregation as pressure was continually brought against it by the government and the worldly community. But Jesus praises the remnant who were shortly to be thrown into prison and subsequently killed. He calls them "rich" and tells them to "fear not," for He endured a similar fate, and He promises them the eternal "crown of life" if they remain faithful to the end of their lives. Notice that He didn't promise to deliver them from their tribulations but rather to stand with them and strengthen them through them. This was a victorious and conquering church in the ongoing spiritual war. They could not be hurt by the "second death." They were steadfast in their calling, and their eternal reward would be tremendous.

Paul Marshall wrote,

- *There are some 200 million Christians worldwide undergoing some form of persecution. The U.S. State Department cites over sixty countries where Christians face the realities of massacre, rape, torture, mutilation, family division, harassment, imprisonment, and slavery, as well as discrimination in education and employment and even death.*[17]

Christians, can you imagine the shame that pretribulation raptured saints would feel when they met the Smyrna-type church people in the eternal kingdom? Are we more privileged, that the Lord would deliver us from a time of persecution when, historically, He strengthens most of His saints to endure it? Wake up to the reality of the times, or the oil in your lamps will be insufficient.[18]

The American churches have been relatively free of persecution and have a tendency to believe that in our "democratic country" it couldn't happen here. However, this mindset can be a catastrophic mistake for us as the Day of the Lord approaches—for Christ Himself alerted us that before His return His people will face tribulation and death and will be hated by all nations for His name's sake.[19] Christian warriors need to remember that <u>the kingdom of the world desires freedom to do what is right in its own eyes without being told it is wrong.</u> Citizens of that kingdom long to rid the world of the restraining influence of the church's light in order to give free reign to deeds of darkness. There is no question that persecution will be coming to the uncompromising Christian church; it is only a matter of time as to when it will come.[20]

Ultimately, what this letter to the Smyrna church teaches us is another aspect of the spiritual character that Jesus Christ values in His people, and that is faithfulness during periods of intense trials. Here were a people who had suffered the loss of their homes and possessions, undergone rejection, blasphemies, and tribulation, and yet had remained steadfastly faithful through it all. They had experienced firsthand what it is like to "walk through the valley of the shadow of death," and they had come through victoriously. Unlike their Ephesian neighbors, they had maintained their first love despite tremendously adverse circumstances.[21] Tribulation experiences not only produce mature and strong Christians, but they also weed out the tares from within their midst. Where is Jesus when Christians are going through this time of tribulation? He's standing right alongside of us, strengthening and encouraging us to keep fighting against the powers of darkness and promising us that the finish line is fast approaching and will bring eternal rewards so great that our finite minds cannot comprehend them.[22]

THE CHURCH OF SARDIS IN AMERICA
(First Read: Revelation 3:1-6)

Among the seven churches addressed by Jesus in Revelation, the church of Sardis did not receive a single word of commendation from the Lord. Something was seriously wrong with this one, yet the Sardis church had a reputation in the community for being "alive."

Envision this in today's commercial society: the parking lot is full every Sunday and the local police are there directing traffic; the senior pastor might host a weekly television program, as well as producing popular and well-attended events during the holiday seasons. Because of these numerous, ongoing, nonstop activities, the church gains a reputation for being "alive." It is a dynamo of activity; programs abound. But it's all done by human effort; so, in reality, it is a church that is "dead." Such churches are led by very gifted communicators—salesmen proclaiming messages of financial prosperity and easy believism and selling insurance policies guaranteeing eternal salvation. They like to call themselves champions in God's army, but they are babes; and because of their lack of spiritual maturity, most of them will compromise the truth of the gospel at the first sign of persecution. At that point, they will align with the coming emergent churches, or "super church" which will join with the worldly government(s) in their war against uncompromising Christians who will not bow down to their idolatrous beliefs.

The Sardis-style ministry is simply an application of big business concepts in the guise of a spiritual move of God. The following scenario is prevalent in these deceptive churches.

- *When you are broken, sick, hurting, or jobless, and a local or TV preacher reaches into your hurt with tears and says, "I sense someone is hurting . . . and if you reach for your checkbook and give your best gift" . . . just dry your tears and write a check for someone or some cause that really needs it— someone worse off than you. Do it, not because you think it will trigger some divine reaction financially, or that God will feel He owes you now. Do it because it is a command to give, especially to the needy and poor. Do it to break the chain of despair and depression you may feel. Do it and laugh because God will take care of all your needs for He can create from nothing.*[23]

Sardis is led by those who have lowered the standard of their message to the level of people's sensitivities and cultural norms in order to make the message nice and inoffensive, and so it remains vague. It's the opinion of many of these church leaders that they need to lure people through the doors with a happy, vague, seeker-friendly message, and then when they have their confidence, they can speak about the tougher, but inoffensive issues. They believe that being consistent and strong in the gospel message will not make friends, fill their wallets, or grow mega-churches. This is outright fraud; it is the "Gospel of Me."[24]

Yes, the Sardis community sends their children to Christian schools, listens to the latest Christian music, and attends church on Sundays, but deep within this people, there is no real hunger for the Lord, no desire to spend personal time growing in the knowledge of the Lord. Sardis believers portray an appearance of spirituality to the world, but God sees into the heart and knows that the Spirit does not reside there. All their works are dead in His sight. How easily people can become attendees of church, rather than abiders in Christ, as programs and routines replace a relationship with Him. This church is no different from any worldly club or organization that continually offers great programs to the community.[25] It is a fraudulent direction these leaders are taking, and it is leading many down the broad road toward destruction. Unless they awake and repent, they will not be prepared for His soon coming, and it will be frightening for this segment of Christianity and especially their leadership.

THE CHURCH OF PHILADELPHIA IN AMERICA

(First Read: Revelation 3:7-13)

Like the church in Smyrna, this was a church beloved by the Lord, who spoke no words of condemnation toward it. A passion for the Lord was the primary focus of their service. It was a church of "little strength," which implies that it was a small congregation with little financial resources. Yet, it was a church that remained faithful to the truth of the gospel, even when they were continually ridiculed by the legalistic Jews, who probably represented great influence and wealth within the city. It takes great spiritual strength to continually proclaim the name of the Lord in the midst of ridicule and threats of persecution. Those who will stand for His truths in such circumstances are the true "overcomers" whom Jesus encourages throughout His letters to the churches.

Jesus told these Philadelphians that because they patiently kept the word of the Lord, He would keep them from the hour of trial that is coming on the whole world. Perhaps this was a church in a province of Asia Minor that was governed by Roman authorities who were not persecutors of Christianity. If so, the church in Philadelphia would likely have been aggressively active in sending forth missionaries throughout the Mediterranean world in the early centuries of Christian growth. It is conceivable that our Lord restrained persecution for the Philadelphia church in order to allow it to freely proclaim the message of the gospel throughout the Mediterranean world.

On the other hand, these words of Jesus to the Philadelphians commonly have been used to support the modern-day theory of a pretribulation rapture. Our first question regarding this should be: Why should the church of Smyrna be cast into the midst of tribulation, while the church of Philadelphia is excused? This "escapism doctrine" of modern-day "rapturists" is dangerous. It puts people to sleep, and the church that expects to be received in the air before the great tribulation does not prepare itself for the battle. And in the coming hour of persecution, many will fall away.

Christ continually warns His people that this hour shall come and we must remain faithful to the end; for it is the faithful church that will have the strength to endure persecution. Jesus is not saying that the faithful church will be kept from tribulation but that in the midst of persecution, when the enemy rages and the temptation to deny the Lord is strong, the Lord will be alongside to encourage, protect, guide, and strengthen His church so that it endures to the very end. It is quite possible that the church in Philadelphia was in a phase that preceded a coming persecution, a phase that the church in Smyrna had earlier experienced.[26]

Additionally, being kept from the "Hour of Trial" may also be representative of the 144,000 who are sealed prior to the Great Tribulation. The purpose for this sealing is also to allow them to powerfully minister throughout the world during the period of Great Tribulation. (Those who are sealed and the purpose for the sealing will be presented in subsequent chapters).

THE CHURCH OF LAODICEA IN AMERICA
(Tone Read: Revelation 3:14-22)

What was missing in Laodicea is very similar to what is still missing in many congregations today: a relationship with Jesus Christ. Although the Lord continues to knock on the door, the Laodicean style of church remains oblivious to His knocking, believing that He is pleased with the various activities that continually occupy its time; it has learned to excel without the abiding presence of Christ.[27] The church, not the Lord, has won the hearts of this people. Their unspoken attitude may be verbalized as follows.

- *Wow, thanks, God, for the gospel of Jesus Christ. We can take it from here. We appreciate the greatness of Your sacrifice, but now we want to show You what we can do. By the way, if Jesus wants to come with us, He's sure welcome. Again, thanks. We'll let you know if we need any additional help.*

When it comes to relationships, lukewarmness is the last thing a lover wants from his or her beloved. Lukewarm, mediocre, or average are not the types of expressions one wants to hear, especially regarding the one a person is about to marry. This is like a woman who dates a man but refuses to marry him because she has other priorities she wants to pursue. Instead, she engages in an off-and-on, shallow relationship with him, keeping him on a string but never really committing to him.

The leaders within this form of church are Christians who know about Him and understand foundational theology, but if anyone speaks with them about pursuing a deeper relationship with Jesus, that one will quickly be labeled a charismatic fanatic. This is a very controlling leadership, and those people who disagree with their direction for the church are strongly encouraged to leave. Their inherent belief is "as long as one's sins are confessed, and the person is baptized and identified with a church congregation, that is all that is necessary." They confess a belief in Jesus, but in actuality, how can one believe in someone they don't really know? Contrary to what they say, the priorities of these church leaders are not intimacy with Christ but watching Sunday attendance climb, along with the size of the offering. More time is spent *organizing* programs than *agonizing* in intercessory prayer. Intercessors give way to intellectuals, and businessmen now run the church like a business.[28] The Laodicean church of today must awaken to the fact that baptism and church attendance is not the end but the very beginning of an ever-progressing relationship with the Lord. We need to become not only His subjects but also His children. He is our Lord and King, but He's also our Father. Yet, despite the lukewarmness of today's Laodiceans, Christ continues to knock on the door of their hearts. But, unless the individuals of this church awaken and respond to His knocking, they will remain lukewarm, and thus a terrifying time lies ahead. He will spit them out of His mouth, for this is a church that is nauseating to the Lord.

Many of the members of Ephesian, Laodicean or Sardis-type churches have common parallels with the Israelites, when they were delivered out of Egypt only to begin a challenging journey through the wilderness. They were very excited and worshipped the Lord when they were delivered across the Red Sea; but as they experienced the bitter waters in the wilderness, they grumbled and complained that the life of slavery in Egypt was far better than the wilderness journey. It is so easy to express joy when things are going well, and this is exactly the scenario that the American church attempts to maintain. We can praise the Lord during a Sunday morning worship service, but do Christians continue to praise Him in the midst of life's wilderness journey? The lukewarm church does not comprehend that it is the wilderness journey that tests and strengthens the hearts of God's people, and thus there is little equipping in these churches for the Christian wilderness journey. This form of leadership simply preaches all the good things that God will do but fails to prepare people for the certainty of a wilderness journey.

While contemplating the differences between churches like Smyrna and the Sardis/Laodicean style of leadership, I was reminded of the following experience of Al Houghton, a minister of the gospel and a former Navy pilot who flew combat missions in Vietnam.

- *During combat in Vietnam, most of the time is spent in routine tasks, but attack can come suddenly. When hours of routine boredom is turned into 10 minutes of panic, two very visible and dramatically different groupings of men emerged. One group (Smyrna) had already made their decision, "this war is worth the sacrifice of our lives" while the other (Sardis/Laodicea) was somewhere in "limbo land" having not yet made any real commitment. The first group functioned without the paralysis of fear and was empowered to do what was necessary to save lives. Those in the second group were literally "locked up" and looked like they were swimming in molasses. **Fear** is the spiritual heritage of the unprepared. **Fear** will be eclipsed by faith if we will embrace the covenant promises of eternal life.[29]*

Semper Fi, Al!

The Laodicean church is commonplace in America today; they have repackaged God so as to make Him user-friendly. The God who deeply desires a relationship with His bride and is jealous for His holiness has been elbowed aside and replaced by a happier-faced model of Christ, who always smiles approvingly at whatever we say or do.[30] How could anyone who has truly met the living God, the all-consuming fire, become lukewarm about Him? [31]

THE "ATTRACTIONAL" CHURCH IN AMERICA

Most contemporary churches probably started out well. They were planted by a pastor motivated for God and in the beginning spent much time in prayer and studies. Unfortunately, many of them get caught up in their success and begin to spend less and less time in their relationship with Christ while spending more and more time building their respective ministries. As they continue down this road, they may soon find themselves loving the Bible more than the Author of the Bible. Knowing the Bible is not the same thing as knowing God, and reading the Bible is not the same thing as hearing from God. The Pharisees knew the Bible, loved the Bible, and read the Bible, but they did not know, love, or hear God.[32]

Eventually, these churches develop techniques of administration and marketing used in the business world. They develop a message of easy-believism that is inoffensive; they market salvation like a life insurance policy; they emphasize attendance and giving as most important in their walk with Christ; and they develop entertaining and fun services that will keep the people coming. Thus, the assurance of salvation is provided to seeds sown on "rocky ground" and in "thorny bushes" rather than alerting them to the dangers of the soil they reside in; it certainly smells like "Sardis and Laodicea"!

A MARINE'S VIEW OF THE PRETRIBULATION RAPTURE

The pretribulation rapture is a modern-day teaching that has helped create the mega-churches within America. It was originally promoted in England by John Nelson Darby, who helped found the Plymouth Brethren movement back in the mid-1800s, and was subsequently popularized in this country by C. I Scofield, a wealthy American attorney who published the *Scofield Reference Bible* in the early 1900s—which contained notes that emphasized this teaching. The Scofield Bible became very popular among evangelicals, many of whom failed to see the difference between a man-made doctrine and the inspired Word of God since it was all included in a single book. Today millions of books promoting this pretribulation rapture teaching have been published and sold worldwide. Also, many seminaries, bible colleges, and churches teach this as being a foundational truth to understanding God's love for His people. It is a popular teaching of mega-ministries, and it has proved extremely profitable for a few in these leadership positions—thus it is promoted in many of the Ephesus, Sardis and Laodicea-style churches of America. This is a teaching that has seriously weakened the contemporary American church, for it has contributed mightily to the popularity of other false gospel messages commonly known as the "easy-believism and prosperity doctrines," which also employ attractional tactics to build their respective ministries. Pretribulation rapture teachings certainly appear to be one of the "myths" that the Lord's Word has warned us about.

- *For the time is coming when people will not endure sound teaching, but having itching ears they will accumulate for themselves teachers to suit their own passions, and <u>will turn away from listening to the truth and wander off into myths.</u> As for you, always be sober-minded, endure suffering, do the work of an evangelist, fulfill your ministry. (**2 Timothy 4:3-5**)*

These pretribulation rapture teachings provide a false degree of comfort to those who correctly discern the "signs of the times" but are fearful of becoming involved, for they know instinctively that they are not prepared. They certainly love reading popular books and watching various movies concerning tribulation-era events, but only if they are continually being assured that they are only reading and watching and will not be participants. Thus, they embrace the lukewarm churches and the television celebrities who emphasize this escapist doctrine. In truth, it is putting the church at ease when, in fact, it should be spiritually preparing itself for the greatest battle in the history of mankind. It is a teaching that robs the church of much of the truth of warfare, for it is embraced by those who wish to be served by God rather than be servants of God. Jesus did forewarn His people concerning doctrines such as this when He stated that in the last days, "many false prophets will arise and lead many astray."[33]

Being a retired Marine Corps officer who spent two tours in the war zones of Vietnam, I disrespect this pretribulation rapture myth for being a wimpy sales presentation designed to please those who are scared of potential conflict. Marines don't leave people behind on the battlefield, and I do get passionately angry when I see Jesus being portrayed as a Commander who calls His people to run from the battle. Jesus Christ is the manliest of men who ever walked this earth, and "retreat" is not in His vocabulary. I can truthfully tell you that in my personal time before the Lord, I have prayerfully requested that if a pretribulation rapture is somehow true for a specific remnant, please leave me behind to stand in support of my Christian and Israelite brothers and sisters who must endure the tribulation.

Imagine being a warrior in the Army of God who was raptured before the great battle begins. How would you feel in the presence of those who, in the midst of the battle, were martyred for the testimony of God? Are those who escape tribulation by being raptured more privileged in God's eyes than they were? Cowards certainly don't think like this; they are just grateful to not have to experience pain and hardships and to teach others that they too can escape the battlefield. <u>Personally, I believe that I would be eternally</u>

ashamed to stand alongside my martyred brothers and sisters if I were among the "privileged" saints who were raptured.

Warriors need to understand that the end-time tribulation is like birth pangs that bring something positive into the world. The tribulation gives birth to the second coming of Jesus, and there can be no birth without pain. The tribulation is not something for believers to enjoy; however, it is not something for us to escape from either. A wonderful purpose for a tribulation is to present an opportunity for lost people to come to repentance, for it is a period of time that will bring in the final harvest. For when God's judgments fall on the world, many will turn to righteousness.[34] Thus, God's warriors need to embrace this opportunity, for it is the most important mission we could possibly be assigned.

CONSEQUENCES OF PRETRIBULATION RAPTURE TEACHINGS

Now, this pretribulation rapture theory is more than simple error; it is a deception that can do great damage to one's faith. Generations of American Christians have been watching the early birth pangs, convinced by their teachers that the next coming event would be the rapture of the church. Yet, in reality, what is coming is intense persecution for those who hold fast to their faith in Christ. A consequence of this mythical teaching will be widespread disillusionment when tribulation descends on this nation and people will realize that they have been deceived by their teachers. There will be a great falling away, and many former churchgoers will align with the world in blaming God for allowing such catastrophe to take place and will then betray many who remain in the fellowship of the church.

All false prophecies are dangerous, and this one carries particular risks. Consider the following testimony of Corrie Ten Boom, who was imprisoned by the German Nazis for hiding Jews from their persecutors. After the war, she spent time as a missionary to the Far East. She wrote,

- *I have been in countries where the saints are already suffering terrible persecution. In China, the Christians were told: "Don't worry, before the tribulation comes, you will be translated, raptured." Then came a terrible persecution. Millions of Christians were tortured to death. Later I heard a bishop from China say, sadly: "We have failed. We should have made the people strong for persecution rather than telling them Jesus would come first." Turning to me, he said: "Tell the people how to be strong in times of persecution, how to stand when the tribulation comes—to stand and not faint." I feel I have a divine mandate to go and tell the people of this world that it is possible to be strong in the Lord Jesus Christ. We are in training for the tribulation. Since I have already gone through prison for Jesus' sake, and since I met that bishop from China, now every time I read a good Bible text I think: "Hey, I can use that in the time of tribulation." Then I write it down and learn it by heart.*[35]

MIGHTY MEN WITHIN THE DISPENSATIONAL COMMUNITY

I do want to mention that several fine men of God, who have been educated in pretribulation rapture doctrines, are among the very best Christian teachers concerning ongoing current events in the twenty-first century. I truly admire and thank men like Hal Lindsey, Greg Laurie, David Reagan, Chuck Missler, Joel Rosenberg, and others for their tremendously fruitful works. These are "watchmen" in the Army of God. They have provided significant strategic information for the American church over the last thirty years. Hal Lindsey's movie *The Late Great Plant Earth* had a tremendous impact upon me when I was still an unbeliever. So, I'm very thankful for men like Hal Lindsey and also Greg Laurie who, unknowingly, pointed me in a direction leading to an overwhelming, "born-again" experience that occurred in 1979. Over the last thirty years, dispensationalists have been the most prominent teachers of the great tribulation events that lie shortly before us. They had the advantage of teaching hard truths without scaring their listeners because of the "rapture" beliefs. Unfortunately, much of their message is falling upon "itchy ears" that see no need to prepare. This is a great danger that I perceive will soon confront the American churches.

THE FRONTLINES OF THE BATTLEFIELD

Jesus is a great army Commander who is giving instructions to His soldiers; however, some of the officers under His command are giving contrary instructions, preparing for a massive retreat. A soldier preparing for war is very different from the one who thinks he will be discharged shortly before the war begins. Many believers today are like soldiers looking forward to an early discharge. Can you imagine David or Joshua preparing their soldiers to retreat when the heat turns up? Can you imagine Peter or Paul looking to escape from preaching the gospel because persecution was coming?[36] Christians must internalize this tough command of Jesus when He tells us that we need to remain faithful even unto death.[37]

THREE GROUPS OF PEOPLE EMERGE DURING TIMES OF WAR

Over the last fifty years in America, every war we have fought (particularly Vietnam) has produced three groups of people within this nation.

- **The first group** is comprised of pacifists - those people who will not fight but neither will they protest. (Wimpy types!)

- **The second group** is comprised of anti-war demonstrators, who rebel against the call of their country and ridicule those who answer the call. Their motto: "Make love, not war!"
- **The third group** is comprised of those who willingly, proudly, and bravely step up to answer the call of their country as well as those who strongly support these American warriors who love and believe in their country.

Now, there is an interesting parallel between these three groups and similar groups found within the American church of today. <u>For example</u>:

The first group regularly attends church and Bible studies, but they have little personal vision for ministry.

- They are content to elect leadership that will be responsible for the church's direction, but don't feel much of a need to be personally involved.
- They have no kingdom vision within themselves. They support their pastor's vision and rely upon the words from the pulpit to guarantee their eternal destiny.
- They just want to sit around, watch television, and wait to go to heaven someday.

The second group actively opposes any talk of warfare. "Make love, not war" is also the motto within their hearts.

- However, their concept of the love of God is not a true, life-changing love but is a false love that leads people away from the fertile soil that produces true disciples of God.
- This type of love is commonly referred to as "tolerance." In other words: "Just continue to march in the same direction you are going – God will understand."
- The sinfulness of man and the need for repentance and obedience to Christ is not a powerful voice in their churches. Their self-indulgent and prosperity teachings appeal to many who place their hope in this world.
- Their primary concern is to not offend people and hurt their feelings, and they repeatedly emphasize that Christ has already accomplished the victory for us; so, we just need to be faithful in our tithing and church attendance, and He will provide for all of our needs.
- Like hippie anti-war demonstrators, they also mock and ridicule Christians who don't agree with them.

The third group comprises warrior-spirited Christians who voluntarily serve in the Army of God.

- They are among those who <u>hunger and thirst for righteousness</u>.

- They are among those who <u>sigh and groan</u> over the abominations that are committed in this country and also in many of our churches.
- They are among those who <u>love their enemies</u> and pray for those who persecute them
- These are disciples who are very passionate for Jesus Christ and the Kingdom of God and are prepared to lay down their lives if called upon to do so.
- These are the ones who will fight the war against the forces of darkness that rules over the kingdom of this world and keeps many of our family, friends, and co-workers in bondage.
- Their heart's desire is to be among their fellow soldiers who embrace the following words of our Lord:
- *Blessed are you when others revile you and persecute you and utter all kinds of evil against you falsely on my account. <u>Rejoice and be glad,</u> for your reward is great in heaven, for so they persecuted the prophets who were before you. <u>You are the light of the world</u>. A city set on a hill cannot be hidden. Nor do people light a lamp and put it under a basket, but on a stand, and it gives light to all in the house. <u>In the same way, let your light shine before others, so that they may see your good works and give glory to your Father who is in heaven</u>. (Matthew 5:11-16)*

MANY WILL "FALL AWAY" AND "BETRAY OTHERS"

Now, how will each of these three groups respond when suddenly, like a thief in the night, catastrophic events occur that destroy this nation's economy and cause the loss of a great number of lives, and robs us of the freedom that we once enjoyed?

Consider the parable of the sower who went out to sow seed – <u>seed being the Word of God</u>:

1. **The first group** of pacifists is like the "seed sown on rocky ground." They can be found in many of the Laodicean-style churches – "Those with a lukewarm faith."
   - *As for what was sown on rocky ground, this is the one who hears the word and immediately receives it with joy, yet he has no root in himself, but endures for a while, and <u>when tribulation or persecution arises on account of the word, immediately he falls away</u>. (Matthew 13:20-21)*
2. **The second group** of liberal, anti-war activists is like the "seed sown among thorns." They love to attend many of the Sardis-style churches – "Those who believe they are rich, but are poor."
   - *As for what was sown among thorns, this is the one who hears the word, but the cares of the world and the deceitfulness of riches choke the word, and it proves unfruitful. (Matthew 13:22-23)*
3. **The third group** of uncompromising Christians who stand strong for the Kingdom of God is like "seed sown in fertile soil." They can be found in many of the Smyrna and Philadelphia-style churches -"Those who overcome the world."

- *As for what was sown on good soil, this is the one who hears the word and understands it. He indeed bears fruit and yields, in one case a hundredfold, in another sixty, and in another thirty." (Matthew 13:23)*

Now, how will each of these groups respond when suddenly, like a thief in the night, catastrophic events occur that destroy this nation's economy and cause the loss of a great number of lives and robs us of the freedom that we once enjoyed? Will tremendous confusion abound with people crying, "Why have we not been raptured?"

Which groups will be disillusioned with church leadership and begin to align with the world in blaming God for allowing such catastrophes to take place? How will they respond when, like Nazi Germany, Russia, and China, the Bible will be outlawed and those who refuse to deny the Lord Jesus will be persecuted?

What will persecution look like? Historically, there has been a confiscation of assets, a separation of families into concentration camps, and execution for those who refuse to deny Christ? How are those who embraced the pretribulation rapture theory going to respond—with deep humility or more like the world because of their anger toward their rapturist-teaching pastors and their disappointment in being a part of a tribulation era? Certainly such events will cause a great apostasy, as many forsake their former beliefs and betray their former friends and family members.

Christians, a time of decision lies shortly before us: During a period of intense tribulation, will we be among those who "will fall away and betray one another?"

- *And then many will fall away and betray one another and hate one another. And many false prophets will arise and lead many astray. And because lawlessness will be increased, the love of many will grow cold. (Matthew 24:10-12)*

Or, will our hearts respond with Isaiah's words?
- *My soul yearns for you in the night; my spirit within me earnestly seeks you. For when your judgments are in the earth, the inhabitants of the world learn righteousness. (Isaiah 26:9)*

Will we see the persecution as an opportunity to honor Christ?
- *Blessed are you when others revile you and persecute you and utter all kinds of evil against you falsely on my account. Rejoice and be glad, for your reward is great in heaven, for so they persecuted the prophets who were before you. (Matthew 5:11-12)*

We are approaching some difficult times ahead as the second coming of Jesus Christ appears to be rapidly approaching. There is a wake-up call from the Lord that is becoming louder and louder, and many are hearing it. Our Lord is searching for warriors who can hear this call and lead His people through the approaching era of end-time events. An old message is being refreshed: The church is being called to the battlefield.

GOD'S ARMY IS STRICTLY FOR VOLUNTEERS ONLY

Our Commander in Chief does not draft His soldiers, but He opens His arms and welcomes all those who volunteer. He does not employ emotional gimmickry but simply speaks out of love and calls each of us to join Him on the battlefield. Although he calls us to join Him in His battle against the forces of evil, He leaves us free to join the enemy against him if we so will. He makes no promises that we will become rich or escape pain in this life. As volunteer soldiers in His army, like our Lord, we will grieve and bleed and perhaps lose our lives for our brothers and sisters who are not yet freed from the enemy. However, we are promised the ultimate victory, and if we fight, His pleasure will rest upon us. Our Lord does not encourage us to join Him simply because we want to be on the winning team, but He wants us to join because we believe in the righteousness of His cause. Volunteers also must understand that we may die in our faith, while not really receiving all of God's promises in this life.

This is not an armchair war, and it will be very difficult for many in our generation to make the adjustment from being spectators to becoming active participants. One of the consequences of television and the internet is that it turns us into "watchers" of world events so that our involvement is simply passive. Many Christians get so carried away with the final victory that they remain blind to the ongoing battle, and the oil in their lamps slowly fritters away. We all need to understand that the way to eternal life with Christ involves the way of the cross. And the way of the cross means there is a great battle to be fought. Who are they who will fall away under the pressure of warfare in these last days? They are the armchair churchgoers who refuse to enlist in the Army of God under such harsh terms. It is extremely challenging to be a committed soldier in the Army of God in this life.[39]

"ABOUT-FACE"

Those with military experience are very familiar with the command "about-face." It is a command to immediately turn sharply 180 degrees from the direction you are currently facing. It is also a command used by our Commander-in-Chief, who calls us to "turn" from our sins. When we obey that command, He will remove the veil which is blinding us from the truth and put us on the path of growing in spiritual maturity. This willingness to turn in an "about-face" will suddenly cause us to see ourselves as we truly are and thus see our need for a Savior. All of God's warriors occasionally will go astray and veer from the course that the Lord directs. However, like Moses, David, or Paul, they all have one thing in common: when confronted with their blindness, they will readily turn in an "about-face" and return to following their Commander.

What will Christians do when our Commander-in-Chief commands us to "about-face"? Will they obey Him or listen to other subordinate commanders, such as some church leaders who tell us that the Commander-in-Chief really meant "right-face" since it is much easier to follow that path. But a partial turn will eventually lead us away from the path that Jesus is going, and even though other commanders tell us that we are moving rightly, we are straying further and further from His direction. Additionally, these other commanders may attempt to convince us that the command was really "At-ease": just keep coming and giving to your church and God will be pleased.

Eventually, the time comes when the Commander in Chief gives the command, "Forward march." Only those who have heard and obeyed the command "about-face" will be equipped to follow the King of Kings and the Lord of Lords in the direction He is heading.[40]

CHAPTER 3

SEALS, HORSEMEN, AND MARTYRDOM

(<u>First Read:</u> Revelation 4—6)

Jesus Christ, our Commander in Chief in the Army of God, has provided His soldiers with detailed intelligence concerning a series of disastrous events that will precede His return to reign over the nations of the earth. He commanded His apostle John to record this information, and certainly one of the main objectives of this intelligence is to provide the people of this generation the opportunity to train and prepare for the raging battles that will attempt to overthrow the kingdom of God and establish a one-world government—a government designed to rid the earth of all who oppose their ungodly objectives.

Yet, this will also be a time of opportunity for that discerning Christian remnant who will *hear and believe* that Jesus is speaking to them - telling them *to prepare* to stand for the kingdom of God in the midst of horrendous tribulations. This intelligence has been primarily recorded in the book of Revelation, which is an inspired writing that has confused many in the church over the centuries; yet it promises great blessings to those who will believe and keep the words of this prophetic book.

- *And behold, I am coming soon. Blessed is the one who keeps the words of the prophecy of this book.* **(Revelation 22:7)**

As previously mentioned, much of the confusion that has arisen in attempts to understand eschatology over the centuries is the result of generations of Christians who could not relate these writings to their respective cultures. However, in our generation technology has developed to a degree that provides us with the ability to relate descriptive events recorded over 1,900 years ago with our twenty-first century culture. Likewise, over 2,500 years ago, the prophet Daniel saw similar events that would confront our present generation, and he was so grieved in his search for understanding that a messenger from the Lord told him to seal up his visions for they were intended for those who live at the "time of the end," when mankind's <u>technological knowledge will greatly increase to the point that communications and travel throughout the world will be commonplace.</u>

- *But you, Daniel, shut up the words and seal the book, until the time of the end. <u>Many shall run to and fro, and knowledge shall increase.</u>"* **(Daniel 12:4)**

Additionally, Daniel was told who would understand those times and who would not.

- *He said, "Go your way, Daniel, for <u>the words are shut up and sealed until the time of the end</u>. Many shall purify themselves and make themselves white and be refined, but the wicked shall act wickedly. <u>And none of the wicked shall understand, but those who are wise shall understand</u>. (**Daniel 12:9-10**)*

Both John and Daniel were shown events that will soon descend upon the world like a "thief in the night," and they were told to record them so that future enlistees in the Army of God, who would use this intelligence to discern these times, would prepare to stand for the kingdom of God. The large majority of mankind in both the church and the nations will soon be overwhelmed by sudden and unexpected catastrophic events that will forever change their habitual lifestyles - from a life rooted in relative ease and comfort, to one of extreme hardships with many challenges that must be confronted in order to survive.

Christian soldiers need to be equipped and ready to be deployed into their respective missional assignments that await them. The following words are meant to encourage this army of warriors.

- *Those who are wise shall shine like the brightness of the sky above; and those who turn many to righteousness, like the stars forever and ever. (**Daniel 12:3**)*

<u>However, in order for Christians to voluntarily enlist in this endeavor, they need to have a foundational understanding of the battles that are coming and the objective of the mission to which they are called.</u> The following chapters are designed to provide a clearer understanding of these challenging events, as viewed through our twenty-first-century eyes, and to provide clarity as to our missional responsibilities during this period of time. The Lord's desire for us is not ignorance of His plans but rather knowledge so that we may prepare the eyes and ears of our hearts through prayer and fasting, whereby He will draw closer to us and become our place of guidance and refuge during this period of severe hardships. Leaders in the Army of God must be committed prayer warriors if they are to have the discernment to understand the times and the commands that they will receive from their Commander in Chief.

As we move forward in the sequence of events recorded in the book of Revelation, let us now continue our quest for understanding by joining with the apostle John as he stands before the throne of God.

THE FATHER GIVES THE SCROLL TO HIS SON
(Revelation 4 and 5)

As John's adventure in the throne room of heaven begins to unfold, he finds himself standing before the throne of almighty God, the highest sovereign of heaven and earth. Obviously, John was overwhelmed by these majestic surroundings in the throne room of God, but when he had calmed somewhat, he noticed a "scroll" held in the right hand of Him who sat upon the heavenly throne. This scroll had writing on both sides, which suggests that events contained within affect both the heavenly and earthly realms; and it also was completely sealed by seven seals.[41] Suddenly a strong angel cries out, "Who is worthy to break the seals and open the scroll?" When no man was found worthy in all of heaven or earth to open the scroll, John was deeply grieved, for he realized that this scroll was of tremendous importance for the manifestation of the coming kingdom of God throughout the earth. Suddenly a Man appeared who was found worthy. It was Jesus Christ, symbolized by a Lamb as though it had been slain. This tells us it was only by His sacrificial death that even this Son of almighty God could qualify to take the scroll from the right hand of His Father and to break open the seven seals, revealing the events that precede the second coming of Jesus Christ to establish the fullness of His kingdom on the earth.

A FALSE PERCEPTION OF THE "LAMB OF GOD"

A false perception of the person of Jesus Christ has been presented by the religiosity of popular church organizations over the centuries. He is portrayed over and over as a little baby in a manger or as a weak-looking, effeminate man walking around in a bathrobe with a halo over his head and little baby angels flying all around, and singing to Him. Their perception of heaven is a place where the "saved" sit on clouds playing musical harps and singing songs forever and ever. Disney World and some Christian movies also have joined with these phony churches in their depiction of the person of Jesus and the angels of heaven. Medieval artworks embraced by churches and cartoonists have seriously weakened the truth that Jesus Christ was the greatest and strongest of warriors who ever walked this earth. These false images certainly don't appeal to many unsaved men who are searching for a strong Leader to provide direction in their lives. The masculine spirit that has not found the true Jesus certainly does not want to follow a "wimpy lord" or live in a "heaven" like that described above. Men, this is a false portrayal of our Lord and His angelic armies. Angels under the command of Jesus Christ are not "wimpy pacifists," for they have historically killed tens of thousands of the enemies of God's people.[42] Also, the response of even the holiest men of God is one of trembling and fear when they are confronted by the glorious presence of our Lord or one of His mighty angels. He is mighty and powerful, and yet He possesses such a deep love for His people that it is just incomprehensible.[43]

A CHRISTIAN WARRIOR'S UNDERSTANDING OF THE "LAMB OF GOD"

Jesus Christ is the "Son of God," who, out of His infinite love for mankind, left the glory of heaven to experience the depths of humiliation upon the earth. He voluntarily left His throne and the presence of His Father and all the citizens of heaven who dearly loved Him in order to receive scorn, hatred, and rejection among the governmental authorities and the religious leaders of mankind and ultimately to die on a cross between two thieves. This occurred over two thousand years ago, when He pulled back the curtain of eternity and stepped out onto the stage of time for approximately thirty-three years, and then He stepped back again into eternity. But in that one brief moment of time, He sealed the fate and fixed the destiny of every man and woman. He split history and divided the ages. Jesus Christ is the "Word of God" who became flesh and dwelt among us, and now He is the only way that one can enter the kingdom of heaven and live eternally in His presence. False religions and false teachers say that there are different paths that can lead to eternal life, but He has said that there is only one way to the Father, and that is through His Son, Jesus Christ. There is no other way! He is the Alpha and Omega, the Beginning and the End. He was dead, but He is now alive forevermore and is currently seated at the right hand of almighty God, His Father.

THE LAMB OF GOD IS ALSO OUR COMMANDER IN CHIEF

Although He is the one and only way to eternal life, and those who receive Him as their eternal Savior are redeemed by this precious blood of the "Lamb of God," He is also the "Lion of Judah." He is a truly mighty Leader who would never delegate assignments to His people that He Himself wouldn't readily embrace—a Commander whom true Christian warriors will readily follow no matter what the danger, what battles have to be confronted, or what costs have to be paid.

Now the days are rapidly approaching when a tremendous separation will take place among mankind. Soldiers in His army will walk through the valley of the shadow of death without a semblance of fear, for He will be with us. And after His victory over the kingdom of darkness, all people who have ever lived will stand before God our Father; and those who have denied Him will be cast into outer darkness, but His sons and daughters, who have been "born again" in the Spirit, will join Him in the eternal kingdom. What will this eternal kingdom be like? It is so wondrous that no eye has seen, no ear has heard, neither has it entered into the mind of man what God our Father and His Son Jesus have prepared for those of us who are redeemed by His blood, which was shed for us.[44] Yet, during this present era of warfare, He reigns as our Commander in Chief, and His name continues to be the battle cry for those warriors who fight daily for righteousness and truth.

His name is Jesus, our Lord and our King. And true Christian warriors will follow Him anywhere and forever. These are warriors whose deepest desire in this life is to love Him with all of their hearts, all of their souls, all of their minds, and all of their strength.[45] Semper Fi, Commander Jesus!

BREAKING THE SEALS OF THE SCROLL

Now, as our Lord Jesus proceeds to break the seals of the scroll, it appears to have two effects. First, it provides us with a clearer view of the purposes of God regarding events that will usher in the kingdom of God throughout the earth, and, second, it physically launches these events. Thus, we observe the launching of a new era with the opening of this scroll - an era in which events will be released that eventually will climax with the coming of the kingdom of God in its fullness.[46]

Now there is a triune series of catastrophic events that are released by the power of our Lord within which much of our discussion will be centered. They are normally referred to as the breaking of the "seven seals," the blowing of the "seven trumpets," and the pouring out of the "seven bowls of the wrath of God." Now the seven seals do not retain their character as seals, for the seventh seal is revealed as seven trumpets, and the seventh trumpet is manifested as the seven bowls of wrath. Looking at the three series together, there is obviously intensification in their severity until that day when the Lord Himself descends from heaven with His army. Additionally, there appears to be acceleration as the events unfold; the seven seals seem quite spread out in time, while the subsequent series of trumpets and bowls appear to be measured in months or even days. Therefore, it appears as if the three series are successive; that is, they follow on the heels of one another.[47] Finally, there are very important interludes within this succession of events. Whereas the threefold series of seals, trumpets, and bowls are primarily concerned with what will happen to the world, the interludes give us insight into how God's people are affected during this tremendous upheaval.

THE SEVEN SEALS—AN OVERVIEW

The opening of the scroll is intended to reveal to this generation the main aspects of our future, as well as the history of the Christian era, as these forces cooperate to bring the kingdom of Christ to its perfect consummation. The spreading of the gospel of Jesus Christ has been the leading factor in shaping the course of Western civilization throughout the last two millennia. In fact, the history of the leading nations of the world is practically the history of Christianity, whereas those nations that have been uninfluenced by the gospel have had no contributing part in the development of civilization. Their condition is best described as one of age-long stagnation.[48]

The breaking of the first four seals began in the first century at the time the gospel of Christ first went out into the world, or very shortly thereafter. Their great power continues to affect the world to this day. Christ refers to these afflictions as "merely the beginning of birth pangs"; yet they appear to continue right up to the period of the great tribulation.

- *All these are but the beginning of the birth pains. Then they will deliver you up to tribulation and put you to death, and you will be hated by all nations for my name's sake.* **(Matthew 24:8-9)**

As will be discussed shortly, the sixth and seventh seals have not yet been broken, but their time is rapidly approaching. First, let's look at the parallelism between the opening of these seals with the events that Jesus described to His disciples on the Mount of Olives.

THE OLIVET DISCOURSE AND SIX SEALS OF THE SCROLL

It was approximately sixty years since the gospel of Jesus Christ had been launched powerfully into the world when John witnesses our Lord opening the seals of His Father's scroll. As the first four seals are broken, four horsemen emerge with individual missions which will bring forth much chaos and confusion into the world. Three of these horsemen are spiritual forces that are obsessed with usurping God's kingdom plans for the earth; yet they are limited by the Lord in their desire to kill and destroy.

Now there is a difference among commentators as to the identity of the first horseman riding the white horse. Some believe this represents the gospel of Jesus Christ going forth into the world, and they have generally sound arguments supporting this belief. Others believe that the white horseman is going forth with the message of the false gospel that Jesus warned us would take place throughout the times leading up to His return. Late in the first century when John witnessed the release of these four horsemen, the New Testament epistles had already been written and the true gospel message had been proclaimed throughout the Roman Empire. Subsequently, false gospel messages became more and more prevalent within the newly formed Christian churches.

Furthermore, the parallelism between the release of the four horsemen and the end-time events which Jesus taught on the Mount of Olives seems to suggest that there are significant elements of truth in both of these scenarios for they both portray a spiritual battle that will be fought until the return of our Lord Jesus who will also appear riding on a white horse.

The teaching of Jesus on the Mt of Olives in Matthew 24 and Luke 21 outlines the chaotic events which precede His 2nd coming to establish the Kingdom of God on this earth. This teaching is widely referred to as the "Olivet Discourse." <u>For example</u>:

1. False messengers of the gospel would arise and deceive many who are seeking truths
2. There would be an increase in worldwide wars and rumors of wars
3. Earthquakes, famines, diseases, and lawlessness would be rampant throughout the world.
4. Uncompromising Christians would be hated among the nations
5. The Christian churches would experience tribulation and many would be killed.

6. This would result in a great falling away within Christianity of those who will betray and hate their former family members and friends who remain steadfast in their faith.

7. But, Jesus tells us to not be terrified by these multiple tribulations for they must take place before the time of the end.

Now these teachings of Jesus concerning the time of the end should provide us with additional insight into the purpose and character of the powers released by the breaking of the six seals of the scroll.

1. <u>The first seal releases the rider on the "White Horse":</u>

- *Now I watched when the Lamb opened one of the seven seals, and I heard one of the four living creatures say with a voice like thunder, "Come!" And I looked, and behold, a white horse! And its rider had a bow, and a crown was given to him, and he came out conquering, and to conquer.* **Revelation 6:1-2**

This picture of a rider on a white horse is a spiritual portrayal of an armed warrior who is being sent onto the battlefield of the world.

- Thus, this horseman on the white horse appears to be symbolic of mighty soldiers in the Army of God who are armed with a bow which will launch numerous arrows carrying the gospel message of Jesus Christ into the hearts of mankind throughout the earth.
- They are conquering warriors that have overcome the world and have a true heart of love for those who are held captive by the forces of darkness.
- Victory is assured as indicated by the crown given to this horseman, yet this conquering Army of God must battle through many generations until that day when the Lord Jesus Christ will also appear riding on a white horse followed by His army who stood strong in the faith throughout the history of the world.

<u>White Horse Mission:</u> To communicate the following message into the hearts of those who will hear throughout the world:

- *"For God so loved the world, that he gave his only Son, that whoever believes in him should not perish but have eternal life.* **John 3:16**

However, the parallelism between the release of the four horsemen and the end-time events which Jesus taught on the Mount of Olives seems to suggest that the spirit of the beast proclaiming false gospel messages will closely follow the rider on the white horse.

The apostle Paul also warns Christians concerning many false teachers who will arise in the midst of the world in order to deceive those who have heard the message of the white horseman.

- *For such men are false apostles, deceitful workmen, disguising themselves as apostles of Christ. And no wonder, for even <u>Satan disguises himself as an angel of light</u>. So it is no surprise if his servants, also, disguise themselves as servants of righteousness. Their end will correspond to their deeds. 2 Corinthians 11:13-15*

These are those who will accept many of the doctrines of the bible, but deny that Jesus Christ is the only way to eternal life.

2. <u>The second seal releases the rider on the "Red Horse"</u>:

- *When he opened the second seal, I heard the second living creature say, "Come!" And out came another horse, bright red. Its rider was permitted to take peace from the earth, so that men should slay one another, and he was given a great sword. Revelation 6:3-4*

<u>Red Horse Mission</u>: To cause continuing worldwide warfare between nations and kingdoms throughout the Christian era.
- This has taken place in many forms throughout the last 2,000 years, but has emerged into worldwide wars beginning in the 20th century.
- Perhaps this is also a portrayal of the "false gospel" message that has evolved into a world of "churchianity" which has continually waged war against the disciples of our Lord Jesus over the centuries. Roman Catholicism and Islamic religions are historical as well as modern day examples of the demonically inspired religious warfare that has continually raged against the kingdom of God.

3. <u>The third seal releases the rider on the "Black Horse"</u>:
- *When he opened the third seal, I heard the third living creature say, "Come!" And I looked, and behold, a black horse! And its rider had a pair of scales in his hand. And I heard what seemed to be a voice in the midst of the four living creatures, saying, "A quart of wheat for a denarius, and three quarts of barley for a denarius, and do not harm the oil and wine!" Revelation 6:5-6*

The scales used for weighing the wheat and the barley are symbolic of limiting food products for the poor populace in various parts of the earth. The oil and wine appears to represent the food products for the wealthy.

<u>Black Horse Mission</u>: To cause continuing social unrest within nations by utilizing earthly products to maintain enmity between the rich and the poor.
- This "black horse" brings drought, famine, and economic hardships to many in the world.

- Oil and wine remains untouched which reveals that the wealthy will remain distinct from the masses.
- Yet the wealthy continually ignore the cries of the poor in their ongoing addiction for more power and riches.
- The time is rapidly approaching when the "black horseman" releases worldwide famine throughout the world resulting in tremendous rioting and hatred among the masses of the nations.

4. **The fourth seal releases the rider on the "pale horse"**

- *When he opened the fourth seal, I heard the voice of the fourth living creature say, "Come!" And I looked, and behold, a pale horse! And its rider's name was Death, and Hades followed him. And they were given authority over a fourth of the earth, to kill with sword and with famine and with pestilence and by wild beasts of the earth.* **Revelation 6:7-8**

Pale Horse Mission: To follow after the first three horsemen and bring about all forms of unnatural death that will continually affect one-fourth of the world's population.

- The "red horseman" is responsible for worldwide wars which have caused millions of casualties over the centuries.
- The poor struggling in hunger, slavery, and various diseases caused by the "black horseman" has resulted in the loss of numerous lives.
- All of these scenarios provide human bodies for the "pale horseman" who joyfully gathers them up.

Additionally, those taking the false gospel into the world has resulted in the martyring of many of God's sons and daughters who would not compromise their faith in the Lord Jesus Christ.

However, even though they experienced death, Hades has no authority over these Christians as indicated by the 5th seal event.

THE COMBINED EFFECT OF THE FOUR HORSEMEN UPON THE WORLD
(Revelation 6:1-8)

The four horsemen that were released with the opening of the first four seals have simultaneously been making their drive throughout the earth from the beginning of the Christian era until the present day. They have repeatedly kept the world in turmoil and will continue to do so with even greater intensity until the kingdom of God comes in fullness.

The Christian church would like to believe that the Lord would not allow His people to be affected by the wars, famines, pestilences, and deaths that are caused by the release of the powers commonly referred to as the "Four Horsemen of the Apocalypse." Obviously, this is not the case, for all these forces are sent into the world in general and they affect all of mankind.[49] However, they do appear to affect the non-Christian nations of the world more adversely than those nations that profess a belief in Christianity.

When the "red horse" appears and brings bloodshed and wars, we, as well as the unbelieving world, see our sons go into battle, where many have and will suffer and die. The same is true of the "black horse," which brings drought, famine, and economic hardships. Whatever steps mankind takes, this economic law cannot be eliminated: as soon as wages increase, the prices of commodities also rise, and the economic division among the people remains the same; rich and poor continue. This causes divisions in society in the form of strikes, protests, uprisings, and so on. The "pale horse" also enters the homes of the righteous and wicked alike and brings death in all its various forms.

Although there is a certain level of protection that our Lord provides, these horsemen appear to exercise their influence upon all mankind without discrimination. We are naturally inclined to reason that the same causes have the same effects: that what is destructive to one segment of society also must be destructive to the other and what is a blessing to one must be equally a blessing to the other. If this were actually the case, nothing positive could be accomplished by the four riders. Let's now examine how differently God's people handle devastations from how people of the world handle them.

THE POSITIVE & NEGATIVE EFFECTS OF THE FOUR HORSEMEN

The Mission of the White Horse:

The proclamation of the true gospel message will have a different effect upon different people groups. Upon those who believe this truth and open their hearts to receive the Lord into their lives; it will mean a transformation from the powers of darkness into the kingdom of light. Thus, Christ's Kingdom grows and is strengthened.

However, this same gospel of truth will also harden the hearts of those who put their faith and trust in the world – many will run to the message proclaimed by the false prophets who follow after the rider on the white horse in order to distort the truths.

The doctrines of this false gospel are found in Roman Catholicism as well as in many liberal protestant denominations who will not accept the inerrancy of the bible. New Age doctrines are rapidly surfacing in many of today's mega-churches which combine the doctrines of worldwide pagan religions with those of Christianity. One of these modern-day religious groups is commonly referred to as the "Emergent Church." Additionally, many of these false gospel teachers are also becoming more vocal in their proclamation that Allah, the Islamic god, is the same as the God of Abraham. These "Liberal, Chrislam and Emergent" teachings are seriously compromising the gospel truths of our Lord Jesus and they appear to be organizing, together with the Roman Catholic Church, into what some theologians refer to as the "super world church."

The Positive Effects of the False Gospel Messages:

The positive effect of these false gospel messages visibly reveals a separation between those who truly love God and those who love the man-made religions within the world of Christianity.

That is:

- Are they seeking God out of a true heart of love with the primary purpose of glorifying Him or seeking Him for worldly riches in this life?
- Does the worship of God take precedence over the worship of their respective churches and denominations?
- Do they desire to follow God as sons and daughters in order to please Him in this life or desire to follow false teachers who tickle their ears and speak guarantees of salvation which allows them to continue in their comfort-seeking, lustful lifestyle?

This division between true and false Christianity must occur in order that God's chosen people will learn to recognize the broad differences between those who are truly sons and daughters of our heavenly Father and those who are "weeds" which the enemy has sown in the midst of the church.

- Without this visible division, it is probable that religious leadership would evolve, much like the Pharisaic church during the time of Jesus, which would attempt to control the world of Christianity with man-made doctrines that must be followed under the threat of persecution and/or losing one's salvation.
- Historically, this has been the mission of Roman Catholicism, but due to this visible separation between the true and false gospel messages, true Christianity has not been deceived and continues to stand firm for the Kingdom of God even in the face of extradition and persecution.

The Positive and Negative Effects of the Red, Black, and Pale Horses:

What is evil to the world may not be evil to the children of God. The same adversities caused by wars, famine, and death cause some to rise in rebellion and curse God while others in the same circumstance humble themselves and patiently seek God. Thus, the same affliction can harden some while it brings others to repentance and sanctifies them. The same tribulation that brings despair to one causes the other to glorify God.

In summary then, what is the effect of the four horsemen upon mankind? They tend to cause a visible separation between the people of darkness and the people of light. The true church grows stronger and purer during times of intense trials, and, conversely, the ungodly grow deeper and stronger in their hatred toward God and His people. This has been a proven effect around the globe throughout the Christian era, and these trials will become even more intense as the world moves toward the second coming of our Lord and King.

A WORLD WITHOUT THE FOUR HORSEMEN

What would be the result in this worldly kingdom if the preaching of the true gospel message was not followed by the four horsemen released by Christ as He broke open the seals of the scroll; or, in other words, what would be the result if there were no wars, no social struggles, and no death in all these forms? Probably the kingdom of darkness would reach the height of its development prematurely. That is, the sinful world, in its attempt to establish a united world kingdom, would soon succeed in organizing into an international federation of nations and would prematurely become this formidable world power that is pictured in the later chapters of the book of Revelation. All things would be under the control of this world power, and it would force the powers of church and state, of home and school, of business and commerce, to comply with the anti-Christian order of things.[50]

Additionally, this tremendous world power would leave no room for the true church of God on earth. It would persecute and, if possible, destroy the kingdom of God in the world. However, the time for all that is not yet, for there are many who are yet to be called out of the kingdom of the world into the kingdom of God. The time will come, and probably quite soon, when the Lord allows a partial realization of this anti-Christian world power to maintain itself for a brief time, and that time is prophesied to be most terrible for the citizens of God's kingdom, for they shall be social outcasts hated by the world. So terrible will be those latter days that even the elect would not persevere were it not that those days were shortened. But as long as nation rises against nation, the world power cannot realize itself, for the simple reason that it labors continually for its own survival amidst ongoing confusion and cannot organize itself in a one-world unity.

A CHRISTIAN PERSPECTIVE ON TRIBULATIONS

Obviously, citizens of the kingdom of God also suffer according to the flesh, for we too are grieved when our sons die on the battlefield, when our homes and jobs are taken from us, or when our loved ones fall into a sinful lifestyle. However, as we continue along our journey through the wilderness of life, we discover that our Lord sees persecution from a different perspective than we do. In fact, He instructs us over and over about expecting and handling persecution, for He knows that affliction brings great strength and maturity to His chosen people.[51] Additionally, He calls us not only to endure persecution from the world but also to actually accept it with great joy, realizing that the glory that awaits us is so great that present times of suffering and persecution are not even worthy of our concern.[52]

Finally, the truth that we do not stand alone but are part of a worldwide army also should bring great courage and strength. Christians need to understand that possessing a spirit of joy in the midst of persecution certainly will have an astonishing effect on those who persecute us and may even awaken many of them to the truth of God. We must remember who the real enemy is, and it is not the ones who physically persecute us. In fact, we should pray and mourn for them, for apart from repentance the destiny that awaits them is eternal suffering. It is Satan and his dark forces that are the enemy.[53]

The life of those in God's kingdom has always been one of persecution and hatred from the world. Only in America has there been a brief reprieve which has allowed missionaries to take the gospel throughout the world over the past 400 years. However, this reprieve is about to end and true believers in America will soon learn that it is during times of tribulation when the church grows greater and stronger, for it is a time when the body of Christ turns fully to the Lord in intercessory prayer. The modern-day churches in China, Africa, the Middle East, and other parts of the world, which continually face life-threatening persecution, reveal tremendous growth and strength among their people. Such churches are obviously much stronger in their love and devotion to the Lord than those in our nation. It is undoubtedly much more difficult for the American Christian to live a fully committed life to the Lord than it would be if they lived in countries where they underwent continual persecution.

Christians realize that all things work together for good for those who love God.[54] In the midst of devastating and grievous circumstances and even when confronted with death, we are never harmed spiritually; for by faith we cling to our Lord, who has a much greater vision for each of us. Therefore, as we experience the trials of life, the eyes of our faith need to be focused more and more on the glory that awaits us. Now it is war, sin, and suffering, but presently it will be righteousness, holiness, peace, and joy when the kingdom of Christ comes. And as far as death is concerned, the pale horse is no terror but merely an instrument to transfer us to the state of glory in the house of many mansions that He has prepared for His people.[55]

So in times of war and trouble, famine and pestilence, when the red horse drives through the earth and the black horse appears in your streets or the pale horse enters into your home, let your heart rest in the power of our Lord Jesus Christ, who holds the scroll with the seven seals and controls all things in heaven and on earth. Remember Paul's words:

- *For I consider that the sufferings of this present time are not worth comparing with the glory that is to be revealed to us.* **(Romans 8:18)**

THE FIFTH SEAL—SOULS OF THE MARTYRS
(Revelation 6:9-11)

John now sees the souls of all of the Lord's martyrs as they rest in the presence of their Father who sits upon His throne. These are all those who had been slain for the word of God since the time of creation—and most certainly their numbers will continue to grow until the return of our Lord, Jesus Christ. A chief purpose for this seal is to clearly show that the martyrdom of saints is under the control of Jesus Christ and is a necessary element in the ongoing war with the enemies of the kingdom of God. The Bible passage literally says that they had been "butchered" for the Word of God by the enemies of Christ and His church. These are committed warriors in the Army of God who did not hide their light under a basket.[56] It is a fact that they not only testified to the Word of God but they also clung to it right up to the point of death.

A very long list of names certainly exists in heaven of those who were slain for the name and the truth of God in Christ Jesus our Lord. Consider the following.

- Those churches pictured in the book of Revelation—Smyrna, Pergamum, and Philadelphia—that were hated and persecuted for Christ's' name.
- The terrible persecutions under the Roman emperors, when those who confessed the name of Christ Jesus were literally butchered and tortured to death.
- The forerunners of the Reformation who refused to return to the mother church of Catholicism and were burned at the stake by that harlot church, which was responsible for the Dark Ages of the middle centuries.
- The countless Christians of our modern-day generation that are continually murdered in various sections of countries that embrace false religions; for example, China, India, Iran, Africa, etc.

They all suffered. They all were persecuted. They were driven from place to place. They were put on the rack and tortured in every conceivable way. They were brought to the scaffold and burned at the stake. As you go through history from its very dawn to the present time, you will find an innumerable host under the altar, slain for their love for God and His Son. And what is the reason for all this? It is an inevitable consequence of the tremendous battle continually being fought between two kingdoms striving for possession of the same world.

THE SPIRIT OF MARTYRDOM

Martyr actually is the Greek word used in the Bible for "witness." A "true spirit" of martyrdom is the willingness to risk all for the benefit of others.[57] I've seen this in action on the battlefield of Vietnam; Marines will not abandon their fellow Marines in the midst of battle. At a certain point in the heat of battle, we are more concerned about the life of another than we are about our own life. The "true spirit" of martyrdom is not about dying but about faithfulness; that is, it is about dying to self in order to accomplish the risky work of living for Jesus.[58]

What about the Muslim martyrs who are sent on suicidal missions in order to kill their supposed enemies in the name of their Allah? Well, look at their motive; it is intentional martyrdom for their own self-glory and what they envision as eternal, carnal delight. Yes, it is a witness unto death, but it is the "false spirit" of martyrdom. Christian martyrs die trying to "save you"; Muslim martyrs die trying to "kill you."[59] The true martyrs are those who lay down their lives for the cause of Christ. They are not the casualties of war; they are the victors. Like champions of God throughout history, they join with their brothers and sisters in the body of Christ who continue to "crush the head of Satan."[60]

The fifth-seal martyrs are those men and women who willingly lay down their lives bearing witness for the truth of the gospel of Jesus Christ without retreat or compromise. These martyred souls under the altar of God are not crying out for vengeance against their enemies but for the glory and righteousness of God, for whom they suffered unto death, to be strongly manifested to the world.

What is meant by "laying down one's life" for the cause of Christ? Just this: Christians who are threatened with being executed will be given an opportunity by their oppressors to deny Him. Certainly many have and will continue to deny Him out of fear for their lives, but the martyrs under the altar are those warriors who made the choice to stand for Christ in the face of death. True martyrdom is a powerful witness to the world; and through such sacrifice, many people turn and come into the kingdom of God. Christians in our generation also will be confronted with this decision, but they must remember this: the reward that awaits their uncompromising witness will be great.

- *Blessed are those who are persecuted for righteousness' sake, for theirs is the kingdom of heaven. Blessed are you when others revile you and persecute you and utter all kinds of evil against you falsely on my account. Rejoice and be glad, for your reward is great in heaven, for so they persecuted the prophets who were before you.(**Matthew 5:10-12**)*

How long must the martyrs wait for the judgment of God to fall on the world? Until the number of all of their brethren who are yet to be killed, even as they were, is complete. In plain language, this simply means that the time is not yet ripe for God's judgment because there are still future witnesses (martyrs) for Christ whose testimony for the gospel must go forth. No, we do not have to seek martyrdom, but we must continue to bear testimony for the Word of God and the kingdom of His Christ. If we do, we may have the hope in our hearts that presently we shall receive the white robes of righteousness, holiness, and victory. Therefore, we need to understand that the enemy who persecutes us merely serves as an instrument to bring us to that eternal state of righteousness and holiness within the kingdom of our Lord. Remember this: potential martyrs for Christ need to maintain a deep joyfulness in the midst of the world's wickedness and persecution since they are tremendously valued in the eyes of God and the eternal reward that awaits them will be great. The Lord rules! He opens the seals, including the fifth one, and so not a hair on your head shall ever be touched against His will.

SCOFFERS WILL PRECEDE THE PERSECUTION OF AMERICAN CHRISTIANS

The time of the end will witness scoffers who deride any message concerning the return of Christ. We will see this as leftist politicians, major news media, many popular movie stars, as well as numerous compromising church leaders embrace worldly socialistic values and denounce those who proclaim that Jesus is the only way to eternal life as being a separatist, hate-filled, and an uncompromising segment of society. When the churches in America are confronted with the choice of standing for Jesus Christ or suffering persecution from the government, many will fall away and betray their former friends who will not compromise their love for the Lord. Today's scoffers will soon become tomorrow's persecutors of the true believers and followers of Jesus Christ.

- *Then they will deliver you up to tribulation and put you to death, and you will be hated by all nations for my name's sake. And then many will fall away and betray one another and hate one another. And many false prophets will arise and lead many astray. And because lawlessness will be increased, the love of many will grow cold. But the one who endures to the end will be saved. And this gospel of the kingdom will be proclaimed throughout the whole world as a testimony to all nations, and then the end will come.* **(Matthew 24:9-14)**

The "gray area" of Christianity is disappearing, and today's churches will shortly be divided by light and darkness as the events described in the above passages accelerate. These are hard truths to handle, and the majority of Christians would rather ignore them with the hope it won't happen in their lifetime rather than face the truth and prepare for it as the Lord commanded. This is the situation in the churches that Christ's warrior leadership must boldly confront.

WHEN WILL THE LORD'S JUDGMENT COME?

The world has not yet shown its real character in the fullness of its hatred of God the Father and His Son, Jesus Christ. In the past, when witnesses for Christ were butchered, the human enemy was not so directly conscious that they rose up against the name of Jesus Christ. However, the time is coming when the world populace will be fully conscious that it is the hateful name of Jesus Christ that is the great obstacle for all their plans of globalization. This will be a time when more than just specific nations rise up against our Lord; it will be the entire world that visibly manifests its dark character. Tribulation and persecution of the saints in the future will become more universal in its character. In other words, the world will attack the true body of Christ fully conscious that it is making an attack on the holiness and the truth of God. There will be no more gray area between good and evil; one either stands with Him or against Him. Separation of the two kingdoms will become completely visible to all. It is at this point that the world is ripe for judgment.[61]

Yet, it will not occur in the United States until the government of this country, which was founded upon Christian values and later became the most influential and strongest nation on earth, joins with the rest of the world in its hatred toward true Christianity and the nation of Israel. Those with discernment understand that contemporary America is currently on the precipice of uniting against the Lord's people.

OPENING THE SIXTH SEAL – A GREAT EARTHQUAKE
(Revelation 6:12-17)

This coming event certainly has to be the greatest and most frightening scenario in the material universe since the days of Noah and that great flood that engulfed the entire world. Yet, this modern-day catastrophe is much different from the flood in Noah's generation, since most of the world's population will initially survive, even though several million people undoubtedly will be killed. Obviously this event is yet future, since nothing as extraordinary as this has occurred in human history since the time that John received this vision. The opening of the sixth seal certainly will cause many of us to wonder how anyone can survive such a catastrophic event, and yet it is just the beginning of numerous catastrophic events that will soon follow.

Observe those who are hiding themselves and trembling in fear of almighty God and His Son, Jesus Christ, whom they now recognize as the King of the universe.[62] They are the mighty ones of the world, who controlled the world's finances and held positions of authority and thus dominated the social and political world. They are also strong in wisdom and learning, people who have always denied the Christ in their worldly philosophies and who, in their imagined strength, opposed and ridiculed the people of the Lord, who believed the message of the gospel.[63]

Eventually this powerful group of worldly leaders will acclimate to this season of chaotic events and will organize, like ancient Babel, to fight against the Lord and His people. But this time they will understand that they are aligning with the world and fighting against almighty God, who is their Creator. This scenario will be discussed in a subsequent chapter.

THE ENTIRE WORLD WILL ACKNOWLEDGE THE REALITY OF GOD

In the past when significant disasters struck different nations of the world, the great majority of people did not see the hand of God in them; they simply assumed them to be natural disasters that continually occur in the world. So what is it about this catastrophe, other than it is so much greater and widespread, that causes mankind to realize that it is a consequence evolving from the wrath of God and not simply a natural disaster? [64] An obvious answer is that this sixth-seal catastrophe is triggered by another event designed to strike at the heart of the Lord—a worldly assault against the kingdom of God so massive and powerful that only the Lord Himself could possibly bring about its defeat.

First, for better understanding, let's take a brief historical look at a time when the Lord delivered His people out from under the bondage of the Egyptian empire. He brought ten plagues against the most powerful nation in the known world and subsequently drowned their mighty army in the Red Sea in the process of delivering His people from the hand of the world's bondage. This deliverance was known throughout the Middle Eastern countries, and they came to know that the God of Israel was truly God. Although this awareness of God brought about a great fear upon these nations, the great majority of them continued to oppose the people of God rather than unite with them.

A similar, but much greater, event is about to take place. It will grab the attention and concern of the entire world and may possibly trigger both the opening of the sixth seal and the subsequent trumpet judgments. <u>A mighty army, greater than the world has ever seen, will soon descend upon the nation of Israel.</u>

CHAPTER 4

A GREAT WAR IS COMING

(<u>First Read:</u> Ezekiel 38 - 39)

INTRODUCTION TO A GREAT WAR

A large percentage of people around the globe do not doubt that a terrible darkness is rapidly creeping into the world. Currently there is no major world war waging between nations, yet the continuing threats of upheavals in the Middle East or potential terrorist attacks here at home seem to dominate the news in today's mainstream media. The word *nuclear* is becoming more and more commonplace in our daily news stories. Even Hollywood appears to be profiting from this mind-set by producing bloodcurdling movies of wars and dark forces threatening the world. They are certainly scary but also quite entertaining; and they blindly encourage masses of moviegoers as their movie-star champions arise to protect the people against these dark forces and thus provide a happy, comfortable ending that allows people to sleep at night.

In truth, there is a growing evil in the world that will continue to gather its forces and strike against the kingdom of God. A remnant of God's people certainly understands that catastrophic times are rapidly approaching, but we need to be active in our preparations. We certainly can learn much by looking through the lenses of politics and economics, but this only provides us with a two-dimensional understanding. We need that third dimension, and this can be found only in the Scriptures, where a much clearer picture emerges. God has provided us with tremendous amounts of information for our generation, but we must search for it. Just because millions of Americans say they believe that Bible prophecy is coming true before their eyes or that they are living in the last days does not mean that they are truly aware of or preparing for events that are right around the corner. The watchmen of God who are burdened to warn the people need to anticipate how, when, and where these forces of darkness will strike next.[65] Now let's look at a coming war that could well be the event that launches the end-times tribulation era.

A GREAT WAR BEGINS IN THE MIDDLE EAST
(Ezekiel 38 and 39)

Approximately 2600 years ago, the Lord spoke to his prophet Ezekiel concerning a great army from the north that was going to descend upon the nation of Israel in order to rid the earth of a people that are despised by the majority of the world's population. This is an army made up of a coalition of several nations, and led by one of the largest and most powerful nations in the world. Ezekiel was told that this attack will occur in the "latter days," when the inhabitants of Israel have been gathered from many nations and have resettled in the land. It is also a time when its citizens live "securely" in the land. During an interview with Joel Rosenberg, the author of the book *Epicenter*, General Amidror, a former head of Israeli Military Intelligence stated,

- *Unless or until Iran gets nuclear weapons, Israel today is more strategically secure than at any other point since her birth.*[66]

Since 1948 Israel has been an established nation whose citizens of Jewish descent have been gathered from various other nations around the world. Israel is quite a small nation, with a population of approximately seven million, yet it is also a prosperous nation that is well armed and nuclear capable, thanks to the United States, who, together with Great Britain, has been its chief ally since its formation over sixty years ago. These "recently established" and "living securely" scenarios, together with other current events seems to indicate that this could well be the time of Ezekiel's war; which is commonly referred as the Gog-Magog war.

Regarding their relationship with God, today's Jewish people are primarily secular or legalistically religious like the Pharisees of Jesus' time; yet in the midst of the people, there are approximately six thousand messianic Jews, who embrace Yeshua (Jesus) as their Messiah. However, as a nation, the great majority of the Jewish people and their government are essentially ignorant of the God of Abraham or don't really care. Some folks may wonder, then, why does God care for them as a nation? Well, primarily, it goes back to His covenant over four thousand years ago, when He made the following promise to Abraham, the father of the people of Israel.

- *I will make of you a great nation, and I will bless you and make your name great, so that you will be a blessing. I will bless those who bless you, and him who dishonors you I will curse, and in you all the families of the earth shall be blessed."* **(Genesis 12:2-3)**

However, that covenant was not made because the Lord holds Israel to be a righteous nation, for He says,

- *And I will vindicate the holiness of my great name, which has been profaned among the nations, and which you have profaned among them. And the nations will know that I am the Lord, declares the*

Lord God, when through you I vindicate my holiness before their eyes. I will take you from the nations and gather you from all the countries and bring you into your own land. **(Ezekiel 36:23-24)**

This has been the historical purpose for establishing Israel as a people of God: that through the Israelites and their testimony and/or their circumstances, God will reveal Himself to all the peoples of the earth. Additionally, there are "numerous prophecies" that tell about a coming time when all of Israel will be saved and ungodliness banished from the land.

The Lord Himself will initiate this great war by putting "hooks" into the jaws of the enemies of Israel and dragging them to a place where He will pour out His wrath to such an extent that the entire world will tremble, and, like the ancient Egyptians, they come to know that the Lord of Israel is surely the one true God.[67]

A GREAT ARMY DESCENDS FROM MAGOG

Although Ezekiel's prophecy was written more than 2600 years ago, chapters 38 and 39 provide us with extraordinary intelligence concerning who will be involved and when it might occur. First let's look at the nations that comprise this massive coalition that descends upon Israel with the intent of wiping out the Jewish race. Of course, the Bible uses ancient names when describing these enemy nations, but most scholars agree on who they are. Rosenberg's book "Epicenter" gives great clarity by providing a table matching the biblical names with the modern names.[68]

Russia is described as the leader of this "Axis of Evil," and Iran is mentioned first among the countries that align with Russia. A summary of the nations follows.

1. Russia	2. Iran	3. Sudan	4. Ethiopia	5. Libya
6. Algeria	7. Tunisia	8. Turkey	9. Gomer = possibly Germany & Eastern Europe	10. Many peoples after you = possibly Palestine, Jordan, Lebanon, Isis Forces

Note that these nations are mostly Islamic and are nations that have harbored a deep hatred for Israel since their formation as a nation. Ezekiel's description of this army suggests that it will be the largest and best-equipped military force ever assembled and, in modern terms, will consist of a countless number of infantry troops, tanks, and aircraft, all armed to the maximum. They will advance on Israel like a "storm" and like a "cloud covering the land." This certainly sounds like a massive onslaught of ground and air forces.

Additionally, it is interesting to note that two nations that have historically been enemies of Israel are not on the list; they are Iraq and Syria. One can surmise that this war will occur when these two countries no longer have the military capability to join their allies in their mission to destroy the nation of Israel. Now the absence of Iraq is understandable if this invasion is to occur in the near future, since their armed forces were dismantled during the war with the United States. However, the absence of Syria presents a very interesting scenario for those who are familiar with the "oracle of Damascus," where Isaiah prophesies that a future time is coming when Damascus will cease to be a city and will become a "heap of ruins." The oracle goes on to describe the terror that will confront Israel and what will happen to their enemies and as a result, mankind will look to the Holy One of Israel.[69] It certainly appears as if a war between Israel and Syria (Isis?) will precede the invasion of Israel by the military forces led by Russia and Iran. In fact, the destruction of Damascus and the defeat of the Syrian army may be the episode that ignites the Gog-Magog invasion of Israel. This could well be another "hook" in the Russians' jaws, for there currently exists a Syrian-Russian treaty whereby Russia has pledged to provide military support in the event that Syria becomes engaged in battle with Israel over the Golan Heights.

RUSSIA'S MOTIVE FOR INVADING ISRAEL

Why would Russia be motivated to commit all of its forces to assist the Middle Eastern countries against their enemy, Israel? Ezekiel tells us that Russia desires "to seize spoil and carry off plunder," which in our day makes a lot of sense since the Middle Eastern countries control the majority of oil resources, which drive the world's economy. Russia has been struggling economically for decades, and if they can successfully align themselves with the Middle Eastern countries, of which Iran is the key power, they will have significant control over the world's oil reserves. Additionally, Russia certainly wants to regain its superpower status among the nations of the world, and this alliance with the Middle Eastern nations may be considered an opportunity to unseat the United States as the strongest and most influential political and economic power in the world. Russia, which had lost its place as a superpower when the communist government disintegrated, is struggling economically but not militarily. Now comes an opportunity to become the greatest and wealthiest nation on earth. This is definitely a "hook" that the Lord uses to draw Russia into this devastating conflict.

IRAN'S MOTIVE FOR INVADING ISRAEL

Former Iranian President Ahmadinejad has said that he believes the end of the world is only a few years away. He also has said that the way to hasten the arrival of the Mahdi (Islamic Messiah) is to launch an apocalyptic holy war against the Christians and Jews. Ahmadinejad also boasted that the Imam gave him the presidency for a single task—to provoke a "clash of civilizations" in which the Muslim world, led by Iran, takes on the "infidel" Western world and defeats the United States. Iran's goals for the war are certainly different from Russia's, so why would Iran and other Middle Eastern countries embrace this Russian influence? No doubt it is because Russia possesses the military capability and technology that these countries need in order to subdue Israel.[70] The Islamic nations have warred against Israel since its formation and have met with hardly any success. They need military help.

These enemies of Israel could easily work together, but Russia is playing with fire. Islamic teaching says, "Listen to the good news about the Mahdi! He will rise at the time when people will be faced with severe conflict and *the earth will be hit by a violent quake*. He will fill the earth with justice and equity as it is filled with injustice and tyranny. He will fill the hearts of his followers with devotion and will spread justice everywhere."[71] Additionally, it is said that those who persist in their disbelief and wickedness shall be killed by the soldiers of the Mahdi. Islam will be the religion of everyone and will enter all the nations of the world. The Mahdi will offer the religion of Islam to the Jews and the Christians; if they accept it, they will be spared, and otherwise they will be killed. It seems unlikely that this catastrophe can be avoided. Warfare and bloodshed are inevitable.[72]

WHY AMERICA WILL ABANDON ITS SUPPORT OF ISRAEL

In his intelligence report, Ezekiel rules out the possibility that any country will come to Israel's defense once Russia and Iran and their allies launch their invasion from the north. Now the United States, England, and other European countries have been staunch supporters of Israel since its formation as a nation in 1948. So what is it that will cause our country to abandon its support for Israel at the moment of their greatest crisis?

Unfortunately, the United States is now a politically divided country. As Americans tire more and more of our Middle Eastern conflicts, the leftist voices grow louder in their support of a Palestinian state with no concern for the consequences to Israel. In fact, there is a rapidly growing belief that if we abandon our support of Israel, we will no longer be endangered by Muslim terrorists. Today, our country has all but abandoned its support of Israel, as we see fewer and fewer Americans supporting the Jewish state. We're starting to hear comments like, "Why should we spend a dime to save Israel?" and "Let the Jews fight their own battles" and "The only reason we as Americans are getting attacked by Muslims is because we support Israel—the sooner we stop, the sooner there will be peace."[73]

It is most probable that the Gog-Magog war will occur when the United States is completely governed by the leftist Democrats and we have a government much like Europe, which may decry an invasion of Israel but would not militarily attempt to stop it. Additionally, the war could be launched at a time when the U.S. is fighting for survival in the throes of unparalleled economic collapse; or perhaps it may come at a time when the U.S. is fighting against chaotic situations in our own country as a result of increased terrorist activity that may render us virtually impotent on the international scene. Actually, all three of the above scenarios could exist simultaneously, feeding off one another. Obviously, this is our current scenario, and I do believe it's probable that this war against Israel could be launched during our present administration.

The real test, of course, will come when Russia, Iran, and all their allies begin to move forces toward Israel.[74] Ezekiel's intelligence indicates that there will be a verbal protest from Saudi Arabia and nations in the West but obviously they will not lift a hand to interfere.[75]

WHY THE EUROPEAN UNION ABANDONS ITS SUPPORT OF ISRAEL

Unfortunately, Europe is a continent where anti-Semitism is rapidly increasing. Jewish schools and synagogues throughout Europe are constantly vandalized and burned, and individual Jews are continually verbally abused and assaulted. Rockwell Schnabel, the U.S. ambassador to the European Union, stated that anti-Semitism in Europe "is as bad as it was in the 1930s."[76] In November 2003, a European poll revealed that the majority of Europeans actually named Israel as the greatest threat to world peace, ahead of Iran and North Korea.[77] Therefore, we can safely assume that Europe would not militarily lift a hand to save Israel.

It is obvious that without the intervention of the United States or a united Europe, there is no one else on the planet who could possibly stand against these tremendous forces that will soon be mustered against the nation of Israel. In short, the kingdom of this world hates the nation of Israel and its citizenry wherever they are living; but in reality, it is a hatred for the God of Israel. Israel is the nation that God uses to make His name known throughout the world.

- *And my holy name I will make known in the midst of my people Israel, and I will not let my holy name be profaned anymore. <u>And the nations shall know that I am the Lord, the Holy One in Israel.</u> (Ezekiel 39:7)*

THE INVASION FROM THE NORTH AND THE LORD'S RESPONSE

Ezekiel's intelligence reports that this military alliance will descend toward the mountains known today as the Golan Heights, which is Israel's northern border adjacent to Syria, Lebanon, and northern Jordan. It is at this place that the Lord launches His offense against this enemy by causing a great earthquake to explode in their midst—an earthquake greater than any the world has ever known. <u>**Note: Perhaps this is the "6th seal event!"**</u> The mountains and cliffs fall upon this invading army, hailstones, fire, and sulfur rain down upon their heads, and pandemic diseases sweep through their ranks as well as through many other peoples who supported these troops in their war of annihilation against Israel.

Tremendous panic and confusion will eliminate discipline among the troops; and during this confusion, they will begin to fire their weapons against one another, resulting in a great massacre within their own ranks. This sudden devastation is so great that all the nations of the earth, together with all animal and sea life, will quake at the presence of the Lord as His fury is poured out on the armies of the enemies of His people. There no longer will be any doubt that the God of Israel and of the committed Christians in the body of Christ is the one and only true God.

This is a very similar scenario to that ancient time when God delivered His people from Egypt and provided safe passage through the Red Sea. Then He wiped out the entire Egyptian army, which was, in that period of history, the most powerful military force in the world. All the nations of that day knew that the God of Israel was God, but this future event will be so much more catastrophic. All the nations shall know that the God of Israel is the Lord and that He will not allow His name to be profaned anymore. That doesn't mean that they won't hate Him, but they certainly will be more careful in their future plans for world domination. This will be the most catastrophic event ever witnessed by mankind since the flood, for this "great earthquake" may also trigger other earthquakes and volcanic eruptions throughout the world, including the western portion of the United States. However, this is not the end for things will soon intensify.

A TIME OF CLEANSING OF THE LAND

Following the earthquake and the devastation that takes place on the Golan Heights, the people of Israel who are unharmed will go out to clean up the land and gather all the wreckage of the weaponry for burning. It will take seven years of constant fires to cleanse the land of the residue of the planes, helicopters, artillery, tanks, trucks, jeeps, trailers, small arms, supplies, and all other equipment that is destroyed. Additionally, the Israelites will gather up many valuable assets that are abandoned from a remnant of survivors who have fled. Much wealth will be accumulated during this cleansing process.

The birds of the air and the beasts of the field will eat the flesh of this once mighty army and drink the blood of those previously considered "princes of the earth." As for the remaining carcasses, we are told that all the people of the land of Israel will assist in burying the bodies in a massive graveyard east of the Dead Sea. Even though the entire population of Israel will be locating and transporting the bodies to this burial site, it will be seven months before the land will be completely clean of all the carcasses. The former leader of this army, identified as Gog, also will be buried. Gog is not a personal name but more likely a title such as prince, or czar, or president, or general. The burial site will be called the Valley of Hamon-Gog.

It appears as if several million soldiers and civilians will be killed during this coming day when the Lord magnifies His holiness as the Defender of His people in Israel. All the house of Israel shall know that the God of Abraham, Isaac, and Jacob is their God. There will be no more secular Jews in Israel.

THE GOG-MAGOG WAR—A SECOND ONE COMING?

The book of Revelation does speak of another Gog-Magog war that occurs at the end of time.[78] However, this is a second war that is yet farther into the future, not the war that is recorded by Ezekiel. We know this for several reasons.

- First, Ezekiel's war occurs relatively soon after the rebirth of the nation of Israel and the ingathering of the Jewish people from around the world. The second Gog-Magog war occurs after Jesus has reigned on earth for one thousand years.
- Second, Ezekiel's war involves a fearsome, but limited, coalition of countries that surround Israel. The war in Revelation involves all the nations from "every corner of the earth" coming to attack Israel.
- Finally, after Ezekiel's war, life continues; bodies are gathered and buried for seven months, and weaponry is gathered and burned for seven years. By contrast, the war in Revelation is followed immediately by the end of the world. Satan and his followers are judged and thrown into the "lake of fire." The heavens and earth are destroyed, and a completely new heaven and new earth are created, and the followers of Jesus Christ will live on this new earth for the rest of eternity.[79]

A CATASTROPHIC EVENT FOLLOWING THIS GOG-MAGOG WAR

There is another very significant event that takes place following the devastation resulting from this great earthquake. The Lord is not yet done, for Ezekiel receives this additional intelligence from the God of Israel:

- *I will send fire on Magog and on those who dwell securely in the coastlands, and they shall know that I am the Lord.* (*Ezekiel 39:6*)

In addition to the destruction of the armies, "fire" is sent north onto the Russian heartland, as well as upon those who dwell "securely" on the coastlands. This implies a sending of "fire" between two groups of people, which sounds very much like a *nuclear exchange.*

A Plausible Scenario

When God's earthquake hits Israel, fear, confusion, and chaos will cause exchanges of fire within the Russian forces. Escalation will ensue, and the Russians may well think that the West is attacking them. Most likely a nuclear exchange will begin inadvertently. Ezekiel also does not identify the people inhabiting the "coastlands in security"; but he does say they will also be on the receiving end of this nuclear war. The Western alliance, led by the United States, is the only group of nations capable of engaging the Soviets in a major nuclear war, and thus it appears that the heartland of Russia will launch the first strike against the West, which will then retaliate.

A Second Plausible Scenario

Muslim terrorists on both Western and Eastern continents could detonate nuclear "suitcase bombs" in various cities in retaliation for what they see as an attack upon the Middle Eastern world.

Experts say that the blast from a single ten-kiloton nuclear bomb (suitcase size) in a major city would destroy everything within a half mile of ground zero, contaminate 3,000 to 5,000 square miles with toxic levels of radiation, and kill 300,000 people within a matter of minutes.[80]

Now, concerning the second scenario, I wish to share something very interesting yet largely unknown in the West. The chief sign that announces the coming of the Mahdi is a **"massive earthquake,"** which will launch a global war to kill and/or to subjugate Jews, Christians, and other "infidels."[81] This Islamic belief may very well cause them to launch an internal nuclear attack on various cities around the country following the great earthquake that the Lord releases in the Golan Heights.

GOG-MAGOG: THE WAR THAT LAUNCHES THE GREAT TRIBULATION ?

As previously mentioned, it is highly probable that this **"earthquake"** described in the book of Ezekiel is the same **"earthquake"** that strikes the earth when the Lord opens the "sixth seal." If so, this Gog-Magog war in Ezekiel is what will launch the great tribulation upon the earth, which will affect all the nations.[82] Finally, the catastrophic effect of a nuclear attack may be what John describes in greater detail in the series of judgments known as "the seven trumpets" which will be addressed in chapter 7.

GOG-MAGOG AND THE CHRISTIAN ATTITUDE

True followers of Jesus Christ may be the only friends Israel and the Jewish people will have left as this terrible war approaches. We need to remain faithful in praying for the peace of Jerusalem on a daily basis. Additionally, the Jews in America undoubtedly will be persecuted during this scheme of events. We must, with all of our heart, align ourselves with them and show our solidarity for their people and their nation.

At the same time, we must remember that God loves the Muslim people of the Middle East as well as the Russians and others living in the former Soviet Union. Lovers of Christ must love and show compassion to all people. This doesn't mean excusing the actions of anti-Christian governments, but it is the believers' hard work to demonstrate and communicate Christ's love during mankind's darkest hours.[83]

CHAPTER 5

GODS WARRIORS IN THE END TIMES = 144,000

(<u>First Read:</u> Revelation 7)

HOPE CONTINUES TO SHINE IN THE MIDST OF DARKNESS

Tremendous devastation will take place on the earth during the coming period of "trumpet judgments." One-third of the earth, the seas, and human beings are targeted for destruction, yet two-thirds will survive. However, if it were God's purpose to destroy the entire earth, He wouldn't do it in stages. These trumpet judgments are unbelievably devastating, yet they are still warnings to mankind and a call for repentance. In fact, God will plant His chosen warriors among the nations to be powerfully anointed ministers for Christ during this time of great suffering. Before the first trumpet sounds, the Lord will send an angel to seal these "servants of God" in order to protect them from the trumpet judgments that will soon descend upon the earth. These comprise a select group of "Warrior-Spirited Christians" whose light will continue to shine mightily in the midst of great darkness throughout the whole earth. They will bring the hope of salvation to millions of people who are scared and searching for answers. These "servants of God" are commonly referred to as the 144,000 from the twelve tribes of Israel.

- *Then I saw another angel ascending from the rising of the sun, with the seal of the living God, and he called with a loud voice to the four angels who had been given power to harm earth and sea, saying, "Do not harm the earth or the sea or the trees, until we have sealed the <u>servants</u> of our God on their foreheads." And I heard the number of the sealed, <u>144,000, sealed from every tribe of the sons of Israel</u>. (Revelation 7:2-4)*

"144,000 SERVANTS" = ARMY OF GOD IN TRIBULATION

<u>Servant</u> is an English word that really doesn't fully communicate the character of these men and women who will receive the seal of God prior to the launching of the trumpet series of events. The Greek and Hebrew words for "servants" are *doulos* and *gibbar* respectively. It is a description applied to the apostles,[84] to the prophets,[85] to Moses,[86] to the true worshippers of Christ,[87] and to anyone who gives himself wholly to another without regard for personal interests.[88]

Thus, these *"doulos* and *gibbar* servants"* are the warriors in the Army of God who are totally sold out to the Lord Jesus Christ and will glorify His name with their lives throughout the latter days of God's judgments. They are the Lord's

disciples of the twenty-first century who have heard and obeyed the Lord's command to "be ready."[89] They represent "God's Anointed Warriors" that, in the author's view, are the disciples who will be empowered and dispatched by Jesus Christ to minister in the midst of the Great Tribulation.

WHO ARE THESE "SONS OF ISRAEL" REFLECTED BY THE TWELVE TRIBES?

There are primarily two opposing views that need to be briefly addressed, since both are widely held in the Western church.

First, there is what many call the "pretribulation dispensational" view. Adherents of this view believe that the twelve tribes of Israel who are sealed prior to the trumpet series are the latter-day people of "natural Israel." Furthermore, they also assume that natural Israel is simply today's "Jews." They teach that this passage describes the beginning of salvation for all Israel (or Jews) recorded by the apostle Paul.[90] Furthermore, this view teaches that only Jewish people will comprise the earthly church during the great tribulation, since the present-day Christian church will have been raptured. Thus, only the Jewish nation in the land of Israel will be the chief object of wrath from the Antichrist.

However, this raises an interesting question: Why are the "lost tribes" of Israel included among those sealed prior to the trumpet judgments? Today's Jews are primarily descendants of only four tribes (Judah, Simeon, Benjamin, and Levi). Yet those who are sealed prior to the trumpet series are the Lord's servants from all twelve tribes of the sons of Israel. Adherents of these dispensational teachings believe the Jews to be the sole representatives of the sons of Jacob. This infers that since the descendants of the northern tribes can no longer be visibly identified, they cannot be counted among the sons of Israel. It is true that descendants of the former northern tribes no longer exist as a single nation, yet they do exist worldwide. God has hidden them among the nations, but He is about to anoint and seal many of them for a future purpose.[91]

A second view is what is commonly known as the "spiritual Israel" view. That is, the twelve tribes of Israel represent the New Testament church, comprised of both Jews and Gentiles. There are some good arguments as to why the present-day church may be identified with Israel; for instance, some New Testament verses address the similarity between Israel and the Church.[92] Yet, many adherents of this teaching tend to misinterpret Scripture when they teach that the Church has totally replaced Israel as the people of God.

Thus, the two most prevalent views of the identity of the 144,000 that is being taught by Western church theologians are:

- *Pre-tribulation dispensational view*, which teaches that the 144,000 who are sealed consists solely of the Jewish nation who will experience the hardships of the great tribulation, while the more privileged church will be celebrating their rapture experience in the heavenlies.
- *Spiritual Israel view*, which teaches that the church has replaced Israel as the chosen people of God. This is commonly called "replacement theology" and has been embraced by many in the church for centuries. This is a false theology that has resulted in a deep hatred toward the Jews, whose descendants are continually blamed for the crucifixion of Christ. This biased teaching has produced many terrible holocausts over the last 1500 years, as millions of Jews have been persecuted by the church, who believed they were doing a service for their God. Roman Catholicism as well as several Protestant denominations continues to adhere to this theology, believing they are solely God's chosen people.

There are elements of truth and deception in both of these views; however, there is another perspective that is much more rational and biblically sound than those teachings outlined above. Because this list of those sealed includes tribes within the northern kingdom of Israel, which were scattered among the nations of the world over 2700 years ago, there remains a nagging sense that the identity of the 144,000 runs much deeper than those traditional views of modern-day theologians, who erroneously teach that Israel means either "the church" or "the Jews." Let's take a look; perhaps you will find the following both intriguing and enlightening.

A BRIEF HISTORY OF THE
NORTHERN KINGDOM OF ISRAEL

The Bible records that King Rehoboam, the son of Solomon, caused the northern tribes to rebel and establish a separate nation. Surprisingly, the Lord commanded the tribes of Judah and Benjamin not to resist that secession.[93]

Thus, approximately 930 BC, Israel was divided into two separate kingdoms composed of the following tribes.

Tribes in the Northern Kingdom of Israel

1. Reuben	2. Gad	3. Asher	4. Naphtali	5. Manasseh
6. Issachar	7. Ephraim	8. Zebulun	9. Levi (partial)	10. Dan

Tribes in the Southern Kingdom of Judah

1. Judah	2. Benjamin	3. Simeon	4. Levi (partial)

Over a period of two hundred plus years, nineteen kings, all of whom "did evil in the sight of the Lord," ruled over the northern kingdom. Consequently, the Lord allowed Assyria, an enemy of Israel, to conquer the northern kingdom in 722 BC. It was a brutal massacre of men, women, and children, but those who survived were all deported from the land and forced to assimilate into other nations and cultures, where they completely lost their religious and national identity. Thus, the northern kingdom of Israel was gone and these ten tribes never reappeared in the pages of history after their defeat by the Assyrians.

The southern kingdom continued to remain in the land, although 130 years later, because they also did evil in the sight of the Lord, were conquered by the Babylonians and went into captivity for 70 years; after which approximately 50,000 people returned to the homeland and Jerusalem. These were the people of Judah, who came to be known as the "Jews." Yet, as many as 95 percent remained in Babylon and were assimilated into the Babylonian culture.

Why is this important? Well, for one thing, it helps us to understand where today's "Jews" come from. This means that the descendants of the northern tribes, as well as those who remained in Babylon, are "not considered Jews." Isn't it somewhat ironic that today's "Jews" are continually referred to as national Israel, yet they represent a very small fraction of Abraham's descendants?

Now this does raise some interesting questions; for example:

- Didn't God make His covenant with "all" the descendants of Abraham, Isaac, and Jacob?
- Because of the disappearance of the northern tribes, does this covenant now apply only to the house of Judah?
- Was the prophet Jeremiah mistaken when he said that God was going to make a new covenant with the house of Judah "and" with the house of Israel?
- Were the prophets mistaken when they heard from the Lord that He was going to forgive and restore (not replace) the house of Israel as a people of God? There are numerous biblical prophecies predicting the restoration and uniting of the twelve tribes once again into one nation who will eternally serve the God of Abraham, Isaac, and Jacob.[94]

ISRAEL (EPHRAIM) NOW LIVING AMONG THE NATIONS

Four thousand years ago, Jacob laid his hands upon his grandson Ephraim (a son of Joseph) and prophesied that the descendants of Ephraim would become a multitude of nations.[95] As most Bible scholars know, the name of Ephraim in Scripture frequently refers to the entire northern kingdom. Certainly, Ephraim was the largest tribe, but as big as it got, it never became a multitude of nations before it disappeared in 722 BC. Since it didn't happen before the disappearance, then Ephraim must have become a multitude of nations after its disappearance. Well, where are they? Where has the Lord hidden them? Obviously, they don't even know themselves.[96]

Just before the fall of the northern kingdom in 722 BC, the Lord sent the prophet Hosea to Israel to prophesy concerning the coming captivity. <u>In his writings, Hosea foretold what was to take place for Ephraim (the ten northern tribes) after their disappearance into captivity:</u>

- The number of their descendants would be more than the "sand of the sea which cannot be measured."[97]
- They were to be rejected and become "wanderers among the nations."[98]
- However, the Lord was not finished with Israel (northern tribes), nor would He ever be finished with them.[99]
- In order to illustrate His long-suffering nature for Ephraim, the Lord told His chosen prophet Hosea to marry a harlot. Subsequently, she was unfaithful to Hosea, which broke his heart, and she left him for other lovers. After a period of time, the Lord told Hosea to forgive her and take her back and restore her as his wife. Likewise, the Lord stated that Ephraim would someday be restored and become His bride.[100]

<u>Now comes another surprise.</u> Not only will the descendants of Ephraim (northern kingdom) suddenly reappear, but after thousands of years of separation, they will once again be united with Judah (southern kingdom).[101] The prophet Ezekiel speaks clearly of this future uniting of Judah and Ephraim, and we also learn from Scripture that when Ephraim returns to the land of Israel, from which they were once cast out, they forever will be called "sons of the Living God."[102]

The fact that we have lost track of these descendants of the northern kingdom is irrelevant. Our Lord has made promises to those people that will be kept. Don't believe these "replacement theologians" who teach that the church has replaced Israel. This is a very misleading doctrine that will confuse a sound understanding of biblical prophecy. A day is coming when a remnant of the descendants of Ephraim will be brought back to the land of Israel, and there they will be reunited with their Judean brothers. That day probably will take place at the second coming of Christ, when He gathers His army together for the Battle of Armageddon. Then we'll reign together with Him in the land of Israel.

AMERICA—A HOME TO THE DESCENDANTS OF EPHRAIM?

Now let's take a look at where these descendants of Ephraim may currently live. There are many stories concerning how the descendants of the ten lost tribes migrated to Europe. Although this cannot be conclusively proved, suffice it to say that many of the heraldic symbols used by the great houses of Europe have their roots in the titles Jacob gave his children. Those coats of arms that people so proudly hang on their walls are straight out of Genesis 49:1-27.[103] Certainly many of these peoples migrated into Europe and subsequently to America. It is interesting to note that the prophet Hosea says that at the time of Ephraim's return to the land of Israel, many will come from "the west."[104]

It is a strong probability that a great number of the descendants of Ephraim are Christians living in the United States. Note the following:

- The covenant of circumcision was required of ancient Israel. Up until the 1980s, babies were routinely circumcised in the United States and millions still are today. This was one of the few nations on earth, besides Israel, to do so. Why us?
- The United States was the first nation to have a five-day workweek, thus observing the Sabbath as well as Sunday. Where did that originate?
- It appears from the prophet Zechariah that Ephraim would be the only ally that Judah will have in their war against the "Greeks."[105] At the time of this prophecy, Ephraim had been lost for two hundred years, but here they are united with Judah. Judah is seen as the bow of war and Ephraim as the arrows. They are fighting against the "sons of Greece." From 332 BC until 65 BC, the Greek Empire included the Middle Eastern countries that are now Lebanon, Iran, Iraq, Syria, and Egypt. Today, these are the homes of the Shiite Muslims.[106] Today the United States is the sole ally of Israel. Perhaps this is the Ephraim of the northern kingdom aligning with Judah of the southern kingdom against their enemies, the sons of Greece.

Finally, Paul tells us in Romans that "all Israel will be saved" when the "fullness of the Gentiles has come in."[107] Perhaps this is because the ten northern tribes are mixed in with the Gentile nations. Think about this! When you consider our own genealogy, can we trace our roots back 200 years? 500 years? How about 2700 years? Modern Israel boasts immigrants from 180 nations. Ephraim, comprising many more peoples than the Judeans were also dispersed some 800 years earlier and therefore, their descendants would be far greater. So, whether one is Hispanic, Asian, African, Indian, or Caucasian, it's more than probable that many of us are physical brothers and sisters descended from Abraham. God knows with certainty. Now, this doesn't mean that every Christian is a descendant from Ephraim, although certainly many are. But, like Rahab, Ruth, and Jethro, many Gentiles are also grafted into the promises of Israel.[108]

THE MEANING OF THE NUMBER 144,000

The delineation of the 12 tribes with that of 12,000 from each tribe can be viewed as a method to universalize the totality of God's anointed disciples residing on the earth at this time. Note that numbering is very significant to understanding much of the symbolism in Scripture.

The number twelve in the bible frequently represents the people of God. For example:

- 12 tribes of Israel in the Old Testament
- 12 apostles of Christ in the New Testament
- The 24 elders before the throne of God in Revelation 4 are probably representatives of God's people from both the Old Testament and the New Testament.

The New Jerusalem will have 12 gates bearing the names of the 12 tribes of Israel and also will have 12 foundation stones bearing the names of the 12 apostles. Also note that the New Jerusalem is laid out as a perfect cube, just like the most holy place in the tabernacle and the temple. The length, width, and height are each 12,000 furlongs or 1500 miles. This is the city that will house the entire people of God.[109]

- 144,000 will be sealed with the names of both the Father and the Son written on their foreheads. Now 144,000 = 12 x 12 x 1,000. The use of the number 144,000 does not necessarily imply an exact number of those who are sealed; it is probably symbolic of a perfect totality of those God has chosen to be sealed.

THE IDENTITY OF THE 144,000
SEALED SERVANTS OF GOD

These are the mighty leaders in the Army of God who will lead His people during the reign of terror that will descend upon the earth. They are the men and women who heard and obeyed the command of Jesus to "be prepared" for His coming.

Just who are they, and where do they come from?

- They are Christians descended from the tribes of the southern kingdom (Jews).
- And they are Christians descended from the tribes of the northern kingdom (Israelites or sons of Ephraim).

- And they are Christians descended from the Gentile nations who have been grafted into God's people.

Currently, they reside in every nation around the world, but a day is coming when they will all gather together with their Commander in Chief, Jesus Christ, on Mount Zion.[110]

The sealing of the 144,000 does not mean that the entire church is sealed. This section of prophecy is not speaking of eternal salvation; it is an anointing of discipleship for those who will be a powerful light in the midst of the darkest period in the history of the world. Many will be eternally saved but not sealed. We see a sign of this immediately after the sealing of the 144,000, when John is shown a numberless multitude from every nation worshipping before the throne of God.

A NUMBERLESS MULTITUDE WORSHIPPING BEFORE THE THRONE
(Revelation 7:9-17)

These are those coming out of the great tribulation who have been cleansed by the blood of the Lamb.[111] This great multitude will be composed of those Christians who were within the church at the launching of the latter-day judgments, as well as many others who are among the great harvest that will take place within the midst of the great tribulation.

Pre-tribulation rapturists believe this multitude to be those privileged Christians removed from the great tribulation because of their faith. Obviously, this view tends to play down the importance that our Lord speaks concerning those Christians who have suffered for the gospel of Christ through the centuries:

- *"Blessed are those who are persecuted for righteousness' sake, for theirs is the kingdom of heaven. Blessed are you when others revile you and persecute you and utter all kinds of evil against you falsely on my account. Rejoice and be glad, for your reward is great in heaven, for so they persecuted the prophets who were before you." (Matthew 5:10-12)*

My perception of this part of the vision is that these are Christians who have suffered tremendous sorrow, grief, hunger, and of course, persecution from the worldly system, but refused to compromise their faith even unto death. Now they stand in glorious holiness before God full of unspeakable joy. They are those who like Paul believe that:

- *The Spirit himself bears witness with our spirit that we are children of God, and if children, then heirs-heirs of God and fellow heirs with Christ, provided we suffer with him in order that we may also be glorified with him. For I consider that the sufferings of this present time are not worth comparing with the glory that is to be revealed to us. (Romans 8:16-18)*

Certainly, this is a depiction of those who are now experiencing His glory, following their suffering and death in the midst of the great tribulation. Now they will reign forever and ever with our Lord because they have truly repented and were reborn into the kingdom of God. Death may be a blessing conferred on people for their faithfulness and to deliver them from evil times.

- *Therefore, behold, I will gather you to your fathers, and <u>you shall be gathered to your grave in peace, and your eyes shall not see all the disaster that I will bring upon this place.</u> (2 Kings 22:20)*

The purpose for John receiving the vision of this numberless multitude and recording it is to continually provide hope for our Christian brothers and sisters who will experience great difficulties during this approaching time of great tribulation. It is intended to encourage them in their sufferings knowing that it is not worthy to be compared with the eternal glory that awaits those who remain steadfast in their faith unto death. Many of these will certainly be among the martyrs who will join their brethren under the heavenly altar (Revelation 6:9-11).

144,000 IS A REMNANT OF THE CHURCH, NOT THE WHOLE

Again, it is a special privilege for some believers, granted by the Lord Himself, that they might suffer for the sake of Christ.[112]

- *Only let your manner of life be worthy of the gospel of Christ, so that whether I come and see you or am absent, I may hear of you that you <u>are standing firm in one spirit, with one mind striving side by side for the faith of the gospel</u>, and <u>not frightened in anything by your opponents.</u> This is a clear sign to them of their destruction, but of your salvation, and that from God. <u>For it has been granted to you that for the sake of Christ you should not only believe in him but also suffer for his sake,</u> (Philippians 1:27-29)*

"Striving side by side" is perhaps, two-by-two proclaiming the gospel in the midst of evil darkness, which has come upon the entire earth. This is publicly proclaiming Jesus Christ without fear of the enemy, even though they are in the midst of severe persecution. Joy remains in the hearts of these warriors. They love Jesus Christ, and they love others more than they value their own lives.

Now the 144,000 who have been sealed for the mission of discipleship during the great tribulation will be severely challenged. As it was with the apostle Paul, hardships, persecution, and imprisonment await this sealed army of Christian knights. Yet, wherever they go proclaiming His name in the midst of chaos, they will go in a powerful anointing that will greatly impact many peoples across the earth.[113] A great harvest lies ahead, but contrary to much modern-day teaching, the greatest harvest will come in the midst of the greatest tribulation.

The 144,000 will be those with the faith of Caleb and Joshua, who were the only two among hundreds of thousands of adult males who were ready to go up against an enemy of giants that appeared unbeatable. They believed that God would give them the victory. Thus, they were the only two among that entire generation who were commissioned to lead God's people into the Promised Land. The remainder of that adult generation perished in the wilderness.[114] Surely many of those who perished in the wilderness received eternal life, but they didn't have the commitment to their God to stand strong in the face of a great enemy. They were not the leaders with the warrior spirit that could lead others into the Promised Land amidst the greatest and most dangerous of circumstances. The 144,000 who will be sealed prior to the coming trumpet judgments possess an uncompromising love for the Lord -they are God's valiant warriors that will be His witnesses in the midst of great tribulation.

LEADERSHIP QUALITIES THAT IDENTIFY THE 144,000 REMNANT

These 144,000 are Christians who continually deny themselves and take up the cross daily and follow Christ.[115] They are His true disciples in the latter days, who view chaos as the greatest opportunity for the light to shine in the midst of darkness.

They are among those historical champions of God who were willing to lay down their lives for the gospel of the kingdom. They understand that they will be persecuted by the world, but it doesn't deter them. Likewise, pressure may be applied to members of their family in order to force them to back off, but their love for the Father and His Son and for the body of Christ will strengthen their commitment to "continue to march."[116]

They are warriors who continue to rejoice in the midst of trials, for they know that it is through the wilderness boot camp that faith and purity of heart is greatly strengthened. Their military mind-set understands that there is no victory without a battle and one is not equipped for battle without the training received in the boot camp of life's tough challenges.[117]

Today, these are those in the body of Christ who recognize the challenging times that are coming quickly, and frequently they can be found strengthening their relationship with the Lord in their respective prayer closets. They are habitual intercessors who understand that in order for true faith to be exercised one needs to let go of the world (in fasting) and lay hold of heaven (in prayer). They are the "watchmen" who are prophets in the Army of God.[118]

These are those who deeply sigh and groan over the sinful abominations that are committed in the midst of the nations. They are being sealed like their brothers and sisters were prior to the destruction of Jerusalem in the days of Ezekiel.[119]

They are also identified with the "overcomers" or "conquerors" Jesus was calling for when He spoke to the churches in Revelation 2 and 3.

Finally, they are the "firstfruits" for God, who follow the Lamb wherever He goes, and in their mouths no lie is found for they are blameless.[120] They will be an anointed light, reflecting the glory of the Lord in the midst of darkness. This is the future glory of Israel.

- *Arise, shine, for your light has come, and the glory of the Lord has risen upon you. For behold, darkness shall cover the earth, and thick darkness the peoples; but the Lord will arise upon you, and his glory will be seen upon you.* **(Isaiah 60:1-2)**

Now many readers may believe that this is not for them, but it is for all who will hear His voice and begin to prepare spiritually. These leadership characteristics are not the result of a bible college or seminary education, nor do they describe the majority of those in present-day, full-time ministry. They are the result of one's quest to become more and more like the Lord Jesus Christ, and we must never settle for a lesser vision in our daily journey.[121] Those who actively and strongly pursue this quest in the daily affairs of life likely will be among those who are sealed.

In summary, the 144,000 "servants of God" do not include the entire church but are the firstfruits of His people - those anointed disciples of Jesus who walk with Him for three and a half years during His latter-day's ministry. Their ministry is addressed in greater detail in chapter 8.

CHAPTER 6

THE "SEVENTY WEEKS" OF DANIEL

(First Read: Daniel 9:24-27)

If twenty-first-century Christian warriors within the body of Christ are to have a clear overview of their mission during the period of the great tribulation, it is important to have a solid grasp of a prophecy that was shown to the prophet Daniel over 2500 years ago. This prophecy, which is revealed in just four verses of Scripture, is one of the most difficult and controversial passages in the bible. But, I truly believe that it is very foundational for a proper understanding of events that appear to provide a timetable for both the first and second comings of Jesus Christ; as well as the objectives that will be accomplished at both comings.

A HISTORICAL BACKGROUND OF THIS "SEVENTY WEEKS" PROPHECY

It was a time in the history of Israel when the southern kingdom of Judah had been in captivity in Babylon for almost 70 years. Approximately 536 BC, Daniel, a prophet of the Lord, understood that Jeremiah, some 50 years earlier, had prophesized that this captivity would last only 70 years.[122] Additionally, some 150 years earlier, Isaiah had prophesized that a leader by the name of Cyrus would decree their deliverance from captivity and allow them to return to Jerusalem.[123] Daniel's heart must have leaped as he heard reports of this chosen Persian leader who was making a name for himself throughout the Middle East. Therefore Daniel, realizing that a man by the name of Cyrus was coming into power, knew that a crucial time was approaching; thus he began to pray fervently that the Lord would soon deliver His people from the bondage of Babylon.[124] This prayer of Daniel primarily acknowledges the sin and guilt of the nation of Israel and its forefathers as he vehemently pleads for the mercy of God and for deliverance from Babylonian captivity.

It is important to understand that the primary issue in Daniel's mind was that the large majority of the Israelite people had become worshippers of the Babylonian gods, which allowed the Babylonian populace to equate the God of Israel with their own gods. Now that the Jewish people were in captivity, they were a reproach before the nations of the world, and thus the God of Israel was considered to be weaker than the pagan gods. Now to Daniel, and surely to a remnant of other Judeans, it was more important that Yahweh, the God of Israel, be manifested as the only true God than it was for guilty Israel to escape the consequences of their infidelity. This was a similar concern that Moses had some nine hundred years earlier, when the Israelites were delivered from Egyptian bondage and shortly afterwards, turned from their God to worship a golden calf.[125]

Daniel understood that if the Lord allowed His people to remain in exile forever and allowed Jerusalem, His holy city, to remain in ruins, that no one would ever believe that this God of Israel was the one and true God, the holy Sovereign of the universe. This was Daniel's burden during this time of prayer. Thus, the stakes were high, and Daniel's prayer received an immediate response from the Lord as He dispatched His holy emissary, Gabriel, to personally communicate His message to Daniel. In one of the most challenging passages in the Bible, the Lord responds to this prayer of Daniel with a mysterious prophecy that addresses both the first and the second comings of the Messiah. It is a prophecy that is frequently referred to as "the seventy weeks" of Daniel.

SEVENTY "WEEKS OF YEARS" WILL BRING ABOUT SIX RESULTS

- *Seventy weeks are decreed about your people and your holy city, to finish the transgression, to put an end to sin, and to atone for iniquity, to bring in everlasting righteousness, to seal both vision and prophet, and to anoint a most holy place.* **(Daniel 9:24)**

Here Daniel was told that "seventy weeks" had been decreed by the Lord to accomplish six results. The first group of *"three results"* appears to be identified with the *first coming* of our Lord Jesus Christ.

- **To "finish the transgression"**: Because of their transgression, the Lord previously had decreed that the Judeans were to be in captivity to the Babylonians for seventy years. Now He says that "seventy weeks of years" will put a complete end to transgression of the law of God. In other words, there is a time coming when the Lord's people will be delivered from the curse of the law.
- **To "put an end of sin"**: This conveys the truth that a time is coming when all sin will be put away from before the face of the Lord.
- **To "atone for iniquity"**: This suggests that a perfect Sacrifice will be made in order to accomplish the first two items.

In summary, transgression, sin, and iniquity represent the nature of the curse, which has separated mankind from the Lord since the fall of Adam in the garden. The crucifixion of Jesus Christ is definitely in view here, even though His people will not experience the fullness of putting away all sin from the earth until His second coming.

The second group of *"three results"* appears to be identified with the *second coming* of our Lord Jesus Christ.

- **To "bring in everlasting righteousness"**: This refers to the state that will exist between the Lord and mankind when sin has been completely removed from the earth.
- **To "seal both vision and prophecy"**: This is the final goal of God's plan for the ages and will culminate when Jesus Christ receives His earthly throne. Then all prophecy, including that dealing with the second coming, will be fulfilled.
- **To "anoint a most holy place"**: This appears to refer to a future temple from which our King, Jesus Christ, will reign over the nations of the earth. Perhaps this is the New Jerusalem discussed in chapter 14 of this book. A detailed description of this coming temple can be found in the book of Ezekiel.[126]

Remember that these six elements will be accomplished at the completion of the "seventy weeks of years"; therefore, it appears as if both the first and the second comings of the Son of God are in view.

SEVENTY WEEKS = SEVENTY "WEEKS OF YEARS"

- *Know therefore and understand that from the going out of the word to restore and build Jerusalem to the coming of an anointed one, a prince, there shall be* **seven weeks**. *Then for* **sixty-two weeks** *it shall be built again with squares and moat, but in a troubled time. And* **after the sixty-two weeks, an anointed one shall be cut off** *and shall have nothing.* **(Daniel 9:25-26)**

For those who are unfamiliar with Hebrew, each of the "weeks" referred to in this prophecy are actually representative of "seven" Hebraic years, which consist of 360 days each. For example, 70 "weeks" equates to 490 "years." There are three groups of weeks in this prophecy, which total "seventy weeks." These are *sixty-two weeks* (= "434 years"), *seven weeks* (= "49 years"), and *one week* (= "7 years").

Both the "sixty-two weeks" and the "seven weeks" refer to a period of time between the issuing of a decree to restore Jerusalem and the coming of the Messiah. The "one week" is a little more difficult, but it appears to be the time frame in which the Messiah, Jesus Christ, ministers upon the earth in order to accomplish the six tasks. The "one week" also is believed by many to be the length of time for the reign of Antichrist. Perhaps this is also true since Satan's purpose for the Antichrist is to replace Jesus Christ in the world as the true messiah. Therefore, he attempts to imitate some of the prophetic events regarding the ministry of Jesus Christ, such as performing great miracles, including resurrection from the dead.

The decree to rebuild Jerusalem appears to originate with the Persian king Artaxerxes in 457 BC. Although this decree by this Persian king emphasizes adorning the temple and enforcing the law of Moses, Ezra took this commission as approval to rebuild the walls of Jerusalem.[127] Now if one were to add the "7 weeks" to the "62 weeks," it would total 483 years, which, using the *solar calendar*, would bring it to AD 27, the approximate beginning point of Jesus' ministry. However, there was a second decree of Artaxerxes that came in 445 BC, when the king granted permission to Nehemiah to rebuild the walls of Jerusalem.[128] If one were to measure 483 years with the *Hebraic calendar*, this would approximate the time of the crucifixion of Jesus—that time when the Messiah was "cutoff" following a three-and-a-half-year ministry.

MYSTERY IN THE NUMBERING OF THE WEEKS (AD 2016?)

This calculation raises a somewhat mysterious question: If 483 years was the supposed time frame, why did Daniel say "sixty-two weeks" and "seven weeks" instead of "sixty-nine weeks"? Something else appears to be involved here. We must remember that both the *first and second comings* of Jesus Christ are involved in this prophecy. It is conceivable that the "seven weeks" also is to be used for calculating a time for the *second coming* of Jesus, the Messiah.

Another interesting scenario that addresses this mysterious *sixty-two-plus-seven-weeks* issue comes from Sir Isaac Newton, a devoted student of the book of Daniel, who, using the *Julian calendar*, calculated 434 years from the decree given to Nehemiah until the birth of Jesus.[129] Thus, approximately 300 years ago, Newton understood that "sixty-two weeks" was appointed for the first coming of Jesus and that the "seven weeks" must represent a time when there would be a second decree to restore Jerusalem.

Thus, it appears that the "seven-week" or "forty-nine-year" period, which is a Jubilee period, has to occur subsequent to the restoration of the Jews to the land of Israel. With this understanding, those in our generation know that on June 7, 1967, the Jewish nation gained control of Jerusalem following the Six-Day War, whereupon they began to rebuild this city. This "forty-nine-year" period of time will then end in 2016, which may very well bring us to the final three-and-a-half-year ministry of Jesus—only this time it appears that He ministers through His body; the "sealed 144,000." (Note: This will be further discussed in subsequent chapters).

A STRONG COVENANT FOR "ONE WEEK"

- *And he shall make a strong covenant with many for one week, and for half of the week he shall put an end to sacrifice and offering.* **(Daniel 9:27...)**

The first coming of Jesus Christ was through a supernatural birth in the natural world. He came to confirm the covenant of His Father and to lay down His life to atone for the sins of His people. His second coming also will be with a supernatural birth, only this time through the spirit indwelling the "firstfruits" within the body of Christ.[130] These Christian warriors will be filled with the Spirit and will powerfully minister throughout the world. These are the 144,000 who are pictured as standing with the Lamb on Mount Zion.[131] Like their King before them, they will be cut off after three and a half years, and, then, three days later, they too will be resurrected and will arise to the heavens to be joined with their Commander in Chief, with whom they will return together in a mighty army that will defeat the kingdom of darkness and establish the kingdom of God throughout the earth. These men are the vanguard of the Lord and will fulfill in their lives the second half of the seven-year ministry of Jesus Christ, which occurs during the great tribulation period.[132]

A COUNTERFEIT COVENANT

- *And on the wing of abominations shall come one who makes desolate, until the decreed end is poured out on the desolator. (Daniel 9:...27)*

Now the first coming of Jesus Christ in His natural body and His soon second coming in His spiritual body fully confirm the true covenant that the Father made with His people. However, the "false prince" who is to come, the Antichrist, also enters into a seven-year covenant with the nation of Israel. That too will be cutoff after three and a half years, when he sets up the abomination of desolation in the physical temple in Jerusalem. Satan will now reign for three and a half years in the hearts of his people. Satan always has attempted to counterfeit the works of the true Messiah; thus he creates his own covenant with Israel, and his false messiah also confirms the covenant for seven years. This covenant will be a peace treaty the nation of Israel will sign with her enemies.[133]

A SUMMARY OF THE MATHEMATICAL CALCULATIONS

Artaxerxes' Decree in 457 BC:
- 62 weeks + 7 weeks = 483 *solar years*, which would end in AD 27, the beginning of Christ's ministry.

Artaxerxes' Decree in 445 BC:
- 62 weeks + 7 weeks = 483 years, which, using the *Hebraic calendar*, would end in AD 32, the time of Christ's crucifixion.

<u>Sir Isaac Newton's theory using the *Julian calendar*</u>:

- Beginning in 445 BC: 62 weeks = 434 years which would end with the birth of Christ.
- ½ week = 3 ½ years: this is the first ministry of Christ ending in His crucifixion.

<u>Jerusalem restored to the nation of Israel on June 7, 1967</u>:

- 7 weeks = 49 years; this would end in 2016.
- ½ week = 3 ½ years: this may be the second ministry of Christ through His body of 144,000, which would end in 2020, when they too will be cut off.

Chapter 8 will address the mission of the 144,000 anointed witnesses in the Army of the Lord ministering during the period of great tribulation.

CHAPTER 7

TRUMPETS, NUKES, AND A LITTLE BOOK

(First Read: Revelation 8—10)

SUMMARY OF THE SIXTH SEAL

The "great earthquake" launched by the Lord against the mighty enemies of Israel will soon rock the entire planet. It will not occur at some unforeseen moment, but will come at a time when the entire world is watching a tremendously large army led by the Russians coming against the nation of Israel in order to purge them from the land once and for all. The events following the opening of the first "five seals" were all initiated by the Son of God, but the world did not recognize them as such. However, with the opening of the sixth seal, the Lord's presence will be manifested to all the nations of this modern era. His concern for His people and His anger toward their enemies will leave no doubt that the God of Abraham, Isaac, and Jacob is truly God.

Many in the church might ask, "Why is the Lord revealing Himself through Israel, a predominately secular nation, and not through His church, who believes that Jesus is the Messiah?" Certainly the church exists worldwide and has in various times and places been under persecution, but the Jewish people also have suffered under continual persecution. Yet, the world does not recognize the reality of God through those events that have continually occurred throughout the last two thousand years of history. So what event could possibly initiate such a catastrophic response by the Lord that the entire world would not doubt His existence and His commitment to oppose the forces that intend to annihilate His people?

- It would be an event that, if not stopped, would forever destroy Israel from the face of the earth.
- It would be an event that would occur at a time when the entire world would witness it.
- An event so impressive that it would clearly reveal that the God of Abraham, Isaac, and Jacob is true to His covenant and that He will deliver His people from the hands of their enemies.
- An event that would turn many in Israel back to their Lord—perhaps not yet to recognizing Jesus as the coming Messiah, but back to the God of their fathers.

THE DAWNING OF THE "DAY OF THE LORD"

The opening of the "sixth seal" appears to be the launching of the Day of the Lord; this is not a twenty-four-hour day but a period of time when the Lord will continually manifest Himself through His people in the midst of the greatest devastation in the history of mankind. It is a day of warfare between the forces of light and darkness.[134] It is a time when "seven trumpets" and "seven bowls" will successively alter world events and continually usurp the world's vision of peace and brotherhood without God. These plagues will fall directly upon those of mankind who do not have the "seal of God" on their foreheads. The purpose of this "sealing," as well as the identity of those who will be sealed (protected) from being casualties of the "trumpet events," will be presented in the following chapter.

The "trumpet events" will cause the powers of unbelief and hostility toward God to break into the open in the person of the Antichrist, and then every person's loyalty will become plain. The "end times" is an era when the forces of both righteousness and evil will be so open and clear that all persons must declare themselves either for Christ or for Antichrist. Thus, these plagues being poured out upon the earth are not simply judicial but also have a merciful purpose: they are designed to turn men, women, and children to God while the time for decision remains.[135] The Day of the Lord eventually will culminate with the second coming of Jesus, the Son of God, and the Commander in Chief who will lead His army of warriors in the final battle.

A NUCLEAR RESPONSE TO THE GOG-MAGOG WAR

The sixth-seal events also appear to include additional devastations that quite possibly result from the "great earthquake." As mentioned in a previous chapter, it is very possible that this "great earthquake" creates such panic and confusion among the world powers that a nuclear war is triggered between Russia and "those who dwell securely in the coastlands."[136] In his book, *Today's Technology in Bible Prophecy*, Charles W. Miller sees events in the sixth seal from a nuclear perspective.

- *When he opened the sixth seal, I looked, and behold, there was a great earthquake, and the <u>sun became black as sackcloth, the full moon became like blood</u>, and the <u>stars of the sky fell to the earth</u> as the fig tree sheds its winter fruit when shaken by a gale. <u>The sky vanished like a scroll that is being rolled up</u>, and every mountain and island was removed from its place.* **(Revelation 6:12-14)**

John's vision of "falling stars" could well be the fiery streak of a rocket exhaust from nuclear tipped missiles as they soar through the atmosphere at speeds up to 8,000 miles/hour. This is followed by a tremendous nuclear blast, which drives everything away from its superheated center with 400 miles/hour winds. These inflowing winds produce strong updrafts just seconds after the explosion. A column of fiery dust and smoke-filled air quickly forms and rises at a speed of nearly 300 miles/hour several miles into the darkening sky. Eventually a gigantic mushroom shaped cloud is formed. The early ascent prior to the mushroom cloud forming gives the visual impression of the "sky departing like a scroll that is being rolled up."[137]

THE RESPONSE OF THE VICTIMS
(Revelation 6:16-17)

Unlike conventional wars, where the privileged people, such as generals, politicians, and the wealthy, often manage to avoid personal catastrophe, all classes of people in the target zones will be victimized. Survivors of the initial blast and heat wave will head for the hills, since staying in the vicinity of the nuclear blast will result in severe and painful radiation poisoning.

"Fall on us" reveals the victims' numbed state of mind and utter hopelessness. When they take stock of injuries, exposure to radiation, and lack of food, water, and medical support, they will consider death from falling rocks a better fate than what they are about to face. They had been rooted in the belief that they were able to live life as their own god. They intended to build their own kingdom of righteousness and peace as viewed by their own concepts and they intended to accomplish all this without any interference from almighty God and His beloved Son. They never knew that His kingdom already was realized in the hearts of His people. They laughed at the idea that this world was principally wicked and that the earth would one day pass away. Their hope was in the stability of the eternal universe, and now that hope is frustrated in a moment.

Additionally, this will be a wake-up call to many professing believers who knew that God's judgment was inevitable but were living as if they would never have to experience it. These are people who voiced a belief in Jesus but lived a life that separated themselves from Him, and thus they were overwhelmingly fearful of seeing His face. This initial calamity will be so severe that they will suppose that the end of the world is upon them. However, this assumption will be incorrect, for it is simply the beginning of the Day of the Lord. Despite the numerous movies and books depicting the horrors of nuclear war, the Bible teaches that the great majority of people will be unprepared to cope with the aftermath of a worldwide nuclear war.[138] However, the remnant among the people of God who will be "prepared" for the Day of the Lord will have understanding of the times and thus will not be filled with fear or consternation, even though this will be a dreadful period from a natural point of view. These are the mighty leaders who will arise and be anointed from on high and will guide many down the narrow road leading into the kingdom of God.

THE OPENING OF THE SEVENTH SEAL
(Revelation 8:1)

With the breaking of this final seal, the entire prophetic book of Revelation is opened for all to see. Viewing this newly opened book leaves those in heaven in stunned silence, for it reveals that the tremendous devastations to be released by the sixth seal is merely a glimpse of an infinitely greater chaotic series of events that are about to descend upon the world. Many in heaven, like the martyrs under the throne, have to be wondering why the Lord would not quickly step in to halt man's senseless violence and put an end to misery. When the book of Revelation is opened to their understanding, they are speechless, for the horrors of this post-nuclear world war will continue on for a much longer time than anyone anticipated. This stunned silence will be the same emotional reaction of the Christian church when they finally come to understand the destructive forces that are about to engulf the world and realize that they are right in the middle of it. Then, the church will finally recognize that we are indeed in the age of the end times and that the judgments of the trumpets and bowls are on the way.

There also will be a large segment of unbelievers who will not harden their hearts and will begin to seek answers from the people of God. However, the great majority of mankind, who have hardened their hearts against God and His Son, eventually will recover from their fear and begin to unify more quickly in their endeavor to create their own kingdom. The coming trumpet judgments will harden them even more, and they will unite to create a world empire much like that in the ancient city of Babel, only instead of Nimrod as its ruler, they will select the Antichrist.

This seventh seal has no plague or judgment content, but its opening actually launches the sounding of the seven trumpets. Thus, the first six seals relate to the forces leading up to the time of the end, while the seven trumpets relate to the beginning of the events of the end.

SILENCE IN HEAVEN AND THE PRAYERS OF THE SAINTS
(Revelation 8:1-5)

During this silence in heaven, seven angels are standing before the throne of God, and they receive seven trumpets. They do not immediately commence blowing these trumpets, but they reverently keep silent until something else has been finished. Subsequently, another angel approaches the altar and receives incense, along with the prayers of the saints. This angel then kindles the incense with the fire from the altar; he stands before the throne of God and causes the incense and the prayers of the saints to ascend up to the Lord almighty. It is very evident that the all-important elements in this period of silence are the prayers of the saints rising up before the Lord. What is the object of these prayers? "Our Father, who art in heaven; blessed be thy Name; Thy kingdom come; Thy will be done upon earth as it is in heaven." This is the cry of the saints who have been calling for His kingdom to come for more than four thousand years. The time has come for the launching of judgments that will prepare the world for the second coming of our Lord to set up His kingdom across the entire earth. Now comes the beginning of God's answer to our prayers.[139]

- *Then the angel took the censer and filled it with fire from the altar and threw it on the earth, and there were peals of thunder, rumblings, flashes of lightning, and an earthquake.* **(Revelation 8:5)**

It is quite possible that this is the heavenly event that launches the great earthquake in the Gog-Magog war. That is when the prayers of the saints over the centuries are united together with the prayers of those interceding today for the protection of Israel from the enemies that are coming against them. A mighty earthquake is coming that will soon shake the entire earth, an earthquake that will ignite an unprecedented, continent-smashing nuclear war.[140]

Christian prayer may delay the start of this war, but it will not prevent it. However, it could allow those who understand the times to personally prepare and to warn others that nuclear war is knocking at our front door. This "period of silence" in heaven most likely will be when the world sees that Russia and Iran are preparing to invade Israel, while the Western world is weakly voicing their opposition to it. And we may very well be in that "period of silence" today. The great earthquake and subsequent nuclear war is then launched when the angel suddenly casts the fire burning with the prayers of the saints down to the earth.

THE FIRST FOUR TRUMPETS
(Revelation 8:6-12)

Trumpets are used in Scripture to awaken people to matters of extreme importance or to summon them to prepare to resist an approaching enemy. Here they are used to alert the world that the Day of the Lord is at hand and will be accompanied by great distress. Listen to the prophecy of Joel concerning this time.

- <u>*Blow a trumpet in Zion*</u>*; sound an alarm on my holy mountain! Let all the inhabitants of the land tremble, for the* <u>*day of the Lord is coming*</u>*; it is near,* <u>*a day of darkness and gloom, a day of clouds and thick darkness!*</u> **(Joel 2:1-2)**

It is likely that the trumpet prophecies foretell seven major events that will occur in the closing period of this nuclear war. Collectively, they document the ferocity of the sixth-seal nuclear war, the war's immediate aftermath, and the continuing, long-term repercussions. These trumpet plagues fall into two separate groups. The first four are directed against the elements of nature and the heavenlies, while the last three, which are called "woes," fall directly upon mankind. A similar division is seen in the breaking of the seals, where there also, the first four were clearly distinguished from the last three.

The First Trumpet Sounds = A Burning of the Land

- *The first angel blew his trumpet, and there followed <u>hail</u> and <u>fire</u>, mixed with <u>blood</u>, and these were thrown upon the earth. And a third of the earth was burned up, and a third of the trees were burned up, and all green grass was burned up. (Revelation 8:7)*

Nuclear hail is formed when large quantities of earth and water are sucked into the fireball and become vaporized. Subsequently, they gradually descend to earth in what we call fallout. John described this nuclear fallout as hail, since it does look like ordinary hailstones. The fallout of hail that falls quickly back to earth within one day is generally the size of marbles. Lighter particles continue to fall like dusty snow, and eventually invisibly, for weeks afterwards. This affects the food crops that are subjected to severe contamination, and they cannot be harvested for decades.

Fire is naturally mentioned, for a single megaton bomb can set ninety-five square miles on fire at the same time. The blood refers to the vaporized remains of people and animals falling back to earth following the blast. Those in the vicinity of an airburst nuclear explosion would be instantly reduced to superheated gases and would eventually fall to the earth as vaporized blood, along with other burning debris. Studies have indicated that a large-scale nuclear war (5,000-10,000 megaton yields) would result in 750 million immediate deaths from the blasts alone. Another 300 million also would die from the heat and radiation coming out of the explosion. But, that's not all. Another billion or so undoubtedly would require medical attention for burns, lost limbs, and other injuries, and yet such overwhelming medical needs could not be met.[141] [248]

Note also that the effect of the first trumpet is imagery from the seventh Egyptian plague during the days of Moses when the Lord sent, thunder, hail, and fire down upon the earth.[142]

The Second Trumpet Sounds = A Burning of the Sea and Marine Life

The second angel blew his trumpet, and something like a great mountain, burning with fire, was thrown into the sea, and a third of the sea became blood. A third of the living creatures in the sea died, and a third of the ships were destroyed. (Revelation 8:8-9)

This appears to be the naval side of the nuclear war. The great mountain burning with fire is not easy to identify. Some commentators think it may be a fiery meteor. However, undersea naval combat with nuclear submarines undoubtedly will be part of this war and thus, the naval vessels at sea will be under attack since that is where the large portion of nuclear weaponry is launched. Thus, like the landmasses, one-third of the seas will be destroyed with much death.

Note also that the effect of the second trumpet is imagery from the first Egyptian plague during the days of Moses when all the water in the Nile river turned to blood causing the fish to die.[143]

The Third Trumpet Sounds = A Burning of the Fresh Water

- *The third angel blew his trumpet, and a great star fell from heaven, blazing like a torch, and it fell on a third of the rivers and on the springs of water. The name of the star is* Wormwood*. A third of the waters became wormwood, and many people died from the water, because it had been made bitter. (Revelation 8:10-11)*

Wormwood is a bitter herb that Scripture employs as a symbol of bitterness and sorrow that God gives to those who forsake Him.[144] Here it is probably used to describe extreme bitterness in the waters caused by radioactive fallout. This certainly pictures the nuclear radiation effect upon the interior of the continents, where the world's rivers and lakes are found. Many survivors will be faced with the dilemma of drinking irradiated waters or dying of thirst. Thus, many undoubtedly will die from these embittered waters. Drinking of irradiated waters will result in a slow, painful death from radiation sickness. Starting with nausea, vomiting, and diarrhea, victims will experience internal bleeding, ulcerations of the lips, and loss of hair within two weeks.[145]

The Fourth Trumpet Sounds = A Darkening of the Heavens

- *The fourth angel blew his trumpet, and a third of the sun was struck, and a third of the moon, and a third of the stars, so that a third of their light might be darkened, and a third of the day might be kept from shining, and likewise a third of the night. (Revelation 8:12)*

A future nuclear war involving the incineration of one-third of the earth will not be the result of a detonation of a few nuclear bombs. Even the twelve-kiloton atomic bomb dropped on Nagasaki in 1945 blocked the sun's rays for a short period of time. However, when we consider the explosion of hundreds of nuclear warheads, each a thousand times more destructive than the Nagasaki bomb, the distinct possibility of there being enough smoke launched into the earth's atmosphere to cause this amount of damage becomes chillingly apparent. Once high-altitude nuclear smoke clouds encircle the earth, they will become a miles-thick, dark curtain throughout the skies. In addition to keeping one-third of the sun's rays from reaching the earth, the thick clouds literally will shorten the length of daylight by a third and the nightlight likewise. Studies of the post-effects of nuclear warfare reveal that the lands would experience subfreezing temperatures over most of the northern hemisphere. These temperatures could remain below freezing for months. No area of the globe could be counted on to be free from this "nuclear winter."[146]

Note also that the effect of the fourth trumpet is imagery from the ninth Egyptian plague during the days of Moses.[147]

THE EAGLE'S WARNING

At the completion of events resulting from the first four trumpets, one-third of mankind's entire physical universe has been decimated. The land, the oceans, the lakes and rivers, and the skies have all suffered tremendous devastation. Sickness and epidemics from a poisoned environment will abound worldwide. However, it is about to get worse. Suddenly, John is shown an eagle flying across the heavens and proclaiming that the next three trumpet judgments will be delivered directly against mankind.

- *Then I looked, and I heard an eagle crying with a loud voice as it flew directly overhead, "Woe, woe, woe to those who dwell on the earth, at the blasts of the other trumpets that the three angels are about to blow!"* **(Revelation 8:13)**

So what are these "woes?"

- *And the fifth angel blew his trumpet, and I saw a star fallen from heaven to earth, and he was given the key to the shaft of the bottomless pit. He opened the shaft of the bottomless pit, and from the shaft rose smoke like the smoke of a great furnace, and the sun and the air were darkened with the smoke from the shaft.* **(Revelation 9:1-2)**

Obviously, this "star" is an "angelic being" that will fall from heaven and come down to the earth. This "angelic being" has also been given powerful, but limited authority over the earth in the midst of tremendous devastation. He has been authorized to release demonic forces that have been imprisoned for centuries in the midst of the earth. My perspective is that this "angelic being" is Satan who will never again be allowed access to heaven, and will attempt to build a massive army and take complete dominion over the entire world. This will launch the "great tribulation" like the world has never before experienced. A very challenging time that Jesus warned His church about in order that they would not be surprised, but prepared:

- *For then there will be great tribulation, such as has not been from the beginning of the world until now, no, and never will be.* **(Matthew 24:21)**

FIFTH TRUMPET WOE: THE NEED FOR MARTIAL LAW

The typical survivor's first reaction to these events will be panic, but this eventually will be replaced by anger. As we have seen in the aftermath of the Twin Towers and Hurricane Katrina, many people will rise up against local authority, angry that government would allow this to happen to them, and demand that something be done to help them. Undoubtedly, there will be a huge outbreak of crime, including robbery and murder among the citizenry. Young people in the prime of life, aware of the lethal effects of radiation, will be angry that they may die in a matter of weeks or months and will want to strike back at the authorities who failed to protect them. Food and water will be scarce, and supplies, transportation, and fuel will be nonexistent. There will be a frantic hoarding of food; neighborhood homes will be attacked by gangs and small groups of criminal bands seeking food and other goods. Eventually, this will be organized by gang leadership, who will recruit these bands to steal for them in order to gain items to sell on the black market. Crops will be highly valued for food, and trees will be highly prized for heating, cooking, and building shelters. Thus, martial law will be the initial measure taken by an existing government to protect the food supplies and to restore order among the survivors to insure their nation's survival.

FIFTH TRUMPET WOE: LOCUSTS STINGING LIKE SCORPIONS
(Revelation 9:3-10)

To begin with, we need to remember that there is an ongoing spiritual war in the heavenlies, as well as in the world. Recall that John saw two sides of the scroll, representing the spiritual heavenly reality and the physical worldly reality. The scroll has been opened and the decrees of the Lord are being released in both the spiritual and physical worlds, revealing that the Lord is controlling the entire situation. Angelic beings are restrained until the time of the Lord's command, and then, in His perfect timing, they are released to carry out their individual missions in this war. This fifth trumpet scenario is designed to reveal what this event will look like from a worldly perspective in the twenty-first century.

Now within this passage there is again the imagery of the smoking after-effects of a nuclear detonation. However, out of the aftermath of a nuclear strike, something will arise to attempt to control and subsequently take advantage of this catastrophic situation.

- *Then from the smoke came locusts on the earth, and they were given power like the power of scorpions of the earth. They were told not to harm the grass of the earth or any green plant or any tree, <u>but only those people who do not have the seal of God on their foreheads</u>. They were allowed to torment them for five months, but not to kill them, and their torment was like the torment of a scorpion when it stings someone. (**Revelation 9:3-5**)*

The Bible has previously referred to locusts as vast destructive armies.[148] In this instance, it is conceivable that the locusts are representative of a vast, perhaps global, military force. This army will not be sent to destroy but to protect environmental property like the trees and crops that survived the nuclear strike. They are allowed to torment mankind but not to kill them. This is not a conquering army but a military peacekeeping force. Their supposed mission is to establish law and order in those communities struggling to survive the chaotic aftermath of the nuclear war. Their initial orders are not to kill anyone, even if violating martial law, which is a typical order given to combat troops sent to restore order during national emergencies. This command is important in preventing an armed revolt from arising among the masses. However, concentration camps certainly will be employed.

These troops will be characteristic of a scorpion army. Scorpions are so bad-tempered that they will lash out at anyone or anything that dare to cross their path. The weaponry used by this peacekeeping force will be like the tail of a scorpion. Although they are ordered not to kill the masses, they certainly will inflict pain and torment, and thus it appears that Taser-gun weaponry will be involved. This is weaponry that will inflict pain like the sting of a scorpion but will not cause death.

The "sealed ones" of God will be exempt from being harmed by this force. It appears as if these are the Christians who are protected from this chaotic environment, and through their leadership, they will be active in bringing peace and understanding to the situation. These are those Christian warriors who have prepared themselves for this "Day of the Lord" and thus are not among the scared, chaotic, and rebellious masses.

THE APPEARANCE OF THE LOCUSTS

- *In appearance the locusts were like horses prepared for battle: on their <u>heads were what looked like crowns of gold</u>; their <u>faces were like human faces</u>, their hair like women's hair, and their <u>teeth like lions' teeth</u>; they had <u>breastplates like breastplates of iron</u>, and the <u>noise of their wings was like the noise of many chariots with horses rushing into battle</u>. They have tails and stings like scorpions, and their power to hurt people for five months is in their tails.* **(Revelation 9:7-10)**

The shape of the locusts described in the fifth trumpet scenario easily can be identified with helicopter gunships, which undoubtedly will be utilized by this peacekeeping force. The whirring noise of the rotor blades and the thump, thump, thump sound of a chopper passing overhead certainly can be identified with the sound of locust wings and the sound of chariots of many horses running to battle. The "crown" of rotor blades, the "faces of men" in the cockpit, the locust-shaped body of the chopper, and the "lion's teeth" armament all foretell the use of numerous helicopter gunships to police the countryside, provide support for the ground troops, and transport Taser-wounded prisoners to concentration camps.

FIFTH TRUMPET WOE: NUCLEAR WINTER

These peacekeeping efforts will last for five months, which seems to coincide with the length of a nuclear winter, a period of time when temperatures are below freezing and a third of the light from the sun and moon has been darkened. Tests reveal that for a ten-thousand-megaton-yield exchange, which is enough firepower to burn up a third of the earth, subfreezing temperatures could last almost six months. John is describing five months of widespread famine and political upheaval in the midst of arctic-type temperatures.[149] It is a period of such grief and hopelessness for the world citizenry that many will seek death, but death will flee from them and they will have to continue in their deep suffering for a time.

Five dreadful months is reemphasized. Why? Christians should pay close attention to its significance in light of God's past warnings regarding major calamities and those who listened and acted. For example, Joseph stored grain for seven years in Egypt before a seven-year famine arrived. We also can look at this example in Noah and the building of the ark. We must respond to John's seven trumpet warnings and make the preparations and commitment necessary to survive as well as minister during the coming nuclear holocaust. We definitely need to store up food and water and other provisions that will last for at least five months.

FIFTH TRUMPET WOE: THE ARRIVAL OF APOLLYON

- *They have as king over them the angel of the bottomless pit. His name in Hebrew is Abaddon, and in Greek he is called Apollyon.* **(Revelation 9:11)**

Now we are introduced to the military commander over this so-called peacekeeping force. It appears that this person will arise from a position of relative obscurity to international importance in the post-nuclear war period. The reference to this king being the "angel of the bottomless pit" describes this world leader's dark character and mission. Both *Abaddon* and *Apollyon* mean "destruction" or "to destroy." His name exposes this demonically empowered leader's evil character and hidden agenda. Perhaps this is the coming world leader who will be claiming that his mission is to bring about worldwide peace. This will certainly be welcomed among the masses that have survived this nuclear war. If this is the Antichrist who is yet to be revealed, he will need to gain the backing of the world's military establishment as his first step toward world power. Subsequently, if he is the chosen one, once he gets control he will overthrow those kings who oppose his dominance and take over the leadership of the world government. One further note: the one who murders the two witnesses in Revelation 11:7-8 is referred to as the "beast that comes up out of the abyss." Thus, this *Apollyon* is very likely the coming Antichrist.

111

SIXTH TRUMPET WOE: 200 MILLION KILLERS
(Revelation 9:13-18)

Five of the seven trumpets have sounded, and the world is now fully aware that these are judgments emanating from the throne of almighty God. During this period, numerous people throughout the world will have repented and committed their lives to serving their Lord Jesus Christ; yet the vast majority will continue in their rebellion and hatred toward Him. Now a voice calls out from the golden altar before the throne of God, indicating that the time finally has come for vengeance against those of mankind who have trampled underfoot and despised the blood of the Savior. Thus, with the sounding of the sixth trumpet, demonic forces are released that will mobilize a murderous army numbering 200 million that will kill approximately two billion of the world's inhabitants.

Many commentators believe this to be an organized army from the East, perhaps from China that rises up out of the turmoil in order to conquer and control the remainder of the earth. That certainly is a possible scenario.

Another possibility is that these are millions of organized Islamic terrorists who reside in countries around the world and may well believe that this long-awaited "great earthquake" launches the coming of their Mahdi; thus, they may launch a worldwide war for their god, Allah.

Regardless of the identity of this army, it does appear to be a nuclear onslaught that kills one-third of mankind.

- *And this is how I saw the horses in my vision and those who rode them: they wore breastplates the color of fire and of sapphire and of sulfur, and the heads of the horses were like lions' heads, and **fire** and **smoke** and **sulfur** came out of their mouths.* **(Revelation 9:17)**

If the trumpet series is indeed nuclear, as previously described, and a third of the earth is destroyed or polluted, then surely that will result in a tremendous loss of lives. The three plagues of fire, smoke, and sulfur certainly sound like the three devastating effects of nuclear devices.

For example:

- Fire = Blast in the immediate proximity.
- Smoke = Heat that travels much farther out than the blast.
- Sulfur = Radiation that travels great distances from the initial explosion.

One can only speculate concerning the specifics of this destructive scenario; however, it is a certainty that these plagues are a supernatural force led by the four demonic angels who have been waiting for centuries for this murderous opportunity to unleash their hatred against humanity. A very clear description of this breathtaking demonic army and its destructive intent is very similar to what is also described by the prophets Joel and Isaiah.[150] Finally, we know that because of the reference to the Euphrates River, where the dark angels are released, that this great war probably will originate in the Middle East.

Certainly the possibility that our generation will experience these trumpet judgments should be an awakening among those in the body of Christ who have ears to hear. The devastating events are obviously punitive in nature, but they are also intended to bring many to repentance.[151] Like the Israelites who were protected against the plagues that came upon their Egyptian captors, the 144,000 who are sealed also will be protected. Nevertheless, they too will be indirectly affected by these plagues, as hardships abound worldwide and unsealed family members and friends become victims. Yet, they are the ones who will not fear and will continually praise the Lord in their circumstances.[152] As a result, the light of Jesus will shine mightily through them, and this will create an astounding, dual effect upon mankind. That is, many will repent and turn to the Lord who protects and provides, but the large majority will be more deeply embittered toward God and the church, whom they will blame for the devastation.

No matter how the scenario unfolds, Christians must be prepared not only to endure but also to minister in the midst of this chaos. Much fear and confusion will be present among the majority of the people of God throughout this period of the trumpets. Such gloom and doubt will cause many to begin to lose sight of their Lord and His revelation as they begin to cry out, "Why does God allow this to happen?" It is at this point that John witnesses the coming of a mighty angel into the midst of this devastation, one who will bring understanding to these times.

A MIGHTY ANGEL BRINGS A LITTLE BOOK
(Revelation 10:1-11)

The identity of this mighty angel who comes down from heaven should be obvious to His people. He appears glorious and very powerful, perhaps as He did when he first appeared to John on Patmos and to Daniel at the Tigris River.[153] Now He comes again in a time of trouble never before experienced upon this earth, and He stands upon the sea and the earth, revealing His control over all things. Nothing happens against His will; the war and the famine and the pestilence and tribulation cannot happen outside of His authority. And He tells us by the rainbow over His head that in the midst of mighty judgments, He never will forget His covenant with His people. This is certainly our Lord Jesus Christ, who is our King and Lord of the entire earth.

He brings with Him a little book, which contains instructions and warns us beforehand what we must do during the tribulation times that are yet to come. That little book must not be merely read and copied; it must be eaten, for it is symbolic of all that John still has to prophesy. Special preparation on the part of John was necessary for this book contains the message of the seventh trumpet, revealing how the kingdom will come and how the purposes of the Father will be done in accomplishing the destruction of the powers of the kingdom of darkness and establishing the eternal kingdom of God upon this earth. Special preparation certainly was needed, for this is not a pleasing message, at least for that period of time leading up to the establishment of His earthly kingdom.

It is a message that reveals (1) severe battles, destruction, persecution and vengeance; (2) the fate of Jerusalem and the temple; (3) the ministry and fate of the two witnesses who are killed for their testimony; (4) the conflict between the woman and the dragon, who attempts to destroy her Child; (5) the beast that arises out of the sea and the beast that arises out of the earth, plus the terrible things they do upon the earth; (6) the overwhelming power of Antichrist and his war upon the people of God; (7) tribulation and oppression for the sake of Christ's kingdom; (8) mystery Babylon and her greatness as well as her destruction; (9) the pouring out of seven vials of wrath, which devastate the entire earth; (10) the coming of the Lord Jesus with his army of saints; (11) the establishment of a millennial kingdom; (12) the binding and subsequent loosing of Satan; (13) the coming down from heaven of the new Jerusalem; and (14) the creation of a new heaven and a new earth where righteousness prevails.

Thus, this little book contains a tremendous, terrible message that has a glorious finale—at least for the people of God. Therefore, John, as well as all the ministers of the gospel in this generation, must be prepared. The seven thunders spoke plainly, but John could not be prepared by simply writing down what he had heard.[154] He must not be merely informed; he must eat the little book, swallow it, and thus make it a part of himself. Here we have the symbolic significance of the preparation of John and every true witness of Christ in the world as a prophet. The message he was to bring was not going to be sweet to the taste of the world but one of tremendous difficulty and sorrow and judgment. Because of this, it will be contradicted and opposed, not only by the wicked world of Antichrist, but also by much of the church as it currently exists. Many who do not truly belong to Christ but are in the church will hate and deny and oppose the message of tribulation and judgment. They will shout, "Peace, peace when there is no peace."[155] Even more, the message may sometimes be opposed by the true people of God, who do not always see and understand that in this world the church must expect tribulation and judgment in order for the kingdom to come. It takes spiritual courage, the courage of a warrior with great faith, to be a prophet of this message. And in order to stand against this opposition, the prophet of this message must "eat" the book of this prophecy.

The prophet Ezekiel had a very similar experience for he also had to "eat" the scroll before he was prepared to proclaim God's message of tribulation and mourning upon the house of Israel. He was told that the house of Israel is stiff-necked and rebellious, so he must expect opposition; and in order to stand for the Lord with this message, it must be part of his very system.[156]

PROPHETIC WARRIORS MUST "EAT THIS BOOK"

If John had simply read the little book, its contents would have remained outside of him and would not have influenced his heart and mind. Thus, he would not have been a true prophet of this message who could stand for the truth in the midst of the world and uphold its testimony in spite of opposition and suffering and tribulation. It had to become part of his flesh and blood, his soul and spirit. It had to transform him, change him, and make a different man out of him. The truth of this message had to so dominate him that he could never believe anything else and could never be silenced about it.

Now, this was not merely revealed to John, in which case the passage would have no significance for us. It contains a lesson for us. It teaches what we must do with the testimony of God in general, but especially with the book of Revelation. We can study the book and listen to various interpretations, and we might find intellectual enjoyment in its interpretation. Perhaps our curiosity will be somewhat satisfied; but that is not sufficient, for the message of this book demands a positive stand.

The question is: Do we believe these things? Is this really true that:

- The world is in iniquity and will fight to the last against Christ and His kingdom?
- There is an apostate part of the church that will align itself with the Antichrist?
- That the kingdom of Christ can come in no other way except through worldwide wars, judgments, and tribulations?

If you believe these things, the book of this prophecy will determine your stand against the world and prepare you for opposition within the church and for a great falling away. Are you ready? If so, you must eat it, appropriate it; it must become part of your entire system and control the direction of your life so that you know only one life, the kingdom of God.

The little book speaks of many woes and tribulations, but it also speaks of joy, peace, and everlasting life. The book tastes sweet to the mouth, but afterward we realize the bitter element, for it is bitter in the belly. Commitment to "eat" this little book does not mean that the Word has no bitter after-effects when it reaches the belly. The process of assimilation and digestion is often painful, for the Word has to battle against the influence of the flesh and its lusts; and it is a painful battle, no matter how sweet it was when first eaten. It causes bitterness and struggle until the medicine of the Word of God has done its work and transformed us.

This is especially true in the book of Revelation for this little book speaks of salvation, redemption, heavenly glory, eternal life, everlasting joy, and a new creation, where our tears are wiped away. This is the also the popular, continuing message of the church. But, the little book speaks of this only after self-denial and suffering and great personal sacrifice has occurred. It holds before us the glory of the future but only at the end of a dark and terrible road to travel.

- *Beloved, do not be surprised at the **fiery trial** when it comes upon you to test you, as though something strange were happening to you. But rejoice insofar as you share Christ's sufferings, that you may also rejoice and be glad when his glory is revealed.* **(1 Peter 4:12-13)**

It is a road of battle for those on earth who are citizens in the kingdom of God. It is a road of persecution and mockery on the part of the world. Jesus Himself tells us, "He that would save his life will lose it, but whoever loses his life for My sake will find it." This is a truth that is hard to grasp. Yet, as it begins its work of transformation, the truth of the "little book" may at first seem painful as it mortifies the old man. But more and more, it leaves nothing but one desire, the coming kingdom of God. This should be the effect of our assimilating this little book of prophecy.[157]

MIGHTY LEADERS WILL ARISE TO GUIDE MANY INTO THE KINGDOM

The time is rapidly approaching when warrior-type leaders, many of whom are outside the traditional American church, will need to network with one another in order to stand together and confront the dark challenges that await this generation. This is a time when numerous disciples of the Lord Jesus, like Peter, Paul, and John, will arise from among His prepared remnant to lead His people toward their respective callings; a time when many true prophets, like Ezekiel, Jeremiah, and Zechariah, also will arise to provide understanding and direction to those with ears to hear. These are the witnesses in the end-time army of God who will stand strong and without compromise for the name of Jesus Christ and His kingdom all across this world. They are numbered among the

144,000 who have been sealed prior to the sounding of the trumpet judgments. There has been much written concerning the identity and purpose of those who are chosen for sealing. Yet, most of those writings have directed attention away from the church, and therefore individual Christians have not been motivated to prepare for a sealing that will anoint them to stand in the midst of tribulation.

The next chapter will address an overview of the mission of the 144,000 witnesses for Christ in the midst of great tribulation.

CHAPTER 8

WARRIORS FOR CHRIST IN THE MIDST OF THE GREAT TRIBULATION

(First Read: Revelation 11)

Going to war for the kingdom of God is very different from going into Iraq or Vietnam. Soldiers in the Army of God are fighting to save people, not kill them. In fact, God's warrior soldiers are fighting to help free and save many of the very ones who will be used to fight against them. Christians are not warring against other people but against the spiritual forces that are using them. Soldiers in the Army of God love their enemies because they are fighting for them, not against them. This is a tough truth that requires a higher vision than just looking at things in the natural; believers must have their spiritual eyes opened to see and live this reality.[158]

Spiritual insight into the events recorded in chapter 11 of the book of Revelation is essential if we are to have a foundational understanding of our leadership role in the Army of God within an evil world system—a system that is committed to erasing the name of Jesus Christ from the earth and establishing its own eternal kingdom. Revelation 11 is not intended to be chronological but presents us with an overview that will enable us to understand much that is to follow in subsequent chapters, which provide more specific details.

Here we are presented with:
- A graphic picture of the church in the end-times generation.
- A probable scenario concerning the identity of the "two witnesses" and their ministry.
- A powerful gospel message that the Lord's chosen people will take throughout the earth.
- A 2nd resurrection following the final gospel proclamation.

THE TEMPLE AND THE HOLY CITY

- *Then I was given a measuring rod like a staff, and I was told, "Rise and measure the <u>temple of God and the altar</u> and those who worship there, but do not measure the <u>court outside the temple</u>; leave that out, for it is given over to the nations, and they will trample the <u>holy city</u> for forty-two months." (**Revelation 11:1-2**)*

There are three significant areas being addressed here. First, there is the temple, which includes the altar where the people of God gather together to worship their Lord. Second, there is the outer court, which is that area that surrounds the temple and where many gather together but do not enter the temple itself. Finally, there is the holy city, which, together with the outer court, will be surrendered to the world's forces for a period of forty-two months (1260 days). Now regarding these three separate areas, John is commanded to measure only the temple with the altar and those who worship within.

Warriors, it is important to remember that the book of Revelation was written to the church in order to provide understanding of coming events so that Christian leadership will be equipped to lead the Lord's people through these tremendously challenging battles that lie before us. Therefore, it should be apparent that it is the church that is in view when this text speaks of both the temple and the holy city.

Passages in the New Testament clearly reveal that the "temple of God" is a spiritual structure composed of every true Christian who trusts only in the blood sacrifice of their Lord Jesus Christ. Jesus Himself is also part of this spiritual temple, for He is the "cornerstone" upon which the entire temple is built. The ancient prophets and apostles of the Lord also are described as being the foundation of this temple. Over the centuries, this temple has continued to be built as our brothers and sisters in Christ have stood uncompromisingly to the point of death for the glory of the Father who sits upon the throne and for His beloved Son. The building of the temple continues today as Christians in this generation proclaim the majestic glory of the Word of God, which allows His light to be manifested in the midst of the darkness of today's world. This holy temple of God will not be completed until the gospel of Christ has gone out to the peoples of all the nations around the globe.[159] Its completion appears to be finished at the time of the sounding of the seventh trumpet.[160] There is nothing more holy to the Lord than this spiritual temple, and all who attempt to destroy it will themselves be destroyed.[161]

Now this spiritual temple resides in the "holy city," which is also a spiritual city whose inhabitants are all those who profess the God of Israel to be their God. In fact, Jesus Christ Himself also has been called the "City of the Lord."[162] Yet within this city reside many rebellious citizens who confess the Lord but do not live in righteousness.

- *Hear this, <u>O house of Jacob, who are called by the name of Israel,</u> and who came from the waters of Judah, who swear by the name of the Lord and confess the <u>God of Israel</u>, but <u>not in truth or right.</u> <u>For they call themselves after the holy city,</u> and stay themselves on the God of Israel; the Lord of hosts is his name. (Isaiah 48:1-2)*

God here admonishes the faithless hypocrites among his chosen people. These seemingly pious Israelites practiced idol-worship on the side and yet, had the audacity to invoke the name of Yahweh as their God also, pretending that they were true citizens of his holy city.[163] Also note that it is Israel, the house of Jacob, and not simply Judah (the Jews) who are mentioned here. These are those who confess the God of Abraham, Isaac, and Jacob throughout the entire earth, not simply those residing in the land of Israel. This city also has been referred to as the "oppressing city" that is rebellious and defiled and will accept no correction or draw near to the Lord.[164]

IDENTIFYING THE TEMPLE AND THE HOLY CITY

The temple and the holy city described in these verses is the contemporary church of the end-times generation, and the altar of atonement within the temple represents the person of Jesus Christ and that place where God's people are redeemed within the holy city. It is on this basis that we should understand that the "holy city" described in this text is representative of the entire world of Christianity—that is, all who have been baptized in the name of Jesus. Recognize the parallelism here: just as many of the ancient citizens of Jerusalem were supposedly inhabitants of the city of God, so also the spiritual Jerusalem of this dispensation is inhabited by nominal Christianity. Therefore, within this great city of the Christian world are three broad classes of Christianity.

- **There is the false church that calls itself Christian.** It performs Christian labors and believes it is responsible for mankind's redemption. It likes to call itself "Christian" but it denies Jesus Christ as the true Son of God and the one and only way to eternal life. This is the false church, similar to those in ancient Jerusalem who continued to worship their man-made theology. This is a city serving the purposes of Satan.

- **There is also a segment of the church that resides in the outer court.** They represent the "show church"—that part of Christianity that outwardly pretends to belong to the true church and feigns to believe in the atonement of Christ but are inwardly hypocritical. These are the tares among the wheat; they go with God's people to His temple for worship, but they never enter that spiritual sanctuary of fellowship with God. They are invited into the temple, but they choose to remain in the outer court. They love to attend the churches in Sardis, Ephesus, and Laodicea. This is where the money changers hang out.[165]

- **Finally, within the temple reside the true people of God who worship at the altar of Christ in spirit and in truth.** These are those who have truly committed their lives to the Lord and are frequently found in their prayer closets alone with God. They have a heart burdened for justice, righteousness, and integrity, and they long to see the name of Jesus Christ glorified throughout the earth. They also have a heart deeply burdened for those who stay in the "outer court" and in the "city proper." Although their words may sound somewhat harsh and cruel to many, they are meant to awaken righteousness among those residing outside the temple.

Just as there were three distinctions in old Jerusalem—the city proper, the outer court, and finally the temple—so there are three distinctions in spiritual Jerusalem of our day: the Christian world, including the false church, the show church, and the true church of God.[166]

A TRUE PHYSICAL TEMPLE
WILL SOON BE BUILT IN JERUSALEM

Finally, I do want to emphasize my belief that a new physical temple will soon be built by the Jewish citizens of physical Jerusalem, which definitely will be a sign of the times. The building of this temple probably will take place following the victory of God's people in the Middle Eastern war described earlier in the sixth-seal event. While Israel is rebuilding their temple, the Lord will be in the process of completing the building of His temple, a spiritual temple made without hands in the hearts of His people.[167] Thus, as we observe these things occurring in the natural, we need to be able to discern what is simultaneously occurring in the spiritual and to be fully prepared to recognize all that will soon follow.

MEASURING THE TEMPLE

Now John was commissioned by the Lord to measure only the temple and not the outer court or the holy city. This is a spiritual act of separating the true church from the false. Here we are taught in symbolic language not only the condition of Christianity within this generation but also how it will undoubtedly manifest itself as the end of the age approaches. Those who remain outside the temple eventually will reveal themselves as enemies of Christ and His true church. We are also told that this will continue for forty-two months; a period of time that the true body of Christ will be in the wilderness outside the reaches of Satan.[168] This is also a designated time for the Antichrist to exercise his authority upon the earth.[169]

THE TWO WITNESSES

Now, within the context of measuring the temple, John is told that two witnesses of the Lord will prophesy for three and a half years.

1. *I will grant authority to my two witnesses, and they will prophesy for 1,260 days, clothed in sackcloth.* **(Revelation 11:3)**

The identity of these two witnesses is one of the more controversial and difficult questions in this section of Revelation. Many modern interpreters believe them to be Moses (or Enoch) and Elijah, who shall literally return to earth to fulfill their ministerial calling and then be killed by the Antichrist. Certainly this interpretation possesses an element of truth, but it also limits our understanding of this passage if we think that it literally refers to two men. Enoch and Elijah were great witnesses of the Lord in their day, and as such they should be viewed as types of those who will be called to proclaim a powerful gospel message in the coming days. Scripture reveals numerous champions of the Lord who stood strong for Him throughout their lives on earth; but their earthly mission has been accomplished, and now they reside eternally with the Lord. Other witnesses soon will arise to be anointed by the Lord to proclaim a great and powerful gospel message to the world in the coming days.

The two witnesses in this text are not two single persons, for they have universal influence throughout the entire world. They are also universally hated, and their eventual death brings universal joy among all the citizens of the world's kingdom. It is certainly not conceivable that two single individuals in a single city could cause so much commotion throughout the world. Then who are these two witnesses?

2. *These are the <u>two olive trees and the two lampstands</u> that stand before the Lord of the earth.* **(Revelation 11:4)**

TWO OLIVE TREES AND TWO LAMPSTANDS

The reference to two olive trees and two lampstands harkens back to a similar vision given to the prophet Zechariah centuries earlier.[170] Zechariah received a vision from an angel of the Lord in which he beheld a candlestick containing seven lamps. Above the candlestick he saw a golden bowl filled with oil, which had pipes connecting to each of the seven lamps, providing each lamp with the oil needed to give light. Now on each side of this oil-filled bowl stood an olive tree. These two olive trees were the source of oil supplied to the golden bowl, which then passed it on to the seven lamps. Thus, we have a candlestick receiving its oil from a bowl above it, which in turn receives its oil from the two olive trees. If the <u>candlesticks, which are representative of the Christian church</u>,[171] are to give true light, then oil must be provided by the two olive trees. <u>These olive trees are symbolic of the Holy Spirit of God</u>, who provides the oil of knowledge necessary to allow the light to shine through the people of God. In summary, what John is seeing is symbolic of God's chosen disciples as they minister in the midst of darkness in the power of the Holy Spirit.

THE POWER OF TWO

It is always the testimony of two that must confirm the Word of God.

3. *<u>If I alone bear witness about myself, my testimony is not deemed true</u>. There is another who bears witness about me, and I know that the testimony that he bears about me is true. You sent to John, and he has borne witness to the truth.* **(John 5:31-33)**

Jesus is always present wherever two or more are gathered together in His name.

4. *Again I say to you, <u>if two of you agree on earth about anything they ask, it will be done for them by my Father in heaven. For where two or three are gathered in my name, there am I among them.</u> (**Matthew 18:19-20**)

When Jesus dispatched His chosen ones to minister among the masses in His authority, it was always two by two. Jesus sends out the apostles two by two.

- *And he called the twelve and began to <u>send them out two by two, and gave them authority over the unclean spirits</u>. . . . And if any place will not receive you and they will not listen to you, when you leave, shake off the dust that is on your feet as a testimony against them. <u>So they went out and proclaimed that people should repent.</u> (**Mark 6:7, 11-12**)*

Jesus also sent out the seventy-two.

- *After this the Lord appointed seventy-two others and sent them on ahead of him, <u>two by two</u>, into every town and place where he himself was about to go. And he said to them, "The harvest is plentiful, but the laborers are few. Therefore pray earnestly to the Lord of the harvest to send out laborers into his harvest. Go your way; behold, <u>I am sending you out as lambs in the midst of wolves.</u> Carry no moneybag, no knapsack, no sandals, and greet no one on the road. Whatever house you enter, first say, 'Peace be to this house!' And if a son of peace is there, your peace will rest upon him. But if not, it will return to you<u>. . . . Heal the sick in it and say to them, 'The kingdom of God has come near to you. . . . The one who hears you hears me, and the one who rejects you rejects me, and the one who rejects me rejects him who sent me.</u>" (**Luke 10:1-6, 9, 16**)*

IDENTITY OF THE TWO WITNESSES IN THE MIDST OF THE GREAT TRIBULATION

Just as Jesus dispatched His chosen disciples two by two throughout the land of Israel, so He will again send out His disciples of this last generation two by two throughout the entire world. I believe that these end-times disciples are the 144,000 (witnessing two by two), who are sealed following the Middle Eastern war and prior to the sounding of the trumpet judgments. Perhaps Moses (or Enoch) and Elijah will also return to earth and be numbered as leaders among the 144,000. If so, their witness would likely be toward those residing in the nation of Israel. We see this army of 144,000 witnesses gathered together with their Commander in Chief on Mount Zion. They are the firstfruits of God's people, and they follow His Son wherever He goes.[172]

Mount Zion, in the literal sense, was the hill in the city of Jerusalem upon which the temple was built and where the Lord dwelt with His people in Israel. However, Mount Zion also is used to describe the true church, where Christ dwells in the hearts of His people. These 144,000 who have been sealed with the name of God on their foreheads come from far countries all around the world, but they will be gathered together with their Lord on Mount Zion (Revelation 14). Perhaps this is a literal gathering prior to being sent out two by two throughout the earth, or perhaps it is a spiritual gathering with their Lord as He speaks to them individually within their hearts. Additionally, this scene also may be a literal gathering together of His disciples following their martyrdom, which will take place following their three-and-a-half-year ministry throughout the earth. At any rate they will receive their marching orders and be commissioned with authority from on high prior to being dispatched into a world that is in the midst of great tribulation. This is the time when His chosen warrior-spirited witnesses will minister in even greater power than was witnessed in the ministry of the Lord Jesus Christ during His three-and-a-half-year ministry two thousand years ago. Such great power has never been consistently manifested since the days when the Lord Jesus walked with mankind.

5. *Truly, truly, I say to you, whoever believes in me will also do the works that I do; and <u>greater works than these will he do, because I am going to the Father</u>. Whatever you ask in my name, this I will do, that the Father may be glorified in the Son. If you ask me anything in my name, I will do it.* **(John 14:12-14)**

Their power won't be greater in quality than that revealed in the ministry of Jesus, but it certainly will be greater in quantity since it will be manifested throughout the entire earth.

Their power over people and the environment will be like that reflected in the ministries of Moses and Elijah. It also may be that they participate in the calling of the trumpet plagues upon the earth.

<u>Note the similarity:</u>

6. *They have the <u>power to shut the sky, that no rain may fall</u> during the days of their prophesying, and they have <u>power over the waters to turn them into blood and to strike the earth with every kind of plague</u>, as often as they desire.* **(Revelation 11:6)**

The gospel message of these 144,000 witnesses will reach every nation and people upon the earth. They also are described as being clothed in "sackcloth," which denotes that their message primarily will be a call for repentance from sin.

7. *Go therefore and make disciples of all nations, baptizing them in the name of the Father and of the Son and of the Holy Spirit,* **(Matthew 28:19)**

8. *And this gospel of the kingdom will be proclaimed throughout the whole world as a testimony to all nations, <u>and then the end will come</u>.* **(Matthew 24:14)**

9. *<u>The glory that you have given me I have given to them</u>, that they may be one even as we are one, I in them and you in me, that they may become perfectly one, so that the world may know that you sent me and loved them even as you loved me.* **(John 17:22-23)**

125

They will go forth in the fullness of the tremendous glory of the Son of God during a time when worldwide technology and transportation will allow all inhabitants of the earth an opportunity to respond.

- *And those who are wise shall shine like the brightness of the sky above; and those who turn many to righteousness, like the stars forever and ever. But you, Daniel, shut up the words and seal the book, until the time of the end. Many shall run to and fro, and knowledge shall increase.* **(Daniel 12:3-4)**

144,000 WILL REPRESENT THE THIRD COMING OF ELIJAH

Approximately 430 years before Christ, The Lord told the prophet Malachi:

- *Behold, I will send you Elijah the prophet before the great and awesome day of the Lord comes.* **(Malachi 4:5)**

The Jewish religious community continues to await the return of Elijah, seeing it as a sign preceding the coming of their Messiah. They believe it to be the literal, physical presence of Elijah rather than one coming in the spirit of Elijah. However, the New Testament shows that it was John the Baptist who came in the spirit of Elijah for the purpose of "preparing the way of the Lord."[173]

As previously shown, the spirit and power of Elijah are also found to be present within the two witnesses. Therefore, as John the Baptist was anointed by God to call the people to repentance and to declare the coming of the Lord, it appears as if many with the anointing of Elijah, who are commissioned to call people from among all the nations to repentance, also shall be the voice of one crying in the wilderness, "Prepare the way [for the second coming] of the Lord; make His paths straight."[174]

These anointed messengers of God will be found in the wilderness, even as John the Baptist came before the first coming of Jesus. Like John, they too will be rejected by the religious leaders and sent instead to the poor and the outcasts, who will hear the true words of God in the midst of tribulation. However, it will not be just one voice this time.[175]

144,000 WILL CHARACTERIZE THE TRUE PROPHETIC SPIRIT

The prophets of God are the eyes of the body of Christ. They are the seers who announce to the people the warnings of the Lord. The true prophets always have had the spiritual discernment to understand their times. It was their assignment to warn, admonish, and call for repentance. The prophets are also called as watchmen. They stand upon the walls of Zion to blow the trumpet and warn of coming danger.

A.W. Tozer also spoke of the tremendous need for the true prophetic ministry:

- *If Christianity is to receive rejuvenation, another kind of religious leader must arise among us. He must be of the old prophet type, a man who has seen visions of God and has heard a voice from the Throne. When he comes (and I pray God there will not be one but many), he will stand in flat contradiction to everything our smirking, smooth civilization holds dear. He will contradict, denounce, and protest in the name of God and will earn the hatred and opposition of a large segment of Christendom. Such a man is likely to be lean, rugged, blunt-spoken and a little bit angry with the world. He will love Christ and the souls of men to the point of willingness to die for the glory of the One and the salvation of the other. But he will fear nothing that breathes with mortal breath.*[176]

The life of the messenger with a genuine prophetic call is not immune to valleys of depression. This is all part of the package. He lives a life that is lonely. The revelation of Christ can come only in the solitary place, away from the crowds and noise of the vendors and their religious wares. These are true prophets who receive their prophetic office directly from the Lord. The prophets are burdened vessels, for they see the vision and the lateness of the hour. The prophet's character is likely to be one of shifting moods, unpredictable at times, and he is not likely to be found mingling with the religious. When a prophet of God speaks a true word of the Lord, it will definitely produce hatred and scorn in the minds of numerous listeners.[177]

The true prophet of God is serious, sober, and not easily persuaded to compromise. His lot is most likely found hidden away on the backside of the desert alone with God. He is the one with a heart for justice, righteousness, honor, and integrity. His words may come across as harsh or cruel, but to the one with spiritual perception, his words are received to awaken righteousness. The higher the calling into his purposes, the hotter the fires required to purify the servant. The greater the responsibility, the greater and more intense are the fires that perfect. This is the cost of prophetic ministry.[178]

THE GOSPEL MESSAGE OF THE TWO WITNESSES

The two witnesses of Christ, who symbolize the 144,000, will boldly and fearlessly stand united against the apostasy of this age as they bear the testimony of Jesus Christ and His truth among all the nations of the earth.[179] As to the contents of their message, this army of "two witnesses" will continually stand before the Lord of the whole earth and will speak nothing but that which their Lord has commissioned them to speak.

- They will speak of Christ and His atoning blood, which is the witness of the righteousness and holiness of God in the midst of a sinful world.

- They will openly condemn all efforts to seek salvation outside of that atoning blood, and this will infuriate the false church and the worldly leadership that is attempting to establish a one-world kingdom.
- This will be a time of tremendous miracles, as the gospel message goes forth in a power greater than the world has ever seen: the blind will see, the deaf will hear, and many of the afflicted will be healed throughout the world.[180]
- But this also will be a time when waters turn to blood, the skies are shut so that no rain may fall, and plagues strike throughout the earth.

The kingdom must come through tribulation and through all kinds of plagues and calamities. Do not think that this is strange; Moses delivered his people from Egypt when God brought great devastating plagues upon the land, which humbled Egypt to its knees. During Elijah's day, the kingdom again was strengthened when he prayed that God would withhold rain from an apostate nation. It also will be that the people of God in the last days will consciously refuse to pray for blessings on the wicked world, and they will beseech God for plagues and judgments that His kingdom may come. And it shall become plain to the entire world, even as it was plain to Pharaoh in the case of Moses and to Ahab in the case of Elijah, that it is the two witnesses of God, ministering throughout the world, who bring about these plagues upon the earth.[181]

The mission of these end-times witnesses for Christ is not to bring peace to the world but to preach an uncompromising kingdom message, not just among nations but within neighborhoods and families.

- *Do not think that I have come to bring peace to the earth. <u>I have not come to bring peace, but a sword.</u> For I have come to set a man against his father, and a daughter against her mother, and a daughter-in-law against her mother-in-law. And a person's enemies will be those of his own household. Whoever loves father or mother more than me is not worthy of me, and whoever loves son or daughter more than me is not worthy of me. And whoever does not take his cross and follow me is not worthy of me. Whoever finds his life will lose it, and whoever loses his life for my sake will find it.* **(Matthew 10:34-39)**

This is a hard teaching that is never heard from the pulpits, but separation has to take place. The pure light of holiness will not compromise with darkness. There can be no middle ground in the kingdom of God. This truth of God is 180 degrees opposite of that which is embraced by the worldly system, which emphasizes "tolerance" as a requirement for world peace. Not surprisingly, the world's government will once again unite with the false church of Christianity to persecute the true church with the objective of erasing the hard gospel message of Jesus Christ from the earth.[182]

However, if we keep our eyes upon the Lord, our attitude in the midst of persecution and suffering will be one of great joy, knowing that the eternal rewards that await us will be great.[183]

Yes, this will be a time of great tribulation never before seen since the creation of the earth, yet this also will be a time of a great harvest of souls such as the world has never before seen. And there will be no more grey areas; one stands either with Christ or against Him. Love and hatred will be clearly visible among all the inhabitants of the earth.

The enemies of Christ will not be able to stop the two witnesses until the end of the forty-two-month period. At that time, when their testimony is complete, the Beast will be allowed to rise up against the two witnesses. The power of the Antichrist may not be fully manifested until the message of the gospel has been preached among all the nations and the testimony against the wicked world and against the false church has been finished. The world must hear the gospel message proclaimed by the church and must hear it repeatedly so that they become fully conscious of their sin and the redemptive work of Jesus Christ. Those who reject Him will do so willingly and deliberately. Then the testimony is finished and may be silenced. At this point the Antichrist will overcome the witnesses and kill many of them but not all, for there will be a remnant of saints who are alive at the second coming of Christ. But for most of the saints of God, this will be a time of terrible persecution as the Antichrist rises up to silence their testimony. Then the Antichrist will reign supreme, and the world will rejoice and send gifts to one another because the church, which spoke of blood and judgment, has finally been overpowered; or so they believe. The world's hatred of God's people, spoken of by Christ, will reach its zenith.

- *If the world hates you, know that it has hated me before it hated you. If you were of the world, the world would love you as its own; but because you are not of the world, but I chose you out of the world, therefore the world hates you. Remember the word that I said to you: "A servant is not greater than his master." If they persecuted me, they will also persecute you. If they kept my word, they will also keep yours. But all these things they will do to you on account of my name, because they do not know him who sent me.* (**John 15:18-21**)

A SECOND DEATH FOLLOWED BY A SECOND RESURRECTION
(Revelation 11:7-13)

These witnesses will have completed their worldwide testimony after forty-two months. During that time many among the world's population will have experienced tremendous "true revival" — yet, the majority of the world who rejected the message will be exploding with anger toward those who have hindered their plans for establishing a worldly kingdom. Now the final three-and-a-half-year ministry of the Messiah has been completed through His body, which moves the world closer to the fulfilling of the last three elements spoken by Daniel in his renowned "seventy weeks" prophecy.[184]

The earthly ministry of Jesus Christ is almost complete; there remains one more event that will be even more glorious than all that preceded it, an event that will bring finality to the gospel of the kingdom. That is the resurrection of the body of Christ. Jesus' first, physical resurrection two thousand years ago initiated a worldwide ministry that has resulted in millions of people entering into eternal life as sons and daughters of God. Now this second, spiritual resurrection, through His body of 144,000, will complete His ministry in this age.

Here we see the first mention of the Antichrist, who at this point in time is the ruler of the kingdom of the world. He is leading the charge to trample the blood of Christ under foot. Prior to the completion of their forty-two-month ministry, the world was not allowed to hinder the 144,000, and certainly many were "burned" who tried to stop them.[185] Just as the veil of protection was removed from Jesus Christ following His three-and-a-half-year ministry, it is also removed from His body of 144,000 chosen prophets following their three-and-a-half-year ministry. They will be slain in view of the entire world in the streets of "the great city that symbolically is called Sodom and Egypt where their Lord was crucified."[186]

Is this "great city" literal Jerusalem? Some commentators say that the city is symbolic of all cities worldwide that are immoral and rebellious against God (Sodom), that enslave God's people (Egypt), and that continually trample the blood of Jesus underfoot (where the Lord was crucified). Thus, they believe that these end-time witnesses are killed in cities throughout the world. Perhaps this scenario is true, but also consider the following possibility that this glorious event will take place in the literal city of Jerusalem with the entire world watching. Recall that Jesus voluntarily went to Jerusalem, knowing that it was time to lay down His life. Likewise, it is quite possible that the 144,000 also will be called by the Lord to travel to Jerusalem, knowing that they too are about to lay down their lives. It appears to be at a time when the Antichrist sets up the "abomination of desolation" on the temple mount and demands that the entire world bow down and worship it. This abomination undoubtedly will be challenged by the people of God, just as Shadrach, Meshach, and Abednego refused to bow down to the image of Nebuchadnezzar in ancient Babylon.[187] Therefore, I perceive that this 144,000 remnant of true Christianity will simultaneously ascend to the temple mount in Jerusalem and refuse to worship this image of the Antichrist. Subsequently, they will be beaten and killed with the entire world watching and cheering and celebrating by giving gifts to one another. Like a Fourth of July party, they will probably set off fireworks around the world, celebrating their supposed victory over the kingdom of God.

However, this is not the end of the ministry of these witnesses, for after three days the entire world will witness the resurrection of this great and numerous body of Christ and watch in horror as they ascend to heaven. Subsequently, a great earthquake rocks the city of Jerusalem, killing seven thousand people. This will result in tremendous worldwide fear and perhaps many, like the Roman soldiers who crucified Jesus, will finally have their eyes opened and will give glory to God and to His Son. Hopefully, these are people who have not yet taken the "mark of the Beast."

This is the second resurrection, and hopefully it will cause more people among the nations to finally have their eyes opened to the truth of the atoning blood of Jesus so that they repent and begin to seek the Lord with their whole heart. It would appear to be the last opportunity for mankind to respond to the gospel of Jesus Christ and enter into the kingdom of God.

CHAPTER 9

CONFRONTATION BETWEEN THE WOMAN AND THE DRAGON

(First Read: Revelation 12)

An overview of over six thousand years of spiritual warfare between the kingdom of God and the kingdom of Satan is depicted in Revelation 12. The object of this stage of John's vision is to provide Christians with a summary of the war that has been taking place between the kingdom of God and the kingdom of Satan since the fall of mankind, a war that will continue until the second coming of our Messiah. Much of what is presented here is revisited in greater detail over the next five chapters. Hopefully this section of the study will provide the Army of Christ with greater insight into the tactics of Satan and his armies of darkness.

THE IDENTITY OF THE WOMAN

(Revelation 12:1-2)

The appearance of this woman is so mighty and glorious that the sun, moon, and stars of heaven all serve as signs to bring out the beauty and the authority that she has been given from on high. John sees her exalted among these heavenly bodies of light, which were all created to rule over the day and the night. Obviously, she is of tremendous importance to the Lord and His kingdom. So, who is this woman? Well, to begin with, listen to the Lord speaking to Satan shortly after he enticed the fall of Adam and Eve into sin:

- *"I will put enmity between you and the woman, and between your offspring and her offspring; he shall bruise your head, and you shall bruise his heel."* (**Genesis 3:15**)

Then the Lord says to the woman:

- *To the woman he said, "I will surely multiply your pain in childbearing; in pain you shall bring forth children".* (**Genesis 3:16**)

This is commonly referred to as the first covenant promise that our God made with mankind. Yet, even with all her glorious appearance, the woman has not yet reached her purpose for existence, which is twofold.

1. First, she is anointed to give birth to the Messiah, the Son of God, who will destroy the effects of sin on mankind.
2. Second, she will give birth, together with the Holy Spirit, to all those who will eternally inhabit the kingdom of God.

Thus, this woman is the symbolic mother of the people of God. She can be identified with true Israel in the old dispensation and with the true Christian church in the new. According to various Old Testament Scriptures, the heavy afflictions upon Israel that preceded the birth of the Savior are represented by these severe birth pains.[188] This woman, in all her glory, is also in a state of tremendous suffering, supported only by the hope of a male offspring she painfully awaits. Suddenly, she sees a terrifying dragon, ready to devour her child as soon as He should be born.

THE DRAGON
(Revelation 12:3-4)

Throughout the four thousand years of the old dispensation, Satan had been totally committed to identifying and annihilating all offspring originating from this woman, who was commissioned to establish a kingdom of God upon the earth. Conversely, God's kingdom, being led by the great King, has been commissioned to destroy the dragon's kingdom, which is very powerful, as indicated by his appearance, having seven heads, ten horns, and the seven crowns upon each of the heads. It is a picture of a monstrous serpent of hideous appearance, terrible power, royal authority, and a bloodthirsty and destructive nature. He is especially focused on the Promised One whom God said would have the power to crush him and destroy his plans for the world.

*   Initially, he probably believed that Abel was the chosen one, and so he had Cain murder him. But then Seth was born, and the spiritual seed of the woman began to multiply in the line of Seth.
*   When Satan realized that his problem was not so simple, he changed his strategy. He got the "sons of God," who were evil "angelic beings," to marry the natural "daughters of men" in order to merge together the human and angelic race and thus eliminate the possibility of a human seed arising from a woman.[189] Again, God counterattacked this tactic through the great flood and saved the seed of the woman through the family of Noah.
*   And so Satan's efforts continued throughout the history of the old dispensation, as he sought to control the population of the entire world at the tower of Babel, to enslave the nation of Israel in Egypt, and to annihilate them as a nation using the Assyrians and the Babylonians. When those early tactics eventually failed, Satan attempted to rule over God's people through the mighty Grecian and Roman empires. (Appendix A: "Historical Empires of the Beast" provides additional an insight into Satan's historical tactics to rid the world of

God's chosen peoples plus our Lord's counterattack's which continually strengthened the Kingdom of God.)

THE BIRTH OF THE MALE CHILD
(Revelation 12: 5)

Throughout this entire period, Satan was intent on either preventing the birth or murdering the child, yet he did not know who the Child would be or when the woman would give birth to Him. The long-awaited time finally arrived when the woman, through the Holy Spirit of God, gave birth to the Savior, who had been promised some four thousand years earlier. Satan didn't know who the natural mother would be, but he did know through earlier prophecies that the birth would be in the town of Bethlehem. When he received intelligence from his sources that the birth had recently occurred, he enticed the Judean king, Herod, a servant of the dragon, to take whatever measures were necessary to have this newborn child slain. Herod then dispatched his soldiers to Bethlehem who murdered all the male children under two years of age so that he might be sure of destroying the one hated Child.[190] But in spite of all this, the Promised One appeared—Christ was born.

The angels of heaven loudly proclaimed the glory of the birth of Christ, and thus Satan learned who He was and directed all his efforts to thwart the purposes of the Son of God throughout His short life among us. The dragon was not certain how Christ intended to gain the victory over him, although he did recognize Him as the Promised One, as he heard the heavenly angels rejoicing over His birth. Therefore, he employed two different methods to usurp the plans of God for His Son.

- First, Satan attempted to subject Him spiritually by offering Christ the kingdoms of the world if He would only bow down and worship Satan.[191]
- When this failed, he aroused the enemies of Christ, the religious leaders of the day, to continually come against Him throughout His three-and-a-half-year ministry. This tactic only caused many within the nation of Israel to come to the knowledge of the truth of their Lord and to recognize the hypocrisy of these religious leaders.

Yet, a time had been ordained from the beginning when Jesus was to be cut off after three and a half years of ministry, and thus His enemies were allowed by God to seize Him. Those enemies vented all their anger and jealousy by severely mocking and beating Him. Eventually they crucified Him between two thieves, intending to display Him as simply another criminal in Israel.

Obviously Satan had to be joyously celebrating while Christ was suffering on the cross, for he certainly believed he had finally won. He thought that he had "crushed the head" of God's chosen Champion and thus turned the tables on God's promise to crush his head. What he didn't realize was that the victory for the people of God's kingdom lay in the way of the sacrifice of the perfect Lamb of God. <u>Sin is what gives the devil his claim for the possession of mankind, and now sin itself has been cast out of those of mankind who embrace the sacrificial Lamb that the Lord Himself has provided. The deceiver himself has been deceived!</u> And now he is about to reap what he has sown, as Michael and his angelic army are about to throw him and his demonic army out from the heavens and from the presence of the Lord and down to earth.

A WAR IN HEAVEN
(Revelation 12:7-12)

The Scriptures of the Old Testament clearly reveal that Satan had access to the courts of heaven and could stand in the presence of almighty God.[192] It is very probable that throughout the four-thousand-year period of the old dispensation, a battle raged in the heavenlies for the souls of those who entered into paradise before the death and resurrection of Christ. Historically, Christ had not yet "crushed the head" of the serpent and thus had not yet assumed dominion over the citizens of the kingdom of God. Satan was still the sovereign ruler of this world, and he argued that all of mankind came under his dominion due to their sin, which disallowed them access before the presence of almighty God.[193] Therefore, according to Satan's view, all the saints of the old dispensation, including Abel, Enoch, Noah, Abraham, Moses, Job, and David, entered into heaven as sinners over whom he had a righteous claim, and they deserved to go to hell, for their sins had not been properly atoned for.

However, the counsel of almighty God countered Satan's argument. That counsel established that Christ's atoning sacrifice applied not only to people who are born on earth following the sacrifice of Christ but also to those who had been born before the crucifixion. Thus, a spiritual war was continually being fought for the souls of the saints of the old dispensation. The head of the Lord's army was Michael, an angelic general who appears in Scripture to be in command of the entire angelic army that is assigned to protect God's chosen people during their life on earth and to confront the claims of Satan for the souls of the Old Testament saints.[194] Finally, when Christ came, suffered, paid the death penalty for the sins of His people, and ascended to heaven to sit at the right hand of almighty God, the battle was finally decided in favor of Michael and his army of angels. The great voice sang out—

- *Now the salvation and the power and the kingdom of our God and the authority of his Christ have come, for the accuser of our brothers has been thrown down, who accuses them day and night before our God.* (**Revelation 12:10**)

This was the deathblow to Satan; it was probably shouted by Michael and his entire army at Satan and his army in a power so great that the mighty enemy was finally cast out of heaven.[195]

Satan has lost the battle in the heavenlies, but he will never surrender; he must be completely defeated. Now that he has been cast down to earth, his wrath is directed toward the woman and her offspring, who remain upon the earth; and the conflict continues to this present day.

THE WAR BETWEEN THE WOMAN AND THE DRAGON
(Revelation 12:6, 13-17)

Now the scene shifts back to the earth, where the woman dwells and continues to bring forth offspring.

- *And when the dragon saw that he had been thrown down to the earth, he pursued the woman who had given birth to the male child.* **(Revelation 12:13)**

The remainder of this chapter is a prophetic picture of all that has and will take place in the Christian era. Satan failed to prevent the birth of Christ, and he failed in his centuries-long war with Michael; and now, being filled with a raging fury, he is intent on pursuing and wiping out Christianity from the face of the earth. His initial and favorite tactic is one of murderous persecution of those who truly profess Jesus as their Lord. However, it isn't just his raging fury that governs his pursuit of the woman; it is his intent to oppose the will of almighty God. The church, symbolized by the woman, is not only the mother of Christ; she is also the mother of all true, spiritual children of God. These are the citizens of the kingdom of God, who continue to oppose Satan and his purposes among mankind. Therefore, he is committed to annihilating true Christianity from the face of the earth.

Satan pursued the woman, but the Lord intervened and enabled the woman, with two wings of the great eagle, to fly into the wilderness, where Satan could not go. This wilderness is representative of that spiritual place where God's people are nourished from on high and, therefore, where neither Satan nor his legions can enter. It lies right in the midst of the world, yet it is separated from the world.[196] Although the people of God reside in the world, they are spiritually separated from the worldly lifestyle. Those in the wilderness live by the principles of God. This wilderness, which is the invisible kingdom of God, is spread all across the world among all nations. Listen to Jesus praying to His Father for His people:

- *I have given them your word, and the world has hated them because they are not of the world, just as I am not of the world. <u>I do not ask that you take them out of the world, but that you keep them from the evil one.</u> They are not of the world, just as I am not of the world. Sanctify them* *in the truth; your word is truth. As you sent me into the world, so I have sent them into the world. John 17:14-18*

BATTLEFIELD TACTICS EMPLOYED BY SATAN

Although Satan cannot pursue the woman into the wilderness, he certainly can employ military tactics against her in his attempts to destroy her or render her impotent on the battlefield. His initial tactic in the first centuries of Christianity was one of persecuting Christians, using segments of the Roman government. It was Satan's plan to murder the leaders of the early Christian movement and to create fear of persecution among the masses, but this tactic backfired on him. Certainly great numbers of Christians were martyred, but the gospel continued to go forth throughout the world on the soaring strength of the "eagle's wings," and this period of intense martyrdom by secular government only resulted in the kingdom of God growing greater and stronger than ever before.

As long as the Christian church remained in a state of separation from the world, the armies of Satan were impotent against it. Thus, he employed a second tactic designed to unite the church with the world. He opened his mouth and cast a huge stream of water into the wilderness, designed to wash the church out of the wilderness and unite it with the world. He can then use that segment of the church that washes back into his world to align with him against those who remain in the wilderness. Like the exodus wilderness in the days of Moses, there is a large segment of people who would rather enjoy the comforts of the world than the hardships of the wilderness, which is designed to prepare His people for entry into the Promised Land. Therefore, a large segment of the church that initially entered the wilderness is now brought out on the floodwaters of Satan. These are a people who verbally profess faith in Christ but actually worship the things of the world. They are used by Satan to establish religious organizations, mock the theology of true Christians, and persecute those who remain faithful in the wilderness. This began with the formation of the Roman Catholic Church, and it continues to this day. The Roman Catholic Church, with the exception of a small believing remnant in its midst, is very much of the world. Her popes have built an unrivaled worldwide empire of property, wealth, and influence. In order to amass their earthly empire, they have repeatedly engaged in spiritual fornication with emperors, kings, and princes. Claiming to be the bride of Christ, the Roman Catholic Church has been in bed with godless rulers throughout eighteen centuries of history. This demonic organization also has been responsible for the murder of millions of men and women dedicated to Christ who would not adhere to the pagan theologies of the pope and his religious leaders.[197]

When the fires of persecution waxed hotter and hotter over the European continent, the Lord again provided a refuge where His people might be nourished from the face of the serpent: the "wilderness" of the Western Hemisphere. He supplied them with "eagles' wings" to the land of America, where they were delivered out of the abyss of Roman Catholicism and where Protestantism was allowed to grow.[198] Immediately thereafter, Christian missionaries were dispatched to take the gospel of Christ to foreign nations all around the globe. Thus, over the last three hundred years, Christianity grew stronger and stronger around the world as Christians in the midst of this Western wilderness proclaimed the gospel protected from the persecution of the enemy.

Again, Satan was forced to change tactics when he failed to merge all the Christian institutions with the world. He now turns to individual believers. He does this by "mouthing" a flood of false doctrines and heresies throughout the Christian institutions in both Europe and America.[199] Such is the present method of satanic attack in the West, as lies from the mouth of Satan have become popular teachings, not only in our country's school system, but also in many false churches that claim to embrace Christian doctrines.

For example, Satan, appearing as an "angel of light," has convinced numerous American institutions that:

- Jesus Christ is not really the Son of God but merely a good man who sets a fine example for us to follow.
- Man is basically righteous, and we must stop listening to those who proclaim that all are born sinners.
- God is really not our Creator; we are merely a product of evolution.
- The Bible was written by ancient men as they perceived the world of their day; and, although it contains many good lessons for us, it really is not the "Word of God."
- Whether we are evangelical Christians, Catholics, Muslims, Buddhists, or Hindus, we all serve the same god.
- Eventually all persons will have eternal life, and we will all become like god.
- Vocalizing that Jesus Christ is the only way to eternal life is detrimental to society and should be outlawed.
- The elimination of both Jews and uncompromising evangelical Christians certainly would be helpful to the establishment of worldwide peace.

Now we are approaching the generation of mankind when Satan is preparing his military forces to completely erase the name of Jesus Christ from the face of the earth and defeat the plans of God, our almighty Father, for His sons and daughters among the human race.

REVIEWING SATAN'S MISSION AND TACTICS FOR THE END TIMES

Satan has been thrown out of the heavenlies, and he knows that his time is short; but he is not about to give up. In fact, the six-thousand-year-old war between the armies of light and darkness is about to intensify. Satan knows that if he can prevent mankind from professing loyalty to God the Father and His Son, then Satan himself would become the recipient of all worship and glory throughout the earth. Thus, he could claim that he is now in control of all those initially created in the "image of God." Perhaps then Satan could argue before both the angelic and earthly populations that he is much more qualified for ruler ship over creation and should occupy the throne of almighty God. The mission that drives his evil heart may be summarized as follows.

- **Satan's Mission Statement:** *"To ascend into the heavens, where I will raise my throne above the stars of God and make myself like the Most High,* [200] *(and where I will continue to challenge His sovereign rule over all of creation.)"*

For four thousand years, Satan attempted to make a frontal attack against God by claiming his authority over all of mankind, both living and dead, because of their sin. But he found that to be an absolute impossibility. The difference between the Creator and the created angelic beings is so vast that Satan's challenge was ludicrous, as proven by the life, death, and resurrection of the Son of God. Of all the living beings created by God, the closest to His heart was mankind. Being "in the image of God," mankind has the capacity for the likeness of God, something Lucifer as an angel did not possess.

- *Beloved, we are God's children now, and what we will be has not yet appeared; but we know that when he appears we shall be like him, because we shall see him as he is.* **(John 3:2)**

Now Satan obviously possesses a heart of immense pride, coupled with a deep bitterness toward our Lord God; yet he was not powerful enough to overthrow Him. However, the "children of God" can be very vulnerable to the supernatural power of Satan.

SATAN'S PRIMARY OBJECTIVES IN HIS WAR ON MANKIND

First, Satan intends to show the entire angelic realm that he is a leader to be worshipped, and he will prove it by controlling those of the Lord's creation who were created in "His image." The principal tactic used to accomplish this was and still is "deception." Satan deceives mankind into believing that the tremendous potential that resides within us can be more fully realized by living life under our own guidance rather than under God's. Thus, Satan convinces the majority of mankind that they have no need for God and that they can be their own gods, doing whatever is pleasing to them, even if it is harmful to others. <u>This self-centered nature is really the nature of Satan.</u>

Second, Satan intends to rid the world of all those who are not deceived and are totally committed to God the Father and to His Son, Jesus Christ. He does this by convincing world governments, together with false religions, that God's people are the only obstacle that keeps them from achieving their worldly goals—so they must be either converted to the world's belief system or killed.

If Satan can defeat the Army of God on earth, then he certainly will claim that God's Word concerning earthly redemption has been voided by the powers of darkness and that he alone is worthy to rule over all of creation. Thus, his commitment to destroy God's beloved witnesses from the face of the earth is tremendously strong.

SUMMARY OF REVELATION 12

Two thousand years are compressed into a few verses in this chapter of Revelation. The intent was to reveal the purposes of Satan, as well as the protection and purposes of God with respect to the war between the kingdoms. This brings us up to the time when the final battle will be fought, but this battle will be greater and more powerful than any previous event in history.

One last supreme effort awaits release of a powerful gospel to peoples of all nations. This will be a gospel released through the body of Christ, His 144,000 witnesses, who have been protected in the wilderness for three and a half years throughout the days of great tribulation. These are those who are nourished (strengthened) by God in the wilderness of this world and hold to the testimony of Jesus right up to that day of their martyrdom – the day when the Antichrist silences their testimony. The next chapter presents an overview of this final battle and the tactics that will soon be released by Satan and his dark forces in both the human and spiritual realms.

CHAPTER 10
THREE BEASTS – AN UNHOLY TRINITY
(First Read: Revelation 13)

The purpose of this chapter is to prepare and strengthen the warriors in the Army of God by providing advance intelligence concerning the dark and terrifying leadership that soon will arise from among the nations of the world. This will be a time of great trouble as evil leaders who have been anointed by Satan will be obsessed with eliminating the kingdom of God from the face of the earth and establishing an anti-Christian kingdom that will reign forever and ever.

Since the creation of man, Satan has been totally focused on wiping out the people of God from the earth and setting up a kingdom totally devoted to himself. Yet to date, he has been unable to complete this evil mission, as Jesus Christ continues to reign in the hearts of millions of His people. Knowing the purposes of the enemy, our Commander in Chief now provides His army with information regarding Satan's future attempt to establish an anti-Christian power throughout the earth. This phase of John's vision begins with Satan, the dragon, standing alongside the sea, knowing that his time is rapidly running out.[201] If he is to successfully complete his mission of worldwide conquest, he must quickly rally the entire world to unify under his lordship. So far he has been unable to destroy the woman in the wilderness, but he has developed a terrible new plan. He is about to establish the greatest and most powerful kingdom in the age of mankind. This kingdom will be led by two men anointed with monumental satanic power, and their primary mission will be to rally the world to rise up and devour all those who faithfully proclaim the name of God the Father and His Son, Jesus Christ.

A BEAST RISES UP FROM THE SEA
(Revelation 13:1)

John is a witness to this yet future event, when he sees a dreadful beast possessing tremendous power rising up out of the sea. The sea here is symbolic of agitated and troubled peoples and nations who are controlled by the power of sin.[202] Therefore, this beast arises from the midst of tumultuous nations that have been experiencing tremendous devastations and are crying out for a worldly savior. It is quite probable that this troublesome period on the earth is the aftermath of the "trumpet series" of events—a time of famine, plagues, and a terrified populace resulting from a short but devastating war that has wiped out a third of mankind and the natural resources of the earth.

Beasts in Scripture are frequently symbolic of great world empires.[203] These empires all have different characteristics, even as wild beasts are different. They may differ in strength, courage, speed, ferocity, and crushing power, just as leopards, bears, and lions differ from one another. Some are nobler than others, and some are more despicable. This final beast combines all the characteristics of the great empires that have historically ruled parts of the world. It will have the courage and ferocity of a lion, it will conquer with the speed of a leopard, and it will possess the merciless, crushing power of a bear. This terrible beast is symbolic of that last evil kingdom that will reign during the time known as the great tribulation. This final world power does not consist of just one nation and one people; rather it combines within itself all the evil character and powers of every worldly kingdom that has historically arisen in opposition to the kingdom of God.

In the previous chapter, Satan, the dragon, was symbolized by seven "crowned heads" and ten horns.[204] Here in this chapter, the beast from the sea is described as having seven heads and ten "crowned horns." This beast from the sea is not Satan, but it resembles him and is submissive to Satan's authority. The dragon is the most ferocious of all beasts, and here we see that he intends to give his power and authority to his "beastly son" (the Antichrist), who will use it in an attempt to carry out his father's purposes. Satan is a spirit, and as such he cannot establish an earthly throne in person. He needs a human agent to be subject to him as a world ruler. However, there is a condition that must be fulfilled: this ruler has to worship and bow down to him; otherwise Satan would lose the very dominion he sought. Thus, the Antichrist is about to receive what Jesus Christ refused when Satan offered Him all the kingdoms of the world in exchange for His allegiance.[205]

Let's now briefly analyze some of the bodily features of this Beast in order to obtain a deeper insight into the character of the Beast and his evil designs for God's chosen people. This will provide soldiers in the Army of God with additional understanding of the battles we will shortly be facing from a worldly society committed to ridding the name of Jesus Christ from the earth and replacing Him with their messiah, the Antichrist.

SEVEN HEADS OF THE BEAST
(Revelation 13:1-2)

The seven heads are representative of great empires that rise above all other nations of the world. These are mighty kingdoms that historically have risen to oppose the kingdom of God. John was told that there is a succession in these seven empires. At the time that John received this vision, around AD 90, he was told that five of these empires already had fallen, one was currently ruling; and the last one was yet to come.[206] The five that had already fallen were the Egyptian Empire, the Assyrian Empire, the Babylonian Empire, the Persian Empire, and the Grecian Empire. The sixth empire that currently was ruling during John's vision was the

Roman Empire. <u>A brief background of the history and character of each of these first six empires is provided in appendix A.</u> The seventh head of this beast, together with the ten horns, represents the "end-times" kingdom, which collides with Jesus Christ and His mighty army in the final conflict preceding His second coming.

Now, none of these previous six "beast empires" ever actually ruled the entire world, but each was the greatest oppressor of God's people during its historical reign. Obviously, these were not the only nations that had been enemies of the Lord and His people. Nations such as Philistia, Edom, and Moab continually despised and warred against God's people, yet none of these nations were of great size or worldly influence. On the other hand, there were other large and powerful empires in the ancient world—China, India, and Mongolia, for example—but these had little if any contact with God's chosen people. There were only six empires that were of such size and influence in the ancient world that figured prominently in the history of God's people up to the time of Christ and the early years of Christianity. All of these empires not only were powerful politically and commercially, but they also were strongholds of idolatrous polytheism. Satan, the dragon, had authority over each of the empires, and he attempted to use these worldly powers to defeat the kingdom of God.

Although these six historical empires have all been great and powerful, none has ever succeeded in attaining universal power over the entire earth or been able to overcome the kingdom of God. Since the discovery of the Western Hemisphere, this has become even more difficult; thus, a worldwide kingdom must be established in an entirely different way. The last kingdom will come by a confederation of prominent nations rather than by military conquest. This is represented by the "ten horns," which are symbolic of a final manifestation of united nations that will all be of one mind.[207] It will be understood that one nation cannot accomplish world domination. It needs to be a league formed of the "seventh head," made up of the "ten horns" who will eventually give their power over to one man, who is the "eighth" and one of the "seven."[208] This is the Beast in its entirety; a confederation of world powers being of one mind and giving all of their power over to a man. This is also the resurrection of the old kingdom of Nimrod's Babel, a united confederation, in modern form.[209]

ANTICHRIST—THE FINAL WORLD RULER
(Revelation 12:2)

From within this seventh kingdom will arise a leader who will perfectly personify the darkness of Satan in the flesh, an "anointed one" whom Satan has chosen to rule over this final demonic kingdom. This is the Antichrist, Satan's messiah to the world, who possesses his father's image and will require all the earth to bow down and worship his spiritual father. Just as Christ is the Son of God who came in the flesh to redeem His people out of the world, now the Antichrist is the son of Satan who comes in the flesh to eliminate the people of God from the face of the earth. Satan believes that by overcoming the people of God, he will have a legitimate claim to be the greatest and most deserving ruler over all of creation. Here we see this dragon in the world working to overthrow the kingdom of God, but his ultimate ambition is to defeat God's plan for His people and thus argue that he is more qualified to rule over all creation.[210]

Antichrist will emerge on the world political scene, bringing new hope through a multitude of promised "changes." He will honor all who acknowledge him and set them up as rulers and reward them with land and wealth taken from among the people.[211] Because of the apparent relationship of the ten horns to the Roman Empire revealed in the book of Daniel, it appears as if the Antichrist may arise out of a modern culture that is descended from the ancient Roman Empire.[212] However, he may or may not presently be a citizen of any contemporary European, Middle Eastern, or northern African nation that was once a part of the Roman Empire. It's possible that he could even be an American whose ancestors came from a region that was once under the control of the Roman Empire.

ANTICHRIST—HIS POPULARITY
(Revelation 12:3-4)

That person who will one day fill the role of the Antichrist is likely a national political figure somewhere in the world today and viewed by his constituents as another popular and successful politician. He will emerge on the world's political scene in the aftermath of worldwide economic, environmental, and military disasters. He gains control by stepping up at this time and mesmerizing the masses into believing that he alone is the one who can lead the world into peace and prosperity through a multitude of promised "changes." He probably is quite handsome and certainly has a charismatic personality that can mesmerize the masses like a popular rock music celebrity. He will seduce many with flatteries to the point that even the wise among the people will stumble and be led astray.[213] These are people who have been raised on "Hollywood stuff" and are schooled in a godless public education system. They have very little conception of the history of the United States or the Middle East. All they know is that when they see and hear this man speak, it makes them feel "warm and fuzzy" inside. They relish hearing vague terms such as *hope* and *change.*

Although the man known as the Antichrist will be charismatic, he also will be very firm in his speech and probably with eyes that appear hypnotic, along the lines of Adolph Hitler's. Being possessed by Satan, he also will have the fierce countenance of a lion—flattering but very dangerous to those who will not idolize him. He will be perceived by the masses as their true savior.

ANTICHRIST—THE APPEARANCE OF INVINCIBILITY
(Revelation 13:3, 14)

Somewhere in his rise to absolute power, Antichrist receives a mortal wound to the head that appears to be fatal. It is possible that he will physically suffer an assassination attempt, which is published in the media as having been fatal. This probably will occur when his popularity is growing, for it appears as if the entire world is aware of this apparently fatal incident. Suddenly he will "miraculously" recover, and the world will marvel as if their heroic messiah has been raised from the dead. They will see this as some sort of divine approval on this man's life. Now the masses will embrace their "savior" with more vehement energy than ever before, and they will begin to see him as a god. This wound may be faked, or it may be real; but nevertheless this perceived resurrection will result in much loyalty from the world. This supposed death of Antichrist and his miraculous recovery is intended to paint a parallel picture with the death of Christ and His resurrection. <u>This tactic of the dragon is designed to weaken the gospel message that the death and the resurrection of Jesus Christ is the only path to eternal life.</u>

Many commentators do not believe that this "wound that was healed" pertains to a human being. They write that it is symbolic of the reincarnation of ancient Babel, or the Roman Empire, or some other power. However, we must ask the question, "Why does the Lord provide so much information concerning this man?" It seems this detail is recorded so that His loyal soldiers will know who and what they are up against. Thus, being familiar with his tactics, we will not be seduced like many in today's church who will be blinded by his hypnotic speech and "miraculous resurrection."

Additionally, he will certainly convince the world that he is invincible when he brings down three powerful nations in his rise to power.[214] Perhaps the assassination attempt will emanate from among these three nations. At any rate, the world will shout, "Who is like the beast, and who can fight against it?"[215]

THE COMING OF THE TWO-HORNED BEAST
(Revelation 13:11-17)

There is a second agent through whom Satan will carry out his war against the kingdom of God. He is symbolized as a beast with two horns like a lamb, but one who speaks with the mouth of a dragon. This second beast is less terrifying in appearance, but he will be anointed by Satan with miraculous power. He is commonly referred to as the False Prophet. He will personify the tenderness and love of a lamb, yet it will be a deceptive form of love, for he will soothingly preach comforting lies intended to gain the loyalty of mankind through trickery.

The primary mission of the False Prophet will be to bring all of mankind to worship the Antichrist. He will have supernatural skills of persuasion, which he will use to promote the Antichrist as a great man with a tremendous love for his people and will bring peace and prosperity to the world. The False Prophet is the workhorse who causes the people to turn to Antichrist. Both delude the masses and exercise their authority over the world. Antichrist represents the kingdom of the world in the political and military realms, while the False Prophet deals with the religious, moral, and commercial aspects of this society.

Together with Satan, the Antichrist and the False Prophet will constitute an unholy trinity of malicious evil. As Christ received authority from His Father, so Antichrist receives authority from the dragon; and as the Holy Spirit glorifies Christ, so the False Prophet glorifies the Antichrist.

THE FALSE PROPHET—HIS THREEFOLD MINISTRY
Signs and Wonders

The False Prophet will publicly perform incredible signs and wonders before the world for the purpose of demonstrating his supernatural authority. This will cause the world to embrace him as a true prophet who deserves great respect and obedience to his every command. These miracle workings of the False Prophet also will persuade the vast majority of people that the god of the False Prophet is greater than all other gods. The result of these "showy miracles" will surely shift the focus of many away from the works of Christian disciples to the person of the Antichrist. He intends to undermine the works and miracles of the disciples of Jesus Christ, who will be sharing the gospel and also performing miraculous works during this period of time. The healing and other miracles of our Lord through the work of His disciples will be directed to needy individuals from a pure heart of love. Their works will stand in opposition to the miracles of the False Prophet, who performs them before the world solely for the purpose of demonstrating supernatural power. Those who experience the miracles of God in their lives probably will not be deceived by the False Prophet, and therefore the kingdom of God will continue to increase. The sincere love for the common people emanating from Christ's anointed disciples will be clearly obvious to many when compared to Satan's disciples, who will resemble popular Hollywood performing stars seeking to elevate their persona and enamor the masses.

The Image of Antichrist

The False Prophet will command the people to make an "image of the Antichrist," which will then be given breath and the ability to speak. When this image is complete, all the inhabitants of the world will be required to worship it. Those who refuse to worship this "speaking image" will be sought out and slain. This scenario is somewhat difficult to envision. Let's look at a couple of possibilities.

- Perhaps this may resemble a "golden image" like that erected by Nebuchadnezzar in ancient Babylon. He too required all persons to bow down and worship it or be put to death.[216] This image is in the likeness of the Antichrist, however. If the image of Antichrist is located in a particular geographic area, then it will require television-type technology to visibly manifest it around the world. If so, there will probably be a law requiring all to gather before a picture of this image and worship it at designated times throughout their daily routine.

- A second scenario could be that a new religious organization will be set up, using existing church facilities around the world, where people can gather and worship the Antichrist. This religious organization itself then will be the "speaking image." Envision this in a nation of Christianity: statues and pictures of Christ, together with any sign of a cross would all be replaced with this image of the Antichrist. All peoples would then be required to join and regularly worship in these churches. Imagine a world of false Christianity, believing that the Antichrist is the true Jesus, and the Islamic people believing him to be the Mahdi. They would be united in worshiping their perception of god.

The Mark of the Beast = 666

The False Prophet will command that mankind receive the mark of the Beast in order to participate in the marketplace. The mark is the number of a man, and this number is 666. This verse probably receives more attention than any single verse in Scripture. The mark not only identifies those who worship the Antichrist, but it also appears as if this number will one day identify the man himself. Over the centuries, many have attempted to identify evil leaders in their day with this number, using Latin, Greek, and Hebrew alphabets, which also can be converted to designated numbers.[217]

As mentioned in an earlier chapter, numbers are frequently used to provide deeper understanding of certain passages in Scripture. In this passage, the number 6 is commonly understood to represent man who was created on the 6th day, while the number 3 is representative of our Triune God. Therefore, 666 is man attempting to be God, though he can never reach the number 7, which represents perfection. However, I wouldn't recommend that we spend time trying to satisfy our curiosity by attempting to identify potential Antichrists. The title the man receives when he obtains worldwide authority probably will be a part of the number. It will be plain to the people of God when he arrives on the world scene as the sole leader.

The purpose for the mark is to control all of the world's commercial activity. In order to legally buy or sell in this anti-Christian kingdom, one must have this mark upon the forehead or the right hand. Who are the ones who receive the mark on their forehead, and who are the ones who receive it on their right hand?

- The forehead is the most exposed and conspicuous part of the body. Perhaps this will be reserved for the leaders in commerce and government so that they may be immediately recognized.
- If so, the mark on the right hand is for the common workers who are also committed to the Antichrist.
- This mark also will be beneficial for those among the body of Christ since its absence provides a visible means of identifying those who remain faithful to the Lord.

The ongoing gospel message being proclaimed during this period most certainly will include warnings against receiving this mark of the Beast. Many will fall away, yet many will remain faithful unto death. They may not be able to buy or sell, but they will faithfully cling to the name of Jesus. Thus, in the midst of tribulation, Christians will be social outcasts in the world, but they will maintain, "The Lord almighty is our God, and Christ alone is our King." And they will not be ashamed.

FALSE TEACHERS ALIGN WITH THE WORLD

False leadership is rapidly "emerging" within the world of evangelical Christendom that has avoided, and will continue to avoid, awkward confrontations with the political system over important biblical truths. It is much easier to speak the words people want to hear, for this gains them popularity among their followers, who will embrace them for supporting their lifestyles. This is parallel to the self-seeking attitude of the Jewish people of the old dispensation when they were warned by God's prophets concerning the coming judgments of God. However, false religious teachers opposed this message of the prophets and preached peace and prosperity and the love of God, asserting that a loving God would never allow His nation to be conquered. Thus, the people vanquished all thoughts of future captivity and continued on their merry way, buying and selling and mocking those messengers God had sent to warn them.

What happened to the Jews in historical Babylon is the same thing that will happen to the spiritually lazy in Mystery Babylon. They will be captivated by the Beast because their hearts will be made drunk with the wine of materialism. These are people who will be churchgoers, neighbors, coworkers, and relatives who may acknowledge Christ, but in reality, they are trusting in money. Paul was certainly including the Christian church of the Western world in his prophetic warnings concerning false teachings.

- *For the time is coming when people <u>will not endure sound teaching</u>, but having itching ears they will accumulate for themselves teachers to suit their own passions, and <u>will turn away from listening to the truth and wander off into myths</u>. As for you, always be sober-minded, endure suffering, do the work of an evangelist, fulfill your ministry. **(2 Timothy 4:3-5)***

Remember this: Whatever people choose to believe, they will somehow find a way to validate it as a truth, regardless of its absurdity.[218]

SATAN'S TACTICS MANIFESTED IN THE HEADS OF THE BEAST

Satan has employed two primary tactics in his zealous rage to obliterate the kingdom of God from the earth.

First, he uses *an all-out frontal assault* with the intent of completely annihilating God's people from the earth. This tactic visibly reveals his deep hatred toward us. This has been historically manifested time and again as God's people frequently have been in danger of complete annihilation. Following is a brief examination of how Satan has employed this frontal assault, using the first six heads of the Beast to attack the kingdom of God. We can expect to see these same methods used in the future.

- Brutal enslavement, which suggests that we can expect mass imprisonment in concentration camps.
- Women and children targeted for slaughter in order to create tremendous fear among the masses. This is certainly a favorite tactic among the cowardly Muslim terrorists.
- Murder of the elderly and newborn babies for the purpose of controlling population growth.
- Brutal and humiliating torture. For example, the <u>Assyrians</u> captured many Israelite army leaders and lifted them up naked but alive on the heads of spears and paraded them in front of their people.
- Attempts to destroy all worship of God by destroying the physical churches; this is parallel to the destruction of Solomon's temple by the <u>Babylonians</u>.
- Destruction of all Christian Bibles, music, and worship under the threat of death. Antiochus Epiphanes of the <u>Grecian Empire</u> outlawed the worship of the God of Israel and declared that all Hebrew Scriptures were to be destroyed.

Second, Satan *entices God's people to voluntarily turn from the worship of the Lord to worshipping the "prince of this world."* This is the more preferable tactic of Satan, since he takes much greater pleasure in turning a man's heart than in killing him. He believes that this proves that he is more worthy of worship than the Lord. Here are some examples of what to expect:

- Satan enticed the Israelites with the Egyptian lifestyle. Instead of trusting the Lord during the hardships encountered in the wilderness, they grumbled and wanted to return to Egypt. This may parallel a great falling away during tribulation times.

- The influences of the Hellenistic culture, which encouraged self-seeking pleasures and immorality, threatened to wipe out the worship of God from the nation of Israel. Many of the youth of that day scorned the traditions of Israel and embraced the pleasures of the Greeks. This is very prevalent in today's Western culture, which emphasizes commercialism, sexual immorality, and entertainment as the epitome of an enviable lifestyle.

- The Roman Empire established a powerful but dark authority within Christianity that was designed to turn Christian worship away from Christ and to a human representative, a pope who is unknowingly controlled by the spirit of Satan. Expect liberal Christianity to be encouraged within the seventh kingdom as long as Jesus Christ is not the focus of worship. These false Christian churches, comprised of Roman Catholicism and liberal Protestantism, will support this anti-Christian kingdom and will be a major player in the betrayal of true believers who refuse to compromise their faith.

"Christian warriors, we must anticipate that similar tactics will be employed by the enemy with even greater power in the seventh kingdom ruled by the Antichrist."

A SEVEN-YEAR COVENANT

As we've seen in a prior chapter, Jesus Christ comes to confirm the true covenant between God, His Father, and all who embrace Him as their Lord. It is a covenant that ushers in everlasting righteousness and ends with the anointing of a most holy place.[219] However, there is also a covenant that will soon be established by Satan, who is intent on counterfeiting the true works of Jesus Christ. A future prince, who is shortly to come upon the worldly scene, will make a seven-year covenant with the secular nation of modern Israel. This covenant, or peace treaty, is made by Israel without the Lord and is described in Scripture as the "covenant with death," because it is made with the sons of darkness and will be confirmed by the Antichrist.[220]

However, after three and a half years, this dark covenant that was founded on lies will be broken by the Antichrist, who will then set up his own image in the Jerusalem temple as another counterfeit anointing of the most holy place. Perhaps the event that triggers the Antichrist's sudden claim to deity will be his miraculous recovery from a head wound. At any rate, the setting up of this satanic image in a newly built temple in Jerusalem will be the sign of the beginning of that great tribulation that will suddenly ensnare the world.[221] Therefore, it appears that Israel will soon begin to rebuild a physical temple to the Lord and again initiate daily sacrifices like their ancestors under the old covenant.

Jesus confirmed His Father's covenant when He kept the law perfectly and then laid down His life at the cross for the sins of mankind. Thus, after three and a half years, Jesus Christ gave His own life as a perfect sacrifice and thereby did away with the need for the sacrificial system of the old covenant.[222] Antichrist appears to be counterfeiting the three-and-a-half-year ministry of Christ with his first three and a half years of uniting world government—afterwards, this will be followed by the mandatory worship of his image.

Perhaps it is when Israel is rebuilding their physical temple that the Lord will rebuild His temple made without hands in the Spirit, a temple in the hearts of His people. This may very well be the time of the anointing of the 144,000, who will represent the body of Christ in the second half of the seven-year covenant that ushers in everlasting righteousness.[223] This may also be the hour when men of wisdom will arise and their voices will be heard in the wilderness, declaring to the whole world, "Make straight the way of the Lord, for the day of the Lord is at hand."[224] These are chosen ones who have been prepared by God Himself. Until this time, they have been hidden away like David and his mighty men in the cave at Adullam. They have been prepared like Joseph in prison, where suffering and sorrow was experienced, until the day they are called to arise. They must first be purged with fire before they can be used at this glorious level.[225]

PURPOSE AND DIFFERENCES BETWEEN TRIBULATION AND THE WRATH OF GOD

Tribulation is a time of warfare between the forces of good and evil. It is God's judgment on the world's evil system. However, tribulation is also the attack of the world's system against the true believers of Jesus Christ. Good and evil cannot coexist. The characteristics of each become more prevalent during a time of conflict. As the battle intensifies, the people on both sides become more visible and neutrality begins to disappear. Weeds among the church are continually exposed, as they fall away and side with the religiosity of the world. The armies of the world become larger and darker and more violent in their hatred against God and His people. At the same time, the Army of God becomes stronger and more radiant as they stand for the truth of God and His Spirit grows stronger and stronger among them.

Tribulation will increase in escalating stages, but so will the strengthening of the Lord's army. Within the church, there will be increasing levels of purging the tares, purifying the people, evangelizing among the nations, and receiving power from on high. This fierce pressure takes place because of God's love for mankind and His desire to bring out of darkness into salvation every single soul possible and to destroy every demonic stronghold that has held the human race captive. Traditional or lukewarm Christianity will collapse during the great tribulation.

The wrath of God is a military action on the part of the armies of heaven to avenge and rescue God's people in the world. God's wrath is directed solely against the forces of darkness. What restrains the outpouring of God's wrath is the ability of His people to maintain their stand and communicate their faith. There are many in the world of darkness who will be called into the light. When this is complete and God's message is shut down within His people, then the full wrath of God will be poured out on the earth. Until then, many warnings are poured out from heaven that tend to either draw people to the Lord or to solidify their hatred toward Him.[226]

OUR LORD'S CALLING: "ENDURE AND REMAIN FAITHFUL"
(Revelation 13:10)

Antichrist is not looking solely for political control of the world; he is intent on receiving worship from every single individual who lives on earth. The working of miracles and the requiring of image worship, together with a marked body, are all designed to visibly identify and unite the individual peoples among the nations in loyalty to Antichrist as well as to one another. They are also intended to help identify those persons who refuse to receive the mark of the Antichrist or bow down to his image. These faithful believers will be classified as enemies among the nations and a hindrance to world peace.

The world system will make war against the people of God who continue to witness during the reign of this Antichrist. These are warriors who refuse to submit to his authority and maintain that it is not Antichrist, but Christ, who is their King. They will be deeply hated, and the world will wage a continuous war against them and eventually overcome them. These will be extremely hard and faith-challenging days of persecution, a time of "wearing out" the people of God. All Bibles and biblically related books will be outlawed, and the peoples will be required to turn them over to the authorities for burning. Those who refuse will be criminally charged and sentenced to imprisonment. Murderous executions, imprisonment in concentration camps, brutal torture, separation from family, and forbidding the purchase of food and water will all be commonly employed tactics of this evil kingdom. These are the days of persecution.

One may wonder why imprisonment of many of God's people is employed by the enemy instead of simply executing them. Imprisonment allows time for the enemy to break down the spirit of people for the purpose of allowing them to voluntarily turn away from the Lord and render allegiance to the Antichrist. Though deep in their heart they may still believe in the Lord, some will give up. Ultimately, their life in this world will mean more to them than their faith in Christ. Satan rejoices when people visibly turn away from almighty God and render allegiance to him, even if it is not from a pure heart. Turning people to him is more important than murdering them, for it means he has defeated what is most important to God—the steadfast faithfulness of His people. The one who has turned away from the Lord undoubtedly will be praised before the world as a newly enlightened hero. This will be a shameful experience.

Our Lord will provide a hiding place for us when the time of persecution arrives. Where is that hiding place?

- For the prophet Daniel, it was both in a king's palace and in a lions' den.
- For Shadrach, Meshach, and Abednego, it was in a fiery furnace.
- For Joseph, it was in an Egyptian prison.
- For David, it was in a cave out in the wilderness.
- For the apostle Paul, it was in prison or shipwrecked in the Mediterranean.
- For the spies sent by Joshua, it was in a harlot's house in Jericho.
- For Corrie Ten Boom, it was in a flea-infested barracks in a Nazi concentration camp.

They were all right where God wanted them, and not a hair on their heads perished. So our hiding place is wherever the center of the Lord's will is for us. The only thing we should fear is being out of God's will. We must trust in the Lord for our individual hiding places, for they will probably be different for every believer in the end times. Meanwhile, let us stand in the gap and prepare our brothers and sisters for the coming hour of trial.[227]

- *If anyone is to be taken captive, to captivity he goes; if anyone is to be slain with the sword, with the sword must he be slain. Here is a call for the endurance and faith of the saints.* **Revelation 13:10**

Although Christians will be physically overcome during this horrendous period of time, they are the ones who are victorious in this war. They have become outcasts from society, mocked by former neighbors, family members, and friends, imprisoned, and killed. This is the body of Christ, having an experience similar to what their Lord Jesus Christ endured two thousand years earlier. They are now glorious participants in His great victory. In the crucial test of faith, they have chosen to relinquish their lives rather than their faith in their God. This is true victory.

REJOICING IN THE MIDST OF PERSECUTION

- *Blessed are those who are persecuted for righteousness' sake, for theirs is the kingdom of heaven. Blessed are you when others revile you and persecute you and utter all kinds of evil against you falsely on my account. Rejoice and be glad, for your reward is great in heaven, for so they persecuted the prophets who were before you.* **Matthew 5:10-12**
- *Indeed, all who desire to live a godly life in Christ Jesus will be persecuted.* **2 Timothy 3:12**

- *Count it all joy, my brothers, when you meet trials of various kinds, for you know that the testing of your faith produces steadfastness. And let steadfastness have its full effect, that you may be perfect and complete, lacking in nothing.* **James 1:2-4**

- *In this you rejoice, though now for a little while, if necessary, you have been grieved by various trials, so that the tested genuineness of your faith—more precious than gold that perishes though it is tested by fire—may be found to result in praise and glory and honor at the revelation of Jesus Christ. Though you have not seen him, you love him. Though you do not now see him, you believe in him and rejoice with joy that is inexpressible and filled with glory, obtaining the outcome of your faith, the salvation of your souls.* **1 Peter 1:6-9**

CHAPTER 11

MYSTERY BABYLON THE GREAT: CAPITAL OF WEALTH, PLEASURE, AND HARLOTRY

(First Read: Revelation 17—18)

As previously mentioned, the book of Revelation is not necessarily chronological. Frequently, a general vision is first recorded, and then later visions are given to provide additional detail. The events recorded in these two chapters concerning Mystery Babylon and the seven-headed beast actually occur prior to the reign of the Antichrist recorded in chapter 13. In fact, the one-world government that will be ruled by the Antichrist will come to "ultimate power" only after the destruction of Mystery Babylon. This is apparent from the crowns on the heads of the ten kings in Revelation 13. Yet, here in chapter 17, as the harlot woman continues to ride the beast, the ten kings have not yet received their royal power.

Now who this ungodly woman is, what she represents, and where she exists today is so important to God's chosen people that more has been recorded concerning her identity and purposes than has been recorded concerning the Antichrist. That is because she is capable of such great deception that everyone who follows her will be eternally lost. Even many people attending today's Christian churches have fallen in love with her.

Christians need to listen to the cry of our Commander in Chief:

- *Come out of her, my people, lest you take part in her sins, lest you share in her plagues; for her sins are heaped high as heaven, and God has remembered her iniquities. (Revelation 18:4-5)*

Mystery Babylon will be burned up prior to the supreme reign of the Antichrist; perhaps she is the target of the "trumpet series," which destroys one-third of the earth. This is very important for our comprehension, as most teachers of Revelation simply warn Christians about receiving the mark of the Beast. Yet, before the time of the "mark," multitudes of peoples who have not come out of Mystery Babylon will be burned up. One needs to understand who, what, and where she currently resides in the world if one plans to survive her destruction.

The identity of this woman, commonly referred to as Mystery Babylon, is of extreme practical importance for our present generation. Yet this continues to be one of the most controversial passages in the book of Revelation, and there have been numerous different interpretations concerning her identity over the last two thousand years. These interpretations have struggled with the fact that Mystery Babylon is pictured as both a woman and a city. However, in order for God's chosen people in our generation to refuse to have fellowship with her, they must be able to discern who and/or what she is during these times.

BABYLON—A CONTROLLING INFLUENCE OVER MIGHTY NATIONS

Now consider the manlike statue in Nebuchadnezzar's dream, which portrayed the different parts of the human body as representative of mighty world empires—empires that would arise and oppress the people of God prior to both the first and the second comings of the Lord Jesus Christ.[228] You may recall that the "head of gold" was representative of the Babylonian Empire. Now we always recognize a person by looking at the person's face, for it provides the identity for the entire body. The head consists of the eyes, the ears, and the brains, all of which develop the vision and guide the body in the direction the head desires to go. Therefore, the successive kingdoms that have risen to power after the fall of the Babylonian Empire are all part of Mystery Babylon. These are also the kingdoms of Satan, which would oppress the people of God in separate places over the centuries. These kingdoms first arose in the Middle East, where they warred against the nation of Israel, and now they have expanded westward as the Christian church has grown over the last two thousand years and moved westward. Babylon is the "head" that controls the affairs of the world and the authority that oppresses the people of God throughout all the ages since the beginning of time.[229]

BABYLON THE GREAT—IDENTIFYING THE CITY

After watching seven bowls of tremendous destruction poured out across the earth, John is summoned by one of the seven-bowl angels to witness the judgment "of the great prostitute who is seated on many waters." Earlier, John had seen a beautiful woman clothed with the sun who was the mother of all true believers. Now when he sees this harlot woman, he is truly astonished. Perhaps his astonishment is because this harlot woman has the same facial features as the woman who was symbolic of the true church. But instead by being clothed with the sun, this woman is adorned with clothing and jewelry symbolic of great riches and tremendous worldly beauty. She also appears to be celebrating, for she is intoxicated from drinking the blood of those martyred for Christ. Remarkably, she is astride the seven-headed beast, which apparently reveals that she is the one who steers the direction of the kingdom of the world.

This evil woman is further described as sitting on many waters, which represent many peoples and nations across the world. Furthermore, she also is referred to five different times as representative of the "great city." Just as the waters are symbolic of peoples and nations, this great city appears to be symbolic of the capital of these peoples and nations, the capital of a gigantic system for the pursuit of wealth and pleasure—Babylon.

Note the following parallel with another woman who is also symbolic of a great city.

- *Then came one of the seven angels who had the seven bowls full of the seven last plagues and spoke to me, saying, "Come, I will show you the Bride, the wife of the Lamb." And he carried me away in the Spirit to a great, high mountain, and showed me the holy city Jerusalem coming down out of heaven from God, having the glory of God, its radiance like a most rare jewel, like a jasper, clear as crystal.* **(Revelation 21:9-11)**

New Jerusalem is symbolic of the bride of Christ, and Mystery Babylon is symbolic of a worldly prostitute. These are two spiritual capital cities; one reigns within the kingdom of God, and the other controls the direction of the kingdom of the world. However, they also have physical locations. Babylon currently exists within the world, while New Jerusalem resides in heaven, awaiting its time to descend to the earth.

Now does the city commonly known as Mystery Babylon have a single geographical location? Well, yes and no! She is that city where the idolatry of commercialism, immorality, and hatred of God exists. She is worldwide, yet she is located more strongly in certain sections of the world. Consider where her primary location exists today.

Similar to Mystery Babylon, the United States of America is also a nation seated on many waters, both physically and symbolically. Physically, she is bordered east, west, and south by the two greatest oceans, and by five great lakes in the north, and through her interior run mighty rivers. Additionally, she rules many diverse peoples, for her population encompasses peoples from every land around the world: Europeans, Asians, Africans, Jews, Arabs, Hispanics, etc. People everywhere dream of a day when they can come to the great land of America. She is the pride of the whole earth, as well as being the focus of great jealousy from nations who envy her riches.

America, a once great nation that exported the gospel of Jesus Christ throughout the earth, has turned from the Lord and now exports pollution among all nations with her adulterous lifestyle. The world watches scenes of lust and greed from Hollywood movies, buys American pornography, listens to the dark lyrics of popular American music, and thus idolizes the American culture comprised of a materialistic and pleasure-seeking spirit. A nation that once proclaimed the righteousness and truth of God among the nations now pollutes the earth with her filth.[230] Our nation may or may not be the final location of Mystery Babylon, but in this generation, the spirit of the whore is most prominent in the great cities of America. There is no doubt among discerning Christians that our once proud and mighty nation is shortly heading for a great and terrible fall.

HISTORICAL ATTEMPTS TO IDENTIFY MYSTERY BABYLON

Recall that John sees this harlot woman sitting on the beast that has seven heads and ten horns. These seven heads are described as seven mountains and also as seven kings. Our early Christian fathers, who experienced the horrendous evils of Roman Catholicism through the dark ages, strongly believed that John was seeing a vision of the power of the Roman papacy represented by this harlot woman seated on seven mountains. They believed that these mountains were representative of the city of Rome, which is known for being built upon seven hills. However, mountains in Scripture are frequently symbolic of mighty empires.[231] Just as a mountain is visibly manifested above the normal surface of the earth, these ancient empires were the greatest among all the surrounding nations in the world. Thus, it appears that this mysterious Babylonian woman, who sits on the top of these symbolic mountains, is the primary controlling influence over all the "seven great empires" that have arisen over the centuries to oppose the kingdom of God.

Certainly the Roman Catholic Church has been in bed with the kings of the earth through the centuries. She has partied with these kings and made both them and their respective nations drunk with the wine of her spiritual fornications. Her cup also is filled with the blood of saints, for she has been responsible for the murder of countless numbers of the Lord's sons and daughters through the centuries. The Catholic Church is very much of this world. Her popes have built a worldwide empire of property, wealth, and influence. They have fought with armies and navies in the name of Christ to build a huge kingdom that is very much of this world. And to amass their earthly empire, they have repeatedly engaged in spiritual fornication with emperors, kings, and princes. Claiming to be the bride of Christ, the Roman Catholic Church has been in bed with godless rulers down through history.[232] Because of her worldwide influence and wealth, every world leader will have to deal with the Catholic Church in order to attain and maintain political power. Therefore, many renowned theologians believe that this harlot woman is representative of the Roman Catholic Church throughout the New Testament age.

Still others believe this harlot is not only representative of Roman Catholicism but also includes the false Protestant churches that claim to be the bride of Jesus Christ. They too have departed to climb into bed with the commercial and political leaders of the world. Although she continues to claim that she is rightfully married to the Lord, she is really the counterfeit church pretending to be the true bride of Christ.

Finally, many have written that Mystery Babylon is representative of the great world cities of today, such as New York, Paris, Chicago, Rome, London, Los Angeles, and Hollywood. These are cities in supposedly Christian nations that have exported evil across the globe. Thus, they see her as the city-prostitute who commits fornication with all the nations of the earth and reigns from a city that is the center of worldwide commerce and industry. However, can we really equate "Babylon the great" with any single city or geographical area? Perhaps! First, let's look deeper into some symbolic truths represented by both the woman and the beast.

BABYLON—UNITING POLITICS, COMMERCIALISM, AND RELIGION

The city of Babylon embraces different public activities that align themselves with one another for a sole purpose; they each want to achieve power and wealth through their own efforts. Every mighty world empire has embraced the following three sources of power within society. <u>These are the ones who will mourn the destruction of the woman, Mystery Babylon.</u>

- The "kings of the earth" represent the <u>political and military</u> arena. (18:9)
- The "merchants of the earth" represent the <u>commercial</u> arena. (18:11)
- The "unfaithful woman" represents the <u>religious</u> arena. (17:5-6)

The uniting of these three elements of society represents a gigantic humanistic system in pursuit of wealth and fleshly pleasures along with the promised assurance of eternal life. The focus of the citizens of Babylon is to achieve more and more earthly riches and comforts without the hand of God. Babylonian laws are continually passed to accommodate their worldly pursuits. These are laws contrary to the laws of God, for they are laws designed to appeal to mankind's desire to be their own gods.

THE WOMAN = COMMERCIALISM AND RELIGIOUS POWER

Now commerce is certainly a legitimate pursuit. Every honest worker has a connection to commerce. The Bible mandates that we work and engage in legitimate business in order to provide for our families.[233] However, while commerce is a legitimate pursuit of profit; *commercialism* is an attitude of the heart that can grow into the religion of money worship. Commercialism is the love of money and luxury that seeps into our psyches, hardening our hearts to needy people and distracting our minds from the priorities of God's kingdom.[234]

The great world of commercialism has become virtually a religion to countless numbers of people; its leaders, who are the captains of industry, are practically the rulers of the world. The world of commercialism is tangible and visible, but the animating spirit behind it all is the love of "money." Money is the god that many worship in our day, for a person's true god is that to which he consecrates his life. Money is the greatest of all the idols in our generation. It is the greatest rival of God for the affections and devotions of man.[235]

The harlot woman appears to be in control of worldly governments because of her great riches and her millions of followers, who continually seek comfortable answers for their lives. These followers of the woman are in pursuit of worldly riches and comforts, but they are also seeking assurance that their happiness will continue in the eternal realm after their death. Both "religion," for its millions of followers, and "commercialism," for its wealth, are extremely powerful and generally control the affairs of public life. Therefore, "politicians" have to climb into bed with the whore in order to gain the support of the people that will allow them to succeed in ruler ship over the various kingdoms of the world.

All the injustices that are committed in the commercial and religious segments of society are symbolized by this harlot woman. Her cup is full of the abominations of an evil, worldly kingdom that has persecuted the true people of God since the beginning of time. Mystery Babylon is the capital city of all humanism, which seeks the unifying and salvation of mankind through his own works. Her merchants are the great ones of the earth, whereas Christ, whose followers have no place in this world, has commanded His people to take the lowest place in it.

THE BEAST = POLITICAL AND MILITARY POWER

This seven-headed beast that is being guided by the harlot woman is the same as the one that will eventually establish that final world empire and murder the two witnesses in the streets of Jerusalem.[236] This beast is representative of the anti-Christian world power from a political and military point of view. It is the attempt of Satan to establish his own kingdom, using the agencies of power that have been instituted in the world. Both political and military powers were initially established by God to help bring social justice and order to the world. However, they have been continually abused by greedy kings and politicians to bring about social chaos and disorder in order to attain power and control over the peoples and wealth of the world.

Now in Revelation 17 and 18, we are presented with a brief historic survey of the development of mighty world powers, as well as a preview of their final defeat and descent into hell. The seven heads represent six stages of development of various kingdoms that existed in the past, plus the coming kingdom of the Antichrist represented by the seventh head. The ten horns represent ten powerful kings who will rule during the final manifestation of the seventh kingdom. They will unite and establish their final anti-Christian kingdom with the Antichrist as the supreme world ruler. This future realization of the kingdom of Antichrist shall come into being through a united confederation of nations rather than through military conquest. Thus, the seventh head is representative of a league of nations that will anoint the Antichrist as the ruling authority over the final world empire. They will be viciously dedicated to wiping out the people of Christ from the face of the earth in order to provide more blood for their rich and beautiful whore.

The eighth beast is obviously distinct from the other seven. He is the Antichrist, not simply another human ruler. Daniel describes him as another horn among the ten, with eyes like a man and a mouth speaking great things. He is even greater than his companions. He blasphemes almighty God and makes war with the followers of Christ. He also overthrows three of the ten horns in his rise to supreme power.[237] He is not a human ruler through whom the power of evil finds expression; he is that evil power itself. He appears to be Satan incarnate.

However, before this eighth beast, the Antichrist, can come into supreme worldwide power, he must control all the commerce and religions of the world. Thus, he must overthrow the woman who symbolizes that great and immoral city of Babylon. This overthrow of Mystery Babylon will take place in a single day without any advance warning. The world will be in tremendous shock and grief as their idols are suddenly swept away and replaced by a single man. This will be a quick and powerful attack on the areas in which the harlot exercises the greatest control—that place where all the merchants of the earth were in bed with her.

THE WOMAN LOVES THE BEAST—
THE BEAST HATES THE WOMAN

The woman is committed to the beast, for it is because of its legislative and military powers that she is enriched. However, unknown to the woman, the beast is not committed to her but is using her to gain power in the world governments. The Antichrist will suddenly attain supreme power by burning the city of Babylon and taking control over all of her commercial and religious activities. This sudden attack appears to be nuclear, for it is described as being a great fire with rising smoke that is seen from far off.

Additionally, the prophet Jeremiah not only spoke of the destruction of ancient Babylon, but also prophesied concerning the future destruction of Mystery Babylon. (Read: Jeremiah 50 & 51).

Following the destruction of Mystery Babylon, the final kingdom will be committed to bringing the following sources of power under the complete control of the Antichrist.

- *Commercialism* will continue to exist for those embracing the "mark of the Beast." But free enterprise among the merchants of the earth will disappear. "No one can buy or sell unless they have the mark of the beast!" In order for this to happen, all economies of the world must merge into one. And for that to occur, the present economies must crumble in order to induce the people of the world to accept the new system. This new world money system will be the lifeblood of the beast government of Antichrist.

- *Religion* will continue to exist for those worshipping the "image of the Beast." But freedom to worship other gods will disappear. Yet a remnant of God's chosen people, previously identified as the 144,000, will not take the mark of the Beast and will not bow down to his image. They will continue to be a strong and powerful light in the midst of this darkest period in the history of mankind.

THE BABYLONIAN WHORE AND FALSE CHRISTIANITY

In Scripture a woman is frequently symbolic of God's chosen people. Time and again His people are represented as a bride who has pledged by covenant to be faithful to Him. In the Old Testament, Israel is the wife of Yahweh, while in the New Testament; the church is the bride of Christ. Also, in the book of Ezekiel, we see the nation of Israel being identified as the wife of the Lord. She was immensely blessed by her Husband but later went whoring after other gods. She also sacrificed her children to these gods, much like today's abortionists.[238] Hosea presents a similar picture. Thus, it is apparent in Scripture that a spiritual harlot is one who claims to be faithful to her Husband yet runs after the gods of other religions. The true church is the spiritual bride of Christ. But the counterfeit church claims to be the true church, and outwardly she may look like the church; but she really embraces the worldly lifestyle. She enjoys the favor of the world, as they bless her with precious jewels and gold. She becomes great and powerful, but she is nothing but a harlot. She fornicates with those who dwell on the earth and laughs at the need for atonement by the blood of Christ. She invents a Christianity of her own, which may not deny Christ as a god but will trample on the need for His redemptive blood. She secretly whores with all that opposes the Lord and His people. Her churches are filled with false teachings that are designed to support her adulterous lifestyle and provide assurance that she is loved by God.

The preaching of "tolerance" is a doctrine promoted by the enemy to effectively weaken the truth of the biblical gospel. There is a fast-growing movement within our nation to ridicule people for being "intolerant" for their Christian beliefs. For example, if Christians proclaim that Jesus Christ is the one and only way to eternal life, they will be maligned as bigots and fanatics, as judgmental and unloving, and therefore a hindrance to the establishment of a peaceful society. The "tolerance" doctrines assume that man is basically good, even if at various times in life people may need counseling help. Tolerance will be communicated around the world as the ultimate expression of love. Eventually it will become unlawful to share the true gospel message with people, because that would be considered offensive. This religious prostitute will side with those governmental authorities that insist that the church must be "tolerant" of those who believe that there are many ways to eternal life. She will help blend Christianity with other faiths and continue to dilute the true gospel of Jesus Christ.

Gradually, she will reveal her character more clearly until a great apostasy takes place. Eventually the false church will openly separate from those who are faithful to the Lord Jesus Christ. Denominations will come to an end; all will unite under a single purpose: the reconstruction of the world. The gospel of Christ will be trampled underfoot by those who insist that they are the true representatives of God. Protestantism will openly join with Catholicism in embracing all religions worldwide. Thus, the woman known as Mystery Babylon is also representative of the apostate church in the present, as well as in past generations. <u>The following sections will provide an overview of why I believe the United States of America is the primary site of Mystery Babylon today.</u>

AMERICA—IN THE WORLD'S SPOTLIGHT

Many say that America is not mentioned in Scripture, and therefore the destiny of our nation is unknown to our generation. It certainly is not specifically mentioned, but why would it be? The Bible was completed two thousand years ago, and the discovery of the Western world would not take place for another thousand years. The Lord does not specifically mention geographical regions of the world before their discovery. Mankind has received a mandate to go out and discover it for themselves, and having done that, more and more clarity emerges from the prophetic scriptures. Jesus commanded His people to take the gospel of the kingdom into all the nations. What country has made the greatest impact upon the growth of Christianity worldwide?

When Jesus teaches on events that precede His second coming, He warns of false teachers who will lead many astray and of many in the church who will betray others. Think about it! What other country has such a large Christian population that will fall away and betray many of His people? America is the greatest representative of Christianity since the last page of the Bible was written. However, the American church also is flooded with false teachers who speak the words people want to hear, for this is what allows them to grow in popularity among those who want to continue in their worldly lifestyles. Paul certainly was speaking to these popular American churches who are led by false teachers.

- *For the time is coming when people will not endure sound teaching, but having itching ears they will accumulate for themselves teachers to suit their own passions, and will turn away from listening to the truth and wander off into myths. As for you, always be sober-minded, endure suffering, do the work of an evangelist, fulfill your ministry.* **(2 Timothy 4:3-5)**

This is similar to the attitude of the Jews, when they were warned by God's prophets concerning the coming invasion by the Babylonian army. In the days of Jeremiah, false teachers among the Jews continued to preach peace and prosperity and insist that the love of God would never allow them to be invaded by the heathen Babylonians. The people listened to these comforting teachings and continued on their merry way, buying and selling until, suddenly, terrible destruction fell upon them and destroyed them as a nation.

Today, in most American churches, the leaders who claim to know His Word fail to recognize that the hour of judgment is at hand. Many of these churches are filled to overflowing to hear their pillow prophets teach a gospel of prosperity and easy believism. These are churches that support their congregations in the idolatrous worship of commercialism, while the few voices declaring the impending judgment of God are ignored. Like the Judeans in the days of Daniel and Jeremiah, Americans today are hardened in sin, embracing the popular but false gospel of peace. The majority of the American church is oblivious to what the Lord is about to do within our country in this generation. Everything is about to change. You will not recognize this nation in the very near future.[239]

AMERICA—WHERE IDOLATRY THRIVES

In America, the voice of demons sounds quite pleasant. They are heard on television, in the newspapers, in theatres, in our classrooms, and even in many of our churches. They are voices that continually speak to us about living a happy and successful life, but in reality they conceal the truth that leads to true eternal happiness. Materialism, entertainment, pleasure seeking, celebrity worship, abnormal sexual relationships, obsession with shopping and eating—these are our idols. We worship those things that provide physical and emotional pleasure, and we worship all those people who contribute to our individual pleasures. Our religion is all about "meism"; we are our own god. These are the worshippers of Mrs. Mystery Babylon, that adulterous whore who pretends to be the bride of Christ.

Even though America has existed only for some three hundred plus years, it is probably the greatest and most prosperous nation in the New Testament era. The age of technology all started with America. Technological equipment and toys have spawned tremendous worldwide commercialism over the past thirty years. America also has had the greatest controlling impact on the commercial sector of the world's culture for several decades leading up to these last days. The world may hate America, but it certainly yearns for its lifestyle. Like Babylon, which was represented by the golden head in Nebuchadnezzar's dream, America certainly appears to be the home of the harlot woman, who is the guiding source of the beast in this era. We are a nation in love with money and toys. The modern temples and altars where we worship are our shopping malls and TV game shows. We bow down to the gods of pleasure, materialism, and money.

The following verse describes the world's social system in the last days. Doesn't this sound like the common lifestyle of today's America?

- *But understand this, <u>that in the last days</u> there will come times of difficulty. For people will be lovers of self, lovers of money, proud, arrogant, abusive, disobedient to their parents, ungrateful, unholy, heartless, unappeasable, slanderous, without self-control, brutal, not loving good, treacherous, reckless, swollen with conceit, lovers of pleasure rather than lovers of God, having the appearance of godliness, but denying its power. Avoid such people. (2 Timothy 3:1-5)*

Is modern America, together with those great historical empires, represented by Mystery Babylon who rides and steers the beast? Probably! At any rate, there can be no doubt that our country loves to fornicate with the lady who rides the beast. And we must be aware that if the rise of the Antichrist is coming within our generation, then obviously America will be the last of the nations represented by this harlot woman. If so, she will soon burn in a single day. That does not mean that the entire population of America will be destroyed, but our nation will no longer exist as a worldwide power. This will be a time of tremendous destruction and grief among Americans, which will open many hearts to the gospel message proclaimed by those warriors in the Army of God.

COME OUT OF HER, MY PEOPLE

The call to come out of Babylon is first heard in the prophecy of Isaiah, and it is heard seven times in all, the last being in this chapter of Revelation.[240] This call implies that the way is open for people to depart from her. The Lord brought His people out of Egypt with a strong hand. This is different with respect to being delivered from Babylon; for here He simply opens the way, and only those who come out are considered His true people.[241] This call to come out of her doesn't mean that we are to physically leave our homes; unless, of course, He calls us to physically relocate. It is a call to depart from the idolatrous pleasures of the world and turn to serving in the army of our Lord Jesus Christ throughout our lifetime.

<u>Here are some examples of false teachings taught in these "Mystery Babylon" churches that we need to be aware of.</u>

- Compromising the truth of the Bible's inerrancy, claiming it is simply a book written by men that contains some truths but also false beliefs. <u>Come out now!</u>
- Teaches that "tolerance" is the ultimate expression of true love for others, that man is basically good, and that we must be tolerant of those who profess different beliefs in God. <u>Come out now!</u>

- Teaches that the God of Abraham, Isaac, and Jacob is the same God as Allah, whom the Muslims worship and that the gods of Buddhism and Hinduism are the same as the God of Christianity; they just have different names depending on one's culture. Come out now!
- Teaches that financial prosperity is available to each of us if we will only begin to tithe our limited resources to their individual ministries and that our personal pleasure and financial security is how we measure success in this life. Come out now!
- If you are among those who are more impressed with their blessings than with our Lord, who gave those blessings, if financial prosperity has priority in their lives, if their comforts have replaced the cross in their lives, and if entertainment has replaced evangelism in the workplace, then come out now!
- If one day you find yourself in a church that is mocking Christians who will not deny their faith in Jesus, you are in Mystery Babylon. Come out now!

These are some of the idolatrous doctrines of Mystery Babylon, and the true people of God must run from these lies that are intended to compromise our faith in God and bring about a great smile on the face of Satan.

There is a day coming when Christians will need to make a definite decision as to whom they will serve. Just as the prophet Elijah spoke to the Israelite on Mount Carmel:

- *How long will you go limping between two different opinions? If the Lord is God, follow him; but if Baal, then follow him.* **(1 Kings 18:21)**

The present-day application of this demand might be:

- One who demands the denying of self and another who allows the gratifying of self cannot both be right.
- One who insists on separation from the world and another who permits you to enjoy its friendship cannot both be right.
- One who came to bring division among the people and another who came to unite the world cannot both be right.
- If the Christ of Scripture is the true Savior, then surrender to Him. But if the false Christ being commonly preached in many pulpits is your savior, then go ahead and follow him.

God will not accept a divided heart; He will have all or none. He will permit no compromise.[242]

- *Then I heard another voice from heaven saying, "Come out of her, my people, lest you take part in her sins, lest you share in her plagues; **Revelation 18:4***

"ABOUT - FACE!"

Those with military experience are very familiar with the command "about-face" which is a command to immediately turn sharply 180 degrees from the direction you are currently facing.

- It is also a command used by our Commander-in-Chief who calls us to "turn" from our sins; then He will remove the veil which is blinding us from the truth and put us on the path of growing in spiritual maturity.
- This willingness to turn in an **"about-face"** will suddenly cause us to see ourselves as we truly are and thus, our need for a Savior.
- All of God's champions will occasionally go astray and veer from the course that the Lord directs. However, like Moses, David, or Paul, they all have one thing in common; when confronted with their blindness, they will readily turn in an "about-face" and return to following their Commander.

What will Christians do when our Commander-in-Chief commands us to "about-face"?

- Will they obey Him or listen to other subordinate commanders, such as some church leaders who tell us that the Commander-in-Chief really meant **"right-face"** since it is much easier to follow that path.
- But a partial turn will eventually lead us away from the path that Jesus is going and even though other leaders tell us that we are moving rightly, we are straying further and further from His direction.
- Some other false commanders may convince us that the command was really **"at-ease"**; just keep coming and giving to the church and God will be pleased.

Eventually the time comes when the Commander-in-Chief gives the command **"forward march"**; only those who heard and obeyed the command **"about-face"** will be equipped

To follow the King of kings and the Lord of lords in the direction that He is heading. [243]

Calling Christian Warriors to "About Face" Now!

CHAPTER 12

THE LAST HARVEST FOLLOWED BY DESTRUCTION

(<u>First Read</u>: Revelation 14—15; 16:1-9)

DARK STORIES ARE ALWAYS FOLLOWED BY THE LIGHT

The entire book of Revelation is the prophetic unveiling of the great war between the kingdom of God and the kingdom of the World for possession of the entire earth. Over and over, readers are presented with several important contrasts between the kingdoms of light and darkness. For example, in chapter 12 we are presented with contrasts between Jesus Christ and Satan, between the woman and the dragon, and between the church in the wilderness and the world in the cities. Throughout the book of Revelation, a story on the dark side is always followed by a story of light. Here are some additional examples.

- Chapter 6 reveals the opening of the sixth seal, releasing a dark and terrible scenario in which all of heaven and earth are shaken and climaxing with the question, "Who can stand?" Then in chapter 7, we see the Lord answering this question by commanding the sealing of 144,000 who will be protected in the midst of great tribulation for the purpose of ministering to the peoples who are confused, scared, and suffering.

- This is followed by the trumpet series, resulting in the destruction of one-third of the natural earth as well as the death of one-third of mankind. Just when one would think that the time of the end is here, we see a mighty Angel come down to earth, indicating that these events that have occurred in the world are under the control of almighty God. He has a purpose for His people during this period of great tribulation that requires our preparedness, for destructive times are about to intensify on the earth.

- Next we see the Antichrist reigning with all power and authority throughout the civilized world. Almost everybody worships this "beast," believing that he is their great hope in life. The people of God are outlaws in his kingdom and are not allowed to buy clothes to wear or food to eat. It is a picture of Satan and Antichrist at the peak of their power, together with a picture of great tribulation for the uncompromising believers in Jesus as the Son of God. Just when this war between the two kingdoms appears to be lost, we see in chapter 14 the great power that opposes this worldly kingdom and its king. We see that glorious spiritual power that will bring salvation and eternal joy to those who stand for the kingdom of God and the great King in the midst of the darkness of the world, a mighty King who will soon destroy this dark worldly kingdom that seems so indestructible.

"BLESSINGS AND WARNINGS" SUMMARIZED IN SEVEN MAJOR EVENTS

Between the devastations of the seven trumpets and the seven bowls of wrath yet to be poured out on the earth, there appears to be another series of "sevens." Chapter 14 presents the reader with a group of seven victorious visions that briefly summarize the events during the final proclamation of the gospel of the kingdom of God throughout the earth. These blessings and warnings culminate with the downfall of the kingdom of this world.[244]

ONE: THE LAMB AND HIS 144,000 TOGETHER ON MOUNT ZION
(Revelation 14:1-5)

In the midst of great evil in the world, the Lamb of God stands on Mount Zion, together with His 144,000 disciples who are the ministers of His light throughout the period of dark tribulations in the latter days. Chapter 13 described the state of the world under the reign of Antichrist, which, from a natural and visible point of view, certainly would appear as if this unholy trinity is completely victorious in their mission to destroy the kingdom of God. However, in chapter 14 the true reality of these events is depicted from our Lord's perspective; for as our eyes are opened to the spiritual realm, we see the people of God safe and secure in the presence of their Lord just before the worldly kingdom of Antichrist is about to be destroyed.

The world demanded that all professing Christians commit spiritual adultery and worship the Antichrist or they would be expelled from the earth. And a great number of professing believers listened to the demands from the world and turned from the Lord.

- *Therefore God gave them up in the lusts of their hearts to impurity, to the dishonoring of their bodies among themselves, because they exchanged the truth about God for a lie and worshiped and served the creature rather than the Creator, who is blessed forever! Amen.* **(Romans 1:24-25)**

However, the 144,000 who are standing with the Lord on Mount Zion are the ones who maintain their spiritual virginity in the midst of great pressures and temptations. Their love for the Lamb of God who sacrificed His life for His people was of much greater value than their own lives. These are the warriors in the kingdom of God who continue to hear the voice of their Commander in Chief.

- *If anyone would come after me, let him deny himself and take up his cross and follow me. For whoever would save his life will lose it, but whoever loses his life for my sake and the gospel's will save it. <u>For what does it profit a man to gain the whole world and forfeit his life?</u> For what can a man give in return for his life? <u>For whoever is ashamed of me and of my words in this</u>*

adulterous and sinful generation, of him will the Son of Man also be ashamed when he comes in the glory of his Father with the holy angels. **(Mark 8:34-38)**

These are those who follow Christ in all of His ways while on earth. They are His disciples. Many will be sealed prior to the judgments, yet many more will enter the kingdom as they hear and believe the gospel message of the 144,000 and stand for Him in the midst of persecutions. Being "sealed" implies protection from the judgments of God that fall upon the earth so that they may proclaim the everlasting gospel during the great tribulation, right up to the end of their lives or until the coming of their Lord. This may or may not lead to martyrdom, but a significant number of those who enter the great tribulation certainly will experience martyrdom. Unlike pagan Christendom, which "exchanged the truth of God for a lie," they make no compromise with the heretical demands of the anti-Christian government. <u>Thus the great question for the people of God is not whether they will undergo great sufferings for the cause of Christ but whether they will remain faithful in the midst of tribulation.</u>

A truth that is not commonly taught in the contemporary church is that there is a distinction among the saints in eternal life. All will be "perfectly" blessed, but all do not reach the same state of glory. God has prepared some of His people to do great things; namely, to fight the kingdom of darkness as mighty warriors. They have been prepared to do more than others, and they will suffer more than others. These are the leaders in His army who, if they remain faithful to their calling, will have a leadership position in the eternal kingdom. Just as He prepared men like David, Elijah, Isaiah, and Paul for special works, and they also suffered more than many others of God's people, so shall it be during the coming period known as the great tribulation.[245] I believe these will include the 144,000 chosen warriors who will openly and boldly proclaim the gospel of Christ with great signs and wonders in the midst of the trumpet series and the first three and a half years of rulership by the Antichrist.

Consider this: Many may have been called to this leadership role, yet they did not forsake their lives and thus did not achieve their full calling. They certainly are among the saints of God, but they did not attain to the leadership role that God had prepared them for. Many of us wrestle with this calling while living in the midst of our blessed comforts. Those who have been called know it deep down inside, yet many are continually excusing their laziness by believing they will start tomorrow. However, tomorrow never seems to come. We need to fight these comforting temptations that impede our calling to make the Lord a priority in our lives. Every one of us faces these temptations toward apathy, as it is an ongoing attack from the enemy. Today we must continually resist and prepare, for the Day of the Lord is shortly before us. Warriors, we must continue to seek the individual destinies He is calling us to and preparing us for!

TWO: THE ANGEL AND THE EVERLASTING GOSPEL
(Revelation 14:6-7)

This section of Scripture does not mean that in the end times angels will proclaim the gospel of Jesus Christ in order to sound the final warning. That is an absurd conclusion some have made, believing that the church has been raptured and that angels are the only ones available to warn the people remaining on earth. The reality is that, like many of the visions in the book of Revelation, this is also symbolic. Here is a picture of a final great evangelistic work of God's people, proclaiming the gospel of the kingdom throughout the earth. It is a last call to repentance!

This angelic vision symbolizes the well-known truth that before the time of the end, the gospel message will be proclaimed to all peoples of different languages residing in every nation throughout the world. This is the mission of the 144,000 who have been anointed on Mount Zion and dispatched by their Commander in Chief into all the nations across the globe. Thus, these verses depict the final proclamation of the gospel to the world. Mankind shall be well acquainted with the gospel message of Jesus Christ before the final judgments fall on the earth. Those who scorn the message will be without excuse when they stand before the judgment seat of almighty God. Certainly many people will respond and be brought into everlasting life, but the great majority of the world will blaspheme this message and persecute those who proclaim it. Finally, this gospel message not only will be a calling to mankind to repent and give glory to God, but it also will contain the prophetic warning that final judgments are soon coming to the world. Therefore, this vision of a gospel-proclaiming angel is symbolic of a short season of vigorous and rapid evangelism across the earth. It is an evangelistic mission that will go out in a power never before seen in the world, the power of Jesus Christ manifested within His body of 144,000. The time is coming when Jesus words will be realized:

- *Truly, truly, I say to you, whoever believes in me will also do the works that I do; and greater works than these will he do, because I am going to the Father. Whatever you ask in my name, this I will do, that the Father may be glorified in the Son. If you ask me anything in my name, I will do it.* **(John 14:12-14)**

Just imagine being a true disciple of Jesus Christ during this time. The earth has experienced great chaos at this point. Some parts of the world have been completely decimated. From out of this chaos, Antichrist has setup his kingdom. Many who have formerly professed belief in Jesus Christ have fallen away and turned to follow the Antichrist. God and His truths are denied by the devoted citizens of this dark kingdom. The sacrifice of Christ is laughed at, and His shed blood has been continually trampled underfoot. Satan and his anointed earthly king shall be the objects of worldwide worship. On every street corner and in every store, you meet with the image of the Beast; his words and his pictures are everywhere, and the people must continually bow down before them or they certainly will be reported to and apprehended by militia forces assigned to seek out and arrest uncompromising Christians. Everywhere you meet with people bearing the visible sign of the Beast on their foreheads and/or their right hands. As one who has refused to take this mark of the Beast, you will not be able to buy nor sell; and you will be continually pushed to the wall. There appears to be no refuge from this darkness, and the suffering is awful. This is a world of tribulation and the blasphemy against God's name appears to go unnoticed from the heavenlies.[246]

Now what questions will be arising in the minds of many Christians? Why does God allow all of this? How long shall the glory of His name be trampled underfoot? How long shall the persecution of His people go unpunished? Doubt will begin to creep into even the most faithful of God's people. It is probable that many of His people will believe that they are the only faithful ones who remain, and they will cry out like Elijah of old, "It is enough O Lord, take away my life. For I've been jealous for my Lord and your people that have not forsaken your name. They have been killed and now I am the only one left." And the Lord responds, "Arise for you have a gospel to proclaim for there are yet (144,000) who have not bowed their knees to the Antichrist."[247]

This is a probable scene into which the final proclamation of the eternal gospel will come. It appears as if Christianity has all but disappeared from the earth. You may feel alone, but He will never leave your side.[248] In the world they will say, "Antichrist has made all things. Who is like unto the Beast, and who can war with him?" But over against this claim, the people of the Lord cry out, "Fear God and give Him glory, for the hour of His judgment has come, and worship Him who made heaven and earth." "For the hour of His judgment has come" clearly indicates that this final message precedes the sounding of the seventh trumpet, which launches the final series of bowls of wrath being poured out upon the earth, a time when the gospel message will no longer be heard.

THREE: THE FALL OF BABYLON
(Revelation 14:8)

This announcement of the judgment of almighty God upon this capital of world secularism is so important to mankind that great detail of her fall has been provided throughout the Scriptures. Since the Garden of Eden, Babylon has been the seat of the power of darkness that has opposed all the works of our Lord in order to draw the hearts of mankind away from Him. There is no greater wrong done to our Lord than to set the affections of our hearts upon other objects. Remember the greatest commandment that He has given to us:

- *You shall love the Lord your God with all your heart and with all your soul and with all your mind and with all your strength.* **(Mark 12:30)**

Babylon possesses that spirit of godlessness that continually lures the hearts of mankind away from their loving Creator. Her allurement is so powerful that she seduces hearts by the fascinating attractiveness of worldly delights, which build that great lie in individual lives that "It's all about me." The people of God have been persecuted continually by Babylonian governments, yet many more of God's people have been enamored and drawn away from the Lord by Babylon's alluring promises. Babylon is a kingdom that makes nations drunk by the wine of her fornication. Being drunk with wine is a depiction of a helpless and shameful condition brought about by excessive drinking. By drinking Babylon's "wine," the worshippers of the Beast shall receive the wrath of God as a burning fire within their souls. This is a spiritual torment that is everlasting, for never shall the worshippers of the Beast receive even one glimpse of God's love. Here upon the earth they receive the things of the world, and God allows His light to shine upon both the wicked and the good alike, but eternal agony awaits all those who choose to follow Satan and the Antichrist. These are Babylonian patriots who loved the excesses offered by the world.

The Lord's call to come out of Babylon appears to be directed to those who have professed faith in Christ—yet continue to revel in the midst of the attractions of the world. Among these are also those religious-minded folks and their feel-good, but false gospel, which claims that there are many ways to eternal life and that a God of love would never relegate anybody to eternal destruction. This gives many great comforts and a green light to continue to drink to excess on the beautiful materialism of Babylon. This is the final warning to come out from her for she is about to be destroyed. Come out now!

FOUR: WARNING AGAINST WORSHIPPING THE BEAST
(Revelation 14:9-11)

Among the strongest of emotions that will bind many in allegiance to the Antichrist is "patriotism." This is a blind and fanatical love for some earthly kingdom. It has been a strong bond in countries such as America and also in Nazi Germany, countries in which allegiance was not forced but taught from their youth. The image of the Beast will be worshipped much like Americans pledge allegiance to the flag.

The fearful punishment that awaits those who worship the beast is twofold.

- They will drink the wine of the wrath of God.
- They shall suffer the fiery punishment of hell.

The first judgment falls upon them while yet alive in this world and will be experienced when the seven bowls are poured out throughout the earth. The second occurs in the world to come. It is a warning that there is a much worse fate for taking the mark, for **the punishment of those who accept the "mark of the Beast" is eternal.**

Our Lord, in His merciful and long-suffering love for mankind, patiently warns people concerning the consequences of rendering allegiance to Antichrist. <u>This warning is not a threat but is the last call from our Lord to leave Babylon and embrace His eternal love.</u>

FIVE: BLESSED ARE THOSE WHO DIE IN THE LORD FROM NOW ON
(Revelation 14:12-13)

"Here is a call for endurance of the saints" is evidently a warning that is expressed in the strongest of terms. Every deceptive and cruel power with which Satan will anoint his Antichrist will be brought into play during this last stage of human affairs in order to draw away the affections of mankind from the Lord and unto the Beast. Remember the instruction given to His people in the midst of the world of Antichrist:

- *If anyone is to be taken captive, to captivity he goes; if anyone is to be slain with the sword, with the sword must he be slain. <u>Here is a call for the endurance and faith of the saints</u>.* **(Revelation 13:10)**

<u>This call for endurance tells us that in the midst of persecution and suffering that God's people are to remain calm and submissive. They do not try to gain control of things by force.</u> Even though they cannot buy or sell, they do not use weapons to obtain what they want. Their suffering will not persuade them to deny their God. Even though the smallest of compromise might gain them favor and keep them out of prison and feed them, they will refuse to compromise. How will they bear this suffering? They know their captors will not escape from eternal destruction and that they themselves will receive an eternal crown of glory for their steadfast righteousness. They trust and embrace these words from the Lord:

- *And I heard a voice from heaven saying, "Write this: Blessed are the dead who die in the Lord from now on." "Blessed indeed," says the Spirit, "that they may rest from their labors, for their deeds follow them!"* **(Revelation 14:13)**

Now not all are equally strong among the people of God. Not all are equally fit to testify and bear the brunt of the battle. It is not because they themselves are less faithful or that those who are stronger are so as a result of any power of their own. They have been prepared for a different mission. Yet the works of all who do not compromise their faith in the Lord will follow them, and all will be eternally rewarded. This does not mean that all attain to the same state of glory. There is a distinction. All those whom God prepared to do more work than others and to suffer more than others may thank the Lord for this great privilege, for their works shall also follow them into the new creation.[249]

177

The Word is clear; faithfulness to Christ may result in martyrdom, but those who persevere are the true victors in the battle between the two kingdoms. This stands in sharp contrast to those professing Christian apostates who will deny their faith and to the pagans, who have never accepted it.

SIX: THE HARVEST OF THE EARTH
(Revelation 14:14-16)

This section of the vision appears to be the fulfillment of Jesus' parable concerning the weeds in the field that were allowed to grow in the midst of the good seeds.[250] The "field" is representative of the world, while the "good seeds" are the people of God's kingdom in the midst of the world. The "weeds" are the people of Satan, who has sown them in the midst of the good seeds. Now the time has come when they will be separated by angelic reapers, who will gather the weeds together to be burned with fire.[251]

Jesus Christ, the Commander in Chief, is the one who supervises the reaping. The actual reapers are the angels. This is the fulfillment of Jesus' words:

- *And he will send out his angels with a loud trumpet call, and they will gather his elect from the four winds, from one end of heaven to the other.* (**Matthew 24:31**)

The harvest definitely will be gathered but not until it is fully ripe, and only almighty God knows this hour. Here we see an angel who comes out from before the presence of the Father and announces to the Son of God that the reaping is to begin. This means that everyone who will come into the eternal kingdom of God has now come in.

Some believe that the gathering of the wheat may well be the removal of God's people from the earth prior to the wrath of God, which brings the reign of the Antichrist to an end. Yet there will be a remnant of His saints who are alive at His coming.[252] However, it is probable that His people who are alive at this time will be separated from those places where God's wrath will fall. Underline For example:

- Noah was separated into an ark prior to the flood.
- Israel was separated and protected when plagues fell upon Egypt.
- Lot was moved prior to the destruction of Sodom and Gomorrah.

Jesus also spoke of this time when He said,

- *Then two men will be in the field; one will be taken and one left. Two women will be grinding at the mill; one will be taken and one left. Therefore, stay awake, for you do not know on what day your Lord is coming.* (**Matthew 24:40-42**)

When the remnant people of God have been separated to places of safety, the destruction of the wicked, symbolized by the harvest of the grapes, may proceed. Thus, it appears that there will be a short period of time during which there are no more Christians living in the midst of the world, for they have been set apart until they behold the coming of the King of Kings. At this point in time, the preaching of the gospel message for the present age will have been completed.

SEVEN: GOD'S WRATH FALLING UPON THE WORLD OF EVIL
(Revelation 14:17-20)

Here we see an angel coming out from the presence of the altar that lies before the throne of God. Underneath this altar is where the martyrs of Christ have been calling out for vengeance against the enemies of the Lord. But the Lord had told them to wait until the number of all their fellow servants who were yet to be martyred was complete. History must first run its course.

- The gospel must first be preached to all nations to allow all of mankind the opportunity to repent and turn to the Lord.
- The kingdom of the Antichrist must be fully manifested so there is no gray area between good and evil.
- The wickedness of the earth must be full, and the remnant of the Lord separated from the worshippers of the Beast.

When that time arrives, the vengeance of almighty God will fall upon all the dark nations of the earth. It will begin with the pouring out of the first five bowls of wrath, resulting in tremendous devastation and suffering throughout the earth. This suffering will not bring repentance, but it will visibly reveal the evil hearts of mankind as they continue to blaspheme the Lord. With the sixth bowl, we witness a gathering together of all the kings of the earth and their dark armies at Armageddon. Unknown to them, this is really the winepress of God's wrath, which will be manifested with the pouring out of the seventh bowl. Here the governing forces of this dark world will be trodden down in God's winepress, resulting in the squashing of millions and millions of those who embraced the Antichrist as their messiah. These are the great and mighty kings of the world who have gathered together with all of their loyal followers for the purpose of wiping out all of the Lord's beloved people from the face of the earth once and for all. The smashing of these kings and their armies will be so great that their blood will run four feet deep over a course of approximately184 miles. The following chapter provides a descriptive scenario of this last great battle.

These seven bowls, called the "wrath of God," are His holiness falling upon the world of sin. The divine work of His kingdom people made great and wonderful changes within this world throughout history, but they could not overcome the darkness, which continued to grow stronger and stronger. Now God the Father and His Son will release their holiness from heaven against this darkness and utterly destroy this world of sin. First, comes great worldwide destruction, but it will soon be followed by a great cleansing that will restore the earth to the days of the Garden of Eden.

HEAVEN CELEBRATES WHILE THE WORLD BLASPHEMES
(Revelation 15)

From the perspective of the saints and angels of God residing in heaven, a "great and amazing" event is about to occur. A few years earlier the sounding of the trumpet judgments resulted in great devastation around the world, yet the kingdom of God continued to be proclaimed in the midst of these chaotic events by His mighty warriors known as the 144,000. This resulted in the awakening of great multitudes of people among all the nations who repented and entered into the gates of the kingdom. Now it is time for the wrath of God to be poured out upon those who refused His word and instead continued to render allegiance to their chosen messiah, the Antichrist, the anointed son of Satan. At God's chosen time, these legions of darkness will be allowed to silence the gospel of Jesus Christ, and the 144,000 will join their martyred brothers and sisters under the altar in heaven. This is a time when the number of all those who are to be martyred for Christ is complete. This then launches the final outpouring of the wrath of almighty God over the kingdom of the World, whose citizens have always despised the Lord and His people. Now their tremendous hatred of the Lord will be manifested in shouted blasphemies in the midst of their sufferings.

The victorious army of those martyred for their testimony stands together in heaven on a sea of glass mingled with fire. During their lifetime on earth, they passed through fiery trials from the enemy until the time came for their martyrdom. Now they stand in victory amidst the fires of heaven, which, like Nebuchadnezzar's fiery furnace, will not harm the children of God but will totally destroy His enemies.[253] Among this victorious army are those who refused to worship the Antichrist even though they could neither buy nor sell nor live in the midst of that society without offering such worship. They were outcasts—many imprisoned and tortured, many betrayed by friends and loved ones, many terribly executed for their faith. They were tested to the extreme, yet they continued to call upon the Lord for their strength. They fought the fiercest of all battles, but they were continuously sustained by their faith in the Lord Jesus, whom they knew would one day come as the victorious King of Kings. Now they stood upon the sea of glass mingled with fire, singing the song of great victory before the throne of God. Yes, this is a time of special privilege for the Army of God, who fought the greatest and most challenging of all battles. They stood up against Satan and his king, the Antichrist, in the midst of the greatest tribulation this world had ever known.

I recently listened to series a of CDs concerning end-time events from a nationally popular pastor who provided some fine insights. Yet, he is a believing rapturist, and when he talked about the 144,000 that will be God's worldwide evangelists, he was adamant when he told his audience, "You do not want to be among the 144,000; you do not want to be among the 144,000." What was his reasoning? They will go through fiery tribulations, and you need to be among those who simply "fly away" to heaven. Ugh! This was a very gifted speaker, but when it comes to warfare he is obviously a pacifist. Hopefully, when the tribulation hits this country, he will be able to overcome his disappointment and minister in the midst of warfare without fear for his own life.

Warriors for Christ, consider the following: Are not soldiers of war the recipients of greater honors when they fight in the thickest of the battle? Should not a soldier of the kingdom of Christ receive great honors for being in the thickest of the fight against the powerful armies of the Antichrist and showing he fears nothing, even though he is hated by all men? To belong to the chosen forces of Christ in the world at the time of Antichrist shall be the greatest honor conceivable. Undoubtedly there will be a special place of privilege in both the new heaven and the new earth for such ones.

- *Blessed are you when others revile you and persecute you and utter all kinds of evil against you falsely on my account. Rejoice and be glad, for your reward is great in heaven, for so they persecuted the prophets who were before you.* **(Matthew 5:11-12)**

But is this multitude limited only to those warriors who fought during the great tribulation? Certainly not! The spirit of the Antichrist has been in the world fighting against the armies of God in all historical dispensations. God's mighty warriors have fought this same battle throughout all the ages, even though it rages most severely during this era of the end-times, anti-Christian kingdom. Abraham fought this battle. Moses fought this battle. David fought this battle. All the witnesses and prophets of the Old Testament era fought this same battle. All the witnesses and martyrs of the New Testament era also fought this same battle. But the battle becomes most severe at the time of the final reign of the Antichrist. Therefore, it is certainly true that all who have remained faithful, from Abel to the very last witness in the kingdom of God on earth, shall stand by the fiery sea of glass singing their song of Moses and of the Lamb. The combining of these two songs embraces both the Old Testament and New Testament eras as one kingdom. Old and new dispensations shall be one; there is no break, no difference between them in glory.

This scene of mighty warriors who have conquered the Beast and its image should remind us of the children of Israel standing on the edge of the Red Sea, looking back over those waters that had just consumed their Egyptian enemies. The greatest and most powerful army in the world of that age had just been completely annihilated because they were attempting to slaughter a nation that God had raised up to manifest His glory throughout the world. At this point Moses and the Israelite people began to sing the "song of Moses" to the Lord, glorifying Him and giving thanks for this miraculous deliverance from their enemies.[254] The heavenly "sea of glass" is a reminder of the Red Sea, which delivered the Israelites and destroyed their enemies. It is also a reminder of the great flood, which delivered Noah and his family and destroyed the enemies of God. These were waters whereby the Lord provided salvation for His people and destruction of their enemies. Fires and waters both save and destroy, depending on which side of the battlefield one has chosen to fight. What a glorious prelude to the destruction that is about to rain down upon the kingdom of Satan and his followers. The physical earth, which also has been worshipped over the centuries, is now about to experience tremendous destruction, along with the inhabitants of this end-times generation.[255]

Warriors for Christ, we too may learn to sing this song of Moses and the Lamb while still in this world. We are in the midst of the battle, which will grow fiercer and fiercer, yet we can continue to sing this song, remembering that one day we will be standing with all our brothers and sisters in Christ alongside this fiery sea of glass, singing and watching the destruction of all wickedness in the kingdom of the world.

THE FINAL JUDGMENTS OF OUR LORD BEGIN
(Revelation 16:1-9)

This final series of plagues that will be poured out upon all of mankind parallels the trumpet judgments that previously tormented the inhabitants of the earth. However, unlike the trumpet judgments, which affected only one-third of the earth and still allowed an opportunity for millions to awaken and embrace the Lord through the testimony of the witnesses of Jesus Christ; these seven bowl judgments will devastate the world at a time when the testimony of Christ has been silenced. This is the time of the final battle in a war that has raged since the fall of mankind in Eden.

It is the time the martyrs under the altar in the heavenly temple are waiting for.

- *They cried out with a loud voice, "O Sovereign Lord, holy and true, how long before you will judge and avenge our blood on those who dwell on the earth?"* **(Revelation 6:10)**

It is the time our sovereign Lord fulfills the promise He made to them.

- *Rest a little longer until the number of their fellow servants and their brothers should be complete, who were to be killed as they themselves had been.* **(Revelation 6:11)**

It is the time for the righteous judgment of God to be poured out across the earth.

- *Since indeed God considers it just to repay with affliction those who afflict you,* (2 *Thessalonians 1:6*)
- *How much worse punishment, do you think, will be deserved by the one who has spurned the Son of God, and has profaned the blood of the covenant by which he was sanctified, and has outraged the Spirit of grace? For we know him who said, "Vengeance is mine; I will repay." And again, "The Lord will judge his people." It is a fearful thing to fall into the hands of the living God.* (*Hebrews 10:29-31*)

First Bowl of God's Wrath Poured Out—On the Earth

Harmful and painful sores will break out upon everybody who bears the "mark of the Beast." This will be very nasty as Job, a servant of God, can testify. Recall that Satan attacked Job, the beloved of God, with boils all over his body.[256] Now Satan's worshippers are suffering a similar fate but without any hope of being healed. Perhaps these sores will be seen as a worldwide plague. Certainly these suffering people will be crying out to their god, the Antichrist, for miraculous healing.

- But, it won't happen!

Second Bowl of God's Wrath Poured Out—On the Seas

All the oceans around the world will become like the "blood of a corpse." Obviously, all sea life will die. Now there can be no question in the minds of all the inhabitants of the earth that this is more than just a passing plague. God is raining judgment down upon the earth. Again, they will turn to their Antichrist and call upon him to heal the seas with his miraculous power.

- But, it won't happen!

Third Bowl of God's Wrath Poured Out—On Rivers and Springs

All the fresh waters, from streams, lakes, and rivers across the earth, will turn into blood. All the promised comforts and necessities of life are being taken away. Listen to the response from God's angel, who is placed in charge of the waters on the earth.

- *They have shed the blood of saints and prophets, and you have given them blood to drink. It is what they deserve!* (*Revelation 16:6*)

These bowls of wrath poured out upon the earth are not all about vengeance. They are an expression of His righteous nature and His intense hatred of sin. Listen to the response to these judgments from out of the altar, where the souls of the martyrs reside and also where the prayers of the saints rise up before the throne of our almighty God.

- *And I heard the altar saying, "Yes, Lord God the Almighty, true and just are your judgments!"* **(Revelation 16:7)**

Contrary to this viewpoint within the kingdom of God, imagine the fear and confusion in the kingdom of the world as suffering and frightened people cry out, "Antichrist, our god, where are you? Remember your promises. Don't you care? Please, help us."

- But, it won't happen!

Fourth Bowl of God's Wrath Poured Out—On the Sun

Here the wrath of God is poured out upon the sun, resulting in tremendous scorching heat falling upon a populace that is covered with painful boils and having only bloody waters to drink. Yet, even in their unimaginable suffering, they will continue to curse almighty God and look to their Antichrist for their deliverance from God's wrath. "O, our beloved Antichrist, please stop this. We've suffered enough. Remember your promises to take care of us."

- But, it won't happen!

CHAPTER 13

THE RETURN OF THE KING

(First Read: Revelation 16:10-21; 19:11-21)

AN OVERVIEW OF THE FIRST FOUR BOWLS OF WRATH

At the time of the outpouring of these bowls of wrath, Antichrist has established a universal kingdom, uniting all the nations of the world under his authority. From a worldly point of view, the kingdom of Antichrist will be the perfect kingdom that "patriotic sinners" have always dreamed about. The nations will have pledged allegiance to Antichrist and his global agenda, and the people will be overjoyed at having silenced the gospel testimony of Jesus Christ and His followers. Now they can live life any way they want, as long as they continue to worship the image of the Beast. Sorcery, idolatry, pornography, adultery, homosexuality, abortion rights, child sacrifice, same-sex marriage, and pedophile acts, will all be acceptable and commonplace. Everything that despises and opposes the commandments of our Lord will be embraced. Antichrist is their messiah and also their eternal hope. Yes, all the civilized nations of the world will enthrone the Antichrist as their hope for eternal security and happiness. They will admire him, worship him, and bow down and acknowledge him as the greatest of all kings. He will have control over the entire civilized world, and his followers will love, trust, and embrace him as their god. The small, surviving remnants throughout the earth that refuse to obey him will become social outcasts and probably forced into hiding while being provided for by the Lord.[257] Many of these will be end-time prayer warriors who are obediently calling for the return of the King.

It is at this point in time that almighty God will come to demonstrate His omnipotent sovereignty. Our Lord now decrees that through these bowl judgments all those who worship the Beast will not be able to buy or sell, for He is taking it all away from them. The crops, the rain, the food, the water, the medicines, the wealth of the earth—it all disappears. Just as Antichrist had done to God's people, so now God does to the people of Antichrist. As the first four bowls of wrath are poured out, the world will continue their hateful blasphemies of God and put their faith for deliverance in their Antichrist. Now it is time to demonstrate the impotence of Antichrist before the world.

FIFTH BOWL OF GOD'S WRATH POURED OUT—ON THE THRONE OF THE BEAST

When the fifth bowl is poured out, a great darkness descends over the Antichrist's throne and spreads throughout his entire kingdom. All of his followers begin to gnaw their

185

tongues in tremendous pain. It is difficult to imagine the effect of this supernatural darkness; but it will certainly intensify the distress of the previous four plagues. Following on the heels of a "scorching sun," this darkness will probably cause a tremendous freezing across his kingdom. Yet, even in the extreme distress that has been launched upon the world of mankind, his people will continue to blaspheme almighty God. Their anger demonstrates that they certainly do not doubt the existence of God, but their hard and rebellious hearts hate Him more and more as bowls of wrath continue to fall upon the earth.

These unstoppable plagues undoubtedly will diminish the glory of the Antichrist; and his supernatural power and authority certainly will begin to be questioned. Up to this point, his people have dedicated both their earthly and eternal lives into his care; but now they will begin to doubt his divinity. These are the same people who had previously declared,

- *Who is like the beast, and who can fight against it?* (*Revelation 13:4*)

Jesus Christ, our true Commander in Chief says, "I can!"

SIXTH BOWL OF GOD'S WRATH
POURED OUT—ON THE EUPHRATES RIVER

During this period of painful darkness, which obliterates the glory of Antichrist in the world, the intensity of hatred toward almighty God will reach a boiling point unlike any period in the history of the world. Many Christians have been taught to believe that the Lord will gradually gain complete victory over the kingdom of the world without a great upheaval. However, the end of this age shall not be a time of peace but of a tremendously bloody war in which armies from all the nations of the earth will gather together with the mission of completely destroying the nation of Israel from the face of the earth. The land of Israel, where the kingdom of God was physically established four thousand years ago, has been chosen to be the location of the final battle between the kingdom of God and the dark armies of Satan's kingdom. That time has now arrived, and our Lord is challenging all of His enemies from around the world to gather together at a location in northern Israel known in the bible as Armageddon.

The sixth bowl poured out upon the earth releases the demonic forces that will allow a gathering of these armies, which are motivated by their tremendous hatred of the Lord. The first event to take place is the drying up of the Euphrates River. After looking at the devastating consequences of the first five bowls, one may wonder what is so significant about the drying up of this river. After all, the Euphrates River, though it is very wide and deep and now flowing with bloody waters for nearly two thousand miles, should not be a major hindrance to modern armies' intent on attacking the nation of Israel. However, the Euphrates has been very significant throughout the history of the Middle Eastern countries. This river always has been the eastern boundary line between Israel and the heathen nations. From a spiritual sense, it is symbolic of the boundary line between God's people and their enemies.[258] The drying up of this river appears to symbolize an invitation from the Lord, calling all the heathen armies to a battlefield located in the land where He has historically manifested His power and glory to His people and their enemies.

The second event that arouses the armies around the world to align together against the kingdom of God are the unclean spirits that proceed out of the mouths of the unholy trinity; that is, Satan, Antichrist, and the False Prophet. This is a powerful spiritual event that will infect millions and millions of kings, religious leaders, generals, and their armed soldiers worldwide with a demonic spirit that will replace any semblance of morality with a deep hatred for, and desire to rape and murder, all those who live in the nation of Israel. The "kings from the east" appear to be representative of the pagan nations of the Eastern world that have never played a major role in the history of civilization. They are the nations with the greatest populations: China, Japan, India, Indonesia, Pakistan, and others. Yet, the majority of these peoples are poor, uneducated, and blindly follow the religious leaders and their wealthy, but corrupt governments. They are worshippers of the gods of Buddhism, Hinduism, and Islam, who have persecuted the Christians in the midst of their countries for centuries. Their armies will surely include millions of foot soldiers who will march across the dried-up riverbed of the Euphrates. They will organize and unite with the forces of Antichrist from the Western and Middle Eastern countries on the plains of Megiddo, commonly referred to as Armageddon.

Armageddon is a Hebrew word that refers to a place known as Mount Megiddo, which overlooks a great valley located about fifty-five miles north of Jerusalem. The Megiddo valley, which also may be viewed from Mount Carmel, is a magnificent sight that captures the imagination of all who visit there. As one stands alongside this great plain, it is easy to envision a gathering of millions of enemy soldiers readying for a great battle against the city of Jerusalem. Now Armageddon is merely the gathering place for the world's armies, not the site of the last great battle. It is the place where they will organize and develop their strategies for the destruction of all of Israel, beginning with the city of Jerusalem. The real battle will take place in the Valley of Jehoshaphat, otherwise known as the Kidron Valley, which lies between Jerusalem and the Mount of Olives.[259]

In the midst of this demonic gathering, our Commander in Chief again alerts His people residing in Israel to remain vigilant and not be fearful or deceived by this tremendous darkness that appears to be unstoppable in its mission to finally annihilate the kingdom of God.

• *Behold, I am coming like a thief! Blessed is the one who stays awake, keeping his garments on, that he may not go about naked and be seen exposed!* (**Revelation 16:15**)

SATAN'S FINAL MISSION STRATEGIES—AN OVERVIEW

Satan knows that his time is short, as he too recognizes the signs that precede the return of Jesus Christ and His mighty army. He knows that he needs to prevent this return of Christ, or He must overwhelm and defeat Him with an earthly and demonic army prepared to engage Him when He sets foot on the Mount of Olives. This is no secret; Satan understands what is shortly ahead, and he needs to defeat the purposes of God and His Son in order to set his throne above that of God and to avoid his eternal destruction.[260]

The historic tactic used to accomplish Satan's purposes has always been *deception*. He has deceived mankind into believing that the tremendous potential that resides within each of us can be more fully realized by living life under our own guidance rather than under God's. Thus, he convinces the majority of mankind that they have no need for God and that they can be their own gods, doing whatever is pleasing to them, even if it is harmful to others. However, in order to truly experience the abundant life, they must remove all those who are not deceived and are totally committed to almighty God and to His Son, Jesus Christ. Satan does this by convincing world governments, together with false religions, that God's people are the only obstacle that keeps them from achieving their worldly goals, and so they must be either converted to the world's belief system or killed. If he could prevent all of mankind from reflecting God's glory upon the earth, then Satan himself would be the recipient of worship and glory throughout the earth. Thus, he could claim that he is now in control of all those initially created in the "image of God," for they have been reborn into the "image of Satan."

However, the time for these tactics of deception has passed. It is now time for a frontal assault on the beloved land of Israel and its inhabitants who have refused to render allegiance to the Antichrist. This was the "Promised Land" created by our Lord to manifest His glory throughout the world, and now it has been chosen to be the final battlefield between the spiritual forces of God and Satan, as well as the physical armies of Jesus Christ and the Antichrist. The powers of good and evil are about to meet head on, and the victor will receive eternal rule over the earth and be glorified in the heavenlies.

FROM ARMAGEDDON TO JERUSALEM

Now comes the launching of the final great battle of this age between the evil kingdom of the world and the holy kingdom of God, a confrontation that has been building for six thousand years. Very little detail depicting this final battle is provided in Revelation;

however, some of the Old Testament prophets, especially Zechariah and Joel, provide additional insights that assist in picturing this end-time event. <u>Let's begin</u>:

Satan gathers together his legions of "human-orcs" for the mission of bringing final defeat to the purposes of the Lord for mankind, which will allow him to grab the reins of control over the entire world. These massive armies are representative of the hatred that has expressed itself throughout human history in hostility toward, and persecution of, the people of God. Those who have seen the movie trilogy *The Lord of the Rings* certainly recognize the deep evil that is manifested in the terrible appearance of the "orcs," which comprise the army of a dark lord. They have a visible murderous and gnawing hatred for those who oppose the reign of their lord over the entire earth. They growl, slobber, and gnaw their teeth while awaiting orders to launch a murderous attack on their enemies. The term "human-orcs" is meant to convey a picture of the inner hearts of these end-times forces that will run to the war when called forth by the demons of Satan, Antichrist, and the False Prophet. This unholy trinity obviously believes that they are the ones initiating this final war against the kingdom of God. However, it is really our Lord who, in His timing, has planned this gathering together of His enemies from out of every tribe and nation.

- *I will gather all the nations and bring them down to the Valley of Jehoshaphat. And I will enter into judgment with them there, on behalf of my people and my heritage Israel, because they have scattered them among the nations and have divided up my land, and have cast lots for my people, and have traded a boy for a prostitute, and have sold a girl for wine and have drunk it.* **(Joel 3:2-3)**

<u>The time has now come:</u>

- To bring about both an external and spiritual cleansing to the land of Israel by purging the nation of its secular idolatry and manifesting the power and the glory of almighty God unto all the nations of the world.
- To remove the powers of darkness from within the nations across the earth and bring them into the valley of God's judgment, where they will be violently destroyed. Those people who remain in all the nations will then have the opportunity to receive and worship the Lord during the coming millennial reign of Jesus Christ.[261]
- To manifest the power and glory of the Son of God as the Lion of Judah, when He comes to bring sudden and total destruction to the enemies of His people and to establish His reign over the nations of the earth.

Now when these massive armies composed of soldiers from around the entire world have organized and coordinated their plans for conquering the land and eliminating the Israelites from the face of the earth, they will begin their march toward Jerusalem, destroying all the peoples and ravaging the land that lies before them. Envision the innumerable Army of Orcs in the *Lord of the Rings*.

- *Fire devours before them, and behind them a flame burns. The land is like the Garden of Eden before them, but behind them a desolate wilderness, and nothing escapes them.* **(Joel 2:3)**

As this murderous Orc army arrives in Jerusalem, they will ravage and rape.

- *For I will gather all the nations against Jerusalem to battle, and the city shall be taken and the houses plundered and the women raped. Half of the city shall go out into exile, but the rest of the people shall not be cut off from the city.* **(Zechariah 14:2)**

Now many believe that this prophetic verse is addressing the violent war that ravaged Jerusalem in 70AD by the Roman army. It is certainly true that this verse is descriptive of those judgments that fell upon the city that crucified our Lord some 40 years earlier. However, these passages in Zechariah are also referring to last-day events that precede the 2nd coming of our Lord. The prophecies found in Zechariah chapters 9 through 14 all focus on the restoration of Israel with Judah as well as the coming day of the Lord.

THE WARRIOR REMNANT OF ISRAEL

Now, the Israel Defense Forces, as well as many of the Israelites who have refused to pledge allegiance to the Antichrist, have no intent to surrender to this evil army, even though they may be outnumbered by as many as 1,000 to 1. Perhaps they have not yet recognized Jesus as their Messiah, but, to their credit many among them have steadfastly refused to take the "mark of the Beast" and to "worship his image."

However, this tremendously large and murderous enemy will still inflict much pain and death in the city of Jerusalem, for two-thirds of the inhabitants of Israel will be killed.

- *In the whole land, declares the Lord, two thirds shall be cut off and perish, and one third shall be left alive.* **(Zechariah 13:8)**

These will be the secular lovers of the Babylonian lifestyle, together with the Pharisaic-type of religious leaders who have voluntarily received the "mark of the beast."

- *All the sinners of my people shall die by the sword, who say, "Disaster shall not overtake or meet us."* **(Amos 9:10)**

However, for the heroic one-third remnant of God's chosen people who battle against these forces of evil, the hand of the Lord will be strong upon them.

- *And I will put this third into the fire, and refine them as one refines silver, and test them as gold is tested. They will call upon my name, and I will answer them. I will say, "They are my people"; And they will say, "The Lord is my God." (Zechariah 13:9)*

These are certainly the ones the Lord will protect and anoint them with the "strength of David" in the midst of the battle.

- *And the Lord will give salvation to the tents of Judah first, that the glory of the house of David and the glory of the inhabitants of Jerusalem may not surpass that of Judah. On that day the Lord will protect the inhabitants of Jerusalem, so that the feeblest among them on that day shall be like David, and the house of David shall be like God, like the angel of the Lord, going before them. And on that day I will seek to destroy all the nations that come against Jerusalem. (Zechariah 12:7-9)*

The Old Testament prophets clearly reveal the contrast between the Israelite peoples who truly belong to Him and those pretenders who do not. The following passages may help clarify who the *two-thirds are who are killed in this final battle* and the *one-third who survive* and eventually escape from the enemy through the Valley of the Lord.

- *Therefore thus says the Lord God: "Behold, **my servants shall eat**, but you shall be hungry; behold, **my servants shall drink**, but you shall be thirsty; behold, **my servants shall rejoice**, but you shall be put to shame; behold, **my servants shall sing for gladness of heart**, but you shall cry out for pain of heart and shall wail for breaking of spirit. You shall leave your name to my chosen for a curse, and the Lord God will put you to death, **but his servants he will call by another name**. (Isaiah 65:13-15)*
- *But you who forsake the Lord, who forget my holy mountain, who set a table for Fortune and fill cups of mixed wine for Destiny, I will destine you to the sword, and all of you shall bow down to the slaughter, because, when I called, you did not answer; when I spoke, you did not listen, but you did what was evil in my eyes and chose what I did not delight in." (Isaiah 65:11)*

His chosen people who will be called by another name include this one-third remnant among the Jews who remained faithful in their hearts to the God of Abraham, Isaac, and Jacob.

- *And it shall come to pass that everyone who calls on the name of the Lord shall be saved. For in Mount Zion and in Jerusalem there shall be those who escape, as the Lord has said, and among the survivors shall be those whom the Lord calls. (Joel 2:32)*

SEVENTH BOWL OF GOD'S WRATH
POURED OUT—INTO THE ATMOSPHERE

As the battle continues, the seventh bowl is poured out into the air. Lightning and thunder are manifested worldwide, followed by an unimaginably great earthquake that shakes the entire planet. Yet the nations continue to fight and rage in great despair for their beloved world. Cities fall, mountains and islands disappear; and great hailstones weighing approximately one hundred pounds each fall upon the masses of people. This plague of hailstones will kill tens of thousands, causing a tremendous fear to arise among the ranks of the enemy. They become insanely scared, and like the orcs in the *Lord of the Rings,* they are at each other's throats, slaughtering their own comrades, for a great panic grips them.

- *And on that day a great panic from the Lord shall fall on them, so that each will seize the hand of another, and the hand of the one will be raised against the hand of the other.* **(Zechariah 14:13)**

These one-hundred-pound hailstones that are poured out onto the heads of the enemy also may be directed against the "principalities and powers of the air" since this seventh bowl is poured out into the air, the air being the abode of armies of evil powers and spirits.[262] Historically, hailstones have been a part of the arsenal of weapons used by our Lord against His adversaries, resulting in mammoth destruction and death.[263] Thus the seventh bowl being poured out into the air appears to represent destruction of the demonic forces of Satan, as well as of the earth.

Suddenly a voice is heard from the temple of God: "**It is finished.**" This was the same voice that spoke those exact words some two thousand years earlier when His work was completed on the cross.[264] Now the judgments of God that have been poured out on the earth are complete. The time of His second coming is being readied. The total redemptive purposes of God will now be consummated, both for salvation and for judgment.[265] Immediately, the Lord brings about a great earthquake in the midst of the battle and causes the Mount of Olives to split in two, allowing His faithful remnant to escape and separate themselves from the enemy who is about to be destroyed.

- *On that day his feet shall stand on the Mount of Olives that lies before Jerusalem on the east, and the Mount of Olives shall be split in two from east to west by a very wide valley, so that one half of the Mount shall move northward, and the other half southward. And you shall flee to the valley of my mountains, for the valley of the mountains shall reach to Azal. And you shall flee as you fled from the earthquake in the days of Uzziah king of Judah. Then the Lord my God will come, and all the holy ones with him.* **(Zechariah 14:4-5)**

This earthquake will be beyond man's comprehension. Isaiah presents us with an eye-opening description.

- *The earth is utterly broken, the earth is split apart, the earth is violently shaken. The earth staggers like a drunken man; it sways like a hut; its transgression lies heavy upon it, and it falls, and will not rise again. On that day the Lord will punish the host of heaven, in heaven, and the kings of the earth, on the earth. They will be gathered together as prisoners in a pit; they will be shut up in a prison, and after many days they will be punished. (Isaiah 24:19-22)*

Up to this point in time, our Commander in Chief has employed three major weapons in this Great War against His enemies.

1. Seven bowls of God's wrath being poured out on the earth, into the seas, into fresh waters, on the sun, on the throne of the beast, into the Euphrates River, and finally, into the atmosphere above the earth.

2. Sending a spirit of fear and madness into the midst of the enemy forces, causing them to fight among themselves. This is the same "sword of the Lord" that was used against His enemies when Gideon and his three-hundred-man army came against the huge army of Midian.[266]

3. Equipping warriors among the Jewish people with a heart of David, so that they become like "a blazing pot in the midst of wood and a flaming torch among sheaves."[267]

In summary, the armies of the Antichrist are experiencing unexpected resistance to their plans for conquest of the kingdom of God, for they have suffered tremendous loss of life to this point. Yet, millions of this enemy still remains alive, and their hatred is raging. They have just slaughtered two-thirds of the Israelites and are intent on pursuing the remaining third that has escaped through the valley of the Mount of Olives, which has split in two. This scenario parallels the pursuit of the Israelites by the Egyptian armies through the Red Sea. There He parted the sea for His people and then destroyed their pursuers, here He parts the Mount of Olives for His people and is about to destroy their pursuers. It is now time for the fourth and most powerful weapon in the arsenal of God to be revealed; a weapon that will completely annihilate the kings of the world and their armies. "**Look up; the Lion of Judah is coming with His mighty army!**"

- *Behold, <u>he is coming with the clouds, and every eye will see him</u>, even those who pierced him, and all tribes of the earth will wail on account of him. Even so. Amen. "I am the Alpha and the Omega," says the Lord God, "<u>who is and who was and who is to come</u>, the Almighty." (Revelation 1:7-8)*

THE COMING OF THE KING OF KINGS
(Revelation 19:11-21)

Many in the church of today believe that Jesus was a pacifist who preached, "Make love, not war." This is a popular belief among the average churchgoing Americans, even though it is contrary to Jesus' own assertion.

- *<u>Do not think that I have come to bring peace to the earth. I have not come to bring peace, but a sword</u>. . . . And whoever does not take his cross and follow me is not worthy of me. Whoever finds his life will lose it, and whoever loses his life for my sake will find it. (Matthew 10:34; 38-39)*

In truth, our Commander in Chief calls His warrior leaders to "make war, because we love." Throughout the New Testament, He calls us time and again to the frontlines of the battlefield. He doesn't tell us that we won't be wounded or even killed; but He does tell us that He will walk alongside of us through the "valley of the shadow of death," assuring us that we will not be killed until our assigned mission is complete. This age is a time of warfare, and peace will never be a true reality in this world until every single enemy of the Lord, both the fallen angels and sinful man, have been thrown into the lake of fire.

At His second coming, Jesus Christ rides down from heaven on a stallion of war rather than a donkey of peace. He is followed by a mighty army, consisting of those who will reign with Him in the 1,000 year millennial kingdom. His weapon is a great sword proceeding from His mouth, which will slaughter thousands of kings, generals, and mighty men among His enemies. This graphic portrayal of Jesus Christ as a vicious destroyer comes as a shock to respectable worshippers used to seeing Him gazing benignly from stained-glass windows, or to those who love to portray Him over and over again as a little baby in a manger.

Has Jesus changed since His first coming? It is not His character or personality that have changed but His mission. His first coming was to "seek and save what was lost"—not to condemn, but to save.[268] He was still the Warrior who challenged the false religions of Israel that were leading His people astray. But He came to give mankind the opportunity to be separated from their sins before all sin has to be destroyed. Now His second coming is for the opposite purpose: to destroy rather than to save, to punish sin rather than to pardon it.[269]

Now, let's visualize this second coming our the Lord Jesus Christ, out Commander-in-Chief:

The Rider on a White Horse

The last time Jesus came to Jerusalem, He came riding on a donkey, a beast of burden, for He was about to suffer an agonizing death for those who had been and would be called into the kingdom of God. He was the King entering Jerusalem, but then His kingdom was not of this world. Now He comes as a victorious warrior King to fight and destroy His enemies, who have murdered millions of His people over the last six thousand years.

He Is Called "Faithful and True"

Since the days of Abraham, the people of the Lord have been looking for His coming to establish the kingdom of God upon the earth. Century after century elapsed, and generation after generation passed away. Dark and troublesome times continually engulfed His people, and yet He did not come. Over time, many of His people who initially awaited His coming fell away and worshipped other gods and even persecuted those who remained faithful to the Lord. This included the Israelites of the old dispensation, as well as the church of this dispensation. Yet He did not come. Why? Because the number of His people who have been chosen to enter the eternal kingdom was not yet complete. At the time of His coming as the warrior King, it is complete. He is called the Faithful One to His people of faith.

He is also called "True," for He is the true Messiah in distinction from all the powers that have ever opposed Him. Antichrist claimed that he was the promised Messiah, but he was simply the last of many wannabes. Jesus Christ is the true Prophet, the true King, the true Word of God, and the true Son of God whom the prophets of the Old Testament and the apostles of the New Testament have told us about.

His Eyes Are Like a "Flame of Fire"

The eyes of Jesus Christ penetrate into the darkness, and the deepest corners of iniquity are completely visible to Him. Nothing remains hidden from the King when He comes for judgment.[270] He is gloriously focused on bringing righteous judgment to the world.

There Are Many Crowns upon His Head

On His head John sees many "crowns," which are symbolic of all of the victories our Lord has won in the historic battles against the forces of Satan. These multiple crowns also leave no doubt that Jesus Christ is the King of Kings who has come to set up His eternal kingdom upon this earth.

He Is Clothed with a Robe Dipped in Blood

Past victories in the kingdom have also been very bloody, as evidenced in both the old and new dispensations. Yes, He is our beloved Lamb of God who sacrificed His life so that His people may have eternal life. But He is also our beloved Lion of Judah, who has continued to walk with His people through the "valley of the shadow of death" for the past six thousand years. This blood is spiritually symbolic of all those in the body of Christ who also laid down their lives for the glory of the Lord.

He Has a Name Written that No One Knows but Himself

This appears to be a name given to Him by His Father, a name that exalts Him above every name in heaven and on earth. He also says to His conquering people that He will give them a white stone with their name written upon it—that no one knows except the one who receives it.[271] These names appear to be known only to the Father and His Son, so when we hear them throughout our eternal lifetime, we will know that He is calling us to His presence.

He Has Other Names

He is known to Himself and to His Father by His hidden name; He is known to the churches as the Faithful and True and as the Word of God; He is known to the world as King of Kings and Lord of Lords.[272]

Armies in Heaven Arrayed in White Linen Follow Him on White Horses

These armies are probably composed of both His holy angels who continually fought against Satan and his traitorous demons and those saints who stood alongside the sea of fiery glass, singing the Song of Moses and the Song of the Lamb.[273] Their numbers also will increase when those of the Lord's people who are alive on the earth at this time will be "caught up in the air" where they will join with their fellow soldiers on their return to the earth.[274] They wear robes of white linen, which are representative of their holiness before God, who gives them their robes.[275] They do not have armor or swords, for they are not entering into the midst of the battle. They are present so that their Lord will be glorified among them, for they are God's witnesses to an event that His people have been anticipating for centuries.[276]

He Treads the Winepress of God the Almighty, Putting His enemies under His Feet

Jesus is the Commander in Chief who treads the winepress of the wrath of God.[277] The gathering of the grapes for the winepress takes place at Armageddon, while the crushing takes place in this final battle. God's generals have crushed the necks of their enemies in the past.

- *And when they brought those kings out to Joshua, Joshua summoned all the men of Israel and said to the chiefs of the men of war who had gone with him, "Come near; put your feet on the necks of these kings." Then they came near and put their feet on their necks. And Joshua said to them, "Do not be afraid or dismayed; be strong and courageous. For thus the Lord will do to all your enemies against whom you fight." (Joshua 10:24-25)*

This is also the time that David spoke of:

- *David himself, in the Holy Spirit, declared, "'The Lord said to my Lord, Sit at my right hand, until I put your enemies under your feet." (Mark 12:36)*

From His Mouth Comes a Sharp Sword

This sword is symbolic of the Word of God, which proceeds from the mouth of Jesus Christ in tremendous power against His enemies. The same omnipotent Word that "spoke" all of creation into being will now destroy these last armies of all those who worshipped the creation yet hated the Creator.

Now when the armies of Antichrist see the coming of the King of Kings, they will gather together to make war against Him and against His holy army of angels and saints coming down from heaven. But they have no chance against them, for immediately, like a mighty sword in the midst of great combat, the "Word" is shouted against the armies of Antichrist.

- *This shall be the plague with which the Lord will strike all the peoples that wage war against Jerusalem: their flesh will rot while they are still standing on their feet, their eyes will rot in their sockets, and their tongues will rot in their mouths.* **(Zechariah 14:12)**

The Lord's enemies are completely consumed by the Word of His mouth, that same powerful Word that created the heavens and the earth.[278] The Army of Christ is witness to this great victory over the millions of human-orcs who were once committed to completely slaughtering the people of God on the face of the earth. Now they see the flesh of their enemies melting from their bodies.

Calling the "Birds of the Air" to the Battlefield

The birds of the air are summoned by the voice of an angel to share in the victory by eating the flesh of those who have been struck down by the Word of God. To give one's flesh to the birds of the atmosphere is expressive of the most complete defeat and shameful subjection of the enemy conceivable.[279] In the past, the enemy has humiliated the dead bodies of God's people by allowing the birds and the beasts to feed upon them.[280] Likewise, Goliath threatened this same humiliation to young David, yet David responded by telling him that it was he and his entire army that would be killed and whose bodies would be given to the birds of the air.[281]

The Lake of Fire Receives Its First Victims

Antichrist and the False Prophet are the first two who are thrown alive into the lake of fire. The Antichrist's army has been totally slain and their flesh eaten by the birds of the air. Yet their souls will suffer in hell while awaiting the final Day of Judgment, at which time they will follow their "beloved" Antichrist into the lake of fire, which burns with sulfur. This is a lake that is probably composed of the same sulfurous fire that the Lord rained down on the cities of Sodom and Gomorrah.[282] This is a torturous lake that is not only intensely hot but also has a foul, putrid smell as well. The Antichrist and the False Prophet are its first inhabitants. Later, Satan himself, together with Death, Hades, and all of sinful mankind will join them in this place of torment.

The Victorious Descending of the Messiah to the Mount of Olives

As Jesus descends, His feet will touch down on the Mount of Olives. The one-third remnant of the Jewish people who survived the Great War will come before Him on the Mount of Olives. Then when they recognize that their promised Messiah is truly Jesus Christ who was proclaimed by the Christian church, they will deeply mourn and weep.

- *And I will pour out on the house of David and the inhabitants of Jerusalem a spirit of grace and pleas for mercy, so that, <u>when they look on me, on him whom they have pierced, they shall mourn for him, as one mourns for an only child,</u> and weep bitterly over him, as one weeps over a firstborn.* **(Zechariah 12:10)**

Then the Lord Jesus will completely cleanse His beloved Jewish people who refused to take the mark of the Beast or to worship the image of the beast.

- *On that day there shall be a fountain opened for the house of David and the inhabitants of Jerusalem, to cleanse them from sin and uncleanness.* **(Zechariah 13:1)**

These are the ones who cried out for His coming, for Jesus had previously told the Jewish people,

- *For I tell you, you will not see me again, until you say, "Blessed is he who comes in the name of the Lord."* **(Matthew 23:39)**

- *For the Lord himself will descend from heaven with <u>a cry of command</u>, with the voice of an archangel, and with the sound of the trumpet of God. And the dead in Christ will rise first.* **(1 Thessalonians 4:16)**

To summarize, the Lord's second coming is an all-out military attack by the armies of heaven against the rebellious angels together with the evil armies from many nations. The Lord Jesus will shout at the head of His armies; He is leading the attack. Can you hear it? There is such passion in it, such anger, and such power.

Surely the mountains will shake, the dead will be raised, and the enemies of God will flee from before Him. Surely the seas will roar and the trees of the field will clap their hands. Let us tremble before Him, for the King is coming. He is coming to judge the earth in righteousness. His shout is like the roar of a lion. Jesus is at one and the same time a sacrificial Lamb and a roaring Lion.

He who died on the cross as a suffering Servant is the same one who's coming back as a conquering King.[283]

CHAPTER 14

THE KINGDOM OF GOD REIGNING UPON THE EARTH

(First Read: Revelation 20—22)

Many in the church have a problem understanding the reign of the kingdom of God during the millennial age, which precedes the coming of the new heaven and new earth. They have been taught that there is no actual future physical kingdom and that the words in Revelation 20 are simply "spiritual." That is, Satan already has been bound since the resurrection of Jesus and we are currently living in the millennial age. If this is true, then there is certainly no ongoing spiritual warfare; it already has been won for us. However, one only has to look at two thousand years of continuing persecution and rampant false teachings within the church in order to understand that this is another deceptive teaching designed to put Christians to sleep while the real war is raging across the world. These "spiritual teachings" of the millennial period first surfaced with the influence of Greek Platonism on the church around the fourth century. They were popularized by Augustine (AD 350–430) and later taught and embraced by the early Roman Catholic Church, which then insisted that any teachings of a physical reign of Christ were heretical.[284] Thus, this has been a spiritually weakening teaching that has been passed down through the ages to this day. My personal experience tells me that most Christians who adhere to views known as amillennial or postmillennial are among those who fail to discern the times for this present generation; they do not see a time of great tribulation and judgment coming upon the Christian church and our nation.

Contrary to those "spiritualized" teachings, the majority of the ancient church understood the millennial period to be an earthly, physical reign of the Lord Jesus Christ and His saints that follows the defeat of the Antichrist and precedes the Day of Judgment and the coming of the new heaven and earth.[285] This is known as "historic (or classical) premillennialism" and was embraced by our most prominent early church fathers, such as Ignatius, Polycarp, Irenaeus, Justin Martyr, and Tertullian. Other respected theologians, such as Sir Isaac Newton, Charles Spurgeon, George Eldon Ladd, Merrill Tenney, Carl Henry, and Francis Schaeffer, also taught the truths of historic premillennialism.[286] They understood Revelation 20 in its plain, simple sense. That is, many saints will be raised at the beginning of this thousand-year period and a second resurrection will occur at the end. A suggestion to my readers: "Read Revelation 19 and 20 without listening to anyone else."

REMOVAL OF SATAN FROM THE EARTH
(Revelation 20:1-3)

Before a millennial kingdom can be established, the deceiver of the nations must be removed. At this time, the human armies of Satan have been completely annihilated. His two human cohorts, Antichrist and the False Prophet, have been thrown into the lake of fire. Now an angel from God has been dispatched from heaven with the authority to remove Satan himself from the earth so that he cannot deceive the nations during the coming millennial reign of Christ. How will Satan be removed from the earth? This mighty angelic representative of almighty God will seize Satan and bind him with a great chain that will not be removed for a thousand years. He will then be thrown into a deep, bottomless pit. When Satan has been cast down, the angel will shut and lock the door to the pit, which no one can open until the proper time. Additionally, it appears that the demonic angels who were the dark agents of Satan for six thousand years also are imprisoned at this time.

- *God did not spare angels when they sinned, but cast them into hell and committed them to chains of gloomy darkness to be kept until the judgment* (**2 Peter 2:4**)

However, Satan's confinement is temporary. At the end of the millennial period, he will again be released to go out among the nations to recruit an army for the final showdown between the kingdom of the world and the kingdom of God.

THE MILLENNIAL AGE— THE SEVENTH DAY OF REST

The millennial age will precede the coming of the new heaven and the new earth and will be a time when the earth is being "restored" for both God and man's eternal dominion. Think of it like this: The time from Adam to Noah was a downward transition of the world away from paradise in the Garden of Eden. The time of the millennium to the new heaven and earth is an upward transition to a paradise restored. Thus, the millennium appears to be a one-thousand-year transition between the life that we now have and the Garden of Eden-type paradise that comes with the new heaven and new earth.[287]

Now, recall that the earth was created in six days and on the seventh day, God rested from all of His works. We have learned that these numbers are symbolic of many truths revealed in the Bible. For example, six days of labor must be followed by a day of rest known as the Sabbath. Also, the number six is symbolic of man, while the number seven symbolizes perfection and completion. Additionally, when the apostle Peter described events that must take place before the end of the age, he declared that a single day with the Lord is as a thousand years to mankind. This prophecy of Peter's also points out that as the earth once perished through a great flood, so will it also perish through a great fire that is yet coming. Following the flood there was a dawning of a new age; and, likewise, after the fires of the "seven bowls of wrath" and the Armageddon war, there also dawns a new age known as the millennium.[288]

There certainly appears to be a parallel between the six days of creation and the first six thousand years of human history. These "sixes" may be described as a period of "labor" — six days of labor for the Creator and six thousand years of labor for mankind. The seventh one-thousand-year period, known as the millennium, represents the Sabbath day of rest when equating the seven thousand years of mankind's history to the seven days of creation. One of our very early church fathers, Polycarp, was discipled by his close friend, the apostle John. Obviously Polycarp would have received tremendous insights from the man who experienced and recorded the book of Revelation. Polycarp was later martyred, but before his death, he also taught others concerning the end of time. One of his well-known disciples was Irenaeus, who wrote a book called *Against Heresies*. <u>In this book, Irenaeus says the following:</u>

- *As God views 1,000 years as a day and He created the earth in 6 days and rested on the 7th, so shall the earth last for 6,000 years and rest under the reign of Christ for the last 1,000 years."*

- Here was a man who was taught by a friend of John's, stating that Jesus Christ would return to reign on earth for one thousand years, which would represent a period of rest from six thousand years of sinful, rebellious living in the world. Also, we should take note that the time frame revealed in the Bible puts us very close to the completion of six thousand years since the time of creation.

THE PURPOSE OF THE MILLENNIUM

Paul provides some additional insights into the purpose of this one-thousand-year millennial period.

- *For as in Adam all die, so also in Christ shall all be made alive. But each in his own order: Christ the firstfruits, then at his coming those who belong to Christ. <u>Then comes the end, when he delivers the kingdom to God the Father</u> after destroying every rule and every authority and power. <u>For he must reign until he has put all his enemies under his feet. The last enemy to be destroyed is death.</u> (1 Corinthians 15:22-26)*

The Son of God must reign until he puts all of His enemies under His feet. During His millennial rule, all evil will eventually be exposed and destroyed forever. Until that time, death still exists, even though it has limited powers during the millennium. The millennium is also a time when Jesus Christ is vindicated before the nation of Israel and the world that persecuted Him. At the end of the millennium, death will be the last enemy destroyed, and then the kingdom is made ready for the Son to deliver it over to His Father. Thus, the millennial age is a time for the rulership of Jesus, while the following age of the new heaven and new earth will be under the rulership of God the Father. Jesus, as the last Adam, brings back obedience and fellowship to the Father, even as the first Adam broke that fellowship by disobedience.[289]

TWO RESURRECTIONS
(Revelation 20:4-6)

Two resurrections are mentioned in these verses, one at the beginning of the millennial reign and one at the end. Now, it seems apparent throughout the church that all Christians who have died through the centuries are immediately raised up to heaven. For example, in Revelation 6 & 7 we are shown a great multitude standing before the throne and before the Lamb of God. Additionally, we are shown that the martyrs that have died for their faith are together under the altar before the throne of God. This all takes place before the millennial period. <u>Thus, it appears that this first resurrection is not speaking about all the saints that have died since they are already in heaven.</u>

The first resurrection appears to be a select group of saints who lost their lives for their testimony of Jesus but will live and reign with Him on this earth for a thousand years. This group certainly consists of those who have been martyred for the gospel of Christ through the centuries, but it is probable that it is also for those who surrendered their lives totally for the kingdom, even though they were not physically martyred. Additionally, this resurrection will include those who are alive at His coming and will be caught up into the air to join His holy army as they descend to the earth. These are also those who refused to worship the Beast and did not receive his mark on their foreheads and hands. These are the strongest and most mature warriors in the army of God. They will be the leaders in His kingdom, helping prepare the world for the final stage of paradise. This first resurrection appears to be a time when this select group of saints will receive their resurrected bodies and will reign with Christ during the millennial period.

The righteous ones that are not included in the "first resurrection" will be joyfully waiting in heaven during the millennial reign of Jesus and then descend with the heavenly Jerusalem at the end of the millennium. Then all those who are the bride of Christ will be united forever.

The unbelievers of the human race will be among those of the second resurrection. The first resurrection is for a chosen group of the righteous only. The second resurrection is for those who denied the Lord during their life upon this earth. It is not my purpose to analyze who are the representatives of the righteous in the first and second resurrections. Yet, it should be our goal to make it to the first resurrection. If it means being physically martyred, so be it. If it means total dedication as if spiritually martyred, so be it.[290]

MILLENNIAL REIGN BEGINS— 45 DAYS AFTER BOWL JUDGMENTS?

The following end-times prophecy in Daniel has been the subject of much speculation over the centuries. Perhaps the understanding of the coming millennial age might provide some insights into the blessings inherent within this prophecy.

- *And from the time that the regular burnt offering is taken away and the abomination that makes desolate is set up, there shall be 1,290 days. Blessed is he who waits and arrives at the 1,335 days. But go your way till the end. And you shall rest and shall stand in your allotted place at the end of the days. (Daniel 12:11-13)*

Since Antichrist is to reign for 1,260 days from the time the abomination of desolation is set up in the temple mount, it would seem as if the additional 30 days represent the period of the "bowl judgments." Thus, it seems as if the 1,290 days mark the end of these bowl judgments. If true, then the reign of Christ appears to begin on day 1,335, which is 45 days after the completion of the bowl judgments.[291] These 45 days may be a time when the earth is being prepared for the millennial kingdom and the first resurrection of those saints who will reign with Him takes place. This will also include those upon the earth who rise up join the Army of the Lord as He returns to the earth. This certainly would explain the blessedness associated with the 1,335 days.

RESURRECTED BODIES OF THE SAINTS

In order to get an idea of what our resurrected bodies will be like, we can look at Jesus' appearance when He walked the earth following His resurrection. He suddenly appears and disappears. Thus during the millennium the natural people on earth will live in different locations and travel by normal means, while the resurrected people will be free to move into different locations as they are led by the Spirit of God. Like the resurrected Jesus, His resurrected saints also will walk, talk, and eat with those in their natural bodies. They will have physical bodies, which can be touched like those in the natural and perform physical functions, but they will be bodies that have great supernatural capabilities. Thus, the resurrected saints will be real people in real bodies—bodies that are incorruptible and eternally free from sin. These will be resurrected bodies of immortality with infinitely greater capabilities than the old physical bodies of this world, which have been corrupted by sin.

NON-RESURRECTED PEOPLES IN THE MILLENNIUM

Within the nations around the world will be innumerable peoples who survived the "bowls of wrath" and were not among the armed forces that gathered at Armageddon and were subsequently killed. These are men, women, and children, both young and old, from all races and cultures who, in their natural bodies, are confused, scared, and wondering what is going to happen next. These will constitute the first generation of human beings living in the millennial kingdom. Prior to this time, the gospel of the kingdom will have been preached throughout the nations, but many may not have heard it or perhaps did not believe. However, after witnessing the Lord's almighty power poured out across the earth, their understanding will have grown and there will no longer be any question in their minds that the God of the Christians is truly God. Many will have suffered tremendous grief at the loss of loved ones during this period, and others undoubtedly are stricken with sickness from the plagues; but a tremendous cleansing of the earth is about to begin. They may not be quickly accepting of Jesus Christ, since initially they will be in a state of shock and confusion, for the world is completely different from what they have known and been taught from birth. But they will undoubtedly listen to the teachings that are about to go forth to the nations.

These are people in various stages of maturity. There will be babies, children, fathers and mothers, aunts and uncles, and grandparents. There may be some whose hearts will never be aligned with God and will eventually be standing on the left side of the judgment seat. The righteous who die during this millennial period will join with their fellow saints in heaven while the unrighteous who die during this period will become part of the second resurrection.

Many questions are in all Christian minds concerning people whom we believe have never had the opportunity to hear the gospel message during their lifetime. These would be peoples living in distant countries in both the old and new dispensations who never had opportunity to hear the truths of the Lord and respond. Ancient peoples in far countries, children who die at a young age, babies that have been aborted: these are examples of human lives that certainly never had the opportunity to know the Lord. Perhaps this millennial period is a time for those people to be resurrected into their natural bodies and experience life under the reign of Christ.

Perhaps these are people who comprise much of the natural population during those times. I know this is speculative, but I believe it to be quite probable.

THE MILLENNIAL AGE—A TIME OF RESTORATION

The thousand-year, millennial, period is a time designated by the Lord to bring about a restoration of all things. This will be a day-to-day restoring of the world to that condition that existed in the Garden of Eden, a perfect world that our Lord calls "very good." It will be a time when Jesus Christ, who reigns and oversees this restoration process, will put all of His enemies under His feet, and mankind will walk in the fullness of Jesus Christ as sons and daughters of our almighty Lord. The earth, which has been groaning for six thousand years, will again rejoice over the righteous reign of the children of God.

- *The creation itself will be set free from its bondage to decay and obtain the freedom of the glory of the children of God. <u>For we know that the whole creation has been groaning together in the pains of childbirth until now</u>. And not only the creation, but we ourselves, who have the firstfruits of the Spirit, groan inwardly as we wait eagerly for adoption as sons, the redemption of our bodies. **(Romans 8:21-23)***

The death and resurrection of Jesus Christ provided the means for the human race to be restored to our Father's design for us.

- *Repent, then, and turn to God, so that your sins may be wiped out, that times of refreshing may come from the Lord, and that he may send the Christ, who has been appointed for you— even Jesus. <u>He must remain in heaven until the time comes for God to restore everything, as he promised long ago through his holy prophets.</u> **(Acts 3:19-21) (NIV)***

Much of the detail concerning this restoration process is found in the prophetic books of the Old Testament. Some examples follow.

<u>The Earth's Dead Waters Will Be Restored</u>

- A large river of fresh water will flow out of the Lord's millennial temple in Jerusalem so deep that one can swim in it. It flows through the eastern part of the land and into the sea, where it will change the seas into fresh water. These seas will again be populated with living creatures and every kind of fish.[292]

<u>The Animal Kingdom Will Be Restored to the Splendor of the Garden of Eden</u>

- *The wolf shall dwell with the lamb, and the leopard shall lie down with the young goat, and the calf and the lion and the fattened calf together; and a little child shall lead them. The cow and the bear shall graze; their young shall lie down together; and the lion shall eat straw like the ox.* **(Isaiah 11:6-7)**

207

The Earth Will Again Yield Tremendous Fruit for the Beloved People of the Creator

- *"Behold, the days are coming," declares the Lord, "when the plowman shall overtake the reaper and the treader of grapes him who sows the seed; the mountains shall drip sweet wine, and all the hills shall flow with it."* **(Amos 9:13)**

Humans and Animals Will Be United in Love for One Another

- *The infant will play near the hole of the cobra, and the young child put his hand into the viper's nest. They will neither harm nor destroy on all my holy mountain, for the earth will be full of the knowledge of the Lord as the waters cover the sea.* **(Isaiah 11:8-9) (NIV)**

Length of Life Will Be as in the Pre-Flood Era

- *Never again will there be in it an infant who lives but a few days, or an old man who does not live out his years; he who dies at a hundred will be thought a mere youth; he who fails to reach a hundred will be considered accursed.* **(Isaiah 65:20) (NIV)**

There Will No Slavery Among Mankind—Each Will Reap the Fruit of Their Own Labors

- *They shall not build and another inhabit; they shall not plant and another eat; for like the days of a tree shall the days of my people be, and my chosen shall long enjoy the work of their hands.* **(Isaiah 65:22)**

These millennial peoples certainly will live long and healthy lives, but all will eventually be subjected to death since they have not yet been resurrected. This will be a period similar to that era between the Garden of Eden and the great flood.

Finally, there is a remarkable parallel between the restoration of the earth during the millennial age and the sanctification process of "born-again" Christians. In both cases, the spiritual regeneration precedes the physical. That is, the earth requires the presence of Christ in order for it to be "born again" and begin the process of physical restoration to its original state. Also, Christians require the "born-again" experience of the Holy Spirit before we can undergo the maturing process of restoration to our sinless state.[293] Pretty interesting!

RESURRECTED SAINTS—THEIR MILLENNIAL MISSION

As previously mentioned, when Jesus was resurrected and appeared before various groups of people, He interacted socially with those who lived in human bodies. He talked with them, ate with them, and cooked for them; they all fellowshipped together, much like they did before His death.[294] There was even a group of Old Testament saints whom Christ brought forth from Hades. They entered Jerusalem in their resurrected bodies and appeared before many believers in the city.[295]

The resurrected saints of the millennial kingdom are going to interact with the peoples of all the nations from a heart of deep, passionate love—a heart of Jesus! The resurrected believers will be governing authorities, evangelists, teachers, and advisors to the nations. They will be in positions of authority at various levels, depending on each person's gifts and proven record of dependability.[296] The more faithful one is during our present natural life determines the degree of leadership authority that will be given in the life to come. Jesus will be the King ruling from His temple in the capital city of Jerusalem.

Those who sit upon the thrones are probably martyrs who were victims of unrighteous judgments in the courtrooms of the world. What an encouragement it is to those hearing the death sentence pronounced on them by earthly judges to know that one day they will be sitting on thrones. Their experiences of injustice in court will strengthen their ambition to be absolutely fair when they come to judge others.[297]

Some of the resurrected saints will be in the King's cabinet, overseeing various areas of government such as the departments of agriculture, commerce, or transportation. Some will be governors over provinces, and some will be mayors over cities. Others will be in charge of leading worship in the temple. Still others will take the message of Jesus out to the peoples worldwide. Jesus will be teaching from the city of Jerusalem, and His evangelists and teachers will be taking His message to the nations around the world. Some teachings will include in-depth lessons on nature in the millennial world—about fish, birds, animals, and vegetation. However, teachings concerning the kingdom of God that is among them will have the greatest impact. These teachings will cause many people to say,

- *"Come, let us go up to the mountain of the Lord, to the house of the God of Jacob, that he may teach us his ways and that we may walk in his paths." For out of Zion shall go the law and the word of the Lord from Jerusalem. He shall judge between the nations, and shall decide disputes for many peoples; and they shall beat their swords into plowshares, and their spears into pruning hooks; nation shall not lift up sword against nation, neither shall they learn war anymore.* **(Isaiah 2:3-4)**

THE MILLENNIAL GOVERNMENT

Unlike the original government established in the United States, the government ruling over the kingdom of God will not be democratic. It will be a glorious monarchy with Jesus Christ, the King of Kings, ruling from His throne in the capital city of Jerusalem. His position of authority is not chosen by popular vote but by the divine choice of almighty God, our Father. The Bible informs us that both Christ and His chosen leaders will rule over the world with a "rod of iron." This is indicative of strong and uncompromising rulership that will establish laws based upon the foundational truths of righteousness and holiness. The character of our Lord will be the ruling character in the lives of His sons and daughters who will live eternally under His kingship. This will be a glorious and righteous government that all of His conquering people will love to be a part of.

God's boundary lines for the nations, which have been usurped by man, may again be reestablished by this government.

- *And he made from one man every nation of mankind to live on all the face of the earth, having determined allotted periods and the boundaries of their dwelling place. (Acts 17:26)*

Perhaps people groups will be broken down into seventy nations, which is the number of the sons of God.

- *All the descendants of Jacob were seventy persons. (Exodus 1:5)*
- *When the Most High gave to the nations their inheritance, when he divided mankind, he fixed the borders of the peoples according to the number of the sons of God. (Deuteronomy 32:8)*

Nevertheless, during the millennial reign of this government, there will be many who will rather pursue the lusts of their hearts rather than the ways of the Lord. Though they will outwardly obey the laws of the kingdom, within their hearts they are hoping that a time will come when they can throw off the shackles of God's righteous laws and pursue their individual desires. These are those whom our Lord describes as:

- *the cowardly, the faithless, the detestable, as for murderers, the sexually immoral, sorcerers, idolaters, and all liars, their portion will be in the lake that burns with fire and sulfur, which is the second death." (Revelation 21:8)*

SATAN RELEASED AND THE LAST WORLD WAR

During the millennium, the earth is restored, peace reigns, and inhabitants of the nations live with great joyous freedom. And it is even going to get better. However, before that time, the true people of God must be separated from those who would rather make their own laws and live life anyway they please. Yes, they are still in the world, but their hearts have not been visibly exposed.

Although the Lord Jesus Christ visibly and physically reigns over mankind during the millennium, when the deceiver is set free from his prison at the end of that period, he will find that the hearts of many will still be responsive to his seductions. This makes it plain that the ultimate root of sin is not found in poverty or inadequate social conditions but in the rebelliousness of the human heart and its hatred for our Lord. <u>The millennial age and the subsequent rebellion of men will prove that people cannot blame their sinfulness on their environment or unfortunate circumstances.</u>[298] Our Lord has always given mankind time to exercise their own free will and thereby choose their destiny. Then he allows circumstances to evolve whereby the intentions of the heart are visibly manifested. People are given the final opportunity to choose sides. In the end, they will have no excuse beyond the sinfulness of their own rebellious heart when they stand before the judgment seat of our righteous and almighty God.

When Satan is released, he will be allowed to move among the nations and tempt people to turn from the Lord, exactly like he tempted Adam and Eve in the garden. The rest of the imprisoned demonic hoards undoubtedly will be released with him and will be employed to deceive and rally mankind to rebel against the kingdom of God. In the end, Satan and his demonic allies build an army so numerous that "their number is like the sand of the sea."

Recall that there appears to be three major battles between the forces of light and darkness described in end-times prophecy.

1. The battle of nations from Magog that comes against Israel. As mentioned in a previous chapter, I believe this to be the sixth-seal event described in Ezekiel 38-39.
2. The second battle is that known as Armageddon and described both in Revelation 19 and Old Testament prophecies. This comes at the end of the six-thousand-year age of mankind and is followed by the second coming of Jesus, our Messiah, to establish a one-thousand-year, millennial, reign.
3. The third battle is the final attempt by Satan and his followers to defeat the purposes of God at the end of the millennial reign of Christ. Here the enemies of God will be quickly consumed by fire. This will be followed by a day of final judgment.

This last attempt to attack and seize Jerusalem, now the capital of the world, fails completely. In fact, the battle is never joined by the people of God on earth. The kingdom of God no longer has need for armies, a Joint Chief of Staff, or a Secretary of Defense. Our Father in heaven sends down fire upon these enemy forces as they surround the city of Jerusalem, and they are completely consumed. The final Great War between the forces of light and darkness is also the shortest ever. The entire army of Satan is killed without the loss of a single human life among those in the kingdom of God. This great climax will occur on the old earth before the new earth appears so that the entire world will witness the final victory of good over evil.

Many of us probably wonder why Satan would arise to lead this final rebellion. Does he not expect his defeat? Does he expect his last bid for earthly sovereignty to succeed? Is he self-deluded, as well as the deceiver of nations? Does he really think he is stronger than God's people and, therefore, God Himself? Or, knowing his fate is sealed, does he seek to take as many as he can to share in his ruin in a last fit of frustrated rage? We may never know! [299] However, we do know that the heart of Satan certainly epitomizes the depths of arrogant pride that refuses to recognize the righteousness of God even in the face of eternal judgment.

HADES OR SHEOL—A TEMPORARY ABODE

Hades, in the New Testament, is the "temporary" holding place for the spirits of unrighteous men and women who have died in their sins. It is not their eternal destiny but a place where they will experience continual unrest and torment until the coming of that day when they will be resurrected to stand before the judgment seat of almighty God. *Sheol* in the Old Testament is the equivalent of *Hades;* however, prior to the resurrection of Jesus Christ, Sheol was the holding place for both the righteous and the unrighteous. It was composed of two entirely separate compartments that may be referred to as paradise for the righteous and torments for the unrighteous. These two compartments are visibly described in the parable of the rich man and Lazarus.[300]

When Jesus laid down His life on the cross, he first descended into Hades, or Sheol, and released the righteous ones, whose spirits had been awaiting His coming. Then the spirits of the righteous in Christ arose and accompanied Him into heaven, although some of them appeared to many of the inhabitants of Jerusalem before they ascended into heaven.[301] The spirits of our faithful brethren of the Old Testament dispensation could not go directly to heaven until their sins had been completely cleansed by the shed blood of Jesus at the cross; thus they had to wait in Hades. But now, all who die in Christ will ascend directly to heaven and stand with all their brethren in the holy presence of our glorious Lord. The spirits of the unrighteous dead will remain in Hades until the end of the millennial reign of Christ and His chosen saints. At that time they will be resurrected to stand before the judgment seat of almighty God, who will then determine their eternal destiny.

"ETERNALLY CONDEMNED" OR "ETERNALLY TORMENTED?"

It is understandable that all of mankind, both believers and unbelievers, have difficulty with the doctrine of eternal punishment. We all shrink from this teaching, for none of us dare visualize how eternal punishment might be experienced by someone we know and love. Yet the Bible does not ignore this teaching, and neither can we. The reality of the fiery torments of hell should spur all of us to continually communicate this truth with great zeal and urgency.[302]

How long will the unrighteous be tormented in the lake of fire? Traditional teachings stick to the view that hell is a place of eternal, conscious torment. That is, a person who is sentenced to hell is doomed to be painfully tormented forever and ever. Wow! Does the Bible "clearly" teach this? Many respected theologians certainly believe so. However, there are others who do not believe that sinners are eternally tortured but that after completing their allotted period of torturous punishment, their souls disintegrate into what they perceive as the "second death." This is called the "conditionalist view." It sees sinners as being punished for a period of time before ceasing to exist. This is opposed to the "traditionalist view," which see sinners as suffering eternal punishment.[303] "Eternally condemned" means that sinners do suffer for a period of time in the lake of fire, but eventually their soul disintegrates into nothingness; however, the memory of their tormenting punishment is never forgotten. At times, the Bible certainly does appear to say the souls of sinners suffer eternally, while in other places it is evident that there are varying degrees of suffering—some suffer more than others. Does that mean some places are hotter than others, or do some suffer longer than others? What the conditionalist view does is magnify:

- The justice of God—each doomed sinner receives precisely what he or she deserves and nothing else.
- The mercy of God— even the worse sinner finally perishes forever.
- The holiness of God— His wrath is real, but it is measured with exact precision in keeping with His own character.[304]

For, readers who want more information on the conditional view as opposed to the traditional view, I would recommend reading "Is Hell Forever?" This is a very interesting booklet addressing an apologetic debate that took place in Federal Way, Washington in September, 2013 between Dr. Phil Fernandes (Traditional View) and Chris Date (Conditional View). Personally, I lean toward the "conditional view" although I tend to remain open-minded to either teaching. There is so much that lies beyond our comprehension, and I find all mysteries of the future to be very exciting and am looking forward to the adventures of discovery awaiting each of us in God's glorious kingdom.

LAKE OF FIRE—
THE PERMANENT ABODE OF THE UNGODLY

When the word *hell* is mentioned in the Bible, it frequently refers to the fire into which the unrighteous are thrown and where they will be eternally punished. Thus, hell appears to be synonymous with the lake of fire. It is described in various sections of the Bible as a place of darkness, sadness, fiery torment, disgrace, and everlasting contempt. The lake of fire is said to burn with sulfur, a yellow substance that burns readily in the air. It is found in its natural state in volcanic areas. A lake of burning sulfur would not only be intensely hot, but it would be stinking and rotten as well. This is a place devoid of the presence of God. However, it is a place that will always be remembered, for even the sons and daughters of the Lord will have opportunity to look upon the dead bodies of those who perished in the lake of fire. This scene will be an eternal witness to the righteousness and holiness of our Lord.

- *And they shall go out and look on the dead bodies of the men who have rebelled against me. For their worm shall not die, their fire shall not be quenched, and they shall be an abhorrence to all flesh.* **Isaiah 66:24**

That their "worm shall not die" may simply refer to the eternal memory of their suffering or perhaps even to the residue of their dead souls, like a skeleton is the residue of dead bodies. At any rate, we are told that we will witness the eternal destruction of our earthly enemies, who once tried to eternally destroy each of us. This will be a visible, eternal reminder of the righteousness of the wrath of God against the enemies of all our brothers and sisters who once suffered under their cruel tyranny.

Death is the last enemy to be defeated. Death lost much of its power when Jesus was raised from the dead, and it will lose even more throughout the millennial period. Death only has power over sinners, and many of the inhabitants of the millennial kingdom are His resurrected sons and daughters. It appears that both Death and Hades, who will be thrown into the lake of fire following the Day of Judgment, are actually powerful fallen angels who are cohorts of Satan. Death appears as the evil angel who is the rider on the pale horse and Hades as another evil angel who follows right behind him.[305] These are probably the two most powerful angels under the rulership of Satan in the demonic realm. They will all join the Antichrist and the false prophet in this horrendous, putrid, and tormenting lake of fire.

The lake of fire is an eternal demonstration of the wrath of God. God's power and glory can be demonstrated both in blessing and in punishment. We have a positive motivation not to fall into sin: the goodness of God. We also have a negative reason not to sin: the severity of God. The eternal witness of the lake of fire is a perfect deterrent to protect us from sin.

- *Note then the kindness and the severity of God: severity toward those who have fallen, but God's kindness to you, provided you continue in his kindness. Otherwise you too will be cut off.* **Romans 11:22**

THE DAY OF JUDGMENT
(Revelation 20:11-15)

Many Christians really don't believe that they will be standing before the judgment seat of our Lord on this glorious day that takes place prior to the coming of the new heaven and new earth. They feel deep in their hearts that there really is no need for judgment since the destiny of a person already has been determined by the time of his or her death. However, the purpose of this final judgment is more than just announcing each person's future destiny before all of creation. To begin, let's briefly examine three points that will provide us with a more complete understanding of the purpose of this coming day of God's judgment.[306]

1. The Day of Judgment will display the perfect sovereignty and glory of God in the determination of each person's destiny; that is, will they live eternally with the Lord in the new heaven and new earth, or will they be consigned to a "second death" in the lake of fire? All will truly understand God's omniscient (all-knowing) and omnipresent (always present) nature. That is, He knows our every thought and the true motives behind our every action, for His eyes not only have been upon us outwardly but also see into our minds and hearts during every second of our entire lives. Nothing that has ever taken place in the actions, minds, and hearts of each man and woman is hidden from the omniscient and omnipresent God of all creation. And as the true heart of each person becomes visible to all, then all will come to understand His righteousness, which determines man's eternal destiny.

2. A second purpose is to reveal the degree of reward as well as the degree of punishment each person shall receive. Some rewards are greater than others, and some punishments are more severe than others. The degrees of reward or punishment are related to the lives that people have lived, and they will be revealed to the world when the "books" are opened before the throne.

3. The third purpose is to execute God's judgment on each person before the entire universe. Are they truly sons and daughters of God who will live together with Him in the new heaven and new earth; or will they be cast into the lake of fire from which they will never leave?

This is a universal judgment over all of mankind, a judgment passed upon the wicked and the righteous at the same time. All will be judged, and this judgment will bring both varying degrees of rewards to His people, as well as varying degrees of punishments to His enemies.[307] From this judgment, there shall be no appeal; it is everlasting.

JUDGMENT DAY—WHO WILL BE THE JUDGE?

Who is the mighty Judge on the great white throne? The Bible clearly reveals that all will appear before the judgment seat of Jesus Christ. However, it also appears that the one who sits on the great white throne, from whose presence both the heavens and earth flee away, is almighty God, the Father of our Lord Jesus Christ. A number of Bible passages ascribe judgment to God the Father. Yet, it is also very clear in the Bible that God the Father judges the world in and through His Son. Jesus Christ who is also the Son of Man, and He is the Father's representative to the entire world. The Father's authority has been given to His Son.

- *The Father judges no one, but has given all judgment to the Son, that all may honor the Son, just as they honor the Father. Whoever does not honor the Son does not honor the Father who sent him.* **(John 5:22-23)**
- *They show that the work of the law is written on their hearts, while their conscience also bears witness, and their conflicting thoughts accuse or even excuse them on that day when, according to my gospel, <u>God judges the secrets of men by Christ Jesus</u>.* **(Romans 2:15-16)**

However, when the entire creation appears before the throne on the great Day of Judgment, it is unquestionable that the Father will personally be present sitting on the great white throne. Therefore, we shall all stand before the Father and His Son, who also sits on His throne at the right hand of the Father; and in the Son's hands will be the Book of Life.[308]

This will be the day when we hear the following words of Jesus spoken in finality before each and every person.

- *So <u>everyone who acknowledges me before men, I also will acknowledge before my Father</u> who is in heaven, <u>but whoever denies me before men, I also will deny before my Father</u> who is in heaven.* **(Matthew 10:32-33)**

JUDGMENT DAY—WHO WILL BE JUDGED?

Who will stand before the great white throne in judgment? All of mankind, from Adam to the very last person who ever lived, shall appear before the final judgment seat. Cain and Abel, Moses and Pharaoh, Elijah and Jezebel, David and Goliath, John the Baptist and Herod, Paul and Nero, Martin Luther and all the Catholic popes, Charles Spurgeon and Karl Marx, Hitler and Corrie Ten Boom, Stalin, Mao, and the millions of Christians they slaughtered, the Clintons and the Reagans, Hollywood celebrities and the homeless, great and small, kings and slaves, rich and poor, young and old—all will appear before the judgment seat of almighty God. Bodies of the dead that were never retrieved, such as those of suicide bombers, those lost at sea, those devoured by beasts, and those who have been dead for thousands of years, all will be resurrected, and their bodies and souls will be reunited.

Following this final resurrection, mankind will appear one-by-one before the throne; the books will be opened, and the thoughts and deeds of every living being will be disclosed to every generation throughout the history of mankind. Obviously, this day of judgment is not a literal twenty-four-hour day but will last until every single being has stood before the throne and their moment-to-moment lives are unfolded before all. Then as judgment is pronounced on each person, they will either go to stand with the righteous at the right hand of God or with the unrighteous on the left.

- *When the Son of Man comes in his glory, and all the angels with him, then he will sit on his glorious throne. Before him will be gathered all the nations, and he will separate people one from another as a shepherd separates the sheep from the goats. And he will place the sheep on his right, but the goats on the left.* <u>*Then the King will say to those on his* **right**, *"Come, you who are blessed by my Father, inherit the kingdom prepared for you from the foundation of the world."*</u> **(Matthew 25:31-34)**
- <u>*Then he will say to those on his* **left**, *"Depart from me, you cursed, into the eternal fire prepared for the devil and his angels."*</u> **(Matthew 25:41)**

And finally, this also may be the day when some of the saints of God will be seated on thrones, for it is they who will judge the angels.[309] And indeed the rebellious angels that aligned with Satan against the Lord also will be judged.

- *And the angels who did not stay within their own position of authority, but left their proper dwelling, he has kept in eternal chains under gloomy darkness until the judgment of the great day.* **(Jude 6)**

Every soul that ever lived will gather together before the great white throne to witness judgments and to be judged. Then all will come to understand the righteousness of God's judgments in the lives of every human being.

JUDGMENT ACCORDING TO "WORKS"

All the works of men must be revealed in their true ethical character. All of our works in their proper light shall be exposed before God, before the world, and before ourselves. The reason is that God must be justified when He judges. He has always declared righteous judgments throughout history, no matter whether mankind agreed or disagreed with the consequences of His judgments. This Day of Judgment is at the end of an age when the thoughts and intents of every heart are exposed and the righteousness of almighty God cannot be disputed by either His people or His enemies. Many times throughout our lives, we see evil people getting away with rape, murder, and all kinds of evil, and we wonder why God does not immediately pour out His wrath upon these people. But on this day, every mouth will be stopped, and all shall acknowledge the perfect justice of God in both His righteousness and His timing. No one shall be dissatisfied with His judgments. Satan and his demonic world, as well as God's people and heaven's angels, will have to acknowledge that God's judgments are perfectly righteous.[310] Although believers have nothing to fear from the judgment, the realization that they will have to give an account for everything they have said, thought, and done should be a continuing incentive to fight against sin.

What will be the standard by which people will be judged? The standard is the revealed will of God in each of our lives, but it is not the same for all. Some have received fuller revelation of the will of God than others.[311] Those who have received a greater revelation of God's will also have greater responsibilities. All of mankind, even those who are ignorant of the Bible, has had the laws of God written on their hearts. This is often referred to as our conscience.[312] What is very clear in the book of Romans is that people will be judged on the basis of the light that they had, and not on the basis of revelation that they did not receive. The reason the Bible teaches that the final judgment will be according to works, even though salvation cannot be earned by works, is the intimate connection between faith and works. Faith will always reveal itself in works; good works are the visible evidence of true faith. If the faith is genuine, the works will be present.[313] For those who profess belief in Jesus Christ but take advantage of His great love and forgiveness in order to maintain their worldly lifestyle, Paul has a warning.

- *Or <u>do you presume on the riches of his kindness and forbearance and patience</u>, not knowing that <u>God's kindness is meant to lead you to repentance</u>? But because of your hard and impenitent heart <u>you are storing up wrath for yourself</u> on the day of wrath when God's righteous judgment will be revealed.* **(Romans 2:4-5)**

THE "BOOKS OF WORKS" AND THE "BOOK OF LIFE"

As previously mentioned, all believers shall stand before the great white throne on judgment day, and we shall see our sins as they have never fully been seen before. We shall one day understand that even our best works were defiled by sin and, therefore, we have no hope for eternal life based upon our perception of "good works." However, there is another book, and it is held in the hands of our Lord Jesus Christ, sitting at the right side of His Father. This is the Book of Life, which contains the names of all His chosen ones who are redeemed by the blood of their Lord and Savior. Following the exposure of their works, the Book of Life will then be opened to determine if their names are recorded. If so, then their sins are removed from the presence of God as far as the "east is from the west."[314] All of our transgressions are removed from before Him, and then we will be clothed in white and will stand on His right side. The opening of this Book of Life has a negative significance for the wicked but a positive significance for the righteous. The great and final decision in judgment shall be whether or not one's name is written in the Book of Life! [315]

However, not all those whose names appear in the Book of Life are alike. They all will be individually judged as righteous, but their works will determine the degree of rewards that each will receive.[316] It is neither unbiblical nor selfish to be motivated by rewards in the world to come. It *is* wrong to be motivated by the honor of man rather than the honor of God or to be motivated by the carnal rewards of this life rather than the eternal rewards of the world to come. But behavioral science teaches that rewards encourage behavior and punishments discourage. The concept of reward and punishment comes from God, and the degree of rewards seems to determine our individual proximity to Jesus in the kingdom. While everyone in the world will have access to meet Jesus, not everyone will have the same proximity to Him on a day-to-day basis. There will be assigned seating at events in the kingdom of God.[317] As citizens of the kingdom, we will have general access to meet with the King. However, only those on His immediate staff can meet with Him every day. Also, those with higher positions in the government can easily obtain an appointment with Him. The degree of one's accessibility to Jesus is considered a great reward in the kingdom of God.[318]

In the sense of being condemned, the true believer in Jesus is not "judged." However, there is another meaning to the word *judge* that does not refer to damnation or salvation but to reward and punishment. In this sense every believer will be judged.

- *For we must all appear before the judgment seat of Christ, so that each one may receive what is due for what he has done in the body, whether good or evil.* (**2 Corinthians 5:10**)

It also appears as if there may be punishments among those who receive eternal life. Any sin that has been repented of is washed away by the blood of Jesus. Yet any sin that is not repented of will be punished. I'm not speaking of losing salvation here but of losing rewards; by punishment, I do not mean damnation but chastisement. If Christians are leading a hidden, carnal life, it will be revealed.[319] The following passage certainly appears to speak to believers who allowed unrepentant sin to remain in their lives.

- *And that servant who knew his master's will but did not get ready or act according to his will, will receive a severe beating. But the one who did not know, and did what deserved a beating, will receive a light beating. Everyone to whom much was given, of him much will be required, and from him to whom they entrusted much, they will demand the more.* (**Luke 12:47-48**)

The significance of the Day of Judgment may be summarized in the following four observations:[320]

- The history of the world is not an endless succession of meaningless cycles but a movement toward a goal that follows the Day of Judgment.
- This day reveals to all that salvation and eternal blessedness is dependent on one's relationship to Jesus Christ.

- This day underscores man's accountability for his life and the opportunities that God has provided to allow one to accept or reject His holy authority over life.
- This day is the final and decisive conquest of all evil and the great revelation of the victory of the Lamb who was slain.

The Day of Judgment will reveal beyond the shadow of a doubt that at the end of this day, the will of God for this age will be perfectly complete.

THE NEW HEAVEN AND NEW EARTH
(Revelation 21:1-8)

Judgment is now complete; the time has arrived that all of the people of God have been yearning for since the fall of Adam. A new heaven and new earth suddenly appears and together they shall be the eternal home of God our Father, the Lord Jesus Christ, the angels of God, and all the overcoming saints, who are God's eternal sons and daughters. Wow! This will be infinitely more glorious than the Garden of Eden. There, it was God walking with man, whom He created in His image. Here, it is our glorious Father and His sons and daughters who have been truly "born again" by the blood of the conquering Lamb of God. This is a picture of a great and glorious family who will live together forever and ever in the kingdom of God, which will reign over the entire universe.

However, a new heaven and new earth does not mean that the present heavens and earth have been completely annihilated and replaced. From the very beginning, God promised man nothing less than the earth itself as his proper habitation and inheritance. When man sinned, his dominion over the earth was not taken away, but the earth over which he now ruled was placed under a curse.[321] At present, the world is a battlefield full of strife and sorrow, for the plan of God has not yet been consummated. The new heaven and new earth is a "restoration" of the old, not a "creation" of a new.

Consider the following four points:[322]

- Here the word *new* is the Greek word *kainos,* which communicates that it is new in nature and quality as opposed to a new creation. If it were "new" in origin, then the Greek word *neos* would have been used. This is a *kainos* heaven and *kainos* earth that is revealed in these passages.
- The book of Romans informs us that this present creation is eagerly awaiting the revealing of the sons of God so that it may be free from its bondage of decay and death.[323] All of creation awaits the coming restoration.
- If God had to annihilate the present cosmos because it has been so corrupted by sin, then Satan would appear to have won a great victory by obliterating the

works of God's original creation. Instead, God will renew this very earth from the results of Satan's evil endeavors.[324]

- Finally, consider our very selves. Our resurrected bodies are not a new creation; we are reborn into new bodies in which sin can no longer enter. We will not be a totally new set of human beings but people of God who formerly lived lives upon the earth. Unrighteousness will never again be found in us, and, likewise, unrighteousness existing in the old creation can never enter the restored creation.

The new earth will still be as much earth as the new us will still be us. The earthly beauty that we now see won't be lost but will become even more beautiful following the restoration of the heaven and the earth. All of the old earth that matters will be drawn into heaven to be part of the new earth. Our mind-set changes when we grasp that everything we love about the old earth will be ours on the new earth—either in one form or another. God is no more done with the earth than He's done with us.[325]

THE NEW JERUSALEM
(Revelation 21:9-26)

The new heaven and new earth will need a capital city from which God the Father and the Son will govern the cosmos. This city is a place where they will dwell with their sons and daughters, as well as the beloved angels who have been guardians of God's people throughout the age of man. It is a city that was being prepared for His people when Jesus first ascended to heaven over two thousand years ago.

- *In my Father's house are many rooms. If it were not so, would I have told you that I go to prepare a place for you? And if I go and prepare a place for you, I will come again and will take you to myself, that where I am you may be also.* **(John 14:2-3)**

John now sees this capital city descending upon the new earth. This is the New Jerusalem, the promised restoration of the beloved city of God. The presence of our Lord within the city is no longer confined to a section of the old temple known as the Holy of Holies, for the glory of God radiates like crystal throughout the entire city as it descends to the new earth. The city also is described as the bride of Christ, which indicates that all of His sons and daughters are within its walls as it descends to the new earth. It is likely that all those whose names were found in Jesus' Book of Life are gathered together following judgment day in preparation for their descent to the new earth.

The beauty of this city is far beyond our most greatest imaginations. Its construction consists of the most precious jewels and metals known to man. It is a city of pure gold, transparent as glass, with foundations adorned with every kind of jewel and with gates composed of a single pearl. Each of the twelve gates is inscribed with the names of the twelve tribes of the sons of Israel, and the twelve foundations under the walls of the city are inscribed with the names of the twelve apostles of the Lord Jesus. Thus, all His sons and daughters, from both the old and new dispensations have entered through the gates and live within these walls surrounding the city of New Jerusalem. This is a city that is approximately 1,400 miles in length and in width, with walls 216 feet high. For an American, this is the distance from the Canadian border to Mexico and from the Appalachian Mountains to the California border. The River of Life flows out from the throne of God throughout the city and perhaps through the gates into the world beyond. Trees of Life, which were denied to Adam following his fall, now grow on both sides of this river and are continually accessible to all of God's people. There will never again be any need for sun or moon, for the glory of the Lord provides a great and glorious light forever. It is quite an amazing picture!

HEAVEN: BORING OR EXCITING?

From the beginning, heaven has been dominant in the thoughts and lives of God's people worldwide. Even the non-believing populace tries to imagine what life will be like in the eternal realm. Unfortunately, most of these thoughts envision the afterlife as simply a spiritual world devoid of any physical environment. This deception crept into the church around the third century with the rise of Gnosticism. One of numerous false teachings of the Gnostics was that both the physical earth and the human body are basically evil, while the spirit world is supposedly good. Thus, the afterlife was depicted as being only a spiritual environment where the "saved" flitted around from cloud to cloud, carrying their harps and singing hymns forever and ever. Failure to understand the goodness of God's creation has blinded countless people from seeing heaven as a place of tremendous pleasure and enjoyment. Instead, they think that for heaven to be "spiritual," it must be drab and unappealing. How could anybody look forward to spending eternity in such an environment, let alone teach it to congregations? Sadly, countless evangelical Christians believe this thin concept of salvation as simply the saving of souls without bodies and without the earth and the rest of God's creation.

The heaven that Jesus described is not some ethereal realm of disembodied spirits. Such a place could never be home for us, because human beings were not created for a nonmaterial existence. Human beings are by nature physical as well as spiritual. Our home that we love is the place that God made for us—earth. We were made from the earth and for the earth. Earth is our home.[326] The coming of the new heaven and new earth is a real event that will visibly combine both the physical and spiritual together forever. The presence of our Lord is in heaven, but at the end of the age, when all evil has been cast away, God will unite the heavens and the earth under the headship of Jesus Christ, and His people will have access to His presence forever.[327]

The great majority of people will admit that they believe in both heaven and hell, yet most have little knowledge concerning the form of afterlife that awaits them in either of these realms. People sometimes say, "I'd rather have a good time in hell than be bored out of my mind in heaven." Many imagine hell as a place where they will hang around and shoot pool and joke with friends. Well, that could happen on the new earth but not in hell. Hell is a place of torment and isolation, where friendship and good times don't exist. Hell will be painfully boring. Everything good, enjoyable, refreshing, fascinating, and interesting originates with God. Outside of God's presence, there is no joy. On the new earth, our Lord will give us renewed minds and marvelously constructed bodies, full of energy and vision. All of our individual giftings and all that we love in this present life will be greatly enhanced on the new earth. Those that are gifted in art, music, farming, construction, accounting, writing, etc. will not abandon these gifts; they will be greatly enhanced and used in their assigned work on the new earth and in other areas of the universe. Those things that one enjoys most in this life will continue to be pursued with endless discoveries that will bring ever increasing satisfaction and enjoyment. The God who created us for good works will not abandon His purposes when He resurrects us to inhabit the new earth. We'll set goals, devise plans, and share ideas. Our best workday on earth, when everything turns out better than we planned, is just a small foretaste of the joy our work will bring us on the new earth. There will never be a moment of boredom among God's people on the new earth.[328]

Deep in our hearts, we all desire a resurrected life on a resurrected earth instead of a disembodied existence in a spiritual realm. We desire it precisely because it is God's plan for us to be raised to a new life on the new earth. It is our Lord who created us to desire what we were made for. He designed us to live on earth and to desire the earthly life.[329]

LIFE ON THE NEW HEAVEN AND NEW EARTH

The incarnation of Jesus Christ brought heaven down to earth. The coming new earth will be God's permanent dwelling place and will be as pure and holy as heaven has ever been. When we deny that the world is our home, we set ourselves up for hypocrisy. For we may pretend to disdain the world while sitting in church, but when we get in the car, we turn on our favorite music and head home to barbeque with friends, watch a ball game, play golf, ride bikes, work in the garden, or curl up with a good cup of coffee and a good book. We do these things, not because we are sinners, but because we are people. We will still be people when we die and go to heaven. This shouldn't be a disappointing reality, for it's God's plan. He made us who we are, except for the sin part, which has nothing to do with friends, eating, sports, gardening, enjoying coffee, or reading.[330]

God's greatest gift to us is "Himself." His presence brings about great joy and is fully satisfying, while His absence brings thirst and longing. One can easily see the joylessness in the unbelieving world. Joylessness is present even among the wealthiest people on earth. Kings, politicians, and celebrities who are worshipped by masses of followers are empty and lonely in their private lives and therefore seek for personal joy in the world of money, sexual immorality, alcohol, drugs and exercising power over others. . Nobody will ever find true joy until they seek the presence of the Lord, who will then open His arms and embrace them.

Curiosity is an inherent part of our character that is also a gift from God. It allows us to daydream, imagine, and speculate about matters in life. This has led to numerous great discoveries in our lives. Curiosity about heaven frequently surfaces as family and friends gather together to socialize. They ask questions such as these.

- *What will our bodies be like? Will we eat and drink on the new earth? What will we know and learn? What will our daily lives be like? Will we desire relationship with anyone except God? Will animals inhabit the new earth? What about our pets? Will there be art, entertainment, and sports? Will we design new technology? What will be the mode of travel? Will we explore the stars and planets in the universe? Whom will we meet, and what will we experience together? Will we be with our family and friends?*[331]

The finest book I have read that addresses these questions and many others is Randy Alcorn's *Heaven*. This is an exceptional work that addresses our curiosities and provides a solid biblical foundation for the author's insightful answers to many questions concerning life in the new heaven and new earth. It also has a study guide that can be used for groups desiring more information on heaven. The more we understand about the truths of heaven, the greater the impact we will have on our neighbors, friends, and fellow employees who may or may not be believers. It will motivate us to talk much more about the great joys that await His people on the new earth.

We will one day pass from this earth to the present heaven through death, but eventually we'll be back to live forever on the restored earth. Yes, we are pilgrims in this life, not because our home will never be on earth, but because our ultimate home isn't on the present earth, which is still under the curse. It was always the plan of our Lord for physical human beings to live on a physical earth; and when sin entered the world of man, God didn't abandon His plan but chose to become a man on this same earth. Why? So that His people would experience His glory forever and that the Lord Himself could enjoy the company of men and women in the world that He made for us.[332]

"BEHOLD, I AM COMING SOON!"
(Revelation 22:7; 12; 20)

Jesus is coming, and He has told us how He will come. He will come accompanied by wars, plagues, famines, persecutions, and sufferings and in a generation when knowledge will greatly increase. And the closer His coming gets, the more intense the power of His enemies will be asserted. Yes, He is coming very soon, but to understand just how rapidly Jesus is coming, we need to consider what must take place before His actual physical coming. Herman Hoeksema, in his book *Behold, He Cometh*, uses an illustration from the Second World War to explain preparations needed prior to the actual coming.

- *When Germany pressed the Allies and pressed them hard, they were for a time in desperate straits. And longingly they looked for the coming of the Americans. The Americans said, "We are coming, and we are coming quickly." But many months elapsed before they actually did come. To the Allies in their desperate condition it seemed a long time before they actually came. Yet, did not the Americans come quickly? Surely, they did; and they came as fast as possible for them to come. But think what was implied in their coming. Many, many things had to be prepared before they could come. An army had to be drafted and trained. Money had to be raised. The army had to be equipped. The material, clothing and ammunition and weapons, had to be manufactured. Ships had to be built. In view of all this, it was absolutely true that they were coming quickly. The same may be applied to the coming of our Lord Jesus Christ. From our point of view it may seem a long time. But look! The children of God must be gathered. The whole church gathered from all nations must be filled: not one of the elect may be lacking.*[333]

All these things, especially over the last decade, are developing right before our very eyes. We see Him coming! The church in the very first century, as well as the church in every age, including our generation, finds itself caught up in a struggle between the kingdom of this world and the kingdom of God. This book of prophecy known as Revelation was written not only to provide essential information for the last generation but also to encourage the church in all generations to maintain their steadfast loyalty in the midst of demonic pressures and persecutions.

We may not know the exact timing of His return, and it will be unexpected to many, for He comes as "a thief in the night." However, for His people who are not in darkness but remain awake, His coming will not be unexpected.[334] Also, there are many followers of Christ today who are awake and like the "sons of Issachar" are discerning that the time of His coming is shortly before us, most probably in this generation.[335]

THE BOOK OF REVELATION
MUST REMAIN OPEN TO BOTH KINGDOMS
(Revelation 22:10-11)

The words of the book of Revelation must never be sealed; they must be communicated by the church in the midst of the world. When this is done, the result will be twofold: there will be those who are saved and those who are hardened. Even among evangelicals, there are those who will have nothing to do with it. They like to say that things will all "pan out" in the end. This is a very dangerous mind-set that may lead them to being like the five virgins who were unprepared for the bridegroom's coming and reacted too late to enter into the marriage feast.[336] It wasn't their unbelief that kept them out; it was their apathetic attitude toward preparedness for his coming.

When this book of Revelation is opened and expounded, it will strengthen the faith and hope of the people of God. However, there will be many who will have nothing to do with it. They will mock and belittle those who proclaim it. They will say, "You are a dreaming, hateful pessimist who is scaring people." It will also arouse opposition among the unbelievers whose hope lies only in the future of this present world, for this prophetic book leaves no hope for their vain dreams. Those who proclaim the end-time prophecies will one day be considered a threat to the national security of our country. What then? Should we keep the book closed because of a threatening and hateful opposition? No! Instead, we are to:

- *Let the evildoer still do evil, and the filthy still be filthy, and the righteous still do right, and the holy still be holy.* **Revelation 22:11**

This book will draw the lines. It will strengthen and emphasize the great difference between the true people of God and the world. It will make the world more conscious of the great difference between its ideal and those of the people of God. And it will also make His people more conscious of the same fact. And for this latter reason, the book must not remain closed but must be open so that all can hear and read it and this twofold effect may be achieved.[337]

Stand fast, Christian warriors; the truths in this prophetic book need to be openly proclaimed to this generation of both believers and nonbelievers.

A FINAL WARNING
(Revelation 22:18-19)

I warn everyone who hears the words of the prophecy of this book: if anyone adds to them, God will add to him the plagues described in this book, and if anyone takes away from the words of the book of this prophecy, God will take away his share in the tree of life and in the holy city, which are described in this book. **Revelation 22:18-19**

There is also a responsibility connected with the reading and the hearing of the book of Revelation. The warning in these verses does not apply to the imperfect understanding of believers who read and teach this book. After all, these words are prophetic and therefore there are inherent difficulties in its interpretation. All who teach this book must clearly understand our fallibility when it comes to interpreting prophecy. No one person is going to have absolute understanding; each of us is just one member of the body of Christ, and we all need to seek truths from others who have different callings and giftings.

No, this "warning" refers to a conscious attitude of unbelief in what is recorded in this book. It is addressed to those who are acquainted with its contents but who would change the message of this book to suit their own purposes so that the kingdom of the world is confused with the kingdom of God. They do it by adding or detracting from it, so that the light of the truth of this prophecy is dimmed. Particularly *they deny the truth of a physical coming of Jesus Christ* by "spiritualizing" these words or by denying the "inerrancy" of these truths. Those who do this must be aware of the punishment that awaits; that is, they will be deprived of their part in the Book of Life. [338]

BLESSED IS THE ONE WHO . . . !"

My brothers and sisters in the Lord, note the following seven beatitudes in the book of Revelation. I would urge you all to memorize them until they are so deeply embedded in your hearts that not even the most severe of challenges could cause you to waver from the path of life or waver from your missional calling in the midst of great tribulation.

SEVEN BEATITUDES IN THE BOOK OF REVELATION

- <u>*Blessed*</u> *is the one who reads aloud the words of this prophecy, and blessed are those who hear, and who keep what is written in it, for the time is near.* **Revelation 1:3**
- <u>*Blessed*</u> *are the dead who die in the Lord from now on. "Blessed indeed," says the Spirit, "that they may rest from their labors, for their deeds follow them!"* **Revelation 14:13**
- *Behold, I am coming like a thief!* <u>*Blessed*</u> *is the one who stays awake, keeping his garments on, that he may not go about naked and be seen exposed!* **Revelation 16:15**
- <u>*Blessed*</u> *are those who are invited to the marriage supper of the Lamb. . . . These are the true words of God.* **Revelation 19:9**
- <u>*Blessed*</u> *and holy is the one who shares in the first resurrection! Over such the second death has no power, but they will be priests of God and of Christ, and they will reign with him for a thousand years.* **Revelation 20:6**
- *And behold, I am coming soon.* <u>*Blessed*</u> *is the one who keeps the words of the prophecy of this book.* **Revelation 22:7**

- <u>Blessed</u> *are those who wash their robes, so that they may have the right to the tree of life and that they may enter the city by the gates.* ***Revelation 22:14***

"The grace of our Lord Jesus Christ be with you all. Amen"

CHAPTER 15

EQUIPPING WARRIOR LEADERSHIP IN THE KINGDOM OF GOD

NEEDED: GREAT LEADERS

Greatness in leadership is not an attribute one is born with; it must be earned. All soldiers in the Army of God have the potential to positively impact other people whom they have been called to lead. Greatness is not pursued for the sake of greatness. It is about one's desire to die to himself, his ambitions, and his personal comforts in order to achieve his calling in life. Our Commander in Chief has a predestined mission for each of His people, and those who actively seek for it will find it; and those who find it must then act upon it. Such actions will produce great leaders who can impact many lives for the kingdom of God.

Good leaders can get things done in normal times, and we can generally get by with good leaders. But we no longer live in normal times, and there is a desperate need for great leaders - leaders who lead by example as they continually display great courage and wisdom in the face of life-threatening challenges. Such leaders have a deep passion to see the kingdom of God manifested in glorious strength, not simply in the institutional churches, but in the workplaces, the neighborhoods, the downtown areas, and individual homes, where "real life" occurs.[339]

Great leaders also recognize that they have weaknesses, but the difference is that they are committed to focusing on their strengths. This creates a spirit of excitement when there is no expectation to continue in one's weaker, less gifted areas. They trust their fellow leaders to provide fruit in those areas where they are less gifted. Thus, great leaders have no desire to control everything, for their sole focus is on God and His kingdom people.

Finally, great leadership has little to do with rank and everything to do with responsibility. Leaders think, envision, and ask questions. Above all, the great leaders "act." Even when leaders don't think they are capable, when they realize they are weak and fear begins to invade their consciousness, they still step up to the plate and "act" like leaders. Where does one go to get these leadership attributes? <u>One must first die to himself, his ambitions, his desires, and all of his needs so that he may live for others and for higher purposes.</u>

Listen to a great leader as he speaks to his followers.

- *Be watchful, stand firm in the faith, <u>act like men</u>, be strong. Let all that you do be done in love.* **1 Corinthians 16:13-14**

So keep yourself on the pathway that leads upward. Stay close to our truly greatest Leader, Jesus Christ, and He will make you a leader that many others will gladly follow.

A MILITARY PERSPECTIVE OF A GREAT LEADER

A leader does not abide in his tent while his men bleed and die upon the battlefield. A leader does not dine while his men go hungry or sleep when they stand at watch upon the wall. A leader does not command his men's loyalty through fear or purchase it with gold; he earns their love by the sweat of his own back and the pains he endures for their sake. That which comprises the harshest burden, a leader lifts first and sets down last. A leader does not require service of those he leads; he provides it to them. He serves them, not they him.[340] These certainly are the leadership traits inherent within the greatest Leader that ever walked on this earth and who currently serves as the true Commander in Chief over the Army of God.

DISCIPLINE IN THE ARMY OF GOD

A priority of great leadership is self-discipline in day-to-day living. Their growing love for the Lord results in their desire for a moment-by-moment walk with Him throughout each day. This certainly requires discipline in Bible study and commitment to continual intercessory prayer; but, even more, soldiers need discipline at those times of the day when they are at their weakest, those times when the spirit of procrastination invariably falls upon them. Great leaders have learned through growing experiences to deal with such issues and not allow worldly temptations to render them impotent during this time. If we do not conquer such temptations, we become POWs in the camp of the enemy for a short period of time. And at some point it becomes recognizable, for it creates a deep emptiness in our spirit and a sense of depression begins to creep into out soul. <u>Great leaders have learned that the "fear of the Lord" certainly means "redeeming the time" for Him.</u>

Sadly, the vast majority of American Christians spend the bulk of their days in these POW camps. Among these are many who may have been called to a leadership role, yet did not forsake their lives and thus did not achieve their full calling. They are certainly among the saints of God, but they did not attain to the leadership role to which God had called them. Every one of us faces these temptations toward apathy, as it is an ongoing attack from the enemy. Today, we must continually resist worldly temptations and prepare to "be ready" for the Day of the Lord lies shortly before us. Warrior leadership in the Army of God in these last days must be totally committed to walk the pathway that the Lord Jesus Christ, our true Commander-in-Chief, has laid before them.

One further note of caution: Christian soldiers are more susceptible to attacks from the enemy immediately following a significant spiritual victory. This is a principle that military leaders learn both in their training and during combat—we are more vulnerable to enemy counterattack immediately after achieving a hard-fought objective. As we begin to internally celebrate our victory, we have a tendency to relax and let down our guard. Be careful here, for this is the most critical time for a counterattack by our enemy.

DEVELOPING OUR MISSION IN THE ARMY OF GOD

Every Christian I have known has a desire to hear our Lord Jesus say, on that day when we enter into His presence,

- *Well done, good and faithful servant. You have been faithful over a little; I will set you over much. Enter into the joy of your master. (**Matthew 25:21**)*

Yet, not every Christian who enters into His presence will hear those words. Now this isn't speaking about our salvation - each of us has a mission assigned that we must pursue; and in order to hear those words, we must move forward in the Lord and His mission for us. This doesn't mean simply being faithful in church attendance and tithing. That is all well and good, but each of us has his or her own mission. Wherever you work, you have a mission—seek for it! Wherever you live, you have a mission—seek for it! We are all called to be partakers of the work God intends to complete, which will usher in the reign of our Lord on this earth. If we don't complete our assigned mission, someone else will, and then that person will reap the reward that was initially set aside for us. Remember this, there can be no victory without entering into the battle – we must see every challenge that comes into our lives as a great opportunity to fulfill our calling to leadership in the Kingdom of God. [341]

The church is about to enter a very challenging time, which is a necessary prerequisite for entry into its most fruitful times. The darkness is gathering its forces, but so is the light. The Lord has given each of us a specific part to play in His overall plan, and it must be our continual quest to search for our individual mission assignment. Almost everyone has a vision for what they want to accomplish, but it's going to require a difficult and continuous work discipline. [342]

OUR MISSIONAL CALLING

As warriors in the Army of God in these last days, we must be totally committed to walk the pathway that our Commander in Chief has laid before each of us. Therefore, it is important for each of us to internalize our personal understanding of the mission to which He has called us. This mission exists in the passion of our hearts, and our direction becomes clearer as it is written down and internalized each day in our hearts. The following is an example of a *general mission statement* that is designed to drive Christian leadership through the wilderness journey of a committed life to the Lord:

Specific mission statements are established when His will is revealed to us each day as we follow Him along the narrow road of a godly life.

> *Day by day, to live out the spirit of the gospel in my life in such a way that it will positively affect others for the strengthening and expanding of the kingdom of God and to stand strong for my Lord Jesus Christ against the forces of darkness in this world.*

When I look at the cities of the United States, I see the Christians as a group of bewildered survivors going about their daily business with little sense of a unifying purpose. In time of war, battles are won by the strategic concentration of force. Soldiers don't just attack along a scattered front. They follow a plan designed by a general with a big map and lots of information. In some of our cities, it's been so long since our soldiers received news about the progress of the battle that they have stopped fighting. They are wandering in the rear of the battlefield, preparing food and generally attending to their own comforts.[346]

Now, let's take a look at the frontlines of the battlefield - that place where Christian soldiers are provided opportunities by their Commander in Chief to make a strong impact for the kingdom of God.

THE FRONTLINES OF THE BATTLEFIELD

Over the last several years, many Christians have awakened to the realization that the traditional church is not where the Lord's soldiers are expected to carry on their respective ministerial assignments. The mission of the traditional church is in the rear, with the responsibility of equipping the troops to be sent to the frontlines of the battlefield. However, for pastors, their respective churches are certainly the frontlines of their battlefield.

The frontlines of the battlefield are where people spend the majority of their time in the presence of others. There is a growing need for Christians to arise and minister to those people who will not be found in Sunday church services. Pastors have influence over a limited number of people for only a small amount of time during the week. Television, movies, computer games, casinos, and such things are much more influential in the individual lives of people in today's culture.

Now Christian soldiers may ask, "Where are the frontlines of our respective battlefields?" Well, ask yourself the following questions:

- Where is that place outside of our homes and churches, where Christian soldiers can have a tremendous impact for the kingdom of God?
- Where is that place that requires so much of our time and effort in life and yet, most of us approach it grudgingly?
- Where is that place where the Lord brings so many people into our lives over the years and yet, most do not envision it as a ministry opportunity?

MINISTERING IN THE WORKPLACE

Early Christians made the workplace their ministerial focus because their occupations regularly took them there. As a result, the workplace played a vital role in establishing and expanding the early church. In fact, most early followers of Jesus remained in full-time business while simultaneously conducting full-time ministry. Christian soldiers need to realize that today millions of God's people are similarly called to full-time ministry in their respective business occupations. Whether one is a business owner, banker, electrician, insurance agent, plumber, landscaper, factory foreman, ditch digger, doctor, lawyer, or government worker, it makes no difference; <u>all can have great influence in their respective areas of employment, for that is where they encounter the world and that is where their lives have been positioned by the Lord.</u>

Unfortunately, many Christians feel like they have a second-class ministerial calling compared to people who serve full-time in a church. This should not be the case, for contrary to what many traditional churches imply, there is no hierarchical distinction between pastors and ordinary people in the eyes of our Lord. The calling to pastoral ministry is not necessarily higher than the blue-collar workers driving daily through rush-hour traffic to get to work on time in order to provide a living for their families. Christians who work in jobs outside the confines of the church need to understand that they are not perpetual privates in God's army just because they have not gone to seminary. They need to discover that they have the potential to become full-fledged "generals" whose ministry influence can grow far beyond the bounds of the workplace and the walls of their local church and into the very heart of the city. Unfortunately, many of these workplace ministers fail to fulfill their divine destiny because they are often derided by others as untrained or uneducated. This is not a new accusation. Both Peter and John, who were fishermen by profession, certainly experienced this ridiculing. Additionally, Jesus, who was a carpenter, recruited His disciples from the workplace rather than from those trained by the synagogues.[347]

Most churches fail to understand that there are significant pastoral communication problems with unbelieving men. Many workingmen refuse to identify with the pastoral culture and therefore will not seek help from the perceived church. Yet, deep within themselves, many of these folks, who may be your fellow employees, or customers, or simply third-party contacts, unknowingly hunger for strong Christian leaders with whom they can relate, namely, peers who engage on the same battleground and who understand their world and their ongoing temptations and struggles. Those with grievances and those who have lost loved ones through death, divorce, or adultery are unknowingly searching to speak with someone who may be able to restore some degree of comfort to their lives. Additionally, there are many people on this battlefield who hopelessly see themselves in dead-end jobs: young men paying fifty percent of their paycheck for child support; blue-collar workers hanging out in casinos, hoping to change their status in life; and small business owners struggling to stay afloat. This sense of hopelessness among a majority of the workforce continues on and on. Yet this provides a tremendous opportunity for Christ's warriors to move toward the front of this battlefield to fight for the souls of their fellow workers.

Christian warriors must free themselves of the American workers' mindset that Monday morning is the lowest point of the week and TGIF is something to embrace. Great missional opportunities present themselves in the workplace on a daily basis, yet a warrior for Christ must take the initiative, or opportunities will be lost. Soldiers become warrior leaders when they commit to making personal sacrifices in order to show a true, loving concern for those people encountered daily in the workplace.

Two examples:

1. As one ministering in his business world, I have written a letter that I send annually to several hundred of my clients. Friendships and trust were built with my client base over several years, and this letter, which communicates a loving concern for them, continues to open several doors for ministry opportunities. A copy of the letter is found in Appendix E. Perhaps it will help you draft a letter communicating your burden for family members, fellow employees, neighbors, or others.
2. In the workplace, you'll come across so many men who are searching for truth, even though they won't admit it, but they would never come to a church believing that it is too "wimpy" for them. So how does one handle their "calling" in the workplace environment? In order to address this question, I've developed scenario that may be effective for witnessing to currently unbelieving, but searching hearts in the workplace. This scenario is found in Appendix F.

Christian warriors, this is a critical time to sound the alarm. Many of our fellow workers, though not Christians, are very concerned about events that are taking place in our country. Taking advantage of opportunities to speak with them concerning today's economic concerns, potential terrorist activity, and increased violence throughout the country definitely will open up most people to serious conversation. Once they realize your concern for them, communication becomes more frequent and open, and then it is only a small step to speak of the warnings given in Scripture and the call of Jesus Christ on their lives.

COMING TO AMERICA – GOD'S RIGHTEOUS JUDGMENT

The United States as a democratic nation is rapidly disappearing – constitutional law will soon be ignored. As Christians, we cannot put our trust in financial institutions or government promises. All this is of the world and God's people need to come out of the world.

Those of us who correctly discern the times recognize that God's righteous judgment will soon descend upon America.

What type of Judgment?

- There have been numerous times in the history of the world when our Lord rained down judgments from heaven. Such as: earthquakes, plagues, hurricanes, tornados, etc.
- However, throughout history our Lord has also chosen to stir up the hearts of nations ruled by evil governments to launch attacks upon a nation that has historically known and worshipped Him, but have fallen into immorality and left Him to pursue their own sinful pleasures.

Think about these scenarios:

- A sudden economic collapse much like the 1929 stock market crash that occurred overnight resulting in sudden bank closures, multiple suicides, famine, diseases, families being thrown out of their homes. All this launched the great depression of the 1930's.
- Multiple nuclear terrorist strikes that will suddenly hit many cities (probably coastal) in our nation and before ordinary folks like us can adjust; the grocery stores, banks, and gas stations will be locked down. It is quite possible that this may happen in the midst of a Middle Eastern war which will affect the entire world.
- Consider what American life would look like a few seconds after and EMP (electromagnetic pulse) incident - a nuclear weapon detonated high above the center of the United States. This would result in a large number of automobiles, airplanes, computers, cellular networks, home electricity, etc. throughout our nation being immediately rendered useless. Over the past couple of years, barely a week goes by when some scientific organization or military expert warns that this scenario is very realistic.

Whatever the scenario, it will certainly be a series of "sudden" catastrophic events unforeseen by the great majority in this country. These event(s) will surely launch more devastation than a thousand Katrina's or 9-11's.

Resulting in:

- Great panic as people swarm to the banks, the grocery stores, the gas stations. They will not have a "customer mentality" – but a panicky, uncontrollable mob with no direction other than to grab and run with no concern for who gets hurt.

Immediate after-effects:

- Neighbors beating on neighbors doors seeking food. Stone throwing – breaking windows. Caring not for who gets hurt.
- Subsequently, after scourging the urban areas, youth gangs will form and go out to the suburban areas. Their intent is to intimidate families, burglarize homes, and murder those who oppose them.
- These "mob-gangs" will eventually organize with one another to kill and rob for food and other products which will become very valuable in a famine-plagued nation.

Governmental Response:

- Government militia forces will eventually unite to bring their "version of order" to the urban areas. Historical events in other countries tell us that militia forces will attempt to confiscate all firearms as well as the storage of foods and supplies.

This time of tremendous challenge is rapidly approaching and in the near future, we will need to stand "shoulder to shoulder" with one another and work together in developing our personal missions focusing upon how we will move forward from here.

I am not trying to be pessimistic; this is a reality that lies before us and I want to alert my family and friends to "prepare now." The ones who are "prepared" are more ready to confront their fears in a period of sudden chaos.

Those who understand the chaotic challenges that will soon confront our generation need to be communicating with their families and friends. The purpose for this communication is to address "physical preparations" that will be needed in the event of a sudden shutdown of banks, stores, gas stations, and subsequent gang violence throughout cities and neighborhoods. I have provided some suggestions for such a physical preparation meeting in Appendix G.

COMING TO AMERICAN – OUTLAWING THE TRUE GOSPEL

In the coming days the American government, together with the United Nations, who view evangelical Christians as the greatest roadblock to establishing their world-wide agenda, will outlaw the gospel proclamation that Jesus Christ is actually the Son of God who will soon return to setup His kingdom throughout the world. They will also make it illegal to profess the following:

- *And there is salvation in no one else, for there is no other name under heaven given among men by which we must be saved." (Acts 4:12)*

It is a time when the great majority of Americans will war against the people of God who continue to stand as warrior-spirited witnesses for Jesus Christ and His kingdom. These are Christian-warriors who refuse to submit to the wicked authority of this world government and maintain that it is Jesus Christ who is their King. They will be deeply hated and the world will wage a continuous war against them.

Even if American cities are struck by terrorists, we Christians may be the first to be blamed and labeled as the greatest enemy to national security. Even if Muslim terrorists are behind these terrorist attacks, Christians may still be blamed for being the major cause of Islamic hatred toward Americans.

Soon, all bibles and biblically related books will be outlawed except for government-supporting leadership in compromising churches - the peoples will be required to turn them over to the authorities for burning. Those who refuse will be criminally charged and sentenced to imprisonment. Torture, executions, imprisonment in concentration camps, separation from family, and forbidding the purchase of food and water will all be commonly employed tactics of this evil kingdom. These will be extremely hard and faith-challenging days and a time of "wearing out" the people of God, but warrior-spirited Christians in the Army of the Lord will remain steadfast throughout this brief period of time.

CHRISTIAN WARRIORS – ENDURING PERSECUTION

My brothers & sisters, the time may come when He calls us to the following:

- *If anyone is to be taken captive, to captivity he goes; if anyone is to be slain with the sword, with the sword must he be slain. <u>Here is a call for the endurance and faith of the saints.</u> (Revelation 13:10)*

In the coming days, true believers in Jesus Christ will be challenged from every direction. Every believer who commits to an all-out relationship with our Lord will come under governmental oppression, various afflictions, and persecution. We may initially struggle in our trials because discipline and suffering is foreign to us, but as we continue to endure – our hearts will continually grow deeper in our love and commitment to Him. At times it may seem unbearable when some friends and even family members become spiteful toward us. Yet, enduring the scorn and persecution from the world joins us in a partnership with Christ as we share in His sufferings in this life.

We need to be mindful that being persecuted is a blessed opportunity to honor Christ?

- *"Blessed are you when others revile you and persecute you and utter all kinds of evil against you falsely on my account. Rejoice and be glad, for your reward is great in heaven, for so they persecuted the prophets who were before you.* (**Matthew 5:11-12**)

Suffering with Christ produces a strong heart bond in our relationship with Him and with one another as we follow Him down the same path that He walked.

Listen to Paul speaking to his disciple, Timothy:

- *Share in suffering as a good soldier of Christ Jesus. No soldier gets entangled in civilian pursuits, since his aim is to please the one who enlisted him.* (**2 Timothy 2:3-4**)

Awareness of one of God's purposes for persecution should strengthen us during these times:

- *For when your judgments are in the earth, the inhabitants of the world learn righteousness.* (**Isaiah 26:9**)

Also, remember that our Lord's mighty hand will be upon us during these times and nothing can touch us without His authorization:

- *You will not fear the terror of the night, nor the arrow that flies by day, nor the pestilence that stalks in darkness, nor the destruction that wastes at noonday. A thousand may fall at your side, and ten thousand at your right hand, but it will not come near you.* (**Psalm 91:5-7**)

Remember David's faith when he said:

- *Even though I walk through the valley of the shadow of death, I will fear no evil, for you are with me; your rod and your staff, they comfort me.* (**Psalm 23:4**)

This is the time when we may be called to glorify our Lord by the laying down of our lives, but it will not happen until our mission in this life is complete.

- *Count it all joy, my brothers, when you meet trials of various kinds, for you know that the testing of your faith produces steadfastness. And let steadfastness have its full effect, that you may be perfect and complete, lacking in nothing. (James 1:2-4)*

EVIL DISGUISED AS DECENCY – "STAND FAST"

Evil disguised as decency in the midst of a lukewarm Christian community, may be strong weapons the enemy will use against you. These are pacifists that will attack your faith and attempt to get you to make compromises so that life won't be so hard. **Stand fast!**

During these times of persecution, the voice of Satan will undoubtedly attack many with, "this is too hard…..it's not fair….God has forsaken me." Be aware that when these thoughts begin to surface that you are a soldier in the Army of God under attack. **Stand fast!**

This will be tough when loved ones embrace you and try to get you to compromise your faith just a little bit by saying, "Daddy please, God will understand." **Stand fast**!

Your steadfastness is of tremendous importance to both you and your loved ones who are considering small compromises. It will have a powerful strengthening effect on all who see your uncompromising testimony which prioritizes the Kingdom of God over the world. Your family and friends may grieve over your steadfastness that leads to persecution, but they too will be strengthened in their lives.

HANDLING SUFFERING IN THE ARMY OF GOD

In the coming days, true believers in Jesus Christ will be challenged from every direction. Every believer who commits to an all-out relationship with our Lord will come under spiritual oppression, various afflictions, and persecution. We may initially struggle in our trials because discipline and suffering is foreign to us, but as we continue to endure, we will recognize how meaningful the discipline of the Lord really is. Our hearts will continually grow deeper in our love and commitment to Him. At times it may seem unbearable when some friends and even family members become spiteful toward us.

The Lord's word tells us that suffering is a necessary experience that His warriors must endure in order to receive His glory. Being "prepared" doesn't mean we won't suffer.

- *The Spirit himself bears witness with our spirit that we are children of God, and if children, then heirs — heirs of God and fellow <u>heirs with Christ, provided we suffer with him</u> in order that we may also be glorified with him. (Romans 8:16-17)*

This truth will be severely tested when the trumpets continue to blast forth devastation upon the earth for then; we will be expected to confront our personal sufferings in order that we will not be derailed from our calling during that critical time.

Suffering is a means by which God breaks the vessel so that His glory might be revealed, but only if we respond in the proper way. <u>One might ask, "What actually is suffering?"</u> Well, suffering may be physical or it may be mental or emotional, but suffering really is anything that we don't like; anything that is uncomfortable or painful for us. Certainly the most painful suffering that may occur would be the loss of our loved ones, but our heavenly Father understands this, for He also experienced the loss of His Son. Our hope in such a grievous situation derives from understanding that - as the Father raised His Son from the dead that our loved ones who die in Christ will also be raised to eternal life with Him.

Enduring the scorn and persecution from the world joins us in a partnership with Christ as we share in His sufferings in this life. Suffering with Christ produces a strong heart bond in our relationship with Him and with one another as we follow Him down the same path that He walked. In order to better comprehend this, consider the following:

- Marines in combat or boot camp who experience really tough trials together eventually grow in strength and closeness with one another. Marines will put their own lives on the line for their fellow Marines.
- Yet a heart that experiences the hardships that Christ also experienced produces a much greater bond than what Marines share with each other. For a deep spiritual love for one another begins to grow which will throw off all the cares of this world and focus only upon the kingdom of God.

It is through suffering in life that warrior-spirited leadership develops the characteristics of holiness that are inherent in His glory and allow them to become more and more conformed to the image of His Son. Characteristics such as a strong compassion for people, a spirit that is slow to anger, a passionate desire for truth and justice, and the ability to forgive our enemies; these all develop within the soul as the leader experiences personal suffering. A proper handling of life's sufferings will burn away inner pride and ego – it purifies His people, especially the one's chosen for leadership.

Sufferings in life should no longer be a surprise, yet leaders must learn to handle them today so we will be prepared tomorrow, when the trumpets begin to blast.

- *… when you do good and **suffer** for it you endure, this is a gracious thing in the sight of God. For to this you have been called, because **Christ also suffered for you**, leaving you an example, so that you might follow in his steps.*

- *He committed no sin, neither was deceit found in his mouth. When he was reviled, he did not revile in return; **when he suffered**, he did not threaten, but continued entrusting himself to him who judges justly.*

- *He himself bore our sins in his body on the tree, that we might die to sin and live to righteousness. By his wounds you have been healed. (**1 Peter 2:20-24**)*

We must stand as warriors in the midst of good times and bad times; for both will be faced in life.

OVERCOMING "FEAR"

Fear has the tendency to cause people to stick their heads in the sand and hope this won't happen. It will keep us from properly preparing and that day of tremendous warfare will then drop on us like a thief in the night.

Our generation is going to face some very challenging times and more and more Christian warriors are needed for a tough battlefield that will bring forth a great multitude of people that will give their lives over to the Lord – People who will be searching for men and women of great spiritual strength in the midst of tremendous tribulations - those who are **not fearful** during these times.

I have learned from my experiences during the Vietnam War that the key to overcoming fear in warfare is by prioritizing the men under your authority over your own life. <u>For example:</u>

- In the midst of a very fierce firefight I learned that when I prioritized the men under my authority ahead of my own life, the spirit of fear could not control my decisions.

Now think about your loved ones in the midst of times when needed supplies will no longer be available and it will free you to make appropriate decisions concerning preparations. This is not the time for God's people to withdraw into passivity – to refuse to look at the reality of a rapidly decaying society that affects all of us and our loved ones. We are not free to play the role of **civilians**, living as if there was no war. Our **military** role is pictured for us throughout the bible; for the history of the saints in every age is one of conflict. <u>Prioritize your family & friends before you and "fear" will no longer be in control of your decisions.</u>

Satan's worldly peoples will always visibly appear to be greater and more powerful than God's mighty warriors for they are usually in positions of worldly authority. Yet, warrior-spirited Christians standing uncompromisingly for our Lord will always prevail in the strength of the Lord. The praying believer will never faint during hard times. On the contrary, he will grow stronger and stronger – because he trusts in God before he trusts in men.

- *He gives power to the faint, and to him who has no might he increases strength. Even youths shall faint and be weary, and young men shall fall exhausted; but they who __wait__ for the Lord shall renew their strength; they shall mount up with wings like eagles; they shall run and not be weary; they shall walk and not faint.* (**Isaiah 40:29-31**)

STEADFAST PRAYER WARRIORS WILL PREVAIL WITH GOD

Christian warriors need to remember that this is a Holy War and that the required power for victory is not found among its human participants, but in the power of God. Thus, believers need to understand the power of prayer which may be likened to that wrestling which took place between God and his chosen warriors throughout history. This is the "ongoing battle" that should be taking place within each member of the Body of Christ.

Believers must prevail with God before Satan can be subdued in their lives. Believers will never prevail by battling in the flesh. The victory is to be the Lord's and Christians can only prevail if they humble themselves before Him in true heart repentance. Prayerlessness is proof that our life is still under the power of the flesh. It proves that the life of God in the soul is mortally sick and weak. The sin of prayerlessness is the cause of a powerless spiritual life. Victory is certain if believers will exercise the patient, long-suffering faith that brought His mighty warriors through the battlefield.

Christians have been brought into the story of life at this time in the history of the world in order to enlist in the Army of God. Believers need to put on the armor of God and allow His Light to shine through them in the workplace, their neighborhoods, and their families. These places are the true front lines of the battlefield.

- *"You are the light of the world. A city set on a hill cannot be hidden. Nor do people light a lamp and put it under a basket, but on a stand, and it gives light to all in the house. In the same way, let your light shine before others, so that they may see your good works and give glory to your Father who is in heaven."* (**Matthew 5:14-16**)

Remember, all of God's biblical warriors did lose some battles now and then, but they continued to be strengthened by their experiences and did not succumb to self-pity. That warrior spirit may be knocked down on occasion, but will always seek the strength of the Lord through prayer and fasting in order to get back up and again "run to the battle." **These are the Christian warriors who will "never quit."**

A PURE CHURCH WILL ARISE IN THE MIDST OF CHAOS

A great apostasy will soon take place bringing a separation between light and darkness in the American churches. The "weeds" within the church will run but those who remain will truly represent the Kingdom of God to the many in our nation who are suffering great loss and grief. This will result in a pure testimony from the true church causing many peoples to embrace the Lord Jesus during the times which precede His 2nd coming to establish His eternal kingdom upon this earth.

I truly foresee a great outpouring of the Holy Spirit upon these warrior-spirited witnesses like never before - even greater in numbers than the 1st century church. This will be the time that Jesus talked about when He said that **"greater works will you do than even I have done"**. He was speaking of worldwide messengers of God ministering in the great and glorious power of His Holy Spirit. This is the Body of Christ that goes forth proclaiming the message of John the Baptist:

- *"The voice of one crying in the wilderness: 'Prepare the way of the Lord; make his paths straight." (**Matthew 3:3**)*

But now it will be calling people to "prepare" for the 2nd coming of our promised Messiah, Jesus Christ.

ANOINTED CHRISTIAN WARRIORS & THE FINAL GOSPEL

Christian warriors of the end-time generation, who I believe are symbolized by the "sealed 144,000" in the Book of Revelation, will boldly and fearlessly stand united against the apostasy of this age as they proclaim the testimony of Jesus Christ and His truths among all the nations of the earth.

- *And this gospel of the kingdom will be proclaimed throughout the whole world as a testimony to all nations, and then the end will come. (**Matthew 24:14**)*

As to the contents of their message during a time of tribulation, these anointed witnesses for Christ will prayerfully stand before the Lord of the whole earth and they will speak nothing but that which their Lord has commissioned them to speak. They will speak of Christ and His atoning blood, which is the witness of the righteousness and holiness of God in the midst of a sinful world.

- *Jesus said to him, "I am the way, and the truth, and the life. No one comes to the Father except through me. (**John 14:6**)*

- *And there is salvation in no one else, for there is no other name under heaven given among men by which we must be saved." (Acts 4:12)*

They will openly condemn all efforts to seek salvation outside of that atoning blood, and this will infuriate the false church and the worldly leadership that is attempting to establish a one-world kingdom together with a one-world religion.

A TIME OF GREAT HARVEST

Yes, this will be a time of great tribulation never before seen since the creation of the earth, yet this also will be a time of a great harvest of souls. A time of tremendous miracles as the gospel message goes forth in a power greater than the world has ever seen: the blind will see, the deaf will hear, and many of the afflicted will be healed throughout the world.

- *"Truly, truly, I say to you, whoever believes in me will also do the works that I do; and greater works than these will he do, because I am going to the Father. Whatever you ask in my name, this I will do, that the Father may be glorified in the Son. (John 14:12-13)*

The world must hear the gospel message proclaimed by His end-time warrior-spirited witnesses and they must hear it repeatedly so that they become fully conscious of their sin and the redemptive work of Jesus Christ:

1. All of mankind shall be well-acquainted with the gospel message of Jesus Christ before the final judgments fall on the earth.
2. There will be no more grey areas; one stands either with Christ or against Him - love and hatred will be clearly visible among all the inhabitants of the earth.
3. Those who reject Him will do so willingly and deliberately - then the testimony is finished and may be silenced.
4. Those who scorn the message will be without excuse when they stand before the judgment seat of almighty God.
5. Certainly many people will respond and be brought into everlasting life, but the great majority of the world will blasphemy this message and will persecute those who proclaim it.

   Finally, this gospel message not only will be a calling to mankind to repent and give glory to God, but it also will contain the prophetic warning that final judgments are soon coming to the world.

COMING TO AMERICA:
CHRISTIAN PERSECUTION AND SPIRITUAL REVIVAL

Many Christian leaders have been teaching that God is preparing a great wave of revival that will allow the restructuring of society, restore all things, and establish the kingdom of God on earth, thus reclaiming the earth so that Christ can return. Of course, this is not what He taught concerning His return. A terrible persecution will precede His coming, and it will cause a great falling away and a separation between false Christians and those who are truly faithful to the Lord. This will be the foundation for the coming, true move of God, a terrifying, but also glorious move of God that will bring the true gospel of Christ to the forefront of humanity.

The great tribulation will produce a final harvest of souls and a revival that will awaken many sincere Christians who have been put to sleep by their teachers. This move of God cannot be purchased, video produced, or manufactured like some movements over the last twenty years, for this move will be accompanied by judgment and persecution. The leaders of this movement will pay the price, like the first disciples, who challenged the falseness that had infiltrated the true church. These leaders will guard the sheep and speak forth in the power of God. There is a showdown coming between true leadership and those false teachers who will attempt to oppose the true movement of God.[343]

For the American believer, it is hard to imagine that Christian persecution could happen in our country, much less preparing for it. Yet it is coming, and it will shortly be commonplace for both Jews and Christians to face imprisonment and death in these last days. It may be even more severe in America than in other nations, for here is where the enemy will concentrate his efforts to stamp out the name of Christ from the Christian church. The political system, the entertainment arena, public schools, the courts, and the media will continue to promote their anti-God agendas. I recommend reading Romans 1:18-31 to see what happens to mankind when they trade the truths of God for lies. This is America in Scripture.[344]

The great majority of Christian teachers in America completely miss the point that the Lord makes in the following passage regarding events at the end of the age.

- *Then they will deliver you up to tribulation and put you to death, and you will be hated by all nations for my name's sake. And then many will fall away and betray one another and hate one another. And many false prophets will arise and lead many astray. And because lawlessness will be increased, the love of many will grow cold. But the one who endures to the end will be saved. And this gospel of the kingdom will be proclaimed throughout the whole world as a testimony to all nations, and then the end will come. (Matthew 24:9-14)*

Jesus Christ, our Commander in Chief is warning His people that in the midst of intense worldwide persecution, masses of "Christian pretenders" will betray one another to government-led persecutors.

A generation of American Christians are watching the early birth pains, convinced by their teachers that the next major event will be the rapture of the church or a sudden, peaceful return of Christ; yet what is actually before us is intense persecution. One day soon, the American church will awaken and realize that they have been deceived by those in church leadership whom they trusted but did not warn them concerning persecution that was coming upon the church. Therefore, most Americans are neither emotionally nor spiritually prepared for the sudden and intense persecution that is shortly before us. Nominal professing Christians will stumble and fall under the threat of persecution and will deny their faith. They will also betray those who were once their friends who continue to stand strong in the Lord. This will happen in America. What other country has such a large Christian population that will "fall away?" Certainly not China, for the Christians there are committed. America is the greatest representative of Christianity in all of history. It is here that these tragedies will occur.

Also, whole American churches that embrace the visions of their forerunners in those liberal Sardis and Laodicea-type churches will unite against the true believers in the Lord Jesus Christ. They want their churches to visibly continue, so they will continue to embrace the universal doctrines of religion that are acceptable to the kingdom of the world. These are beliefs that will deny the need for man's redemption from sin and mock those who proclaim that Jesus Christ is the eternal Son of God and the only way to eternal life. We know from history that these harlot churches will rejoice when true believers are imprisoned and killed for the gospel of Jesus Christ. They are a part of the religious nature of Mystery Babylon. They will join with the whore on top of the seven-headed beast in order to continue sharing in her riches and beauty and to retain their popular position in American society. Don't be fooled by the smooth words of these false teachers. They will tell you that all it takes to be pleasing to God is to do certain good things and abstain from certain bad things. Over the centuries, these teachers have deceived many into believing that they are true Christians.

OUR LORD TARRIES – "WHY?"

Day and night, God's intercessors have cried out to the Lord that His kingdom will come and righteous judgment will occur on the earth. Yet our Lord tarries. Though He is at work every moment of every day, it is not always as we wish or in ways that are visible to us. He is on the throne of justice; so we may wonder just how long justice can be postponed. Yet we must remember that He is also on the throne of grace. This grace is intended not only for those being persecuted but also for the persecutors. If postponement of justice for one more day results in bringing one more person into the kingdom of Christ, then so be it. We must remember, for the Lord a thousand years is like a single day.

If a million years from now we were to ask ourselves whether our momentary suffering during our earthly life was an acceptable exchange for one more life to enter eternal glory, how would we answer? When considering these hard but wonderful truths, I am reminded of the Roman centurion who was in charge of the crucifixion of Christ. Listen to him.

- *When the centurion and those who were with him, keeping watch over Jesus, saw the earthquake and what took place, they were filled with awe and said, "Truly this was the Son of God!"* **(Matthew 27:54)**

I wouldn't be surprised if this Roman centurion and some of his men, who led the military unit assigned to crucify our Lord, subsequently searched for and found the truth that Jesus Christ was the Son of God. If so, these Roman persecutors certainly repented and will reign with us in glory. Such is the long-suffering of Him who sits on the throne of grace.

Christians, consider this:

Being imprisoned is not so bad, for prisoners are not as distracted as those on the outside, and therefore the message of the gospel can be more powerful in a prison environment. They do not put hope in their plans for worldly success, and they think about the end of life more than those on the outside. Tell them about Jesus, and they are much more eager to hear. "If the Son sets you free, you are free indeed." That is real freedom. One man stands inside a prison and is free. Another man stands outside a prison in luxurious living and is in bondage.[345]

Christian warriors - remember this well: we are alive this day because Jesus has a mission for us that is yet to be fulfilled. When we die, that will be a sign that He wishes us to do something else. Eternal missions await each of us. We must move forward in our assignments each and every day of our short lives in this world. Our deepest motivation must be to hear Him tell us face to face,

- *Well done, good and faithful servant. You have been faithful over a little; I will set you over much. Enter into the joy of your master.'* **(Matthew 25:21)**

WALKING AS GOD'S WARRIORS DAY TO DAY

Redeeming the time may be extremely difficult, but it is also one of the most important areas of daily life that champion leaders must master. Stay on the offensive; take the sword of the Spirit, which is the Word of God, and know it, memorize it, and take it up daily. Stand firm; when under daily fire, remember Job. Intercessory prayer must become heart driven, for this is where your one-on-one relationship with the Lord truly grows powerful.

Additionally, we need to embrace our biblical calling to **"fast"** for this is a great channel for spiritual power. Important insights into understanding our call to biblical fasting is found in Appendix D. Fasting, together with pray, is a very critical area for those who are called to warrior leadership in the coming days.

Let your faith shine within your environment; remove the basket, and be the light that you are called to be in the world. Anticipate the battle, and allow it to cause growth in strength and intimacy with the Lord.

This is our call, though perhaps it is not for everyone. But for those who hear this call to be warriors and overcomers, this is an opportunity that was offered to warriors like Paul, David, and Elijah, and it is offered to each of us in our lives. We only have one life and thus, one opportunity to stand for our Lord on the front lines of the battlefield and fight against His enemies. The rewards that are promised in the afterlife are predicated upon our kingdom work during this lifetime. Some will rule ten cities, some five, and some one, but most will be citizens, not leaders. All will receive rewards, but there is a difference—His warriors will be called to eternal leadership in the eternal kingdom. Let us not go to the grave wishing that we had answered this call. Now is the time, not tomorrow or next week; the call is now to "those who hear."

GOD'S VALIANT WARRIORS TAKE HEAVEN BY FORCE

Of all men and women who live on the earth, the Christian needs continual courage and resolve for there is nothing that one can do as a Christian that is not an act of valor. It requires more prowess and greatness of spirit to obey God faithfully, than to command an army of men.

Matthew 11:12

- *From the days of John the Baptist until now the kingdom of heaven has suffered violence, and the violent take it by force.*

Ephesians 6:10-12

- *Finally, be strong in the Lord and in the strength of his might. Put on the whole armor of God that you may be able to stand against the schemes of the devil. For we do not wrestle against flesh and blood, but against the rulers, against the authorities, against the cosmic powers over this present darkness, against the spiritual forces of evil in the heavenly places.*

Isaiah 35:4

- *Say to those who have an anxious heart, "Be strong; fear not!*

Proverbs 16:32

- *Whoever is slow to anger is better than the mighty, and he who rules his spirit than he who takes a city.*

It may seem like a little thing for a Christian to pray, yet prayer cannot be performed properly without a princely spirit. The Christian in prayer comes up close to God and takes hold of Him and wrestles with him. He will not let go without a blessing. There is no duty in a Christian's walk with God that is not lined with difficulties.

The Christian is to proclaim an irreconcilable war against his bosom sins; which are those sins that lay closest to the heart; they must be trampled underfoot. <u>Now what kind of courage do you think this requires?</u>

Genesis 22:2

- *He said, "Take your son, your only son Isaac, whom you love, and go to the land of Moriah, and offer him there as a burnt offering on one of the mountains of which I shall tell you."*

Do you think Abraham was being tried when he was called to take his son, his only son whom he loves dearly and waited so long for his birth? Yet what was that to this:

> *"Soul, take your lust, your only lust, which is a child of your love; a lust that has caused most joy and laughter, from which you receive the greatest return of pleasure. Lay hands on it and offer it up; pour out its blood before Me, and do it freely and joyfully for it is no pleasing sacrifice which is offered with a countenance which is cast down; and do this before you have one last embrace."*

Truly, this is hard – flesh & blood cannot bear this. Our lust will not lie as patiently on the altar as Isaac or as a sacrificial lamb, but it will roar and shriek. The Christian will experience great wrestling of the spirit before they can bring their heart to this work.

Such a lust will plead for itself and Satan will extenuate the matter when he says:

> "It is but a little lust and the soul will not surely perish because of it. It will not be seen in public to shame you. Shut it up and then you can embrace it once in a while in secret."

The unwillingness to deal with the lust(s) of the flesh is a primary reason why there are so few conquerors even though many enter the race. All have a desire to be happy, but few have the courage and resolution to deal with the difficulties that they meet. Satan is tireless in this war upon the saints.

The violent and the valiant are they that take heaven by force. The coward will never win it for he will falter and eventually quit. They may follow Christ for a mile or two while He leads them away from their worldly course and bids them to prepare for hardship. One's courage will be tested by the Lord.

It is a disgusting thing to see a bold sinner and a fearful saint; one resolved to wickedness and the Christian wavering in his presence. The guilty puts the innocent to flight and hell keeps the battlefield.

In a sense, God and the angelic kingdom are spectators. They observe how we acquit ourselves as children of the Most High. Every exploit that your faith does against sin causes heaven to rejoice. The heart of Christ (who is standing by with your reserve) leaps for joy to see the proof of your love for Him. When you come out of the field, He will receive you with the same joy that He received at His return to heaven.

However, principals and self-discipline must be well fixed, or the heart will be unstable. Blind zealousness is soon put to a shameful retreat. Hypocrites show spurts of courage, but cannot prevail in a long battle.

Take heed of any worldly profit, pleasure, or honor beneath Christ or heaven, for they will soon capture your heart and take away your love. And if our love be taken away, there will be little courage left for Christ.

THE ARMY OF GOD IS FOR "VOLUNTEERS ONLY:"

Obviously, my approach to addressing these end-time events is from a military perspective since much of who I am today is the result of my 20 years in the Marine Corps.

- The common purpose for all volunteers in the Army of God is to **prepare in the boot camp of our prayer closets** in order to allow the light and glory of our Commander-in-Chief, Jesus Christ to be clearly manifested on the spiritual battlefield which lies in the midst of this world.

- Our Commander-in-Chief does not draft His soldiers, but He opens His arms and welcomes all those who volunteer. He does not employ emotional strategies, but simply speaks out of love and calls each of us to join Him on the battlefield.
- Although he calls us to join Him in His battle against the forces of evil, He leaves us free to join the enemy against Him if we so will. He makes no promises that we will become rich or not experience pain in this life.
- Christian warriors who will stand fast in teaching others and will not compromise the true gospel are His disciples whom He values deeply.

Our Choice – Will We or Won't We?

We are faced with the option of greatness as a leader in the Kingdom of God, but we can choose to settle for less. If we decide for greatness, it will cost us everything we have and are. We will have to surrender our life. The choice is momentous, but amazingly, it is ours to make.

LEADERSHIP PRIORITIES IN THE KINGDOM OF GOD

- **1st** – We fight for the glory of His wondrous Name in the midst of a world of darkness.
- **2nd** – We fight for the salvation of those in bondage to the enemy. Family, friends, co-workers and strangers that our Lord brings into our lives.
- **3rd** – We fight without fear for ourselves for we are called to let go of this life and not be concerned for the consequences that may befall us.

Finally, my dear brothers and sisters who are hearing this message – may our Lord powerfully anoint you to be mighty warrior-spirited witnesses for the Lord Jesus Christ and the Kingdom of God as you travel though the wilderness of this life.

- *Arise, shine, for your light has come, and the glory of the Lord has risen upon you. For behold, darkness shall cover the earth, and thick darkness the peoples; but the Lord will arise upon you, and his glory will be seen upon you. (* **Isaiah 60:1-2***)*

PRAYER FOR SPIRITUAL STRENGTH

Ephesians 3:14-21

For this reason I bow my knees before the Father, from whom every family in heaven and on earth is named, that according to the riches of his glory he may grant you to be strengthened with power through his Spirit in your inner being, so that Christ may dwell in your hearts through faith—that you, being rooted and grounded in love, may have strength to comprehend with all the saints what is the breadth and length and height and depth, and to know the love of Christ that surpasses knowledge, that you may be filled with all the fullness of God. Now to him who is able to do far more abundantly than all that we ask or think, according to the power at work within us, to him be glory in the church and in Christ Jesus throughout all generations, forever and ever. Amen.

CHAPTER 16

UNDERSTANDING "THE PROBLEM OF EVIL"

CALLING FOR CHRISTIAN WARRIORS

The Lord is calling many among His people to champion His kingdom purposes, both in the spiritual and on earthly battlefields. Those who respond are His warrior-spirited Christians who really want to stand strong for the Lord in the face of a world that is becoming increasingly darker year by year. These are soldiers in the Army of God who will not shy away from being counted among those in His army who can identify with the following passage:

- *"If the world hates you, know that it has hated me before it hated you. If you were of the world, the world would love you as its own; but because you are not of the world, but I chose you out of the world, therefore the world hates you. Remember the word that I said to you: 'A servant is not greater than his master.' If they persecuted me, they will also persecute you. If they kept my word, they will also keep yours. (John 15:18-20)*

This chapter is intended to speak to Christians about becoming a true champion leader equipped with a warrior spirit. This type of champion will not be idolized, but will compete on a battlefield where one's age, gender, or physical handicap is not an issue; a champion leader in the Army of God. The opportunity to become that champion leader that our Commander-in-Chief is looking for is available to all, but history and experience shows that very few have the desire to step onto this battlefield.

First of all, Christian warriors must recognize that they are up against an enemy who is incredibly powerful; one whom the great majority of the world's population ignorantly embraces. Since the days of mankind's fall in the Garden of Eden, there has been ongoing warfare between Satan and his vast and powerful army of darkness and the eternal purposes of our Lord. Over and over, the Scriptures reveal that there is a violent, ongoing war occurring in the spiritual realm in which the people of God on earth must actively participate. The New Testament Christian, like the Old Testament Israelite, continues to be engaged in a battle, and it is a battle…….

- …….*not directed against flesh and blood, but against the rulers, against the authorities, against the powers of this dark world, and against the spiritual forces of evil in the heavenly realms" (Ephesians 6:12)*

Many within God's Kingdom recognize that a tremendously violent war is increasing in intensity; that the world is rapidly becoming darker than ever before and yet, these Christian warriors, like the sons of Issachar who understood their times, are deeply concerned that the traditional western church is asleep at the most critical time since the beginning of creation.

DEAFNESS WITHIN NUMEROUS CHURCHES

The Lord has been calling His people to champion His truths during their day-to-day lives on the worldly battlefields and yet, it is obvious that the voice of the enemy is becoming more and more influential throughout America. <u>What is causing this deafness to His calling?</u> Are believers not hearing the call because of their day to day busyness with worldly issues and their continuing pursuit of worldly pleasures? Is the church not listening because they do not want to hear that difficult times may be approaching? There certainly appears to be a strong tendency on behalf of believers to stick their heads in the sand and simply enjoy the social aspect of church life and ignore the wickedness that is rapidly overtaking America.

Perhaps a significant roadblock causing deafness among many in the church can be attributed to the following mindset among many in church leadership:

> Why has Christ's church been called into an offensive role in spiritual warfare when we serve a sovereign God who doesn't need our help to ensure victory? Doesn't the Word of God teach that God is all-powerful? Therefore, there is no reason to believe that He needs us to fight any battle.

However, there is another extremely critical issue that causes Christians to subconsciously back away from the battlefield and that is a lack of understanding of what is commonly described as the **"problem of evil."** This is a question that allows many unbelievers to continually mock Christians for their belief in a righteous and omnipotent (all-powerful) God by saying:

> *"If the God of Christianity is so loving and all-powerful, then why is there so much evil and suffering in the world?"*

- This is a centuries old issue that worldly philosophers continually use to confront the church in order to support their non-belief of God.

Christians need to understand that the problem is not evil itself; the problem is the failure to confront evil in their individual lives. This chapter is meant to examine some of these issues which continually hinder Christians from taking their combat role seriously. Hopefully, with insight into these historically perplexing questions, warrior-spirited Christians will be better equipped to hear the trumpet of God summoning His people to the battlefield.

Now, in order to gain deeper insight into this invisible realm of spiritual warfare and the problem of evil, let's examine three separate, historical eras where Satan and his demonic allies attempted to usurp the purposes of Almighty God:

1. Before the Foundation of the World.
2. In the Garden of Eden
3. The Tribulation of Righteous Job

BEFORE THE FOUNDATION OF THE WORLD

What is evil and where did it come from? This is a great and important question from the standpoint of our belief in God. Many people say they don't believe in God mainly because the problem of evil and its origin perplex them. One certainly cannot understand the course of biblical history nor grasp their individual role in mankind's story without having insight into the origin of evil. Let's begin with the Word Himself who teaches that He is the beginning of all things and that all was created to perfection.

- *In the beginning was the Word, and the Word was with God, and the Word was God. He was in the beginning with God. <u>All things were made through him, and without Him was not anything made that was made</u>. (John 1:1-3)*
- *And God saw everything that he had made, and behold, it was very good.... (Genesis 1:31)*

However, sometime prior to the creation of our world as we know it, God created the heavens and its citizens known as angels. God created all and thus, all things were created in perfection and evil did not exist. So, there was a time when evil did not exist; when the heavenly principalities and powers were all perfect, all glorious, and all worshipping and serving their Creator. However, in the course of time, a rebellion occurred in the heavens that brought about the advent of evil into the creation. A rebellion led by Lucifer (Day-Star), who was perhaps the highest ranking angelic being in the angelic world.

Who was this Lucifer (Satan) who would lead a rebellion against his Creator? It is inconceivable that God would have created something other than a cosmos endowed with a perfect harmony of righteousness, joy, peace, and love; and He didn't. Scripture appears to indicate that Satan was the most beautiful and powerful angelic being in the creation. Listen to an abbreviated description of Satan (Accuser) as spoken by the Lord before the rebellion:

- *"You had the seal of perfection, full of wisdom and perfect in beauty and you were covered with every precious stone. You were an anointed guardian cherub and you were on the holy mountain of God where you walked in the midst of the stones of fire. <u>You were blameless in your ways from the day you were created, until unrighteousness was found in you</u>" (Ezekiel 28:11-15)*

So, what occurred in Satan's life to cause him to rebel against his Creator? The Lord goes on to say to Satan:

- *"<u>Your heart was lifted up because of your beauty</u> and thus, you corrupted your wisdom by reason of your splendor. You were filled with violence and you sinned so I cast you as a profane thing from the mountain of God. <u>How you have fallen O Day Star, son of Dawn</u>!" (Ezekiel 28:16; Isaiah 14:12)*

What did Satan desire that he did not already have?

- *"But you said in your heart,": "I will ascend to heaven – I will raise my throne above the stars of God – I will ascend above the heights of the clouds – <u>I will make myself like the Most High.</u>" (Isaiah 14:13-14)*

Prior to his rebellion, Satan appears to have been one of the most powerful angelic beings created by God. However, as time evolved, Satan became more and more dissatisfied with his position; he came to believe that greater personal fulfillment was available if only he could be free to pursue it. Thus, he conspired against his Creator God and began to recruit allies among his angelic friends and built an army designed to overthrow the Lord and assert his contention that he was the one most qualified to rule the universe.

How did Satan proceed with this desire to take the "Throne of God'? One can only speculate, but it certainly is reasonable to assume that Satan raised support for his cause by convincing other angelic beings that their Creator was not allowing them to reach their fullest potential. Thus, if they were to achieve their desired destiny, they would need to take matters into their own hands. In other words, Satan is saying, "God doesn't care about us. We need to stand up against Him and do what is right in our own eyes". <u>Sound familiar?</u> Satan challenged God's authority to the heavenly throne by claiming that he had just as much right to rule over the creation and secondly, he convinced a multitude of his angelic friends to join him in his rebellion against their Creator.

So how did the Lord handle this rebellion? Listen to a summarization of His words as spoken to Satan:

- *"How you have fallen from heaven O' star of the morning, son of the dawn. <u>You said in your heart that you would make yourself like the most High</u>. Nevertheless you will be thrust down to hell. I have brought fire from the midst of you and it has consumed you – and you will be no more. You have come to a dreadful end and will be no more forever."* (**Isaiah 14:9-11; Ezekiel 28:18-19**)

But not yet, for God still had a purpose for Satan within His eternal plan for the creation.

THE REBELLION OF SATAN CONTINUES! WHY?

Now here is an important question before us that we need to consider in order to get a deeper understanding of our role in today's spiritual warfare:

> *"Why didn't God cast Satan and the other usurpers into the lake of fire immediately after their heavenly rebellion and protect mankind from his deception?"*

The great principle that we must lay hold of here is that God, in His wisdom, allowed this to happen. <u>Think about this:</u>

> *If God had destroyed Satan and his angelic allies at the point of rebellion, would He have proved Himself as being the Righteous One in this conflict, and having the sovereign right to rule over all creation?*

Certainly, He would have proved His power over this rebellious army of angels, but would the unleashing of this power have created questions in the hearts of the remaining angelic populace? Might some of these remaining angels also doubt the love of God toward them and His Creation? Would they secretly believe that their destroyed kin had some legitimate points in their claim against God? Perhaps, they too needed to be confirmed in righteousness. If so, then the immediate crushing of the rebellion would not change the scenario that caused the initial uprising. Therefore, the possibility of subsequent angelic rebellions must be considered.

<u>The inescapable truth is that it was our sovereign Lord's eternal plan to allow evil to enter the creation, but because we know of His tremendous hatred of sin, we can conclude that a greater purpose is in view by the allowed presence of sin.</u>

Now, with these insights, let's examine the confrontation that took place in the Garden of Eden.

IN THE GARDEN OF EDEN

In the biblical story of the creation of our world, we learn that man was created in the image of his God; a creature of perfection who walked with God daily in the Garden and enjoyed close communion and fellowship with his Creator. Thus, in the beginning, there was a deep, loving relationship between Adam and the Lord. Subsequently God, the Creator of the entire cosmos, gave man dominion over all of His earthly creation. Then one day, Satan suddenly appears before Adam and Eve and alleges that God had deceived them by misleading and withholding greatness from them. Satan then promises that if they would listen to him, they too could become like gods.

It is certainly feasible to believe that both Adam and Eve began to think, "I will make myself like the most high!" Subsequently, they both rebelled against their Creator by believing the words of Satan. Their action alleges God to be a lying deceiver and Satan to be their real friend who wants them to have more greatness. The consequence of this choice meant that they now assumed the image of Satan and his sinful nature and established him as their lord. Thus, Satan becomes the Prince of this world and all human offspring inherit this sinful nature which results in a separation from their Creator, and introduces death into the creation.

1. What did God do about this sudden turn of events? After cursing the serpent Satan and condemning our first parents for their rebellion, He then promises that mankind would be redeemed from this sinful nature and would again be restored to a close relationship with the Lord. This would be accomplished when a mighty Warrior Leader from God would be born from the seed of the woman; a Warrior who would perfectly reflect the true image of God throughout His life and thus, with His sacrifice for mankind, crush the head of Satan and gain a complete victory over sin and death.[349]
2. As a result, mankind had an opportunity to be restored unto their relationship with Almighty God and Satan would then be defeated and eventually thrust into the Lake of Fire.

QUESTIONS TO CONSIDER FOR THE ARMY OF GOD

In light of this rebellion in the Garden, there are some key questions to consider if warrior leadership is going to gain deeper insight into the mission of the Army of God.

1. Even if God did not throw Satan and his legions in the Lake of Fire following their initial rebellion, why did our omnipotent (all-powerful) Lord allow Satan to enter into the Garden of Eden and entice mankind into sin?

2. Didn't our omniscient (all-knowing) Lord know that Satan would deceive mankind into sin? Wouldn't mankind have benefited if Satan had been cast in the Lake of Fire prior to God's creation of the earth and mankind?

3. Why would a Tree of Knowledge of Good and Evil even be placed in the Garden if mankind was commanded not to eat any of its fruit?

4. Was it the eternal plan of our Lord that mankind would fall into sin at the beginning? Wow!

These questions must be prayerfully contemplated in light of the Scripture that reveals that the redemption of mankind from sin was in view even before the world was created:

- .....*as __he chose us in him before the foundation of the world,__ that we should be holy and blameless before him. In love __he predestined us for adoption through Jesus Christ,__ according to the purpose of his will,* (**Ephesians 1:4-5**)

 <u>In light of the above, did Adam pass or fail the "test" when he ate the fruit of the Tree?</u> Perhaps the answer is not as simple as it appears on the surface. He certainly failed if viewed from a perspective of disobedience to the Lord's command but, perhaps he passed when viewed by the bigger picture which we will continue to explore.

Obviously, one's perceptions of all these questions affect what one thinks about God. For example, those who would argue against the sovereignty of God would claim that either He was not able to put down the rebellion at its origin; or that He is not concerned with the resultant death and suffering which sin has ushered in; or that He was simply outsmarted by Satan. Even many faithful believers in God wrestle with this problem of evil, but believe that it is not for them to understand. Some may even call this attitude being faithful. Christians need to stop hiding behind the excuse that "it's not for us to know;" for, "it is for us to know." It is my firm belief that these questions are for us to understand and the understanding of them helps to build warrior leaders in the Kingdom of God.

Now let's continue further into a biblical period which might aid our understanding of the ongoing conflict between Almighty God and Satan, and the believers' part in it. Insight into the conflict in the life of Job, where we see behind the spiritual veil, can shed much light upon the ongoing spiritual conflict and the purpose behind it.

JOB – A MIGHTY WARRIOR OF GOD

A brief overview of the background of Job, reveals that he was a man who received a loving and powerful testimony from God for being "blameless, upright, fearing God, and turning away from evil." Additionally, Job was an extremely wealthy man who was known to be the "greatest of all the men of the east"; and he was the head of a large family consisting of seven sons and three daughters for whom he continually interceded before God. Thus, Job was a loving, righteous man in the eyes of God as well as within his family and circle of friends. [250]

However, a grievous tribulation was about to erupt in the life of Job and his family that is probably unparalleled in the life of any family. Our Lord, who dearly loved His servant Job, gives permission for Satan to slaughter his family and destroy all of his possessions. Shortly after this devastation, Satan, with God's permission, attacks Job's physical body with innumerable painful boils.

Now how could a loving God allow such a thing to happen to one of the most righteous men of that age? When confronted with this question, many Christians would respond that God doesn't really care what we have to go through in this life for only eternal salvation is His focus and it should be ours. This mindset is simply a form of religious deism; meaning God does not interfere in our earthly lives. Obviously, there is so much to learn here concerning the Christian role in spiritual warfare that it is vitally important for warrior leadership to look closer at this devastating and largely misunderstood event in the life of Job; by examining what is simultaneously taking place in the heavenly realm.

The first chapter in the Book of Job reveals that the court of heaven, where our Lord has His throne, was the control center where all decisions were made involving the warfare that took place in the life of Job and his family. It began on a day when all the sons of God came and presented themselves before the Lord; Satan was also among them and as he was questioned by God concerning where he had been, Satan responded that he had been walking back and forth across the earth. Then the Lord said to Satan.......[251]

- ....*"Have you considered my servant Job, that there is none like him on the earth, a blameless and upright man, who fears God and turns away from evil?"* (**Job 1:8**)

Obviously it is not possible for servants of Satan to be blameless before God and therefore, this statement implies that the Lord is in the process of reconciling to Himself a new mankind by delivering man from his covenant of death with Satan. God is on the offensive in this spiritual battle and Satan is challenged to confess that God can redeem mankind from under his power or prove otherwise. Thus, Satan is backed into a corner, although he doesn't know it. <u>It is important to understand that by making this statement the Lord is the One who initiates all that is to follow in the saga of Job.</u> This scenario is very similar to the confrontation with Adam and Eve where God sets the stage and allows man to be put to the test. However, the purpose here is not to test Job's allegiance to God, but to allow him the opportunity to honor his Lord before all the hosts of heaven; also, to be an example to future generations of those who enter into the Kingdom of God. Satan then responds by questioning the genuineness of Job's allegiance to God for he answers the Lord saying.......

- ....*"Does Job fear God for no reason? Have you not put a hedge around him and his house and all that he has, on every side? You have blessed the work of his hands, and his possessions have increased in the land."* (**Job 1:9-10**)

Here Satan is saying that the Lord is simply creating the appearance of righteousness by blessing Job so abundantly and thus, Satan is intent on accusing the Lord of being a deceiver rather than a God of truth.

Satan then proposes a challenge to God by responding with.......

- ....*"But stretch out your hand and touch all that he has, and he will curse you to your face."* (**Job 1:11**)

This challenge was intended to expose the Lord before all the heavenly hosts as a deceiver who's Word cannot be trusted. In effect, Satan is saying that what he did to Adam, he will also do to Job. He is out to prove that he can thwart the purposes of God in creation. The Lord accepts this challenge and grants permission for Satan to proceed against all of Job's family and wealth with the exception that Satan was not allowed to take Job's life. [252]

Thus, the battle in the life of Job begins. This challenge by God and acceptance by Satan was to be settled by a spiritual battle designed to demonstrate whose power actually prevailed in the life of Job. Also, this battle is being fought before the entire heavenly host; they are all witnesses to this event. What will determine the outcome of this battle?

- **Answer**: Will Job curse God in the midst of his grievous suffering or will he remain faithful even though he has lost everything in life?

It is extremely important to understand what is at stake here: The Lord's Word says that His servant Job is a blameless and upright man; a man that loves God with all of his heart, soul, mind, and strength. Satan's word says, "Not true and I can prove otherwise."

- The Word of God is at stake and it's amazing that our Lord has chosen a common man, who is about to endure tremendous suffering, to demonstrate the truth and righteousness of the Word of God.

- On the other hand, Satan's mission is to make void the Word of God. If he is victorious the curse pronounced against him in the Garden becomes questionable for then the Word of God cannot be relied upon. Therefore, Satan's attack is primarily against God, not Job.

- The only way that Satan can be proven false is through Job maintaining a positive response during a prolonged, painful trial.

The Lord God had entrusted the honor of His holy Name with a man. Job was selected to champion the truth of God and he doesn't even know it. The battle was about to reveal that Job's devotion to his Lord was genuine and was not prompted by temporal benefits. He was in a condition of tremendous misery, both physical and emotional, without any hint of improving his circumstance, but in the face of continuing temptations, he remained faithful in his love for God.

Whose word will prevail; the Lord's or Satan's? This is what spiritual warfare is about.

It is important for Christian warriors to remember this lesson: We serve a God who not only gives His Word, but He allows it to be tested under the most difficult of conditions. Now having received these insights into the spiritual battle, let's return to the Garden of Eden with this renewed perspective.

RETURNING TO THE CONFRONTATION IN THE GARDEN OF EDEN

What if Adam & Eve had remained obedient to God and rebuked Satan as the deceiver; would it have proved that they loved God with all their heart, mind, soul, and strength?[253] Would it have proved they did so from a heart of "free-will"? Could not Satan have made the following statement to God?

- *.......Have you not put a hedge around him and his house and all that he has, on every side? You have blessed the work of his hands, and his possessions have increased in the land. (Job 1:10)*

Satan could have accused the Lord of practicing deception by denying the free-will aspect of mankind by claiming that God had created obedience. Adam was not God's intended champion! Champions are warriors in the Army of God who fight the battle using the Lord's strength. [254]

Adam was a good man and he possessed the authority to deal with Satan but he was not trusting in God for the victory. Adam stood by his own strength; but Job stood by God's strength.

Additionally, God did not place the Tree of Knowledge of Good and Evil in the Garden for the primary purpose of testing man, but it was more an invitation to Satan to engage in warfare for the dominion of creation. This becomes even clearer when we consider the pre-creation covenant between God the Father and His Son, Jesus Christ.

A PRE-CREATION COVENANT

BETWEEN FATHER AND SON

It certainly appears that the Lord, in His absolute sovereignty, had already ordained the fall of mankind in the Garden long before it actually occurred. His Word tells us that the sacrifice of the Son of God was foreknown before the foundation of the world and that the names of those who have been chosen for eternal salvation were written in the book of life prior to the creation. For example:

- *He was <u>foreknown before the foundation of the world</u> but was made manifest in the last times for your sake, who through him are believers in God, who raised him from the dead and gave him glory, so that your faith and hope are in God.* **(1 Peter 1:20-21)**
- *For those whom he <u>foreknew he also predestined to be conformed to the image of his Son</u>, in order that he might be the firstborn among many brothers.* **(Romans 8:29)**

The provision for grace which God made for His people before the foundation of the world involved His own Son and His assumption of human nature, the offering of Himself as a sacrifice for sin, His resurrection, and His supremacy over all the Church.[255] Clearly, these were matters of arrangement between God the Father and His Son prior to the creation. The first pronouncement of this redemptive plan was to Satan himself immediately after the fall of mankind when God told him:

- *.......I will put enmity between you and the woman, and between your offspring and her offspring; he shall bruise your head, and you shall bruise his heel."* **(Genesis 3:15)**

Since we recognize the scenario that the Lord placed the tree of the knowledge of good and evil in the garden and also allowed Satan access to mankind, we may now ask, "Was it the Lord's eternal plan that Adam fell into sin?" Answer: "Yes, it certainly was." But, because we know of the Lord's tremendous hatred of sin, we can easily conclude that a higher purpose is being served by the allowed presence of sin into His creation.[256] Now with this background in mind, let's examine some glorious truths that may provide a clearer understanding of the problem of evil.

SEVEN WONDROUS TRUTHS UNVEILED BY ADAM'S FALL

<u>First Truth Unveiled:</u>

- Adam's fall revealed that mankind did not yet have a true heart of love for his Creator, even though he was blessed with all that one could desire in this world.

God cannot create a heart of true love and thus, the weakness of the heart of mankind would not have been revealed without the fall. It is through periods of tribulation that we grow nearer to our Lord for it is mostly during these hard times when His people cry out to Him and discover that He hears and acts on their behalf. Thus, that love which is not a created thing grows within us as we see Him deliver from evil and bless us. Yes, the problem of evil causes much suffering, but it's not only mankind who suffers; the Lord has suffered alongside of us.

Second Truth Unveiled:

• The fullness of our Lord's attributes would not have been seen and understood without the fall and thus, we would not have known Him as He desired nor would we have understood what "love" truly means.

• *"Who is like you, O Lord, among the gods? Who is like you, majestic in holiness, awesome in glorious deeds, doing wonders?* (Exodus 15:11)*

We learn throughout Scripture that He is righteous in all of His ways and He will never violate His laws; yet, He is overwhelming in His love for His people. How could believers know about the patience and long-suffering of our Lord without it being demonstrated toward His people as they rebelled against Him century after century? Or, how could they know the depths of His love when after years of rebellion, He continually reconciles mankind unto Himself and casts their past sins as far from Him as the east is from the west.

• *The glory that you have given me I have given to them, that they may be one even as we are one, I in them and you in me, that they may become perfectly one, so that the world may know that you sent me and loved them even as you loved me. (John 17:22-23)*

Our Lord has taught us that true, holy love is sacrificial – that is, we are to place others as more important than ourselves. This sacrificial love of God for mankind was ultimately demonstrated at the Cross of Calvary when Jesus Christ, the Son of God, in obedience to His Father's predestined plan, willingly sacrificed Himself in order to free His people, whom He dearly loved, from the bondage of Satan.

Third Truth Unveiled:

• The fall of mankind demonstrates the dependency upon God that is needed to sustain life. Even the perfect creature is fully dependent upon his Creator for continued perfection.

This is a truth that would never have been known if the rebellion had been squashed at its source. The sin of Satan was that, in his perfection, he saw no need for God. If evil had not been present in the Garden of Eden, perhaps it was only a matter of time before Adam, in all of his splendor, or one of Adam's posterity would have committed the same rebellious sin as Satan.

Fourth Truth Unveiled:

- Knowledge of good and evil is necessary in order to truly understand and fully appreciate the perfect world in which believers will eternally live.

How can perfection be known unless it is contrasted in some way with its diametric opposite? For example, can one know righteousness unless he is familiar with unrighteousness? In the same way, can love, joy, and peace be truly known and appreciated without knowledge of hatred, sorrow, and war which are experienced within this life?

Fifth Truth Unveiled:

- Without the "fall", would we really understand true faith that would prioritize the Lord above all of creation?

Like Adam, each of us is provided with the same opportunity to choose who to follow; God or Satan. The fall provided the opportunity to bring forth Kingdom Warriors from mankind empowered by God for battle - an opportunity during our short life on earth, to join the Army of God against this ancient arch-enemy.

Additionally, like Job, we need to understand that it is during times of tribulation when believers can truly have a strong impact in the heavenlies; for it is during these times that the following words of the enemy come into our hearts, "If God is real and loves you, why does He allow these things to happen to you?" Christians must recognize that the spiritual battle is upon us and how we respond to these difficult times determines whether or not we are standing alongside our Lord on the battlefield.

Sixth Truth Unveiled:

- The "fall" provided the opportunity for our heavenly Father to introduce His Son who would perfectly reflect God's holy and righteous character in a way that mankind can understand.

Although, our Lord Jesus is the eternal Son of God, He had to become a Son of Man from the seed of Adam in order to fight the enemy. In other words, He must be fully Man who defeats Satan, but He must also be fully God, for He must be free of the sin nature in order to destroy the Adversary whose servants are slaves to sin. <u>We would not have come to truly know Jesus and His sacrificial love for us without the fall.</u>

There were other victories as mighty warriors standing strong for the Lord were brought forth in redemptive history, but the essence of sin in man thwarted any opportunity of obtaining perfect victory over the Adversary. The nature of the battle to be fought between Jesus Christ and Satan was that man was to exhibit the full image of God throughout his lifetime and in the face of constant assault.

Seventh Truth Unveiled:

- Those who are born again by the blood of Christ have a new relationship with God that was not available to Adam in his original state.

This is a relationship of family purchased by the blood of God Himself. The blood of the Lord Jesus that provides redemption has given birth to sons and daughters of God that are in such an intimate relationship with Him that they are called the Body of Christ.

Mankind no longer appears simply in the image of God, as Adam was before the fall; we have been born again and our identity is now sons and daughters of God. God walked with Adam in the Garden. In the new creation, God lives within His people. <u>A former friend now becomes a son.</u>

Thus, soldiers in the Army of God can say:

> *"Thank you Father, for allowing the Fall to occur which has provided us with the opportunity to grow more and more into the likeness of Your glorious Son through our ongoing understanding of good and evil; and to allow us to stand against the darkness of evil as we allow the Light of Christ to shine through us. Also, thank you Father for introducing your Son and providing the opportunity for us to be "born again" into your beloved family."*

This provides some answers to the previous questions regarding the problem of evil if believers truly understand and accept the fact that their righteous and omnipotent Lord frequently chooses to tie His hands while awaiting His Army of Warriors to come forth onto the battlefield.

TRIAL BY ORDEAL – AN HISTORICAL PERSPECTIVE

Ancient pagan kingdoms frequently elected to have judicial disputes resolved by an appeal to their respective gods. The idea being that divine intervention would take place and the party in the right would be vindicated.

A common method used to call their pagan gods into a dispute was to engage in a trial by ordeal whereby the dispute was settled by combat. The kings involved in the dispute would select their individual champions who would physically fight until a winner was proclaimed; usually this was a fight to the death. Although the champions were pitted against each other, it was believed that the divine power of their respective gods was what determined the outcome. [257]

History appears to reveal that our Lord also condescends to handle disputes arising from the lips of His accuser by similar ordeals.

BIBLICAL EXAMPLES OF ORDEALS BY COMBAT

God's Champion(s)	versus	Satan's Champion(s)
David	versus	Goliath
Moses	versus	Pharaoh
Elijah on Mount Carmel	versus	450 Prophets of Baal

These single events certainly stand out, but we need to remember that life is a battlefield where God's people are confronted again and again by Satan's chosen vessels. Other examples include the trials of Jacob, Joseph, Jonathan, Joshua, Gideon, Abraham, Hannah, Ruth, Esther, the Prophets, the Apostles, Irenaeus, Eusebius, Polycarp, the Martyrs, Luther, Calvin, George Whitfield, Jonathan Edwards, Watchman Nee, Corrie Ten Boom, David Wilkerson, etc., etc.

The whole history of the church is the arena of God versus Satan in trials by ordeal. It hasn't changed; running the 21st century race of champions is likewise, a trial by ordeal. Satan's champions will always visibly appear to be greater and more powerful than God's champions; fear is a tremendous power utilized against Christians and the only way that leaders will develop a champion mentality is by spending our time in His presence. That brings us to the second ordeal.

A SECOND ORDEAL

God's potential champions must first prevail with the Lord Himself. We see this important truth demonstrated in the life of Job. The primary ordeal between God and Satan is to be decided by God's ordeal with Job; for in order to subdue Satan by the hand of Job, God must first subdue Job. Job can prevail with God only as he is brought to his knees in submission before Him. Listen to Job's confession at the end of his terrible ordeal:

- ......*I had heard of you by the hearing of the ear, but now my eye sees you; therefore I despise myself, and repent in dust and ashes." (Job 42:5-6)*

It is God, not Job, who is the real conqueror of Satan, but Job will be eternally honored as a type of overcoming champion that our Lord is searching for among His people.

CONTINUING WARFARE UPON THE CHURCH

The armies of Satan continually fight to thwart God's purposes and to prevent the return of Jesus Christ in victory. Satan's very survival depends upon it. As always, this battle is directed against those whom God has declared righteous through the Blood of Christ. Therefore, Christians continue to be called upon to wage war against their spiritual adversaries and the worldly kingdom that is committed to the defeat of Christianity among the nations of the world.

Christians have been brought into the story of life at this time in the history of the world in order to enlist in the Army of God. Believers need to put on the armor of God and allow His Light to shine through them in the workplace, their neighborhoods, and their families. These places are the true front lines of the battlefield.

- *"You are the light of the world. A city set on a hill cannot be hidden. Nor do people light a lamp and put it under a basket, but on a stand, and it gives light to all in the house. In the same way, <u>let your light shine before others, so that they may see your good works and give glory to your Father who is in heaven.</u>"* (**Matthew 5:14-16**)

Participants need to remember that this is a Holy War and that the required power for victory is not found among its human participants, but in the power of God. Thus, believers need to understand the power of prayer which may be likened to that wrestling which took place between God and Job. This is the "second ordeal" that should be taking place within each member of the Body of Christ. Believers must prevail with God before Satan can be subdued in their lives. Believers will never prevail by battling in the flesh. The victory is to be the Lord's and Christians can only prevail if they humble themselves before Him in true heart repentance. Prayerlessness is proof that our life is still under the power of the flesh. It proves that the life of God in the soul is mortally sick and weak. The sin of prayerlessness is the cause of a powerless spiritual life. [258]

<u>For God to subdue Satan through the hand of His people, God must first subdue His people.</u> But, just as Job wrestled long with God, the Christian may, at times, have to wrestle long in prayer. However, the victory is certain if believers will exercise the patient, long-suffering faith that brought Job through the battlefield. The Job testing in our lives is a daily one; certainly not to the depth that we read about in Job, but all that happened to Job happens to many of us over a period of time. Yet, since it happened to Job all at once and with much greater severity, his reaction as a Champion of God should influence all believers.

It is important to remember that Adam did not rely upon God in the battle and lost. All of God's champions do lose some battles now and then, but they continue to be strengthened by their experiences and do not succumb to self-pity. That champion spirit may be knocked down on occasion, but will always seek the strength of the Lord in order to get back up and again run to the battle. These are the Christian warriors who will never quit.

REMEMBER THIS WELL !

God may choose to tie His hands since he is fighting the battle through His Warrior Army. Otherwise the Accuser can cry out before God..........:

- *.......Have you not put a hedge around him and his house and all that he has, on every side? You have blessed the work of his hands, and his possessions have increased in the land.* (*Job 1:10*)

Soldiers in the Army of God should not allow the Accuser to say that they are not truly righteous, but that they profess Christ because of our earthly prosperity or our desire to achieve earthly prosperity. They must stand as champions in the midst of prosperity and adversity; for both will be faced in life.

EMBRACE THIS TRUTH:
"LIFE IS MEANT TO BE CHALLENGING"

The "easy believism" gospel message that is so popular today is not true. This is the belief that we can have spiritual power and prosperity and be pleasing to God in this life without sacrifice and suffering. Those who embrace this popular message will live a life of whining and self-pity and will not really grow in their understanding of God and His ways. It's a self-focused gospel message and its teaching will cause many to "fall away" during the times of deep tribulation.

One might ask, "What actually is suffering?"-----Well, suffering may be physical or it may be mental or emotional, but suffering really is anything that we don't like; anything that is uncomfortable or painful for us.

In the wilderness, Israel lived a wandering lifestyle that God had led them into for a season of time. They were on their way to being restored, but they continually responded in a negative way. They developed a victim mentality and constantly grumbled about their state of discomfort. They had sunk into a maintenance mentality, trying to stay alive, rather than a victory mentality of ruling and reigning with God. They seemed to believe that when they entered the Promised Land that all fighting would cease and their worries would disappear. They had no idea that they were the weapon in God's hands that would establish the rule of God on earth. This sounds like much of the contemporary church. [259]

Believers have not been put on this earth simply to be saved, and then sit around living life as usual. We are being presented with the opportunity that Jesus offered His disciples; making an eternal impact on the Kingdom of God and becoming a warrior-spirited soldier in His Army. If believers decide for greatness, it will cost everything they have and are; for they may even have to give up their very lives. The choice is momentous, but amazingly, it is for every believer to make. [260]

CONCLUDING THOUGHTS

Regarding the problem of evil:

Hopefully, this chapter provides some answers to the problem of evil as we see our righteous and omnipotent Lord tying His own hands while awaiting His champions to come forth into the battle.

Regarding the importance of intercessory prayer:

Even though God knows our needs, there may not be an unleashing of divine blessing to meet these needs until we demonstrate a meaningful relationship which continues to seek and obey our Heavenly Father in our day-to-day activities. Otherwise, Satan can cry "Foul!"

Encouraging us to the battle:

The idea that we are called as individuals to champion the Lord as His truth and righteousness are being called into question should encourage us to the battle. Also, the believer's strength and determination during times of hardship has a profound impact upon the world. Many have come to acknowledge God as they witness the attitude of God's warriors during periods of tribulation.

A FINAL PRAYER

Our Father in heaven, hallowed be your name. Your kingdom come, your will be done, on earth as it is in heaven. **(Matthew 6:9-10)**

Dear Father, we thank You for quickening our hearts once more with this message. We await this day with great expectation. Come, Lord Jesus, even today in the person of the Holy Spirit, and prepare us for the work that You have chosen for each one of us to do.

As a watchman waits for the dawn, so we also wait and long for You. Move as You have in the days of old. Summon Your power, and show us Your strength as You have done before.

Be exalted once more in the midst of the nations. Raise up the standard of Your people. Pour out Your favor upon us so that people around us will know that Your presence is with us and will be able to distinguish Your soldiers from the people of the world. May the labors of Your army of warriors glorify Your name and be a bright light and a strong salt that will bring a mighty increase of people into the kingdom of almighty God.

Thank You for revealing Your plans and Your heart to us for the coming days. We wait for Your coming with great expectation and with thanksgiving in our hearts. Now, unto You and You alone, be all glory and power for all that You have done, are doing, and will do in our lives.

In Jesus Christ's name, we say, Amen!

APPENDIX "A"

HISTORICAL EMPIRES OF THE BEAST

FIRST HEAD OF THE BEAST = EGYPT

A Brief Background

God's chosen people, the family of Jacob, migrated to Egypt sometime between 1900 BC and 1800 BC. They numbered only seventy persons at that time, but the Lord blessed the wombs of the mothers, and their numbers rapidly increased. Some two hundred years later, the spirit of the Beast began its work in the Egyptian rulers; this resulted in a brutal enslavement of these descendants of Jacob.

Satan's Objective

- The tactics of Satan included the enslavement of these people of God so that they might be used to build up the world's kingdom.
- To control the growth of the sons of Abraham by slaughtering newly born babies and to take pleasure in the suffering of their families.
- Thus, he undoubtedly rejoiced, believing that he openly humiliated and defeated the purposes of God for His people.

Our Lord's Objective

- However, it was Satan who was unknowingly being controlled. Because of slavery, the Israelites did not marry among the heathen Egyptians, and so the experience of enslavement allowed them to grow in numbers and bond together as one people. This is like men in the military who go through difficult and traumatic times together; they bond for a lifetime.
- Thus, this long period of enslavement of God's people created a national identity for Israel. So 430 years after the family of Jacob migrated from the Promised Land into Egypt, they now numbered more than two million, and the time had come for almighty God to raise up a champion warrior (Moses) who would confront Satan's champion (Pharaoh).

Certainly our Israelite brothers and sisters in the Lord suffered tremendous affliction during this period of brutal enslavement, but it was a sacrifice that resulted in the Lord establishing a large and mighty nation in the midst of the world. Through this nation He would reveal His almighty power and glory to the world and make this spiritual war

273

visible to those with eyes to see and a heart to understand. And through the newly formed nation of Israel, He would eventually bring forth the Messiah, who would lead a numberless multitude into the glory of the eternal kingdom.[1]

SECOND HEAD OF THE BEAST = ASSYRIA

A Brief Background

Approximately 900 BC, following the death of King Solomon, the nation of Israel split into ten northern and two southern tribes. Thus, two nations were formed. The northern tribes immediately turned from God and followed the idolatrous practices of the Beast. Our Lord continually sent prophets into the land of the northern tribes, calling them to repent and return to the Lord who led them out of Egypt. However, every northern king ignored the prophets and continued to lead their people along the path of darkness. Finally, in the year 722 BC, after 280 years of warnings, the Lord withdrew His hand of protection from the ten northern tribes and allowed a mighty Assyrian army to conquer the land of the north.

Satan's Objective

- This Assyrian invasion led to a brutal massacre including thousands of women, children, and babies. Military leaders of the northern army were tortured, stripped naked, and lifted up alive on the heads of spears in a horrendous display before their families and friends. Thus, Satan visibly manifested his merciless hatred for these sons of Abraham.
- Rejoicing in his supposed victory, Satan subsequently directed the Assyrian army to launch an invasion into the southern kingdom, but during this siege the Angel of the Lord went out at night and struck down 185,000 Assyrians, resulting in a tremendous defeat that would severely weaken their empire.

Our Lord's Objective

- Our Lord's divine judgment over sin is visibly manifested to the remainder of His people in the southern tribes as well as the survivors in the northern tribes.
- The northern survivors were carried off to foreign lands, but the Lord has not forgotten them and, as discussed in chapter five, many of their descendants who now reside in countries throughout the world will once again be reunited with the southern tribes to form one holy kingdom under the reign of the Lord Jesus Christ. Certainly, many contemporary Christians are among these descendants of Ephraim, the former northern kingdom.

---

[1] Deuteronomy 29:4

THIRD HEAD OF THE BEAST = BABYLON

A Brief Background

God's remaining nation in the south, consisting primarily of the tribes of Judah and Benjamin, also fell into idolatry. Under evil leadership, the nation established cultic worship and developed contempt for God, whom they blamed for the catastrophe that decimated the northern kingdom. They did this in the face of continuing warnings from all the messengers God sent. It is said that their abominations exceeded those of the northern tribes and even those of ancient Sodom.[2] But like their northern brethren, the tribes of the south would not escape judgment. God would allow another army to invade Jerusalem and the southern territories.

However, it would not be the Assyrians this time, for the third head of the Beast, the Babylonian Empire, had recently defeated the Assyrian army and established itself as the great empire in the Middle Eastern world. So in 605 BC, the Babylonian army, under the command of King Nebuchadnezzar, captured Jerusalem and removed the great riches of silver and gold from Solomon's temple. Over the next eighteen years, prophets from God (Jeremiah and Ezekiel) continually proclaimed that this was a judgment allowed by God and that the Judean nation should humble themselves and submit to the Babylonian kingship. However, many false prophets arose and convinced the godless Judean leadership that God was on their side and they should not serve the Babylonians. Subsequently, the glory of God departed from the temple, and the protecting shield of heaven was lifted. Then in 587 BC, King Nebuchadnezzar came again to Jerusalem and brutally seized the city. Only this time he showed no mercy to the inhabitants; the temple was completely destroyed, the walls surrounding Jerusalem were leveled, and many of those who escaped the sword were carried captive back to Babylon.

Satan's Objectives

- To weaken the power of God upon the earth by destroying a nation through whom God could manifest Himself.
- To assimilate the Judeans into the Babylonian culture, believing this would effectively wipe out the sons of Abraham from the earth.
- To annihilate Solomon's temple, which had housed the glory of God upon the earth, and thus wipe out all worship of the Lord.
- To eliminate the people through whom the promised Messiah would come and thus prevent the crushing of the serpent's head.

---

[2] Ezekiel 16

There was no more nation of Israel. The testimony of the Lord who worked on behalf of His people was visibly wiped out as the country became desolate and its survivors taken captive. It would appear as if the spirit of the Beast had won the war. The nation that was to bring forth the Messiah was no more, and its people were being assimilated into the Babylonian culture.

Our Lord's Objective

- To righteously judge His people for their disobedience to the Mosaic covenant and for ignoring the warnings of His true messengers.
- To raise up a faithful remnant that would have a tremendous influence over the government of the Babylonian Empire and provide impacting prophetic insights to future generations of believers.
- To expose the idolatry of the Babylonian system and manifest Himself as the one true God by working through this faithful remnant.
- To purify the Holy Land and its people by rebuilding a nation from a faithful remnant out of a seemingly impossible situation.

The Lord previously had decreed some 150 years earlier that this captivity would not be permanent and that they would be delivered after seventy years by a man named Cyrus.[3] Thus, in 536 BC, Cyrus, the commander of the Persian army, invaded the city of Babylon and assumed control over the Mediterranean world and subsequently, allowed the Jewish people to return to Israel.

THE FOURTH HEAD OF THE BEAST = PERSIA

A Brief Background

Under the leadership of Cyrus, the Jews were allowed to return to their homeland. However, only a faithful remnant of approximately 50,000 actually chose to leave Babylon and rebuild the city of Jerusalem and their nation. The vast majority decided to stay, for they had assimilated into the worldly culture of Babylon and chose to no longer be Jews.

Satan's Objectives

- To annihilate the entire Jewish race using a high-ranking Persian authority by the name of Haman to deceive the king and turn him against the Jews. However, God overturned this deceitful attempt by raising up His champions, Esther and Mordecai, who exposed the lies of Haman before the king, resulting in Haman's execution.

---

[3] Isaiah 44:48; 45:1-13; Jeremiah 25:11-12

Our Lord's Objective

- To rebuild a nation using a small remnant of loyal Jews who were willing to leave the comforts of Babylon in order to settle a land that had been desolate for seventy years.
- To rebuild the temple for the Lord in Jerusalem; construction began around 520 BC.
- To rebuild the walls of Jerusalem; construction began around 440 BC.

Thus, the "Jewish nation" was established in the land of Israel, even though it remained under the authority of the Persian government.

THE FIFTH HEAD OF THE BEAST = GREECE

A Brief Background

As time progressed, the Persian government had more and more trouble keeping its wide empire in submission. Meanwhile, the Greeks had been building a powerful kingdom for some decades, and in 333 BC, under the leadership of Alexander the Great, they defeated the Persian armies. With the swiftness of a leopard, they extended their borders all the way to India and became the largest empire up to that time. Alexander died ten years later, and the Greek Empire was then divided into four geographical provinces. During this time, Israel was made subject to the Hellenistic culture because of its geographic location between two of these provinces: the Seleucid province of the north, comprised of Syria and much of the Middle East, and the Ptolemaic province of the south, comprised of Egypt and Palestine. While initially under Ptolemaic rule, conflicts also brought the Jews under Seleucid rule. Descendants of both Seleucus and Ptolemy were intent upon infusing the Greek way of life (Hellenism) over their respective domains.

Hellenism constituted a lifestyle of "eat, drink, and be merry for tomorrow we die." Merchants could amass great wealth; public eating halls serving rich foods and wines were very popular; music filled the cities from end to end; and gymnasiums were very popular among the youth, and many of the young Jewish men who were ashamed of their heritage had operations to undo their circumcisions.

Satan's Objectives

- To create the mentality, "Take pleasure today; don't worry about tomorrow."
- To move 100,000 Jews to Alexandria in 312 BC in an attempt to train them in Greek practices and destroy Jewish traditions.
- To raise up a new king out of the northern province in 175 BC with a passionate dedication to enforce Greek Hellenism over the entire nation of Israel. This was Antiochus IV Epiphanes, who launched one of the darkest periods in Israel's history. He is widely considered to be a "type" of the latter-day Antichrist.

- Under the reign of Antiochus, Jews were forbidden under the penalty of death to (1) practice circumcision, (2) observe the Sabbath, (3) observe Jewish feasts, and (4) destroy all copies of the Hebrew Scriptures. This created a greater apostasy among the Jews, but at the same time the resistance toward Hellenism grew stronger.
- In 168 BC, Antiochus rode into Jerusalem and ordered a pagan deity (perhaps Jupiter) to be erected in the Holy of Holies. This event has been called the "abomination of desolation" by the Jews and is believed by many to refer to the prophecy in Daniel 11:31.
- Additionally, pigs and not lambs, were to be sacrificed on the temple altar, a drunken orgy was made compulsory with the temple sacrifices, and a pagan priest was appointed to oversee this new form of worship.
- All Israelites were required to pay homage to this form of worship or they were killed. Many died, including women who continued to have their children circumcised.

Our Lord's Objectives

- To raise up a resistance force to oppose the cultural impact of Hellenism and to stand fast to their Jewish heritage.
- To use the 100,000 Jews who were shipped to Alexandria to influence the other cultures. This was accomplished when they translated the Hebrew Bible into Greek (Septuagint), which allowed it to be read in the Gentile provinces.
- To initiate a rebellion under the leadership of the Maccabees, which eventually forced the Syrian Greeks to withdraw from Jerusalem. This began as a small group of guerilla fighters who had continuing success, and with each victory, their army grew until forty-two months later, they threw off the Hellenistic yoke. On December 25, 165 BC, the Levite priesthood began cleansing the temple and reinstating the worship of their Lord. This event is still celebrated as Hanukkah. The power of Antiochus had waned, and he was no longer involved in Israel's affairs.

SIXTH HEAD OF THE BEAST = ROME

A Brief Background of the Roman Empire and Israel

In 63 BC, the Roman Empire under General Pompey threw off the Greek yoke in the Middle East. This officially exchanged Grecian influence for Roman power over Israel. Rome was the Beast empire that established Herod as king over Israel. He was reigning at the birth of Jesus Christ and failed in his attempt to locate and murder Him. Thirty years later, this sixth Beast kingdom allowed the crucifixion of Jesus Christ. Subsequently, in AD 70, Rome completely sacked Jerusalem, which had rebelled against its authority. A great slaughter took place as the wrath of the Beast was directed against the Jewish populace. It was during this time that the Jews began to lose their national identity, as many were forced to flee to other countries. Yet a remnant of the Jewish populace still remained. Later, in AD 135, following a second Jewish revolt, Rome banned all the Jews from Jerusalem. They would not gather again as a nation until 1948.

A Brief Background of the Roman Empire and Christianity

Rome saw the early Christians as an unauthorized, separate religion that they couldn't control. In those days, the Roman Empire mandated "emperor worship," and those who refused to recognize the emperor as a god were viewed as traitors to Rome. Christians were accused of cannibalism and incest because of their talk of "eating flesh, drinking blood, and loving one another." Thus, Christianity became a capital offense, and many suffered martyrdom. This murderous persecution was extremely brutal, yet Christianity continued to experience rapid growth throughout the Roman Empire.

In the third century, Constantine became the Roman emperor and embraced Christianity. Under his reign, Christianity became the "official religion" of Rome. Constantine was actively involved in key church decisions, and as a result the church became very politically oriented. Additionally, in order to appease the angry pagan religious sects within the empire, many of their pagan traditions were allowed into the Christian environment and remain today. Thus, Christianity became identified with the Roman Catholic Church, which was a tremendously powerful force in the religious and political worlds. This power continued to grow over the centuries, for it was ruled that the Catholic priesthood held the power of "eternal life or damnation." This allowed people to live any lifestyle they chose because they could always be forgiven by a priest. Throughout the Dark Ages, the Catholic Church persecuted millions of Christians who refused to embrace Catholicism. They also were committed to killing the Jewish population. Thus, the intent of the sixth head of the Beast was to annihilate all aspects of Christianity not under the control of Catholicism. This slowed down greatly when Christians migrated to America to avoid persecution. Later, their descendants established a Christian government that has been a powerful factor in the expansion of the kingdom of God throughout the world. Yet the spiritual and political arm of the ancient Roman Empire continues into the twenty-first century and remains a force within the world today. That is why many Christian teachers believe that the seventh head of the Beast is a "revived Roman Empire." An empire that judged and persecuted the Lord at His first coming would then be judged and destroyed by the Lord at His second coming.

ONE WORLD - TWO KINGDOMS

THE KINGDOM OF GOD

The Kingdom of God was one of the most prominent, teachings of Jesus during His time upon earth and yet, it is a biblical teaching that is largely overlooked by the contemporary church. Perhaps this is understandable for Jesus Himself refers to the Kingdom of God as a mystery, yet it is a mystery that He expects His people to understand.[4] As Christians, our Lord continually admonishes us to be awake and prepared for the coming Kingdom of God; a time when all things both in heaven and upon earth will be united in Jesus Christ, the Son of our living God.[5] An insightful understanding of our Lord's Kingdom is more important today than at any other time in the history of the church for it appears that we are rapidly approaching the days preceding the second coming of our King, Jesus Christ. Therefore, in order to have a clearer understanding of the events that usher in the second coming of the King of kings, Christians need to have a clearer understanding of the meaning and the purpose for the Kingdom of God.

THE MYSTERY OF THE KINGDOM

The Jews of antiquity expected that the coming of God's Kingdom, which their Messiah would usher in, would bring a mighty manifestation of divine power that would break apart the godless nations of the earth - a power from God that would overthrow Rome and sweep away the godless Gentiles - a power that would purge the earth of unrighteousness and exalt God's people, Israel, in their own land over all the nations of the earth. However, the reality is that the Kingdom of God did come in fulfillment of the Old Testament promises, but in different terms than was anticipated by the religious leaders of Israel. The Kingdom of God had arrived, but as a mystery that they failed to comprehend.

This mystery of the Kingdom of God may be summarized as follows: During the era between the first and the second coming of the Jesus Christ, the promised Messiah, the power of His kingdom will enter into His people and launch a powerful offensive against the kingdom of darkness, which will <u>deliver many out of the world and into the blessings</u>

---

[4] Mark 4:11-12
[5] Ephesians 1:9

of the reign of Jesus Christ. This has been happening for two thousand years as millions of people have responded to the Gospel of the Kingdom.

However, it is important to note that the Kingdom of God is with us only in part, but not yet in fullness although it has greatly expanded over the past two thousand years. It is necessary to understand that this Kingdom can only be comprehended by the Spirit of God residing within us. It requires our individual response in order to be intelligible. That is, even though the activity of this Kingdom is an objective fact, its recognition by mankind requires individual personal participation; in other words, one must be born again as a child of God in order to enter into the eternal Kingdom of God.[6] He calls each one of us individually and we must respond individually; not through a third party intermediary such as a priest or a church, but we must respond directly to the person of Jesus Christ for He is our one and only intermediary before almighty God.[7]

OUR KING PROVIDES INSIGHT INTO THE MYSTERY OF HIS KINGDOM

The parable of the "four soils" describes how the Kingdom of God currently operates in today's world:[8]

Parable of The Four Soils (Matthew 13:3-23)

Jesus taught that this transitional period between His first and second coming is a period of seed sowing in which different soils will respond differently to the message of the Kingdom.

This teaching informs us that there are four ways for hearers to receive the gospel message, but that three of these ways will not result in a true heart response:

1. **Seed own in the first soil** is the heart that hears the word, but doesn't understand it. The evil one then comes and quickly snatches away whatever was temporarily sown in the heart. This is seed that is sown but quickly devoured by birds.
2. **Seed sown in the second soil** is the heart that initially receives the gospel message with great excitement, but this is only a superficial emotional experience; for when challenges arise in their lives they will fall away. This is seed sown on rocky ground

---

[6] John 3:3

[7] George Eldon Ladd, *The Presence of the Future*, (Grand Rapids: William B. Eerdmans Publishing Co., 1974), 225

[8] Dan Juster & Keith Intrater, *Israel, the Church and the Last Days*, (Shippensburg, PA: Destiny Image Publishers, 1990) p.40-45

and thus, has no root in itself. These are people who gravitate to the entertaining, easy-believism churches, but they continue to live like the world.

3. **Seed sown in the third soil** is the heart that receives the gospel message, but the cares and riches of this world continue to dominate their lives and chokes out the Word. These also are people that may be regular church-goers and undoubtedly, many are currently pastors, elders and deacons which take a business-like approach to building their individual churches. These are seeds sown in thorny areas of the ground that are focused on the riches of this world and when these thorns rise up, it chokes the truth of God's word out of their hearts.

4. **Seed sown in the fourth soil** is a heart that receives and turns from the cares of this world and through its allegiance to Jesus Christ, the Kingdom expands throughout the world. This is the true "born again" believer that certainly spends time in church, but considerably more in the prayer closet growing in intimacy with the Lord. This is seed sown on fertile ground which the evil one cannot uproot.

Thus, the Kingdom of God is present among us in a stage of seed sowing and extends an offer to people to enter the Kingdom and be fruit bearers. Three kinds of people are "pretenders" and will not come in, but one kind will and they will manifest the gospel throughout their remaining lives resulting in the Kingdom of God being greatly strengthened both in growth and power among the nations of the world.

EVIL SEED SOWN IN FERTILE SOIL

The Kingdom of God has indeed come among men but not for the immediate purpose of shattering evil in the world. It is like a farmer sowing seed; for it is working quietly and secretly among men and it does not force itself upon them for it must be willingly received. Eventually, both a harvest of wrath and a harvest of salvation will take place at the end of the age. However, until then, the evil one is intent upon weakening and rendering the good seed of God's Kingdom impotent by sowing bad seeds in their midst. Warrior leadership must recognize that an evil society continues to exist in the midst of God's people. Shortly however, a great tribulation that is coming will cause a visible separation between those that are truly people of God and those that are "wannabees" but are not willing to submit in total repentance.[9]

HANDLING SUFFERING IN GOD'S KINGDOM

Christian soldiers need to get over the tendency to view evil and suffering from an individual perspective; e.g. when I suffer or when my family suffers. We may ask why are babies starving, women raped, and innocents slaughtered while wicked and greedy

---

[9] Matthew 13:24-30

people continue to live in luxury; but when we are able to see the broad picture, it is easier to make sense of suffering. Everything depends on where you start, if you begin by envying the prosperity of the wicked, we will charge God with unfairness. But, if you begin by delighting in God, you are far from being a victim of injustice; you trust that justice will prevail in God's timing. The point is that God is entirely just and therefore, a time is coming when all of mankind will appear before the Throne of God and His judgment and sentencing will determine the eternal destiny of every human being that was born from the beginning. Since this entails awaiting the End, it involves walking by faith. Christians need to develop a kind of "homesickness" for heaven.[10]

A scene from the popular movie "The Fellowship of the Ring" also provides some insights into the mystery of suffering and injustice. There we see Gandalf counseling Frodo as they are confronting dark forces within the caves of Moria: Gandalf is saying, "Many that are living deserve to die and some that died deserved to live. So do not be too eager to deal out death and judgment for even the very wisest of men cannot see all the ends." Frodo then says, "I wished none of this had happened." Gandalf replies, "So do all that live to see such times but it's not for us to decide. All that we have to decide is what to do with the time that is given to us. There are other forces at work in this world besides the forces of evil."

THE KINGDOM OF GOD IS COSMOLOGICAL

Finally, we need to be aware that the establishment of God's kingdom encompasses more than just the redemption of His people; this redemption process includes the entire creation "which labors and groans awaiting the revealing of the sons of God."[11] All of creation requires cleansing from the effects of sin. This cosmological view of salvation helps us to better understand the coming massive destruction, which occurs in the heavenlies as well as upon this world prior to the second coming of our Lord.

The contemporary American church is accustomed to focus only upon our individual salvation. Simply put, we must be born again, sanctified and delivered from sin, and then we will go to heaven. End of story. In brief, this is the entire story of our salvation lodged in the minds of many. Of course, all of this is important and perfectly true as far as it goes. Nevertheless, it is only part of the truth, not the whole of it. Instead, believers must realize the biblical truth that all the world, the entire kingdom, including the earthly environment and the animal kingdom, which God originally created and which fell under the power of sin and the devil, will again be restored and even raised to a higher glory than it originally possessed, even as we shall be.

---

[10] D.A.Carson, *How Long O Lord?*, (Grand Rapids, MI: Baker Book House, 1990) c.8
[11] Romans 8:19-21

THE KINGDOM OF THIS WORLD

An overview of some significant differences which separate the Kingdom of this World from the Kingdom of our Lord will help in the understanding of those events which will confront the church preceding the second coming of our Lord.

To begin, there are not two worlds; there is only one. There is but one world and from the fall of Adam to this day, there are two powers that fight for dominion over that one world. On the one hand, there is the dominion of Satan, who apparently gained the victory in the Garden of Eden; on the other hand, there is the dominion of Christ, Who is called to restore the kingdom to the Father. Now the Kingdom of God in the Christian era breaks the bounds of Israel's national existence and becomes international. Christ now gathers His subjects from all parts of the world and out of every nation and tongue and tribe for it is no more a battle between nations as in the Old Testament era.

Both kingdoms reside in the same world and outwardly enjoy the same benefits. They enjoy the same rain and sunshine and it is here that our view often becomes obscured, but needs to be clarified. Understand that because the Kingdom of God lies within the hearts of His people and not within geographical boundaries, as does the Kingdom of Satan, both powers make use of all outward institutions that God has setup in the world. For in this world where both the principles of sin and grace operate simultaneously, God created various institutions designed to maintain the possibility of an orderly life which would allow the human race to develop as far as possible in spite of the inherent presence of sin.[12]

These institutions are summarized as follows:

1. **The institution of various forms of government** were established by God and equipped with the sword to maintain order in society and to punish the evildoer, in order that the Kingdom of God might have a place to develop. Without this restraint upon the development of sin, the principle of evil would develop prematurely, and life on earth would soon prove impossible as it did in the pre-flood era.
2. **The institution of the church** has been established in the world for the upbringing and edification of the saints of God and for the extension of God's Kingdom throughout the world.
3. **The institution of society in general: the home, the school, and the business workplace** were all established to bring order and progress in society.

---

[12] Tal Brooke, *When the World will be As One*, (Eugene: Harvest House Publishers, Inc., 1989)

The two powers fight for nothing less than possession of the whole world and in this fight they both make use of all the institutions that God has established in this dispensation. Therefore, we see that the battle against the forces of darkness rages along a huge frontline.

INSTITUTIONS IN THE KINGDOM OF THE WORLD

The antichristian world has also established a kingdom using the institutions that God has established. However, theirs is a kingdom without Christ and without His atoning sacrifice. Instead of God, man is the absolute sovereign within this kingdom. Progress in business, industry, commerce, as well as the arts and sciences is characteristic of this kingdom, all without God and without His Son. Moreover, they will speak of righteousness and brotherly love and strive to realize the universal brotherhood of man. They want to abolish the effects of sin and usher in a universal blissful state. Thus, they essentially strive for the consummation of what they call the Kingdom of Mankind in the world.

In order to accomplish their purposes for a perfect world, these children of darkness manipulate the institutions that God has setup in the world:

1. **Institution of the State:**
   A worldly view of the institution of the state reveals that governments are encouraged to emphasize the rights of humans even at the expense of justice. The acceptable philosophy is that all mankind is basically good and committed acts of evil are the result of living in a poor environment. Accepted and encouraged within this worldview are the individual rights, which approve of abortions, same-sex marriages, releasing of criminals on legal technicalities, etc. They believe that a caring society along with psychiatric counseling is what is needed to properly reduce acts of evil within the world.

2. **Institution of the Church:**
   A worldly view of the institution of the church reveals that the cooperation of the church is also invited to assist in the establishment of this worldly kingdom. However, the acceptable gospel of the church is a social gospel. That old message of sin and guilt and total depravity that one can only be cleansed by the blood of Jesus Christ has become antiquated and will not satisfy the needs of the modern generation. Thus, a new gospel has come to the forefront, a gospel of love and peace for all men, without Christ. Not that man is spiritually impotent, but that he is divine; not that he is by nature a sinner, but that he is by nature righteous as a child of God.

   In order to function in this kingdom mindset, the church must allow itself to become a powerful agency for the establishment of this universal kingdom of peace and righteousness. Today, the vast majority of churches and seminaries do not accept the truth of the inerrancy of Scripture. Non-evangelicals maintain that scripture is of human origin, which could possibly communicate a divine message and thus, it could be profitable even though it contains many errors. As pertains to eternal salvation, they maintain that either all are saved (universalism) or that the saved ones are those who work for the welfare of others in various social programs. They may even encourage imitating Christ as an example of a good man who performs good works for society. Finally, the liberal churches believe Jesus was a good man who was aligned with God in nebulous ways. However, actual miracles and a resurrection are not really necessary, but can be symbolic of a higher reality. What they believe is truly important is the example He portrayed in His love toward men. They love the hymn, "Peace on earth, goodwill toward men".

3. **Institution of the Home, the School, and the Workplace:**

   A worldly view of the institution of society in general as characterized by the <u>home</u>, the <u>school</u>, and the <u>business workplace</u> are summarized as follows:

   - If family life would obstruct the development of their ideal worldview, it also must be transformed. If free love, homosexual marriages, and the murder of unborn children are advantageous to the establishment of this kingdom, its practice must be encouraged. Child discipline is viewed as archaic and criminal; divorce is acceptable in this society and adultery is certainly not frowned upon.
   - Schools are required to adhere and teach this worldview. They may not teach a definite religion, nor allow prayer for that would not be in harmony with a universal brotherhood. Differences must be removed and competition must cease and an acceptable socialistic state of things must be established and taught. Scholarship is encouraged, but is secondary to one's social standing or athletic ability when it comes to applying for acceptance to a university.
   - Business is largely motivated by the desire to acquire rather than to serve the consumer as well as their employees. Who gets hurt in the process of commercialism is not all that important for what is important is the financial power that can be achieved.

In summary, the great aim of this worldview is to establish a kingdom that is in outward form like the kingdom of God as pictured in the Bible, but the principal motive is enmity against God and against His Son together with the promoting of mankind as the being a truly divine people.

APPENDIX "C"

INSIGHTS INTO "DISCERNING THE TIMES"

This is not the time for God's people to withdraw into passivity – to refuse to look at the reality of <u>a rapidly decaying society</u> that affects all of us and our loved ones.

We are not free to play the role of <u>civilians</u>, living as if there was no war. Our <u>military</u> role is pictured for us throughout the bible; for the history of the saints in every age is one of conflict.

Therefore, we must have a deeper understanding of the spiritual warfare in light of our 21st century <u>technology</u> if we are to properly prepare for His coming; for we have been commanded to stay ready and alert by the Commander-in-Chief Himself.

<u>Listen to Jesus scolding those who fail to discern the times:</u>

- *He also said to the crowds, "When you see a cloud rising in the west, you say at once, 'A shower is coming.' And so it happens. And when you see the south wind blowing, you say, 'There will be scorching heat,' and it happens.* **You hypocrites***! <u>You know how to interpret the appearance of earth and sky, but why do you not know how to interpret the present time?</u> (Luke 12:54-56)*

THE PROPHET DANIEL

Now, the prophet Daniel, who saw similar events over 2,500 years ago that would confront a future, end-time generation, was told by the Angel of the Lord when these events would take place:

<u>The Time of the End</u>

- *And those who are wise shall shine like the brightness of the sky above; and those who turn many to righteousness, like the stars forever and ever. But you, Daniel, shut up the words and seal the book, until the <u>time of the end</u>.* **<u>Many shall run to and fro, and knowledge shall increase</u>***." (Daniel 12:3-4)*

I submit to you that in our generation, technology has developed to a degree that allows us to relate such visions that both John and Daniel saw and recorded many centuries ago to our 21st century culture.

For example – in the Last Days:

"Many shall run to and fro"

- **"Many"** – The world now has a population of approximately 7 billion peoples. This world's population has tripled in my lifetime.
- **"Run to and fro"** - Airplanes, trains, automobiles, etc. allow people to easily travel from country to country as well as daily visit shopping malls and movies that may be miles away.

"Knowledge shall increase" = consider the technology of today:

- **Television, radios, and computers** - Allows people to witness and participate in daily activities throughout the world.
- **Telecommunications** – Allows people to communicate with anyone, anytime, anywhere in the world.
- **Weaponry** – Today's nuclear technology endangers the great majority of the world's population.

Additionally, Daniel was told who would understand the times and who would not:

- *The Angel of the Lord said, "Go your way, Daniel, for the words are shut up and sealed until the time of the end. Many shall purify themselves and make themselves white and be refined, but the wicked shall act wickedly. **And none of the wicked shall understand, but those who are wise shall understand.** (Daniel 12:9-10)*

NOW, WHEN WILL THE LORD RETURN?

No One Knows That Day and Hour

- *"But concerning that day and hour no one knows, not even the angels of heaven, nor the Son, but the Father only. (**Matthew 24:36**)*

However, Jesus does provide some clues concerning the season of His coming! In Matthew 24, together with Luke 21, Jesus provides numerous signs that will take place prior to His 2nd coming to establish a righteous kingdom upon this earth.

The following examples should provide us with insights that our Lord spoke and expects our generation to understand:

WARS & RUMORS OF WARS

- *And you will hear of wars and rumors of wars. See that you are not alarmed, for this must take place, but the end is not yet. (**Matthew 24:6**)*

Obviously, our world has never before experienced such world-wide wars and rumors of wars. In the 20th century, two world-wide wars arose that affected almost every country around the globe including the United States of America. Since then, our country has been actively involved in wars in Vietnam and the Middle East.

Today, in the 21st century, the rumors of wars are daily news headlines in our country as well as around the world. These "rumors" will soon end for a tremendous world-wide war lies shortly before us. This coming war was discussed in both chapters 4 and 7 of this book.

NATION WILL RISE AGAINST NATION

- *For <u>nation will rise against nation</u>, and kingdom against kingdom, and there will be famines and earthquakes in various places. (Matthew 24:7)*

The English word "nation" does not express the warning that our Lord intends for us to visualize. The Greek word for "nation" is "ethnos" which is representative of different people groups rather than separate nations, which is represented by the word "kingdom."

These same "people groups" or "ethnic groups" exist in many nations, but none more so than in the United States. <u>For example:</u>

- Racism is rampant in our country. Tremendous hatred exists between numerous large people groups within both the <u>black</u> and <u>white</u> communities as well as <u>Hispanic</u> communities. Racial wars are occurring throughout our country.
- Groups of <u>Muslims</u> also have a tremendous hatred toward <u>Jews</u> and <u>Christians</u>. This is especially evident in European countries, but it is growing in our country as well.
- The political world of <u>liberalism</u> and <u>conservatives</u> is tremendously divisive. This is no longer a country of Republicans and Democrats who can work together in unity, but we have developed into a divisive government which refuses to work together for the people of our country.
- <u>Homosexuality</u> embracing "same-sex marriage" has no respect for those who hold to the <u>biblical morals of Christianity</u>. With the recent Supreme Court ruling on gay marriage, America has taken another step toward judgment. This landmark decision is certainly part of the fulfillment of several end-time predictions describing the moral downfall of the world. For many sincere Christians, it is a hard fact to swallow that America leads the way in this rising sickness of wickedness and perversion. Thus:

TODAY WE ARE THE "DIVIDED STATES OF AMERICA"

- *If a kingdom is divided against itself, that kingdom cannot stand. (Mark 3:24)*
- *And if a house is divided against itself, that house will not be able to stand. (Mark 3:25)*

- -----"*Every kingdom divided against itself is laid waste, and a divided household falls. (Luke 11:17)*

However:

- *All these are but the beginning of the birth pains. (Matthew 24:8)*

So, what comes next?

- *"Then they will deliver you up to tribulation and put you to death, and you will be hated by all nations for my name's sake.*
- *And then many will fall away and betray one another and hate one another. And many false prophets will arise and lead many astray.*
- *And because lawlessness will be increased, the love of many will grow cold. (Matthew 24:9-12)*

What is our calling throughout this time of persecution?

- *But the one who endures to the end will be saved.*
- *And this gospel of the kingdom will be proclaimed throughout the whole world as a testimony to all nations, and then the end will come. (Matthew 24:13-14)*

Dear fellow Americans – the warning signs contained in Matthew 24 and Romans 1 are unfolding before our very eyes today. Certainly, the urge for many patriotic Americans is to step up and fight against these immoral laws that have been instituted over the past fifty years. However, for Christians and moral conservatives, this fight was lost a long time ago. To continue to fight legally, in the public square, or pointing the finger will only incur more wrath from the wicked which also controls our government. Our fight must now, more than ever, be directed towards our own purity and obedience to Christ, and become engaged in His war against the powers of darkness.

We are called to be ambassadors for Christ, to sojourn in the world and not become part of the world, but live as citizens of the kingdom of God. Any further attempts to stop this tsunami of wickedness will just incur further abuse, harassment, mocking, and persecution. The rainbow coalition along with the far political left will not simply stop coming after us, but will inflict persecution towards anyone who rejects their agenda. Unfortunately, many fellowships and denominations are succumbing to these pressures by the rainbow coalition. Many are falling away from the living God and accepting this perversion as a lifestyle sanctioned by God. Don't be among them! For now, let the wicked have America – we get it all back in the end. [13]

---

[13] Charles B. Pretlow, *Walk as Citizens of Christ's Kingdom*

THE "TIME OF THE GENTILES"

- *...For there will be great distress upon the earth and wrath against this people. They will fall by the edge of the sword and be led captive among all nations, and Jerusalem will be trampled underfoot by the Gentiles, until the times of the Gentiles are fulfilled. (**Luke 21:23-24**)*

The time of the Gentiles is that period of time when the holy city of Jerusalem is under the dominion of Gentiles (non-Jewish people).

- It was 70AD when the Romans warred against the Jews and destroyed the holy temple. Then in 135AD, following another Jewish rebellion, the Romans dispersed the Jewish people from the city of Jerusalem and from the land of Israel.

The city of Jerusalem was then under the control of a multitude of nations for over 1800 years. Finally, in 1967 following the six-day war, the Jews once again took control of the West Bank and the city of Jerusalem.

- Thus, the time of the Gentiles ended in June, 1967. This had to happen before the 2nd coming of our Lord.

THE LESSON OF THE FIG TREE

Jesus used the "fig tree" parable when teaching His disciples concerning the last days:

- *"From the fig tree learn its lesson: as soon as its branch becomes tender and puts out its leaves, you know that summer is near. So also, when you see all these things, you know that he is near, at the very gates. Truly, I say to you, this generation will not pass away until all these things take place. (**Matthew 24:32-34**)*

It is commonly understood by many theologians that the usage of "fig tree" in Scripture is frequently representative of the nation of Israel.

Now, the coming forth of the leaves is prophetically accepted by many to be the establishment of Israel as a nation on May 14, 1948.

Verse 34 tells us that this generation (those born in 1948 forward) would not pass away until all these things take place. "All these things" include His 2nd coming to establish the millennial kingdom on earth.

So, how long is a generation?

- *The years of our life are seventy, or even by reason of strength eighty; (**Psalms 90:10**)*

We are now 67 years into the generation that was born on that date and thus, using this perspective one can expect Him to return on or before the year "2028."

ANOTHER INTERESTING INSIGHT

One of our very early church fathers by the name of Polycarp, was a disciple and also a close friend of the Apostle John. Obviously Polycarp would have received tremendous insights from the man who experienced and recorded the Book of Revelation. Now, Polycarp was later martyred, but before his death, he also taught others concerning the end of times. One of his well-known disciples was Irenaeus who wrote a book called "Against Heresies."

In this book, Irenaeus says the following:

> "As God views 1,000 years as a day and He created the earth in 6 days and rested on the 7th, so shall the earth last for 6,000 years and rest under the reign of Christ for the last 1,000 years".

Here was a man who was taught by a friend of John's stating that Jesus Christ would return to reign on earth for one-thousand years which would represent a period of rest from six-thousand years of sinful, rebellious living in the world.

Also, we should take note that the timeframe revealed in the Bible puts us very close to the completion of six-thousand years since the time of creation as recorded in the bible. In fact, some theologians have calculated that the 6,000 years will end in "2028."

Finally, I feel compelled to share an additional insight that may or may not be meaningful. One night in the year 2001, I had a very brief dream (1 minute) where a 29-year-old African-American pastor was scolding me for not knowing when the Lord would return. At the end of the dream he said the following, "He's coming back in 25 years, that's when He's coming back!" I suddenly awoke and sat up in bed considering what I had just dreamed. Obviously, this dream was telling me that the year of the Lord's return would be 2026. Now I do not know whether this was from the Lord or not and I'm not setting dates. However, there are so many signs that are unfolding before us that I do believe we are in the generation that will not only go through great tribulations, but also in the generation in which the Lord will return.

These are end-times events which are quite mystifying for the great majority of God's chosen ones - but it is extremely critical for our generation of Christians who will play a leadership role to discern the times and **"be ready."**

- *Therefore you also must **be ready**, for the Son of Man is coming at an hour you do not expect. "Who then is the faithful and wise servant, whom his master has set over his household, to give* *them their food at the proper time? Blessed is that servant whom his master will find so doing when he comes. Truly, I say to you, he will set him over all his possessions.* (**Matthew 24:44-47**)

However, prior to the 2nd coming of Jesus, the following will occur:

- *For then there will be great tribulation, such as has not been from the beginning of the world until now, no, and never will be.*
- *And if those days had not been cut short, no human being would be saved. But for the sake of the elect those days will be cut short.* (**Matthew 24:21-22**)

Be among the following:

"God's Valiant Warriors are called to stand strong for the Kingdom of God!"

In Summary:

- Daniel was told that the time of the end would occur when "many shall run to and fro; and knowledge would increase." (Obviously, our generation can relate to this)
- Wars and Rumors of Wars are commonplace in today's world
- Ethnos will rise against Ethnos which is happening throughout America
- The time of the Gentiles ended in 1967 following the 6 day war.
- The fig tree began producing fruit in 1948 and it was told that the time of the end would take place within the generation that was born within that time. That is – today's generation.
- The warning signs in Matthew 24 and Romans 1 are unfolding before the eyes of those who truly have spiritual discernment of the times.
- Irenaeus prediction of the time of the millennial kingdom would occur 6,000 years from the beginning of the creation of mankind.

APPENDIX "D"

CHRISTIAN WARRIORS – WE ARE CALLED TO "FAST"

In the early centuries, the disciples of Jesus were called to "fast" for it was a channel of power. However, as time went on and paganism began creeping into the church, more and more emphasis was placed upon the outward act of fasting as a sign of piety among the priestly leadership. This certainly has been a contributing factor causing the power and gifts of the Holy Spirit to be withdrawn from the traditional churches. Paul's prediction about a form of religion "having the appearance of godliness, but denying its power" (2 Tim.3:5) was being fulfilled.

But, as we approach the end of this age, many of God's people are awakening and seeking His face for spiritual renewal. It is my conviction that many will rediscover one of the lost secrets of the early church; that is, the power that is released through the biblical practice of "fasting unto God."

<u>What is Biblical Fasting?</u> Many have been taught that it is to do without, to practice self-denial. They say that it is not necessarily to abstain from food, but from anything that hinders our communion with God. Yes – it is true that there are many things besides food that may hinder our communion with God and it is also true that we need to practice self-denial. However, the biblical truth still remains that "to fast" means primarily "not to eat." The Greek word for "fast" is "nesteuo" which means "not to eat." If we continue to widen the meaning of a biblical fast, the cutting edge will be gone.

Now let's examine three main forms of biblical fasting, but each involves literal abstinence from food.

TYPES OF BIBLICAL FASTING

1. THE "NORMAL" FAST = ABSTAINING FROM FOOD

- *And after fasting forty days and forty nights, he was hungry. (Matthew 4:2)*

Jesus fasted – and afterwards He was hungry. We are told (Matthew 4:2 & Luke 4:2) that He ate nothing, but not that He drank nothing. After 40 days Satan tempted Him to eat, but not to drink. This all suggests that this fast was abstinence from food, but not from water. Thus, the "normal fast" involves abstaining from all forms of food, but not from water.

2. THE "ABSOLUTE" FAST = ABSTAINING FROM FOOD & WATER

- *And for three days he was without sight, and neither ate nor drank. (Acts 9:9)*

This is just an example of what we call the "absolute fast." Normally this was never more than three days. The body can go long periods without food and with physical benefit, but only a very short time without water.

- *"Go, gather all the Jews to be found in Susa, and hold a fast on my behalf, and do not eat or drink for three days, night or day. I and my young women will also fast as you do. Then I will go to the king, though it is against the law, and if I perish, I perish." (Esther 4:16)*

Here a tremendous crisis threatened the whole Jewish race with extermination. This "absolute fast" was called because desperate situations require desperate measures.

There are examples in scripture of "absolute fasts" which must have been supernatural because of their long duration. For two separate periods of forty days, with little duration in between, Moses was in the presence of God neither eating nor drinking. This also occurred in the life of Elijah (1 Kings 19:8).

Conclusion: The "absolute fast" is an exceptional act for an exceptional situation. It is probably something reserved for spiritual emergencies - a need that has not yielded to normal prayer and fasting. This may be needed in cases of powerful possession by evil spirits.

We need to be very sure of the leading of God to undertake an "absolute fast" for any period longer than three days.

3. THE "PARTIAL" FAST

- *"I ate no delicacies, no meat or wine entered my mouth"(Daniel 10:3)*

Here, the emphasis is on restriction of diet rather than total abstinence. Daniel and his friends did not want to defile themselves with rich food or wine as these would have first been offered to the Babylonian gods. Instead they asked for vegetables to eat and water to drink. At the end of ten days, they were in better appearance and strength than all the youths that ate the king's rich food.

Years later, when Daniel received a prophetic vision, he sought the Lord for understanding of this vision for three full weeks on a "partial fast" (Dan.10:2-3). We are not told why he didn't do a "normal fast" – perhaps affairs of state or other circumstances precluded this, or perhaps God guided him otherwise. But, undoubtedly there is a definite spiritual value in a season of seeking God with such a restricted diet.

Elijah was also on a "partial fast" at the brook Cherith for a lengthy period of time. However, this is certainly appropriate during a time when there was a famine in the land and many of his fellow countrymen were facing starvation. To minister effectively to those in need, we must be able to identify with their needs by having undergone similar experiences.

Others have partially fasted by omitting a certain meal each day. However, one must be vigilant to ensure that the value of omitting the one meal is not offset by increasing the intake at others.

Conclusion: The partial fast is of great value, especially where circumstances make it difficult to undertake a "normal fast." Also, it can be used as a stepping stone to a normal fast by those who have never fasted before.

PURPOSES FOR FASTING

1. SEEKING PERSONAL HOLINESS

Humility is foundational for true holiness. Fasting is a corrective to a prideful heart. Pride and a too-full stomach are old bedfellows. Because of our natural tendency toward self-pride, we need to, like King David, humble ourselves with fasting from time to time.

Sodom – her sin was not just homosexuality, but she was a prideful people, with excessive food, and a prosperous easy life (Ezek. 16:49). God foresaw that these same circumstances of pride and fullness of stomach would be one of Israel's pitfalls when they entered the Promised Land. Moses reminded them prior to entering the land:

- *And you shall remember the whole way that the Lord your God has led you these forty years in the wilderness, that he might humble you, testing you to know what was in your heart, whether you would keep his commandments or not. And he humbled you and let you hunger and fed you with manna, which you did not know, nor did your fathers know, that he might make you know that man does not live by bread alone, but man lives by every word that comes from the mouth of the Lord.* **(Deuteronomy 8:2-3)**

- *Humble yourselves, therefore, under the mighty hand of God so that at the proper time he may exalt you,* **(1 Peter 5:6)**
- *Do nothing from rivalry or conceit, but in humility count others more significant than yourselves.* **(Philippians 2:3)**
- *"Blessed are the meek (Humble), for they shall inherit the earth.* **(Matthew 5:5)**

Fasting is equated with "humility." Setting aside time when you would rather watch television = humility. Putting the Lord before any of your bodily desires = humility.

Humility is NOT weakness! Just the opposite: it takes great strength to pick up your cross and follow the Lord.

<u>Mourning</u> over our sins and failures is also a process leading to our sanctification. There is a natural sequence as we move from self-humbling to mourning for the sins of others.

The eyes of the Lord continually search the earth for the Ezras who will weep and pray for the sins of a faithless people; or for the Nehemiahs who weep and mourn, fast and pray over the broken city of Jerusalem.

Prior to the complete Babylonian destruction of Jerusalem, Ezekiel was told to:

- *And the Lord said to him, "Pass through the city, through Jerusalem, and put a mark on the foreheads of the men who sigh and groan over all the abominations that are committed in it." (Ezekiel 9:4)*

These were the ones protected from the massive destruction that soon came upon Jerusalem.

Heaven marks the men who mourn with God for the sins that break His heart and turn His face away from us. This will also be a future event as the Lord "seals" the 144,000 prior to the Great tribulation. These are the ones chosen to be His witnesses throughout the whole earth during that destructive time that lies shortly ahead.

<u>Consecrating ourselves to God</u> through fasting is also an act of personal sanctity.

The best biblical example is that of Jesus undertaking a forty day fast in the wilderness prior to His public ministry. He received the power of the Holy Spirit at His baptism but by His accepting of the six weeks of fasting, He was reaffirming His determination to do the will of His Father right to the end.

Paul and Barnabas were also set apart by a consecrated fast. This was there anointing for their future ministry:

- *Then after fasting and praying they laid their hands on them and sent them off. (Acts 13:3)*

2. <u>FASTING TO BE HEARD BY GOD</u>

In ancient Israel there was so much formalism and hypocrisy within the church that it rendered the religious exercise of "fasting" obnoxious to the Lord. This was true of their tithing, their prayers, and their worship.

Isaiah 58:3-4 uncovers the self-seeking and self-pleasing desires that lay in the hearts of these exercises of piety:

The religious cry out:

- *'Why have we fasted, and you see it not?*
- *Why have we humbled ourselves, and you take no knowledge of it?'*

Then God answers:

- *Behold, in the day of your fast you seek your own pleasure,*
- *Fasting like yours this day will not make your voice to be heard on high.*

   It then goes on to show us the character of the "fast" that God Himself chooses.

- *"Is not this the fast that I choose: to loose the bonds of wickedness, to undo the straps of the yoke, to let the oppressed go free, and to break every yoke?* **(Isaiah 58:6)**

- *Then you shall call, and the Lord will answer; you shall cry, and he will say, 'Here I am.'* **(Isaiah 58:9)**

   True fasting is designed to make your prayers mount up as on "eagle wings."

- *Have you not known? Have you not heard? The Lord is the everlasting God, the Creator of the ends of the earth. He does not faint or grow weary; his understanding is unsearchable. He gives power to the faint, and to him who has no might he increases strength. Even youths shall faint and be weary, and young men shall fall exhausted;* **BUT** *they who wait for the Lord shall renew their strength; they shall mount up with wings like eagles; they shall run and not be weary; they shall walk and not faint.* **(Isaiah 40:28-31)**

   Fasting is connected with the desire to:

- Seek God with all your heart – then
- Draw near to Him – then
- Prevail with Him in prayer

When a person is willing to set aside the legitimate appetites of his body to concentrate on the work of praying, he is demonstrating that he means business. That he is seeking with all his heart and will not let go until he gets answers from God. Fasting confirms one's resolution to sacrifice anything to attain what we seek from the Kingdom of God.

Of course we must not think of fasting as a hunger strike to force God's hand and get our own way. Prayer is much more complex than asking a loving Father to supply His child's needs. Prayer is warfare! Prayer is wrestling! There are opposing forces.

- *For we do not wrestle against flesh and blood, but against the rulers, against the authorities, against the cosmic powers over this present darkness, against the spiritual forces of evil in the heavenly places.* **(Ephesians 6:12)**

This is a realm of deep mystery – Scripture states the facts but does not explain them.

Now all this is no reflection on our Lord to fulfill the desires of those who love Him. Fasting is calculated to bring a sense of urgency into our praying. It is our expression of earnestness employing God's appointed way. He is using the means that God has chosen to make his voice to be heard in the heavens. Prayer with fasting is giving heaven notice that we are truly in earnest.

Many times we may wonder why our prayers are not being answered. We think we are waiting for heaven to respond, but heaven is really waiting for us. Are our prayers truly in earnest from the bottom of our hearts?

God has given His sons and daughters the blessed privilege of entering into His presence. And to do this, He has given us the weapons of prayer and fasting to add to our spiritual armory.

- *If my people who are called by my name __humble themselves__, and __pray and seek my face__ and __turn from their wicked ways__, then I will hear from heaven and will forgive their sin and heal their land.* **(2 Chronicles 7:14)**

3. FASTING TO FREE THE CAPTIVES

- *"Is not this the fast that I choose: to loose the bonds of wickedness, to undo the straps of the yoke, to let the oppressed go free, and to break every yoke?* **(Isaiah 58:6)**

The nature of "fasting" is not to bring man into bondage, but to loose them from it. So many peoples among mankind are bound with invisible shackles of the enemy.

Many discerning Christians recognize that many who we encounter in the path of life are oppressed by the devil and his legions. They are bound by forces they do not understand. In many cases they feel guilty for their actions and when alone, they weep out of sheer frustration.

A large and continually growing proportion of our generation is hopelessly bound by alcohol, drugs, gambling, pornography, and illicit sexual desires. Others are secretly entangled in satanically inspired cults and various forms of witchcraft, black magic, and godless spiritualism.

Many professing Christians are also bound by anger, fear, jealousy, resentment and such things that continually bind them from truly walking with Christ. But how to get free?

They may try hard to pray, to believe, to claim, yet they remain bound. More often than not, the gospel that is preached to them is deficient. Forgiveness through the death of Christ though vital, is not the whole gospel. Often, a person in Satan's grip is incapable of responding to this message:

- *When anyone hears the word of the kingdom and does not understand it, the evil one comes and snatches away what has been sown in his heart.* **(Matthew 13:19)**

Today, we send people to the psychiatrist when the root of their troubles is satanic. How can they possibly be cured by the treatment of mental or physical symptoms, when the problem is spiritual? Undoubtedly, many today who spend years in the mental institutions need, not drugs or electro-shock treatment, but deliverance from satanic bondage.

Understandably, we need to seek the Lord's anointing for such a ministry of deliverance which He promises to His faithful disciples. **Discipleship fasting is a powerful weapon appointed by God, to break the enemy's hold over people.** A "fast" undertaken at God's direction will strengthen an intercessory prayer warrior to maintain pressure on the enemy until he is compelled to loosen his grip on the captive(s). Then "fasting" will give authority, when God's moment comes, to speak the commanding word that generates the release from bondage.

Our Lord wants us to know His own deep compassion for these tormented souls and He has given us the authority to deliver them which is part of the "great commission" (Mark 16:17).

Yet, it is true that deliverance is seldom possible unless the one possessed truly desires it and is ready to repent of any sin(s) that have opened the door to Satan. But, so often there is a deep, inner desire on the part of those afflicted, but do not know what they can do nor whom they can turn to who will pay the price in prayer and fasting, and command the deliverance.

4. FASTING FOR REVELATION

- *I, Daniel…turned my face to the Lord God, seeking Him by prayer and supplications with fasting…Gabriel…said to me, O Daniel, I have now come out to give you wisdom and understanding…* **(Daniel 9:2,3,21,22)**

There should be no doubt that there is a very close connection between the practice of "fasting" and receiving spiritual revelation. Many non-Christian religions such as Buddhism, Hinduism, and Islam practice "fasting" because they realize its power to detach one's mind from bodily desires and to sharpen one's sensitivity to the spiritual realm.

It has been said that in the last days:

- *And in the last days it shall be, God declares, that I will pour out my Spirit on all flesh, and your sons and your daughters shall prophesy, and your young men shall see visions, and your old men shall dream dreams.* *(Acts 2:17)*

Surely this will apply to many who seek God with "fasting." However, these are not the only revelations that our Lord provides His seeking people – we may get it as He brings fresh light through His holy word or by some other means such as bringing a prophetic word from another Christian.

But the need for these challenging times is the "spirit of wisdom and revelation" which is given to those who continually seek God with "prayer and fasting." Certainly the promise given long ago to those who keep God's chosen fast is still true:

- *Then shall your light rise in the darkness and your gloom be as the noonday. And the Lord will guide you continually and satisfy your desire in scorched places and make your bones strong; and you shall be like a watered garden, like a spring of water, whose waters do not fail.* *(Isaiah 58:10-11)*

ENSLAVEMENT OF THE SPIRIT TO THE BODY

It has been said that the quickest way to a man's heart is through his stomach. Satan certainly realized this was equally true for a woman when he tempted Eve with the forbidden fruit. The cry of a man and woman's stomach helped drown the voice of God in the Garden of Eden.

Following their miraculous deliverance from Egyptian bondage, many of the people of Israel cried out that they would rather be in bondage to the Egyptians than go hungry in the wilderness.

- *And the whole congregation of the people of Israel grumbled against Moses and Aaron in the wilderness, and the people of Israel said to them, "Would that we had died by the hand of the Lord in the land of Egypt, when we sat by the meat pots and ate bread to the full, for you have brought us out into this wilderness to kill this whole assembly with hunger."* *(Exodus 16:2-3)*

This is an amazingly, disgusting attitude following such a tremendous deliverance. A people that would rather feed their bodies and remain in bondage than to be in the presence of the Lord guiding them toward the Promised Land—a land flowing with "milk and honey" which was provided by the Lord.

Though God has planted instinctive appetites within our bodies for our ongoing well-being, we are required to keep our physical bodies subservient to our spirit. The body is to be our servant, not our master. For each believer, there is a fine line between satisfying the normal desires of the body from a fleshly craving that stifles our inner spirit. In our western culture, food is an ever present temptation to which we constantly yield and to which we overindulge.

Unlike the "first Adam" who could not withstand the fleshly temptations of Satan, the "last Adam" met the attack of the same tempter, not in a perfect paradise, but in a desolate wilderness with a body weakened by prolonged fasting and gripped by intense hunger. Where the first Adam failed the "last Adam" triumphed.

So many Christians are oblivious of their bondage to food and to the fact that there is a leakage of spiritual power in their lives. What they believe is a natural and healthy appetite is really a lust that enslaves them to their physical bodies. The truth that Christian discipleship involves self-discipline in this realm has been put out of their minds. **For the Christian to be a warrior in the Army of Christ, he must take control over his body through self-discipline. He cannot allow his body to dictate his direction in life.** Maintaining physical fitness is also a responsibility of the spiritual-warrior.

- *Do you not know that in a race all the runners compete, but only one receives the prize? So run that you may obtain it. Every athlete exercises self-control in all things. They do it to receive a perishable wreath, but we an imperishable. So I do not run aimlessly; I do not box as one beating the air. But I discipline my body and keep it under control, lest after preaching to others I myself should be disqualified.* **(1 Corinthians 9:24-27)**

Beware of Asceticism – when disciplines such as "fasting" are enforced by man-made rules, it cannot deal effectively with the bodily lusts. Self-control, on the other hand, is the fruit of the Spirit, springing up from the divine life within us. The physical is not to be ruthlessly depressed, but it is to be firmly disciplined, not by rules but by our hearts desire to please our Father and continually seek His will. Thus, our physical bodies need to be continually subordinated to our spiritual needs.

FASTING & THE BODY

- *Or do you not know that your body is a temple of the Holy Spirit within you, whom you have from God? You are not your own, for you were bought with a price. So glorify God in your body.* **(1 Corinthians 6:19-20)**

1. OBSTACLES TO OVERCOME

There is a great deal of opposition to a prolonged "fast" because of common misconceptions that we must keep eating to live and that, "fasting" is starving.

Those who undertake a prolonged "fast" must be aware that well-meaning friends and family will present "health" arguments to show that "prolonged fasting" is a foolish venture.

Of course food is necessary for the sustaining of life, but air, water, and sleep are more urgently needed. The body cannot live more than a few minutes without air; or a few days without water and sleep – but under normal circumstances the body can exist quite satisfactorily for several weeks without food.

2. GOD HAS EQUIPPED HUMAN BODIES WITH SELF-NOURISHMENT

A well-nourished body can exist for several weeks without any harmful effects. During a "prolonged fast" the body is living on surplus fat and at the same time, it is burning up wasteful and decaying tissues of the body. Only when this refining process is complete does the body begin to consume healthy living cells, and that is when starvation begins.

Fasting is not harmful to the body – in fact the very opposite is true. Fasting is a process of physical therapy – it releases the body to naturally cleanse and heal itself.

3. THREE PHASES THE BODY PASSES THROUGH DURING A PROLONGED FAST

The first phase is marked by a "craving" for food, which lasts for three to four days. Once it passes, there may be a pleasurable sensation at the thought of food, but there is no more craving or strong temptation. It is here we must differentiate between a "desire for food" and a "hunger for food."

- When the stomach is suddenly denied what it is used to, it tends to cry out like a spoiled child while true hunger is a cry from the whole body stemming not from habit, but from need.

The second phase is marked by a feeling of weakness and tiredness which may also last for three to four days. This may be the most difficult phase of the fast and some may find it necessary to rest a good deal. On a positive note, the gradual disappearance of this sense of weakness is a signal that the body has eliminated its grosser wastes and poisons.

The third and easiest phase is one of growing strength, with little or no concern for food, and only occasional spasms of weakness. At this stage, the person fasting often feels he can continue his fast indefinitely without any great effort.

The termination of this final phase is marked by the beginning of hunger pangs showing that toxic elimination has been completed and the body is beginning to draw on healthy tissue. The appearance of hunger after the third phase is the warning that the body is beginning to "starve." In certain cases, this may occur as early as the 21st day, but often it is not until the 40th day or longer.

FASTING FOR HEALTH & HEALING

Included in many of the blessed results of God's chosen fast in Isaiah 58 is the promise:

- *Then shall your light break forth like the dawn, and your healing shall spring up speedily; Your righteousness shall go before you; the glory of the Lord shall be your rear guard. **(Isaiah 58:8)***

Is this a natural; and/or supernatural healing? I believe the promise embraces both possibilities.

Certainly there are ills that can be cured or even prevented if fasting coupled with reformed eating habits were practiced.

When the eating of food ceases, the body no longer engages in the work of assimilation; it therefore concentrates on the work of elimination. This is more evident during the initial stages of a prolonged fast when there is a more rapid loss of weight, but the process continues throughout the fasting period. Oblivious to this, man continues to dig his grave with his knife and fork.

As previously mentioned, fasting has a way of detaching us from the natural world so we can focus more on God and the spiritual world. The discomforts one must endure in the earlier stages of a prolonged fast can result in a valuable purifying of our physical bodies, not to mention the spiritual benefits. The unpleasant taste in the mouth together with bad breath and headaches are all part of the process during the early phase.

Fasting is not easy or pleasant; at least during the early stages. However, it is both a physical and spiritual medicine.

WHAT ARE THE GENERAL PHYSICAL BENEFITS?

The cleansing process of a prolonged fast usually produces:
- Brightness of the eyes and pure breath
- Clear skin and a sense of physical well-being
- Our taste and smelling senses are much sharper
- Mental powers become more clear and active

However, we need to have our motives clear and make sure that, whatever we may hope to gain in health and healing, our major concern must be the glorifying of God and the spiritual issues which prompted the fast.

HOW TO BEGIN & BREAK A FAST

Now there are pitfalls both in beginning a fast and breaking a fast that must be avoided. The body grows accustomed to fasting by degrees.

Some ideas:

- Start with a partial fast, then
- Fast all day until supper, then
- Fast a day with a very light meal or with fruit only

When you can manage a full, one day fast without feeling faint, though you certainly will feel hungry, you will be ready for longer fasts of three, five, or seven days. If you envision a longer fast, you should be quite certain that God has called you to it.

There are two important things that have happened to the digestive system during a prolonged fast:

- The stomach has been slowly shrinking so that it has nothing like its previous capacity for food.
- The organs of the body (liver, kidneys, etc) that are usually engaged in assimilating food go into a kind of sleep.

When breaking a fast, the stomach must be given time to return to its normal size and the organs must be gently awakened. Thus, a normal fast of some length should be broken with fruit or vegetable juices (probably diluted during the first day) and taken every two to three hours. Eventually you will gravitate slowly to solid fruit and vegetables. A little bread may be eaten with these meals but stay away from pastries. Protein is best introduced first in the form of cheese, eggs, or nuts; with fish or meat last of all.

Your foods must be eaten slowly and reduced to a liquid before swallowing. Stop at the first sensation of fullness in your stomach. Your body will tell you how to proceed, but you need to continue to exercise self-discipline.

SETTING PURPOSE-ORIENTED GOALS

1. Is it God's desire that I undertake a partial, normal, or absolute fast.
2. Are my motives right? Is there any hidden desire to impress others?
3. What are my spiritual objectives?
   - Personal sanctification? Fullness of the Spirit?
   - Intercession? What special burdens?
   - To loose the captives? Who is on the list?
   - Special ministerial calling? Direction for a calling?

- Receive God's revelation concerning a challenging time?

4. Am I determined above all else to glorify the Lord in my fast?

Be aware of this – a season of fasting will be a time of increased conflict with the powers of darkness. Satan will attempt to take advantage of your physical condition to launch an attack. Discouragement is one of his weapons—guard against it by maintaining a spirit of praise. Put on the whole armor of God and expect a battle (Eph. 6).

Do not make the mistake of judging the effectiveness of your prayers by what you feel. Frequently in seasons of fasting and prayer, you will find the going harder rather than easier. This is often when most is happening – this is wrestling – this is spiritual warfare.

Finally, it is recommended that you keep a day to day diary during the fast and record events concerning your spiritual objectives. Also record how your physical body responds on a day to day basis. This will be valuable information for your friends who make a decision to fast.

CONCLUDING NOTES

Be aware—when we cannot say "no" to a second helping of the food we like, though we do not need it; when we are always having "snacks" between regular meals; when we crave special foods that tickle the palate; when food is an ever-present temptation to which we constantly yield—then it is a certainty that we are in bondage to our physical bodies which will surely have a negative effect on our spiritual nature and thus, our fellowship with the Lord.

How can we expect the power of the Holy Spirit to flow if we do not prepare the channels? We are the temple of the Holy Spirit and fasting certainly assists us in preparing our bodies and souls (wineskins) for the "new wine."

If there is a call in your life to a deeper purifying of your soul or some new task for which you feel ill-equipped – then you need to inquire of God by separating yourself unto Him in prayer and fasting.

Fasting strengthens the intensity and power of prayer and becomes a ceaseless expression of a "prayer without words." Such a prayer warrior can be such a great spiritual influence in other people's lives without being physically present with the one who is the target of prayer.

<u>One last note of caution:</u>

Those who profess belief in Christ, yet continue in their sinful lifestyles (drugs, pornography, sexual immorality, etc.) are not truly Christians. One must "humble" themselves and forsake these things or the door to the Kingdom of God will not be open to you.

Prioritize your relationship with God, but also enjoy those things that He has given us. Just don't over-indulge. For example: If you want to watch the Seahawks, do it! But after the game, turn it off. Do not let fleshly desires control your time.

FASTING IDEAS FOR SPIRITUAL BREAKTHROUGH

Arthur Blessitt:

- After 3 days – no hunger pains or desire for food
- After 12-14 days – sense of complete cleanliness & mental clarity
- After 21 days – seems to be a sense of an outpouring of spiritual power that is indescribable that continues until the fast is ended.
- After the 3rd week there is no longer any interest in the physical world. One's mind is filled exclusively with spiritual ideas & truths.

<u>The mind will concentrate on one thing w/o wavering or being distracted. If the fast is controlled by the Holy Spirit and Jesus is foremost, then fasting is a beautiful & powerful experience.</u>

Andrew Murray:

- Fasting & prayer together bring about a separation from the spirit of worldly pleasures... <u>Also, prayer together with fasting brings about a deeper fellowship with God.</u>

J. Oswald Sanders:

- One value of fasting is that it tends to keep the body in submission to the spirit. <u>Also in prayer, the mind becomes unusually clear and vigorous.</u> There is a noticeable spiritual quickening and increased power of concentration on the things of the spirit.

J. Harold Smith:

- God impressed on his heart that he would never have the God-given anointing to reach the worst of sinners until he could fast for 40 days and read the bible through at least once. He did this and his life has never been the same. God helped him to win people to Christ that were on his prayer list for 20 years.

- He never entered a prolonged fast w/o first knowing it was the will of God. The greatest bible conferences that he experienced were when he did not eat one bite of food from the time he got off the plane until he got back on to return home.
- <u>Fasting will make a significant difference in winning souls to Christ.</u>

Charles Stanley:

- Fasting brings about a supernatural work in our lives. God will not entrust supernatural power to those whose lives are not under total control…<u>The Christian who would have the supernatural power of God must be under the total control of the Holy Spirit.</u>

C. Peter Wagner:

- Fasting is an intentional practice of self-denial and throughout the centuries, it has been a means of opening ourselves to God and drawing closer to Him…To the degree that fasting becomes more of a norm in our day-to-day Christian life, <u>we will become more effective in spiritual warfare.</u>

John Wesley:

- Let fasting be done with our motive singly fixed upon the Lord. To glorify our Father in heaven / to express sorrow and shame for our transgressions / to add seriousness and earnestness to prayers / to obtain all the great promises that He has made to us in Jesus Christ.

AN URGENT MESSAGE FOR TRULY VALUED FRIENDS

Preparing for the challenging times that lie shortly before us by encouraging Physical & Spiritual Preparations in 2016

> **Please set aside some quiet time for this critically important message from Don Bell who is not only your CPA, but your Christian friend!**

Dear <u>Friend</u>,

I have a number of close friends, but over my years in business, I have developed a deep caring heart for my clients whom I see less often. It has developed into something much more than just a business relationship, it is truly a friendship. As a former Marine, I understand the value of a friendship; it's more than simply kind words, for a true friend is one who will sacrifice oneself to stand alongside of those who are experiencing difficulties in life; and we all know that life can definitely be a battlefield.

Obviously, you know that I am available to assist with tax and financial issues, but you probably don't know that I am also available as your friend to support you during times of challenges that we all face in life. Everyone faces difficult challenges in life; our level of joy, prosperity, maturity all depends on how we handle those events which periodically confront each of us. None of us can handle these things alone. We all need true friendship.

I realize many of you are very concerned about the economic future of our nation and rightfully so. It is also my strong belief that we are right on the verge of devastating events that will create great fear and chaos in our nation as well as in many other countries. Those who have seriously "prepared" will be among those who will stand strong and guide their families who will be experiencing great fear in the midst of these catastrophic times which may soon descend upon us.

I am not trying to be pessimistic; this is a very probable reality that lies before us and I want to alert my family and friends to "prepare now." The ones who are "prepared" are more ready to confront their fears in a period of sudden chaos.

Preparation Overcomes Fear

Fear has a tendency to cause the majority of people to stick their heads in the sand and hope these things will not happen. It will keep them from properly preparing for that coming event(s) that will bring great panic among the unprepared.

However, as a former Marine commander serving on the frontlines of Vietnam, I learned that when you prioritize others before yourself, then **"fear"** will have much less control over your decision-making. Remove yourself from the picture of a future devastating scenario and only consider your family, children, etc. whom you are responsible for and **"fear"** will no longer be an issue. Your love for others overcomes **"fear"** which should encourage preparation for these probable future events.

How Do We Begin To "Physically Prepare"?

Those who understand the chaotic challenges that will soon confront our generation need to be communicating with their families and friends. The first step is to meet with them individually and lay out a scenario of a sudden shutdown of banks, stores, gas stations resulting in tremendous panic followed by gang violence, etc. throughout the cities across our nation.

Then, at that meeting, discuss in detail how each family would acquire preparation supplies. Get feedback from those in the group. Each person is to take notes and receive individual assignments to bring to the subsequent meeting. (The next meeting will go through all notes and make assignments).

If you would like additional insights concerning physical preparation – contact me and I'll provide more specific suggestions that I have written and also presented in various places.

A CPA—But Also A Disciple Of My Lord, Jesus Christ

As a concerned friend, I truly believe that it is time that I share some things with you about God, our Father and Creator, and about His Son, Jesus Christ. First of all, I want to assure you that I have no motive for writing to you except out of a loving concern for my friends and my passion for the Lord. This isn't about religion or about choosing a particular church; it's about you and your eternal destiny which hinges on your relationship with the Lord during this lifetime. This is something that the Lord Himself has put into my heart, for the times we are facing in today's world are visibly becoming more and more troubling; and I believe that the future for ourselves and our families will present some very challenging circumstances. Yet we can overcome these challenges by placing ourselves in the hands of the Lord:

As my relationship with the Lord grew over the years, I started attending seminary part-time as well as attending to my business responsibilities. I share this with you because I want you to know that I too have the same biblical educational background of most pastors; not that I want you to think more highly of me, but that my message to you might be received with more credibility. Actually, in 2008, I received a Doctorate in Ministry from Tacoma's Faith Seminary in the area of "Strategic Leadership." My passion for Jesus encouraged me through these studies while simultaneously pursuing my business responsibilities due to my passion for my client-friends. A few years ago, I chose to minister in the business world rather than taking a church pastoral position because I knew that this was what the Lord called me to.

Recently, I completed a book newly entitled "God's Anointed Warriors." This is the result of many years of study and prayer. It has now been published and is available for those who are interested in what some of the prophetic books in the Bible have to say concerning our generation. We really need to prepare ourselves and our families for the fallout from economic and/or terrorist events that will suddenly confront us.

Most Important Element of Preparation – "Spiritual"

My friends, tough days await us and our loved ones. We must be prepared, not just physically, but more importantly, spiritually. I exhort you not to continue forward in life "hoping" that one day when you leave this earth you will find eternal life in heaven. <u>You must come to the place where you "know" not "hope" that your eternal destination is with our Lord in heaven.</u> How do we know when we've arrived at that point in life when we are counted among the citizens of the Kingdom of God? <u>Answer</u>: When the Holy Spirit of God bears witness within our spirit while in this life, that we belong to Him:

- *<u>The Spirit himself bears witness with our spirit that we are children of God</u>, and if children, then heirs—heirs of God and fellow heirs with Christ…* **Romans 8:16-17**

Today's World & Eternal Preparation Message

Again, I want to assure you that I have no other motive for writing this letter than my sincere love and concern for my "client friends" that the Lord has brought to me over the years of my business life. Friend, it is so important to understand a basic biblical truth which so many governmental and educational arenas continually ignore, that is:

- *Jesus said, "I am the way, and the truth, and the life. <u>No one comes to the Father except through me.</u>* **John 14:6**

<u>Why Do So Many In Our 21st Century Schools, Government, And Media Refuse To Recognize This "Truth?"</u>

- Because they have embraced the worldly pleasures and do not want to hear that their chosen lifestyle is leading them down a dark, sinful road.

- They want to believe that man is basically "good" so they can choose to live their lives without interference from God.
- They do not want to hear the true gospel message that reveals them to be "sinners."

Thus, they hate God the Father and His Son Jesus Christ who calls them out of the world and they are becoming more and more hateful toward committed Christians.

The Hatred of the World Toward Jesus & Uncompromising Christians:

- *"If the world hates you, know that it has hated me before it hated you. If you were of the world, the world would love you as its own; but because you are not of the world, but I chose you out of the world, therefore the world hates you.* **John 15:18-19**

Who Is JESUS, Really?

The Eternal "SON OF GOD" Who came in the Flesh to provide each of us with the Opportunity to spend Eternal Life in the Kingdom of God!

The Word Created the Entire Cosmos

- *In the beginning was the Word, and the Word was with God, and the Word was God. He was in the beginning with God. All things were made through him, and without him was not anything made that was made.* **John 1:1-3**

Who is the Word?

- *And the Word became flesh and dwelt among us, and we have seen his glory, glory as of the only Son from the Father, full of grace and truth.* **John 1:14**

Why did the Son of God come into the World?

For God so Loved the World

- *"For God so loved the world, that he gave his only Son, that whoever believes in him should not perish but have eternal life. For God did not send his Son into the world to condemn the world, but in order that the world might be saved through him. Whoever believes in him is not condemned, but whoever does not believe is condemned already, because he has not believed in the name of the only Son of God .* **John 3:16-18**

My friends, we cannot be looking in another direction for eternal life; those who try to enter the heavenly kingdom another way, Jesus calls *"thieves and robbers"* and they will not be allowed to enter. Jesus is the only "doorway" into the eternal kingdom! Do not buy into the worldly gospel that there are many ways to eternal life. There is only one and I do pray that each one of you and your loved ones find it.

- So how do you, my friends, enter into the family of our Lord? Very simply:
- *If you confess with your mouth that Jesus is Lord and believe in your heart that God raised him from the dead, you will be saved.* **Romans 10:9**

Sound simple, yes? Yet, why does Jesus say this?

- *Jesus said "Enter by the narrow gate. For the gate is wide and the way is easy that leads to destruction, and those who enter by it are many. For the gate is narrow and the way is hard that leads to life, and those who find it are few.* **Matthew 7:13-14**
- Why so few?
- Answer: Because even those who "profess belief" may not truly believe with their whole hearts and they refuse to die to their sinful, bodily desires that are so rampant in this world!

Listen:

- *Put to death therefore what is earthly in you: sexual immorality, impurity, passion, evil desire, and covetousness, which is idolatry. On account of these the wrath of God is coming. In these you too once walked, when you were living in them. But now you must put them all away: anger, wrath, malice, slander, and obscene talk from your mouth. Do not lie to one another, seeing that you have put off the old self with its practices and have put on the new self, which is being renewed in knowledge after the image of its creator.* **Colossians 3:5-10**

- *Do you not know that the unrighteous will not inherit the kingdom of God? Do not be deceived: neither the sexually immoral, nor idolaters, nor adulterers, nor men who practice homosexuality, nor thieves, nor the greedy, nor drunkards, nor revilers, nor swindlers will inherit the kingdom of God. And such were some of you. But you were washed, you were sanctified, you were justified in the name of the Lord Jesus Christ and by the Spirit of our God.* **1 Corinthians 6:9-11**

Note: We can certainly add to this list the 21st century sins of internet pornography, drug addiction, and lovers of today's worldly pleasures more than lovers of God.

My friends, I strongly and lovingly exhort you to not shrug off these words and think that all things will work out in time and continue to live out your life as if tomorrow will be no different than today. A time is coming for all of us when there will be no tomorrow.

Different Age Groups

I have numerous client friends who range in age from teenagers to the elderly in their 90's. To each of you I say that it makes no difference where you are in your stage of life;

it makes no difference how great you think your sins have been; if you call out to Him for forgiveness with all your heart, He promises to remove all of your transgressions as far from him as the east is from the west (Psalm 103:11-12).

I can personally vouch for that, for in 1979, when the "born again" experience happened to me it was like 10,000 pounds was removed from off my back that I never realized was there until it was gone and a tremendous love for the Lord began to fill my heart. This all happened following the Vietnam War after which I was living a very wild and sinful life. Today, I am so thankful that friendships came into my life and pointed me in a direction that led to an overwhelming experience with the Lord that changed my life as I put off the things of the world and embraced the things of the Kingdom of God.

The rewards and forgiveness is the same for those who are elderly as it is for those who are young. So, don't let your age or deep feelings of guilt keep you from opening your heart and asking for forgiveness for a lifetime of sins in the name of Jesus Christ, the son of God, who at the Cross on Calvary hill, atoned for the sins of all who will confess and believe. <u>We are all youngsters in the light of eternity.</u>

<u>Those who call upon Him with a sincere seeking heart will never be the same again.</u>

Do Not Be In Bondage To "Anger" – "Bitterness" - "Unforgiveness"

Over my years in the CPA business, I have had thousands of interviews with people and have witnessed divorce, adultery, loss of jobs, children fighting over parent's estate, etc., etc., etc. All of this creates anger and hurt among family and former friends and I've learned that we all tend to hold onto this anger in our hearts. This is such a deep hindrance in our desire to live a life of joy.

I would exhort each of you to rid yourselves of this heavy weight in your inner being by "forgiving those" who have hurt you. <u>It's not a question of who is right or wrong; it doesn't matter,</u> just forgive and release the weight from <u>your</u> spirit and allow the Lord to handle matters. Forgive others even if they refuse to forgive you; the important thing is that you forgive. <u>Then stand back and watch the weight come off of your back that you never realized was there.</u>

For Non-Christians: Our Relationship Is Not a Coincidence

My dear client-friend, you've been brought into my life and it's not a coincidence. The Lord is definitely calling you to join Him and His people in the Kingdom of God. No matter how much you believe that you have sinned in this life, it will all be washed away forever and ever if you will turn, repent of your sins, and allow yourself to be cleansed by the mighty blood of Jesus Christ, the Son of almighty God.

The essence of who we are as human beings consist of three parts: body, soul, and spirit. We need to be aligned with the Lord who birthed us into this world. Our spirit has to awaken to our past sinful lifestyle which has controlled our walk and then - "repent" in order to come alive in the spirit. Awaken dear friend while there is still breath in our earthly body.

This is called being **"born-again."**

- ..... *unless one is born of water and the Spirit, he cannot enter the kingdom of God. That which is born of the flesh is flesh, and that which is born of the Spirit is spirit. Do not marvel that I said to you, 'You must be born again.'* **John 3:5-7**

FINAL RECOMMENDATION FOR THOSE WHO WISH TO SEEK THE LORD

So if you've read to this point and want to know how to proceed, I would suggest that you get a bible, if you don't already have one, and open to the Gospel of John found in the New Testament section. Then ask God to open your heart to His truth and begin to read. Read with an open heart believing that Jesus is right alongside of you and your direction will be made plain. See what happens when you ask if Jesus is truly the Lord. Eventually, you will feel a deep desire to cry out for forgiveness and that will be the time when He removes the weight of sin from your soul and He will remember your sins no more; they are completely gone from your life and from His remembrance. There is no way of finding the Lord except to seek Him – He stands at the door of your heart and knocks, but you must open up.

If you have never truly sought the Lord for forgiveness in your life, try opening your heart up to Him and call out for forgiveness.

The following prayer is an example for those who wish to open up to Him for the first time:

Pray the following prayer from a seeking heart:

A sinner's prayer

"It is hard for me to believe in you, Jesus. Yet I do believe what is written. It has the ring of truth. You are the One I have run from. You are what I have longed for all of these years. Maybe I never believed even when I thought I did. You're the King, not me. I'm tired of trying to run my life. I'm not qualified. I've messed up everything. I do believe now that Jesus is the Christ, the Son of God. I ask for the life you promised. I ask for your Holy Spirit inside me. Please wash me from my sins. Please fill the hole in my heart, Jesus. Please be to me what I've always longed for. I can't make it on my own. I need You."

319

FOR ALL OF YOU NO MATTER YOUR BELIEF

If you are currently facing grievous circumstances, no matter what it is, I will make myself available to listen and intercede for you, or with you, before the Lord. I can also share your petition(s) with others who will also faithfully meet and/or pray with you.

Perhaps you have a deep hunger inside (a sense of emptiness) for something more in life (I call it an unfulfilled warrior spirit) – let me know! I will be an intercessor who stands with you in prayer before God the Father and His Son, the Lord Jesus Christ. Don't hold onto grief and sorrow – I will be your private disciple if you desire.

APPENDIX "F"

MINISTERING IN THE WORKPLACE

The Sunday church gatherings are not the frontlines of our spiritual battlefield. They have an important part to play in this war, but they are behind the frontlines.

From a military perspective the organized church is:

- Boot-camp training meant to prepare young Christians for the frontlines of the battlefield. (Such as: Teaching through the bible)
- A medical center for treating the hurting & wounded (Such as: Celebrate Recovery).
- A place that provides memorial services for those who die. (By the way, a funeral service is a place that provides great opportunities to capture hearts for the kingdom.) Attack here: for the enemy is at his weakest in the midst of grieving hearts searching for answers.

Where are the Frontlines of the Spiritual Warfare?

- The real frontlines of the battlefield are where Christians live out life - in your family, and perhaps in your neighborhood.
- However, the workplace is where one can be a tremendous witness for the Kingdom of God.
- This is where we can impact many people in the truth of the Lord.
- In the workplace, you'll come across so many men who are searching for truth, even though they won't admit it, but they would never come to a church believing that it is too "wimpy" for them.

  So – How do We Handle Our Calling in the Workplace
  Be watchful – and when you see the Lord open a door to speak with someone, you might begin by saying the following:

- As a concerned friend, I truly believe that it is time that I share some things with you about God, our Father and Creator, and about His Son, Jesus Christ.
- First of all, I want to assure you that I have no motive for speaking to you except out of a loving concern for my friends and my passion for the Lord.
- This isn't about religion or about choosing a particular church; it's about you and your eternal destiny which hinges on your relationship with the Lord during this lifetime.
- This is something that the Lord Himself has put into my heart, for the times we are facing in today's world are visibly becoming more and more troubling; and I believe

that the future for ourselves and our families will present some very challenging circumstances.

- Yet we can stand strong during these times by placing ourselves in the hands of the Lord.

My friend, tough days await us and our loved ones. We must be prepared, not just physically, but more importantly, spiritually.

- I exhort you not to continue forward in life "hoping" that one day when you leave this earth you will find eternal life in heaven.
- You must come to the place where you "know" not "hope" that your eternal destination is with our Lord in heaven.

At this point – you will know if you have their attention. If so – then continue as follows:

Again, I want to assure you that I have no other motive for this conversation than my sincere love and concern for my friends that the Lord has brought to me over the years of my life.

Now, I want to share with you a basic biblical truth which so many governmental and educational arenas continually ignore, that is:

Who Is JESUS, Really?

He is The Eternal "SON OF GOD" Who came in the Flesh to provide each of us with the Opportunity to spend Eternal Life in the Kingdom of God!

- **Then quote the following (you should have them memorized:**

The Word Became Flesh

- *In the beginning was the Word, and the Word was with God, and the Word was God. He was in the beginning with God. All things were made through him, and without him was not any thing made that was made. (John 1:1-3)*

Who is the Word?

- *And the Word became flesh and dwelt among us, and we have seen his glory, glory as of the only Son from the Father, full of grace and truth. (John 1:14)*

Why did the Son of God come into the world?

For God so Loved the World

- *"For God so loved the world, that he gave his only Son, that whoever believes in him should not perish but have eternal life. For God did not send his Son into the world to condemn the world, but in order that the world might be saved through him. Whoever believes in him is not condemned, but whoever does not believe is condemned already, because he has not believed in the name of the only Son of God. (John 3:16-18)*

Dear friend, we cannot be looking in another direction for eternal life; those who try to enter the heavenly kingdom another way, Jesus calls *"thieves and robbers"* and they will not be allowed to enter.

- Jesus is the only "doorway" into the eternal kingdom! Do not buy into the worldly teachings that there are many ways to eternal life. There is only one and I do pray that you and your loved ones find it.

So how do you, my friend, enter into the family of our Lord? Well:

- *If you confess with your mouth that Jesus is Lord and believe in your heart that God raised him from the dead, you will be saved. (Romans 10:9)*

Sound simple, yes? Yet, why does Jesus say this?

- *Jesus said "Enter by the narrow gate. For the gate is wide and the way is easy that leads to destruction, and those who enter by it are many. For the gate is narrow and the way is hard that leads to life, and those who find it are few. (Matthew 7:13-14)*

Why so few?

- Answer: Because even those who "profess belief" may not truly believe with their whole hearts and they refuse to die to the sinful pleasures in the world!

My friend, I strongly and lovingly exhort you to not shrug off these words and think that all things will work out in time and continue to live out your life as if tomorrow will be no different than today. **A time is coming for all of us when there will be no tomorrow.**

Now if your friend has had a long life of sinful living, he might believe that the Lord would never forgive him. At this point, you could tell him that:

I have numerous friends who range in age from teenagers to the elderly in their 90's.

- To each one I say that it makes no difference where you are in your stage of life.
- It makes no difference how terrible you think your sins have been.
- If you call out to Him for forgiveness with all your heart, He promises to remove all of your transgressions as far from him as the east is from the west (Psalm 103:11-12).

The rewards and forgiveness is the same for those who are elderly as it is for those who are young.

- So, don't let your age or deep feelings of guilt keep you from opening your heart and asking for forgiveness for a lifetime of sins in the name of Jesus Christ, the son of God, who at the Cross on Calvary hill, atoned for the sins of all who will confess and believe.
- <u>We are all youngsters in the light of eternity.</u>

<u>Those who call upon Him with a sincere seeking heart will never be the same again.</u>

Additionally, do not be in bondage To "Anger" – "Bitterness" - "Unforgiveness"

Over my years, I have numerous peoples who have experienced divorce, adultery, loss of jobs, fighting among family members, etc., etc., etc.

- All of this creates anger and hurt among family and former friends and I've learned that we all tend to hold onto this anger in our hearts.
- This is such a deep hindrance in our desire to live a life of joy.

So, after confessing your sins before God and asking for forgiveness in the name of the Lord Jesus Christ, I would exhort you to rid yourselves of this heavy weight in your inner being by "forgiving those" who have hurt you.

- It's not a question of who is right or wrong; it doesn't matter, just forgive and release the weight from your spirit and allow the Lord to handle matters.
- Forgive others even if they refuse to forgive you; the important thing is that you forgive.
- Then stand back and watch the weight come off of your back that you never realized was there.

My dear friend, you've been brought into my life and it's not a coincidence. The Lord is definitely calling you to join Him and His people in the Kingdom of God.

- No matter how much you believe that you have sinned in this life, it will all be washed away forever and ever if you will turn, repent of your sins, and allow yourself to be cleansed by the mighty blood of Jesus Christ, the Son of almighty God.

The essence of who we are as human beings consist of three parts: body, soul, and spirit. We need to be aligned with the Lord who birthed us into this world.

- Our spirit has to awaken to our past sinful lifestyle which has controlled our walk and then - "repent" in order to come alive in the spirit.
- Awaken dear friend while there is still breath in our earthly body.
- This is called being **"born-again."**

However, your impact in the workplace will depend upon the strength of your relationship with your Lord.

- For our light to shine in life-changing brightness, we need to continually seek the oil for our lamps.
- As more and more oil is provided, the bigger the lamp and the brighter the light shines in the midst of darkness in the workplace.
- This oil is continually provided as we spend time alone with Him seeking the battlefield intelligence from our Lord needed to minister on the frontlines.

The toughest battle in the young Christian life is maintaining the discipline to spend quality time alone in fasting, praying, and studying His Word.

- There certainly is nothing wrong with going to the movies and eating popcorn, or enjoying a beer with your friends on occasion. In fact, these can be important ways of deepening relationships with your co-workers, friends, and family members.
- However, these things cannot control the time in your life. Time alone with family is extremely important, but the quality time you set aside in your private area to be alone with the Lord will determine the power of your light on the battlefield of life.

HOW DO WE BEGIN TO PHYSICALLY PREPARE?

Those who understand the chaotic challenges that will soon confront our generation need to be communicating with their families and friends. The first step is to meet with them individually and lay out a scenario of a sudden shutdown of banks, stores, gas stations followed by gang violence, etc. throughout the cities across our nation. (Note: Perhaps the initial meeting should only be 4 - 5 of your closest friends who are like-minded concerning the approaching chaos).

Then, at that meeting, discuss in detail how each family would acquire the following preparation supplies. Get feedback from those in the group. Each person is to take notes and receive individual assignments to bring to the subsequent meeting. (The next meeting will go through all notes and make assignments).

Food supplies for a minimum of six to twelve months:

- What type of food supplies should be made for long-term storage?
- How long would supplies last that they currently have in their homes? Inventory!
- Are they financially able to acquire the required food supplies?
- Discuss need for secretive storage of foods & supplies. Why?

Drinking & cleansing water for an indefinite period of time:

- Discuss methods of storing and purifying water.
- Costco 55 gallon water containers with a purifying agent called "Aquamira" which has a 5 year life.

Medical supplies, batteries, toilet paper, gasoline, propane, tools, flashlights, radios, etc.:

- Discuss what may be needed for an indefinite period of time.
- Costco also has emergency first-aid kits.

Supplies to survive a lengthy, cold winter without electrical power.

- Items such as clothing and sleeping bags.
- What items are needed for young children and babies?
- Survival kits kept in cars.
- Briefly speak of "nuclear winter." (Sub-zero temperature for six months).

- Perhaps you should discuss plans for handling nuclear "fallout." You only need to stay sheltered for a few days; just long enough for the "fallout" to lose its radioactivity.

Also, consider that our prepared supplies may be a great blessing to many unprepared families that will be suffering from shock and hunger:

- We need to be equipped to "share." <u>However, we must be careful here!</u> If those who have not prepared know about your preparations, it could get nasty.

Discuss the probability of gang violence that will undoubtedly occur in cities and neighborhoods for each individual family could certainly be exposed to tremendous dangers:

- Plan for each family to gather together on a pre-determined property and live in community?
- A community of friends and family who have gathered together are more capable of fending off gang-related assaults.
- If so, family supplies should be inventoried and ready to move to the selected property(s) on a moment's notice.
- Telephone communications may not be possible so the timing of this gathering must be well planned in advance.
- Networking with your close neighbors may also be critically important.

Discuss the ownership and use of firearms in a volatile situation:

- Discuss if and when firearms may be used for protection.
- Only those who are properly trained and experienced in the use of firearms should be allowed to handle them.
- Suggest only mature adults handle guns since younger men and women are more panicky in a dangerous confrontation with gangs or burglars. Many of the younger folks have not yet learned important disciplines in life and are more prone to be aggressive without wisdom.
- Suggest those with military experience be assigned to develop and oversee a group security plan within your gathered community.
- Discuss your response if government militia forces arrive to confiscate your weapons.

Finally, discuss the relationship that each individual member of the gathered family(s) has with the Lord and develop a plan of how to proceed with the deepening of each relationship.

- Areas of solitary prayer / gathering together / bible studies / teachings.

At the end of the meeting, set a date when all will again meet together with five to six other families in order to present their recommendations and finalize their plans.

- At this meeting, it is very important that the 4 – 5 leaders who initiated this movement act as the facilitators to help the group see and think about things that they would normally never consider.
- Facilitators must assist in helping individual families see where they fit in the bigger picture as well as monitoring the progress of the meeting with periodic summarization, group encouragement, and affirming each member's input, yet not allowing the meeting to lose focus on its intended mission.
- Now there are plenty of websites that provide information as well as sell products to those who intend to make preparations, so it is recommended that each family do some researching.
- Also, assign responsibilities and get individual commitments from each family and set a date for completion, whereupon another meeting is scheduled to affirm completion.
- Remember, you cannot micro-manage the situation; you need to assign responsibility to each individual within the family unit.
- Finally, those who initially show interest, but do not follow up on their assigned responsibilities should not be part of the team. Their responsibilities need to be assigned to others.

The only trustworthy preparations are those for the heart, not the body. If you love the Lord, this is where all preparations must begin.

- Those who set their hearts to seek the Lord and cleave to Christ more and more – are better prepared for the coming storm than anyone. They are more secure than the wealthy that have stored guns and years of food away in some remote country haven; yet are not focused on Christ.

Many believers have put their eternity destiny into the Lord's hands – but most have not done the same with their earthly destiny.

Think about it: How much can you stockpile and for how long? There is no possible, failsafe way to prepare for what's coming.

But if you are making spiritual preparations – getting your heart in order, dealing with sin, calling on the Lord with greater intensity, trusting in His Word – then you are readying yourselves for anything.

- You'll be ready for economic meltdown, crop failures, closed stores, droughts, sicknesses, and persecution from government.

- Those who are spiritually prepared will also discern that it's time to equip yourselves and your families with physical preparations as well.

Now what we have talked about here will not resonate with many. They want to blindly excuse themselves by believing that we can all relax - live life as usual, and when the chaos strikes, God will immediately supply heavenly manna for us. This mindset comes from an inward "disbelief" that chaotic times are approaching. Many of these will be the ones who "fall away" from the church and trust in the government to take care of them.

This is the "sluggard" mindset that refuses to take action.

- *Go to the ant, O sluggard; consider her ways, and be wise. Without having any chief, officer, or ruler, she prepares her bread in summer and gathers her food in harvest. How long will you lie there, O sluggard? When will you arise from your sleep? A little sleep, a little slumber, a little folding of the hands to rest, and poverty will come upon you like a robber, and want like an armed man.* **(Proverbs 6:6-11)**

---

1 Thessalonians 5:2-9

For you yourselves are fully aware that **the day of the Lord will come like a thief in the night**.

While people are saying, "There is peace and security," then sudden destruction will come upon them as labor pains come upon a pregnant woman, and they will not escape.

But you are not in darkness, brothers, for that day to surprise you like a thief. For you are all children of light, children of the day. We are not of the night or of the darkness.

So then let us not sleep, as others do, but let us keep awake and be sober. For those who sleep, sleep at night, and those who get drunk, are drunk at night. but since we belong to the day, let us be sober, having put on the breastplate of faith and love, and for a helmet the hope of salvation.

For God has not destined us for wrath, but to obtain salvation through our Lord Jesus Christ.

NOTES

Introduction

[1] Luke 12:35-59; Joel 2 and 3.

[2] 1 Chronicles 12:32

[3] Matthew 24:21

[4] Isaiah 60:1-2

[5] Ezekiel 9:4-6

[6] Psalm 23:4

[7] 1 Peter 4:17

[8] Luke 21:28-31; Daniel 12:10

Chapter 1
AMERICA – "A FORMER CHRISTIAN NATION"

[9] Matthew 25:1-13

[10] This point is made by Greg Austin, pastor of Gardiner Community Church, Gardiner, Washington.

[11] Ryan Wyatt, "The Kingdom Time Is Now," *Visionary Advancement Newsletter*, n.d.

[12] Reggie McNeal, *Practicing Greatness* (San Francisco: Jossey-Bass, 2006), 8.

Chapter 2
WARNINGS FOR THE CHURCH IN AMERICA

[13] Matthew 24:9-11

[14] Charles Stanley, *A Touch of His Freedom* (Grand Rapids: Zondervan, 1991).

[15] Matthew 23:2

[16] Herman Hoeksema, *Behold He Cometh: An Exposition of the Book of Revelation* (Grand Rapids: Reformed Free Publishing Association, 1969), 61.

[17] Paul Marshall, *Their Blood Cries Out* (Dallas: Word, 1997), 4.

[18] Matthew 25:1-13

[19] Matthew 24:9; Mark 13:13; Luke 21:17

[20] David Ravenhill, *The Jesus Letters* (Shippensburg, PA: Destiny Image, 2003), 80-81.

[21] Ibid, 86.

[22] Psalm 23:4; 1 Corinthians 2:9

[23] Gregory R. Reid, *The Gospel of Vague* (Enemies of the Cross – Prosperity Movement: www.etpv.org/2008).

[24] Ibid

[25] Ravenhill, *The Jesus Letters*, 115-16, 120-21.

[26] Hoeksema, *Behold He Cometh*, 132-33.

[27] Ravenhill, *The Jesus Letters*,139.

[28] Ibid, 142-44.

[29] Al Houghton, *"Word at Work* Newsletter, Volume XXI, Ch. 7.

[30] Ravenhill, *The Jesus Letters*, 151.

[31] Rick Joyner, "The Army of God Mobilizes, " Part 9, www.morningstarministries.org

[32] Jack Deere, *Surprised by the Power of the Spirit* (Grand Rapids: Zondervan, 1993).

[33] Matthew 24:11

[34] Isaiah 26:9

[35] Quoted in David Pawson, *When Jesus Returns* (London: Hodder & Stoughton; 1995), 199-200.

[36] Keith Intrater, *From Iraq to Armageddon* (Shippensburg, PA: Destiny Image, 2003), 141-42.

[37] Revelation 2:10; 12:10; 2 Timothy 3:12; John 17:15; Acts 14:22

[38] Tim Taylor of Watchman Ministries, e-mail to the author.

[39] Andrew Walker, *Enemy Territory* (Wilmore, KY: Bristol Books, 1990), 15-16.

[40] Al Houghton, *Word at Work* Newsletter, Volume XXI, Number IX, Chapter 10.

Chapter 3
SEALS, HORSEMEN, AND MARTYRDOM

[41] Philip Mauro, *Things Which Soon Must Come to Pass* (Swengel, PA: Reiner Publications, 1974), 182.

[42] 2 Kings 19:35; Isaiah 37:36

[43] Revelation 1:12-18; Daniel 10:5-12

[44] 1 Corinthians 2:9-10

[45] Mark 12:28-30

[46] Mauro, *Things Which Soon Must Come to Pass*, 180.

[47] David Pawson, *When Jesus Returns* (London: Hodder & Stoughton, 1995), 133.

[48] Mauro, *Things Which Soon Must Come to Pass*, 187-89.

[49] Matthew 13:24-30 (The Parable of the Weeds)

[50] Herman Hoeksema, *Behold, He Cometh: An Exposition of the Book of Revelation* (Grand Rapids: Reformed Free Publishing Association, 1969), 216.

[51] 2 Timothy 3:12; Romans 5:3-4

[52] James 1:2-4; Romans 8:16-18

[53] Ephesians 6:12

[54] Romans 8:28; 1 Corinthians 2:9

[55] John 14:2-3

[56] Matthew 5:14-16

[57] Roderick Graciano, "The True Spirit of Martyrdom," Timothy Ministries, www.tmin.org.

[58] Ibid.

[59] Ibid.

[60] Genesis 3:15

[61] Hoeksema, *Behold, He Cometh*, 230-31.

[62] Revelation 6:15

[63] Hoeksema, *Behold, He Cometh*, 244.

[64] Revelation 6:16

Chapter 4
A GREAT WAR IS COMING

[65] Ezekiel 3:17-20

[66] Joel C. Rosenberg, *Epicenter: Why the Current Rumblings in the Middle East Will Change Your Future* (Tyndale House, 2006), 68-69.

[67] Ezekiel 38:4

[68] Rosenberg, *Epicenter*, 132.

[69] Isaiah 17

[70] Rosenberg, *Epicenter*, 114 –19.

[71] Ayatollah Ibrahim Amini, *Al-Imam, al-Mahdi, The Just Leader of Humanity*, trans. Dr.Abdulaziz Sachedina (Qum, Iran: Ahul Bayt Digital Islamic Library Project, al-islam.org/Mahdi/nontl/Toc htm (accessed April 15, 2006, emphasis mine).

[72] Ibid.

[73] Rosenberg, *Epicenter*, 249-50.

[74] Ibid.

[75] Ezekiel 38:13

[76] Reuters, "U.S. Envoy: Anti-Semitism in Europe Nearly as Bad as in 1930s," February 13, 2004.

[77] Robin Shepherd, "In Europe, an Unhealthy Fixation on Israel," *Washington Post*, January 30, 2005.

[78] Revelation 20:7-10

[79] Rosenberg, *Epicenter*, 254.

[80] John Mintz, "U.S. Called Unprepared for Nuclear Terrorism," *Washington Post*, May 3, 2005.

[81] Rosenberg, *Epicenter*, 120-23.

[82] Charles W. Miller, *Today's Technology in Bible Prophecy* (Lansing, MI: TIP, 1990), 135.

[83] Rosenberg, *Epicenter*, 250.

Chapter 5
GOD'S WARRIORS IN THE END TIMES = 144,000

[84] Romans 1:1; Galatians 1:10; James 1:1; 2 Peter 1:1; Acts 4:29; 16:17

[85] Revelation 1:1; 10:7; 11:18; Jeremiah 7:25; 25:4

[86] Joshua 1:1; Revelation 15:3

[87] Acts 10:36; Ephesians 6:6

[88] 1 Corinthians 7:23

[89] Matthew 24:44; Luke 12:40

[90] Romans 11:25-29

[91] Micah 5:7-8; Hosea 1:10

[92] Galatians 3:29; Philippians 3:3; Romans 2:28-29; 9:6

[93] 1 Kings 12:24

[94] Hosea 11:8-9; Zechariah 10:6; Ezekiel 37: 16-22; Micah 5:7-8

[95] Genesis 48:19

[96] Ellis H. Skolfield, *Hidden Beast 2* (Fort Myers, FL: Fish House, 1990), 130-31.

[97] Hosea 1:10

[98] Hosea 7:8, 8:8, 9:17; Micah 5:7-8

[99] Hosea 11:8-9

[100] Hosea 2:14-23; Zechariah 10:6

[101] Larry Simmons, *42 Months to Glory* (Oklahoma City: Ephraim House, 1994), 86.

[102] Ezekiel 37:19-21; Romans 10:26; Hosea 1:10

[103] Skolfield, *Hidden Beast 2*, 140.

[104] Hosea 11:10; Douglas S. Winnail, *Early Christianity and Europe's Western Isles*, www.tomorrowsworld.org.

[105] Zechariah 9:13-14

[106] Skolfield, *Hidden Beast 2*, 135-36.

[107] Romans 11:25-27

[108] Simmons, *42 Months to Glory*, 91-92.

[109] Revelation 21:9-26

[110] Revelation 14:1-5

[111] Revelation 7:9-17

[112] Joel C. Graves, *Gathering Over Jerusalem*, (Xulon, 2003), 6.

[113] John 14:12-14

[114] Numbers 13 and 14

[115] Luke 9:23

[116] John 15:20-21; Genesis 22; Matthew 10:37

[117] James 1:2-4

[118] Isaiah 21:6; Ezekiel 3:17

[119] Ezekiel 9:4

[120] Revelation 14:1-5

[121] Ephesians 4:15

Chapter 6
THE "SEVENTY WEEKS" OF DANIEL

[122] Jeremiah 25:11-12; 29:10

[123] Isaiah 45:13

[124] Daniel 9:1-23

[125] Exodus 32:12-13

[126] Ezekiel 40-46

[127] Ezra 7:12-26; 9:9

[128] Nehemiah 2:5-8

[129] Isaac Newton, *Observations upon the Prophecies of Daniel and the Apocalypse of St. John* (London, 1733), 135.

[130] Revelation 14:4-5

[131] Revelation 14:1-5

[132] Benjamin Baruch, *The Day of the Lord Is at Hand* (Baruch Publishing, 2004), 21.

[133] Ibid, 28-29.

Chapter 7
TRUMPETS, NUKES, AND A LITTLE BOOK

[134] Joel 2; Jeremiah 46:10; 2 Peter 3:10; 1 Thessalonians 5:2; Isaiah 13:6-9; Acts 2:19-21; Amos 5:18

[135] Acts 2:20-21

[136] Ezekiel 39:6

[137] Charles W. Miller, *Today's Technology in Bible Prophecy* (Lansing, MI: TIP, 1990), 142.

[138] Ibid.

[139] Herman Hoeksema. *Behold, He Cometh: An Exposition of the Book of Revelation* (Grand Rapids: Reformed Free Publishing Association, 1969), 296-97.

[140] Revelation 6:12; 8:5; Ezekiel 38:19

[141] Miller, *Today's Technology in Bible Prophecy*, 161-65.

[142] Exodus 9:23-26

[143] Exodus 7:20-21

[144] Jeremiah 9:15

[145] Miller, *Today's Technology in Bible Prophecy*, 176.

[146] Ibid., 178-82

[147] Exodus 10:21-23

[148] Judges 6:3-5

[149] Miller, *Today's Technology in Bible Prophecy*, 196-213.

[150] Joel 2:1-11 and Isaiah 24:1-15

[151] Revelation 9:20-21

[152] Psalm 23; Job 1:21

[153] Revelation 1:10-16; Daniel 10:5-6

[154] Revelation 10:4

[155] Jeremiah 6:14

[156] Ezekiel 2:8—3:3

[157] Hoeksema. *Behold, He Cometh*, 23.

Chapter 8
WARRIORS FOR CHRIST IN THE MIDST OF THE GREAT TRIBULATION

[158] Rick Joyner, "The Church will Begin to Take On More of a Military Mentality in the Coming Times," *MorningStar Newsletter*, April, 2008.

[159] Matthew 24:14

[160] Revelation 11:15-19

[161] 1 Corinthians 3:16-17; Ephesians 2:19-22

[162] Isaiah 60:14

[163] Gleason L. Archer, "Isaiah" in *The Wycliffe Bible Commentary*, ed. Charles F. Pfeiffer and Everett F. Harrison (Chicago: Moody, 1962), 642-43.

[164] Zephaniah 3:1-2

[165] Matthew 21:12-13

[166] Herman Hoeksema, *Behold, He Cometh: An Exposition of the Book of Revelation* (Grand Rapids: Reformed Free Publishing Assn, 1969), 369-70.

[167] Benjamin Baruch, *The Day of the Lord Is at Hand* (Baruch Publishing, 2004), 27.

[168] Revelation 12:6

[169] Revelation 13:5-7

[170] Zechariah 4

[171] Revelation 1:20

[172] Revelation 14:1-5

[173] Like 1:17; Matthew 11:14

[174] Matthew 3:3

[175] Baruch, *The Day of the Lord Is at Hand*, 48

[176] A.W. Tozer, "'Prophetic Preaching,' This Is the Need of Our Day and It will Come," quoted in "A New Breed of Modern Preachers," sermon by Greg Gordon, www.sermonindex.net

[177] Baruch, *The Day of the Lord Is at Hand*, 76-77.

[178] Rosha Judah, *Prophets Still Speak* (The Sound of a Trumpet, 1991).

[179] Matthew 24:14

[180] John 14:12

[181] Hoeksema, *Behold, He Cometh*, 390-92.

[182] John 15:20; Matthew 24:10

[183] Matthew 5:11-12

[184] Daniel 9:24

[185] Revelation 11:5

[186] Revelation 11:8

[187] Daniel 3:8-12

Chapter 9
CONFRONTATION BETWEEN THE WOMAN & THE DRAGOM

[188] Jeremiah 4:31; Micah 4:8-9

[189] Genesis 6:1-4

[190] Matthew 2:1-18

[191] Matthew 4:1-11

[192] Job 1:6; 2:1; Zechariah 3:1

[193] John 14:30; Ephesians 2:1-3

[194] Jude 9; Matthew 24:31; Luke 4: 10-11; Daniel 12:1

195 Herman Hoeksema, *Behold, He Cometh: An Exposition of the Book of Revelation* (Grand Rapids: Reformed Free Publishing Assn, 1969), 431-35.

196 John 15:19; 17:16

197 Dave Hunt, *A Woman Rides the Beast* (Harvest House, 1994), 70-79.

198 Philip Mauro, *Things Which Soon Must Come to Pass* (Swengel, PA: Reiner Publications, 1974), 384-389

199 Hoeksema, *Behold, He Cometh*, 448-49.

200 Isaiah 14:12-14 (emphasis mine)

Chapter 10
THREE BEASTS – AN UNHOLY TRINITY

201 Revelation 12:12

202 Isaiah 57:20; Revelation 17:15

203 Daniel 7-8

204 Revelation 12:3

205 Matthew 4:8-10

206 Revelation 17:9-10

207 Revelation 17:13; 17

208 Revelation 17:11; Daniel 7:8

209 Herman Hoeksema, *Behold, He Cometh: An Exposition of the Book of Revelation* (Grand Rapids: Reformed Free Publishing Association, 1969), 576.

210 Isaiah 14:13-14

211 Daniel 11:39

212 Daniel 7:8

213 Daniel 11:32

214 Daniel 7:7-8

215 Revelation 13:4

216 Daniel 3:1-7

217 Benjamin Baruch offers the example of *"Prince Charles of Wales,"* which equals 666 when calculated using the Hebrew alphabet. Prince Charles seems an unlikely candidate in today's political arena. However, this is an example of how one's name can be translated into a number (*The Day of the Lord Is at Hand* [Baruch Publishing, 2004], 178).

218 Matthew 11:19

219 Daniel 9:24

220 Daniel 9:27; 11:22-24; Isaiah 28:15-22

221 Matthew 24:15-22

222 Hebrews 10:8-10

223 Baruch, *The Day of the Lord Is at Hand*, 26-29.

224 Daniel 11:33;

225 Baruch, *The Day of the Lord Is at Hand*, 44-46.

226 Dan Juster and Keith Intrater, *Israel, the Church and the Last Days* (Destiny Image, 1991), 137-47.

227 Ellis H. Skolfield, *Hidden Beast 2* (Fort Myers, FL: Fish House, 1990), 175.

Chapter 11
MYSTERY BABYLON THE GREAT: CAPITOL OF WEALTH, PLEASURE, & HARLOTRY

228 Daniel 2

229 Benjamin Baruch, *The Day of the Lord Is at Hand* (Baruch Publishing, 2004), 52-56.

230 Ibid., 124-27.

231 Jeremiah 51:25; Daniel 2:35; Zechariah 4:7

[232] Dave Hunt, *A Woman Rides the Beast* (Eugene: Harvest House, 1994), 70-71.

[233] 1 Timothy 5:8

[234] Roderick Graciano, "Battling Babylons," Timothy Ministries, www.tmin.org, 49.

[235] Matthew 6:24

[236] Revelation 13 and Revelation 11

[237] Daniel 7:8; 20-22; 24-25

[238] Ezekiel 16:8-22

[239] Ibid. p.96

[240] Isaiah 48:20; 52:11; Jeremiah 50:8-9; 51:6-8; Zechariah 2:6-7; 2 Corinthians 6:17-18; Revelation 18:4-8

[241] Philip Mauro, *Things Which Must Soon Come to Pass* (Swengel, PA: Reiner Publications, 1974), 494.

[242] Arthur W. Pink, *Elijah* (Edinburgh: The Banner of Truth Trust, 1956), 129-33.

[243] Al Houghton, *Word at Work* (Newsletter Volume XXI, Number IX, Chapter 10).

Chapter 12
THE LAST HARVEST FOLLOWED BY DESTRUCTION

[244] Philip Mauro, *Things Which Must Soon Come to Pass* (Swengel, PA: Reiner Publications, 1974), 432-34.

[245] Luke 19:17-19

[246] Herman Hoeksema, *Behold, He Cometh*, 494.

[247] 1 Kings 19 (modified for this scenario)

[248] Psalm 23:4

[249] Hoeksema, *Behold, He Cometh*, 501.

[250] Matthew 13:24-30

[251] Matthew 13:36-43

[252] 1 Thessalonians 4:15-17

[253] Daniel 3:8-30

[254] Exodus 15:1-18

[255] Hoeksema, *Behold, He Cometh*, 521-23.

[256] Job 2:7-8

Chapter 13
THE RETURN OF THE KING

[257] Psalm 23:5

[258] Herman Hoeksema, *Behold, He Cometh*, 546.

[259] Joel 3:1-3; 12

[260] Isaiah 14:12-21; Ezekiel 28:13-19

[261] Zechariah 14:16; Isaiah 52:10; 66:20; Psalm 86:9

[262] Ephesians 2:2; 6:12

[263] Joshua 10:11; Ezekiel 38:18-22)

[264] John 19:30

[265] George Eldon Ladd, *A Commentary on the Revelation of John* (Grand Rapids: Eerdmans, 1972), 214.

[266] Judges 7:20-22

[267] Zechariah 12:6

[268] Luke 19:10; John 3:17

[269] David Pawson, *When Jesus Returns* (London: Hodder & Stoughton, 1995), 166.

[270] Amos 9:1-4

[271] Revelation 2:17

[272] Ladd, *A Commentary on the Revelation of John*, 256.

[273] Revelation 15:2-3; Mark 8:38; Luke 9:26; 1 Thessalonians 3:13; 2 Thessalonians 1:7-8

[274] 1 Thessalonians 4:17

[275] Revelation 6:11

[276] 2 Thessalonians 1:10

[277] Revelation 14:20

[278] John 1:1-2; 14

[279] Hoeksema, *Behold, He Cometh*, 634.

[280] Psalm 79:1-2

[281] 1 Samuel 17:44-47

[282] Genesis 19:24

[283] Keith Intrater, *From Iraq to Armageddon* (Shippensburg, PA: Destiny Image, 2003), 216.

Chapter 14
THE KINGDOM OF GOD REIGNING UPON THE EARTH

[284] David Pawson, *When Jesus Returns* (London: Hodder & Stoughton, 1995), 260.

[285] Alan F. Johnson, "Revelation" in *The Expositor's Bible Commentary*, ed. Frank E Gaebelein (Grand Rapids: Zondervan, 1981), 12:578.

[286] Pawson, *When Jesus Returns*, 259.

[287] Dan Juster and Keith Intrater, *Israel, the Church and the Last Days* (Shippensburg, PA: Destiny Image, 1990), 193.

[288] 2 Peter 3:4-8

[289] Juster and Intrater, *Israel, the Church and the Last Days*, 195.

[290] Keith Intrater, *From Iraq to Armageddon*, (Shippensburg, PA: Destiny Image, 2003), 154-55.

[291] William R. Villanueva, *Signs of the End of the Age: Revelation Unravelled*, (Ramseur, NC: Solid Rock Publishing, 1996), 176-77.

[292] Ezekiel 47:1-9

[293] Pawson, *When Jesus Returns*, 228.

[294] Luke 24; John 20

[295] Matthew 27:53

[296] Matthew 25:21; Luke 19:17

[297] Pawson, *When Jesus Returns*, 222.

[298] George Eldon Ladd, *A Commentary on the Revelation of John* (Grand Rapids: Eerdmans, 1972), 269.

[299] Pawson, *When Jesus Returns*, 226-27.

[300] Luke 16:19-31

[301] Matthew 27:52-53; Ephesians 4:8-9; 2 Corinthians 12:1-4

[302] Anthony A. Hoekema, *The Bible and the Future* (Grand Rapids: Eerdmans, 1979), 273.

[303] David Reagan, "The Reality of Hell," *Lamplighter*, Mar-Apr 2006, 3-6.

[304] Ibid., 212

[305] Revelation 6:8

[306] Hoekema, *The Bible and the Future*, 253-54.

[307] Herman Hoeksema, *Behold, He Cometh: An Exposition of the Book of Revelation* (Grand Rapids: Reformed Free Publishing Assn, 1969), 659.

[308] Hebrews 1:13; 8:1; 12:2; 1 Peter 3:22

[309] 1 Corinthians 6:3

[310] Hoeksema, *Behold, He Cometh*, 665.

[311] Matthew 11;20-24

[312] Romans 1;18-21

[313] Hoekema, *The Bible and the Future*, 260-61; James 2:26.

[314] Psalm 103:12

315 Hoekema, *The Bible and the Future*, 265-67.

316 Luke 19:12-19; 1 Corinthians 3:10-15

317 Matthew 6:20; 20:21-23

318 Intrater, *From Iraq to Armageddon*, 210-11.

319 Ibid., 212.

320 Hoekema, *The Bible and the Future*, 264.

321 Genesis 1:28; 3:17

322 Hoekema, *The Bible and the Future*, 280-81.

323 Romans 8:20-23

324 Isaiah 50:2

325 Randy Alcorn, *Heaven* (Carol Stream, IL: Tyndale House, 2004), 245-48.

326 Randy Alcorn, *50 Days of Heaven*, (Carol Stream, IL: Tyndale House, 2006), xii.

327 1 Corinthians 1:10

328 Alcorn, *50 Days of Heaven*, Day 44.

329 Ibid., 92.

330 Ibid., 114-15.

331 Alcorn, *Heaven*, Table of Contents.

332 Alcorn, *50 Days of Heaven*, Day 14.

333 Hoeksema, *Behold, He Cometh*, 718.

334 1 Thessalonians 5:1-5

335 1 Chronicles 12:32

336 Matthew 25:1-13

337 Hoeksema, *Behold, He Cometh*, 722.

338 Ibid., 723.

Chapter 15
EQUIPPING WARRIOR LEADERSHIP IN THE KINGDOM OF GOD

339 Reggie McNeal, *Practicing Greatness* (San Francisco: Jossey-Bass, 2006), 5.

340 This point is made by Greg Austin, pastor of Gardiner Community Church, Gardiner, Washington.

341 Matthew 25:14-30 (parable of the talents)

342 Rick Joyner, *50 Days for a Soaring Vision* (Shippensberg, PA: Destiny Image, 2003).

343 Charles Pretlow, *Revelation Six, Get Ready* (Westcliffe, CO: Get Ready Publishing, 2004), 282-83.

344 Larry Simmons, *42 Months to Glory* (Oklahoma City: Ephraim House, 1994), 215-18.

345 Randy Alcorn, *Safely Home* (Carol Stream, IL: Tyndale House, 2001), 277-85.

346 John Dawson, *Taking Our Cities for God; How to Break Spiritual Strongholds* (Lake Mary, FL: Creation House, 1989), 136.

347 Ed Silvoso, "Ministry in the Marketplace," *Visionary Advancement Strategies Newsletter*, August, 2006.

348 See Michael Novelli & Caesar Kalinowski, "Bible Storying", Soma Community Church, Tacoma, 2003-

Chapter 16
UNDERSTANDING THE PROBLEM OF EVIL

349 Genesis 3:15

250 Job 1:1-5

251 Kline, Meredith G., "Trial by Ordeal" in Through Christ's Word: a Festschrift for Dr. Philip E. Hughes, (Phillipsburg: Presbyterian and Reformed, 1985) c.6

252 Job 1:1-2

[253] Matthew 22:37; Mark 12:30; Luke 10:27

[254] Revelation 12:11

[255] Arthur W. Pink, *The Divine Covenants* (Grand Rapids: Baker Book House, 1973), 31.

[256] Arthur W. Pink, *The Sovereignty of God* (Grand Rapids: Baker Book House, 1973), 247-252.

[257] Kline, Meredith G., "Trial by Ordeal" in Through Christ's Word: a Festschrift for Dr. Philip E. Hughes, (Phillipsburg: Presbyterian and Reformed, 1985) c.6

[258] Andrew Murray, *The Believer's Prayer Life* (Minneapolis: Bethany House Publishers, 1983), 20-21

[259] Ryan Wyatt, *Visionary Advancement Newsletter*

[260] Reggie McNeal, *Practicing Greatness*, (San Francisco: Jossey-Bass, 2006), 8.

SELECTED BIBLIOGRAPHY

Alcorn, Randy. *50 Days of Heaven*. Carol Stream, IL: Tyndale House, 2006.

------. *Heaven*. Carol Stream, IL: Tyndale House, 2004.

------. *Safely Home*. Carol Stream, IL: Tyndale House, 2001.

Barna, George. *Revolution*. Wheaton, IL: Tyndale House, 2005.

Baruch, Benjamin. *The Day of the Lord is at Hand*. Baruch Publishing, 2004.

Bass, Clarence B. *Backgrounds to Dispensationalism*. Grand Rapids: Baker, 1960.

Brooke, Tal. *One World*. Berkeley: End Run Publishing, 2000.

------. *When the World Will Be As One*. Eugene: Harvest House, 1989.

Butler, Phill. *Well Connected*. Colorado Springs: Authentic, 2005.

Carson, D. A. *How Long, O Lord?* Grand Rapids: Baker, 1990.

Clinton, J. Robert. *The Making of a Leader*. Colorado Springs: NavPress, 1988.

Frost, Michael, and Alan, Hirsch. *The Shaping of Things to Come*. Peabody, MA: Hendrickson, 2003.

Gaebelein, Frank E., ed. *The Expositor's Bible Commentary*, vols.7 and 12. Grand Rapids: Zondervan, 1981.

Graciano, Roderick. *Battling Babylons*. Tacoma: Timothy Ministries (www.tmin.org), n.d.

------. *The True Spirit of Martyrdom*. Tacoma: Timothy Ministries (www.tmin.org), n.d.

Graves, Joel C. *Gathering Over Jerusalem*. Xulon, 2003.

Hitchcock, Mark. *Iran, the Coming Crisis* (Sisters, OR: Multnomah, 2006.

Hoekema, Anthony A. *The Bible and the Future*. Grand Rapids: Eerdmans, 1979.

Hoeksema, Herman. *Behold, He Cometh*. Grand Rapids: Reformed Free Publishing Assn, 1969.

Hunt, Dave. *A Woman Rides the Beast*. Eugene: Harvest House, 1994.

Intrater, Keith. *From Iraq to Armageddon*. Shippensburg, PA: Destiny Image, 2003.

Jensen, Richard A. *Thinking in Story*. Lima, OH: CSS Publishing, 1993.

Joyner, Rick. *Epic Battles of the Last Days*. New Kensington, PA: Whitaker House, 1995.

------. *Overcoming Evil in the Last Days*. Shippensburg, PA: Destiny Image, 2003.

Juster, Dan, and Keith Intrater. *Israel, the Church and the Last Days*. Shippensburg, PA: Destiny Image, 1990.

Kah, Gary H. *En Route to Global Occupation*. Lafayette, LA: Huntington House, 1991.

Kern, Lynn R. *Jesus Is Coming! But When?* Proctor, MN: Know the Truth Publications, 1999.

Kline, Meredith G. *"Trial by Ordeal" in Through Christ's Word: A Festschrift for Dr. Philip E. Hughes.* Phillipsburg, NJ: Presbyterian and Reformed, 1985.

Ladd, George Eldon. *A Commentary on the Revelation of John.* Grand Rapids: Eerdmans, 1972.

------. *The Presence of the Future.* Grand Rapids: Eerdmans, 1974.

MacPherson, Dave. *The Unbelievable Pre-Trib Origin.* Kansas City: Heart of America Bible Society, 1973.

Mathews, R. Arthur. *Born For Battle.* Wheaton, IL: Harold Shaw Publishers, 1978

McNeal, Reggie. *Practicing Greatness.* San Francisco: Jossey-Bass, 2006.

Mauro, Philip. *Things Which Must Soon Come to Pass.* Swengel, PA: Reiner Publications, 1974.

Miller, Charles W. *Today's Technology in Bible Prophecy.* Lansing, MI: TIP, 1990.

Morris, Henry M. *The Revelation Record.* Wheaton, IL: Tyndale House, 1983.

Mounce, Robert H. *The Book of Revelation.* Grand Rapids: Eerdmans, 1977.

Murrow, David. *Why Men Hate Going to Church.* Nashville: Nelson, 2005.

Newell, William R. *The Book of Revelation.* Chicago: Moody, 1935.

Pawson, David. *When Jesus Returns.* London: Hodder & Stoughton, 1995.

Pink, Arthur W. *Elijah.* Edinburgh: The Banner of Truth Trust, 1956.

------. *The Sovereignty of God* Grand Rapids: Baker, 1973.

Poythress, Vern S. *Understanding Dispensationalists.* Grand Rapids: Zondervan, 1987.

Pretlow, Charles. *Discernment.* Canon City: Wilderness Voice Publishing, LLC, 2013

------. *Revelation Six, Get Ready.* Westcliffe, CO: Get Ready Publishing, 2004.

Ravenhill, David. *The Jesus Letters.* Shippensburg, PA: Destiny Image, 2003.

Reagan, David. *Living for Christ in the End Times.* Green Forest, AR: New Leaf, 2000.

------. *"The Reality of Hell,"* Lamplighter, Mar-Apr 2006.

------. *Wrath and Glory.* Green Forest, AR: New Leaf, 2001.

Richardson, Joel. *Antichrist, Islam's Awaited Messiah.* Enumclaw, WA: Pleasant Word, 2006.

Roberts, Vaughn. *God's Big Picture.* Downers Grove, IL: InterVarsity, 2002.

Rosenberg, Joel C. *Epicenter.* Carol Stream, IL: Tyndale House, 2006.

Rosenthal, Marvin. *The Pre-Wrath Rapture of the Church.* Nashville: Thomas Nelson, 1990.

Roxburgh, Alan J., and Fred Romanuk. *The Missional Leader.* San Francisco: Jossey-Bass, 2006.

Simmons, Larry. *42 Months to Glory.* Oklahoma City: Ephraim House, 1994.

Skolfield, Ellis H. *Hidden Beast 2.* Fort Myers, FL: Fish House, 1990.

Stetzer, Ed. *Planting Missional Churches.* Nashville: Broadman and Holman, 2006.

Stetzer, Ed, and David Putman. *Breaking the Missional Code.* Nashville: Broadman and Holman, 2006.

Towns, Elmer H. *Fasting for Spiritual Break Through.* Ventura: Regal Books, 1996

Vandergriff, Henry. *Mystery Babylon.* Raleigh: Lamb Publishing, 2000.

Van Kampen, Robert. *The Sign.* Wheaton, IL: Crossway, 1992.

Villanueva, William R. *Signs of the End of the Age: Revelation Unravelled.* Ramseur, NC: Solid Rock Publishing, 1996.

Wagner, C. Peter. *The Church in the Workplace.* Ventura, CA: Regal, 2006.

Walker, Andrew. *Enemy Territory: The Christian Struggle in the Modern World.* Wilmore, KY: Bristol Books, 1990.

Wallis, Arthur. *God's Chosen Fast.* Fort Washington: CLC Publications, 1975

ABOUT THE AUTHOR

Don Bell is currently a partner in a CPA firm in the Pacific Northwest. He has been in the business world for approximately 30 years and specializes in training small business owners in the essentials of tax and accounting. Earlier Don had served 20 years in the U.S. Marine Corps where he retired as a major - however, he was also enlisted for six of those years. During his Marine Corps career he served two tours within the combat environment of Vietnam and was a small unit commander during his 2nd tour in 1969. He is the recipient of a number of medals including the Bronze Star and the Presidential Unit Citation. He was also the selected "honor man" in his class at Officer Candidate School at Quantico.

Don is currently married to Geraldine Bell (Gery) and has four grown children plus several grandchildren. Following his "born again" experience outlined in chapter one of this book, Don felt called by the Lord to attend seminary where he received a Masters degree in Divinity (MDiv) and sometime later, a Doctor of Ministry (DMin) specializing in Strategic Leadership. Don's passion to see the glory of the Lord Jesus manifested in the workplace encouraged him through these studies while simultaneously pursuing his business responsibilities with the mission of reaching out to his client-friends.

Don's approach to addressing these end-time events is from a military perspective since much of who he is today is the result of his 20 years in the Marine Corps. The Lord has put a deep burden in his heart to arouse a remnant of Christian warriors to visualize their heritage and purpose in life. Don sees the Book of Revelation as a prophetic field guide to help prepare Christians to minister in the midst of the great tribulations which will precede the coming of the Lord Jesus Christ. This book is designed to bring insight into the Lord's purposes for these recorded tribulations and the mission of the Army of God in the midst of chaotic events.

The common purpose for all volunteers in the Army of God is to prepare in the boot camp of life in order to allow the light and glory of our true Commander-in-Chief, Jesus Christ to be

clearly manifested on the battlefield which lies in the midst of this world. Don's passionate desire is to play a role in assisting the kingdom of God being manifested in glorious strength outside of the institutional churches and in the workplaces, neighborhoods, downtown areas, and individual homes where "real life" occurs. He also hopes to network with a band of brothers who have a similar vision for kingdom ministry.

Don's website:　●　www.equippingwatchmen.com

CPSIA information can be obtained
at www.ICGtesting.com
Printed in the USA
FSHW021720021220
76321FS

9 781943 412082